RAILWAYS
OF
THE ANDES

By

BRIAN FAWCETT M.I.Loco.E., F.R.G.S.

PLATEWAY PRESS

ISBN 1 871980 31 3

First published 1963

Second Edition published 1997

ISBN 1 871980 31 3

PLATEWAY PRESS

Taverner House, Harling Road, East Harling, Norfolk NR16 2QR

Cover artwork by ROY C. LINK

Book design by KEITH TAYLORSON

Printed in England by POSTPRINT
Taverner House, Harling Road, East Harling, Norfolk NR16 2QR

FRONT COVER ILLUSTRATION:
The official opening of the second verrugas bridge, on the Central Railway of Peru, in 1890.
(Collection – Keith Taylorson)

BACK COVER ILLUSTRATION:
Ticlio station, on the mountain section of the Central Railway of Peru, junction for the Morococha
branch – the highest railroad in the world.
(Collection – Keith Taylorson)

FRONTISPIECE:
Cerro de Pasco Railway No. 99, a Rhode Island
(American Locomotive Company) 2-8-0 of 1902, pictured at Oroya.
(Brian Fawcett)

CONTENTS

When commissioning illustrations for the advertising of locomotives, rolling stock or railway materials, you will of course require realistic atmosphere as well as accuracy of detail.   What artist could be better prepared for such work than one who specialises in this field, being also a locomotive engineer with a quarter of a century's practical experience ?

If it is a "thumb-nail" line sketch you want, an elaborate coloured advertisement, or a locomotive that IS a locomotive, apply to :

BRIAN FAWCETT. M. Inst. Loco. Eng.

ENGINEER   ARTIST

"Grovedale," Blackwell, Carlisle.

PREFACE

Brian Fawcett was born at Spike Island, Cobh, County Cork, Ireland on 26 May 1906. He was the son of the celebrated Andean explorer, Colonel Percy H. Fawcett, later to be tragically lost during an expedition to the Matto Grosso in 1925. His early education was at Newton College, Newton Abbot, and in Jamaica and California. On the family's return to England, Fawcett, lacking formal professional qualifications, apprenticed himself to an iron foundry and worked there until, in 1923, he obtained a position with the Central Railway of Peru. This was achieved through a recommendation from Mr Oliver Bury, Chairman of the Peruvian Corporation, a London company with numerous interests – including railways – in Peru.

Present day readers may consider Fawcett's move to be an odd career path. But in the 1920's many of the major South American railways were largely owned by British shareholders, and all managerial, and many senior technical, posts were filled as a matter of course by British nationals. In common with the 'Colonial' service, it was a means by which young men who were willing to endure the often spartan living and working conditions could acquire responsibility at an early age, with a touch of adventure as well.

Fawcett, still only 17, set sail for Callao, Peru in March 1924. In his early autobiography *"Ruins in the Sky"* (Hutchinson, 1958) he tells how his hopes of appointment to the Locomotive Department were dashed when on arrival in Lima he was attached at first to the Central Railway's Traffic Department. The Central was one of the premier railways of Peru. Of standard (4ft 8½in) gauge, its main line connected Callao and Lima with Huancayo, and crossed the Andes at a height of almost 16,000 feet. Fawcett's duties included the checking of station accounts, discipline, and investigation of the frequent hair raising accidents, mostly involving gravity cars.

After a month Fawcett was transferred to Oroya, a tough mining town in the Andes, where he became intimately involved with the operation of the 'Mountain Section', and also came across the Cerro de Pasco Railway, an American-owned railroad serving copper mines at 14,000 feet. At Oroya Fawcett experienced at first hand the special character of Andean railroading, combining elements of British and American railway practice, custom and jargon into a bizarre but fascinating mix that was without parallel anywhere in the world.

Soon Fawcett achieved his eagerly awaited transfer to the Locomotive Department, initially as Day Shed Foreman at Chosica. In 1927 promotion took him – still only 21 – back to Oroya. Here he made the acquaintance of the hard bitten railroad engineers and workshop staff, a fiercely individualistic breed who combined antipathy to discipline with respect for an official – such as Fawcett – prepared to 'lead from the front' and insist on standards being maintained. While in Oroya Fawcett had the frightening experience of helping to defend the expatriate community against armed attack by strikers, during a bitter industrial dispute. This culminated in a dash for freedom on board a specially assembled train behind station pilot No. 67. This extraordinary episode – which included the birth of a baby to one of the English women on the train – and which climaxed in the triumphal arrival of the train (driven by Fawcett, protected by colleagues brandishing six-shooters) in Lima, is breathtakingly recounted[1] in *"Ruins in the Sky."*

This was not to be Fawcett's only brush with death. Later in his career he was supervising the testing of steam railcars then being introduced on the Central. In 1937 he was in the cab of railcar No. 6 at Encalada when a bank of thistle tubes – carrying a pressure of 460psi – exploded. Narrowly escaping being scalded by the exploding steam – the cabs had *sliding doors* – Fawcett clambered to the outside of the cab and, in trying to smash the windows to activate the vacuum brake, slipped and fell, cheating death a second time when the pilot (cowcatcher) flung him clear of the train. Taken by track car to Guadalupe, and then to hospital, Fawcett suffered months of painful treatment for his burns before fortunately making a full recovery.

Fawcett had long been an enthusiast for air brakes, and had been astonished to find the Central – one of the world's premier mountain railways – still following 'British' tradition and using vacuum brakes.

His lunch hours were spent working on plans for his own design of low pressure automatic air brake. Following his accident in 1937, he was given the job of designing and implementing a complete programme for converting all the Central's locomotives and rolling stock to Westinghouse air brake operation, which he successfully carried out over the next few years. The text book which he wrote entitled *"Manejo del Freno de Aire Westinghouse"* published by Gil of Lima in 1941 (in the Spanish language) was the first book of his own work to appear.

Fawcett eventually rose to the rank of Assistant Chief Engineer, but deteriorating economic conditions on the railways after World War Two caused disillusionment to set in, and he retired from railway work in 1947. He was elected a Fellow of the Institution of Mechanical Engineers and of the Royal Geographical Society, and died on 10th August 1984, after a life full of adventure and achievement.

Despite the heavy responsibilities of his railway career, Fawcett found time for his favourite pastime, drawing, and took every opportunity to produce sketches of locations his duties took him to. He was also a keen photographer and assembled a priceless collection of images of Andean railways at a time when few outside enthusiasts were able to explore them. Following his return to England in 1947, he pursued a new career as a commercial artist and author. He produced work for several railway magazines and articles for the US magazine *"Trains"*. His first commercially-published book, *"Let Me Drive,"* an instruction book on how to drive a steam locomotive, aimed at teenage boys, was published in 1951. In 1953 his account of his father's expeditions *"Exploration Fawcett"* became an immediate best seller was translated into at least eighteen different languages. The English version was reprinted twice before publication and many times since. It is considered to be a classic of its genre.

The first edition of *"Railways of the Andes"* was published in 1963, and is also regarded as a classic. The book was never reprinted but a later volume of photographs under the title *"Steam in the Andes"* was published by D. Bradford Barton in 1973, and is now a much sought-after item. In 1994, steps were put in train to republish *"Railways of the Andes"*. Through the good offices of the I. Mech. E., and of Mr Alistair Goldie, of Carlisle, a personal friend of Fawcett, the present publishers were put in touch with Fawcett's executors. Full co-operation was given to the publication of this second edition, which utilises Fawcett's original text, with no attempt to update or amend it[2]. However a new Foreword by D. Trevor Rowe summarises developments in the 50 years since Fawcett's 'retirement'. Regrettably a number of photographs used in the first edition have not survived into the present day, but we have been privileged to have full access to the photographs featured in *"Steam in the Andes"* together with some unpublished material. This selection, supplemented by views from Plateway Press' own archive, forms the basis of the illustrations for this new edition. Also featured are examples of Brian Fawcett's own artwork (generously provided by Mr Goldie), period advertisements, and some excellent maps of Andean and associated railways. For permission to reprint these we are indebted to the Railway Gazette, London.

KEITH TAYLORSON
Brighton
England
September 1996

[1] *Chapter 6, "Spontaneous Combustion on the World's Roof".*
[2] *No record has been found of the "small North British Engines" used in Ecuador, remembered by Mr John L. Macintyre and referred to in Chapter 13.*

FOREWORD

by D. Trevor Rowe

"Railways of the Andes" was published in 1963, when it is very doubtful if any of those reading it had ever visited South America, although they may well have heard of railways such as the Central of Peru, which featured in the type of *"Boys' Adventure Annual"* of patriotic style on which the youth of my generation was nurtured in the 1930's. South America was well beyond the range of the annual two-week holiday before the jet age, although it must not be forgotten that many expatriates had spent much of their life there and, like Brian Fawcett, could recite exciting tales of their experiences. More of these have been published than may be thought, a superb and fairly recent example being *"Railway Engineer in Brazil"* by T. Hanson (Excalibur Press, 1989). This describes life on the Great Western of Brazil, where banditry and local revolution added to the excitement of strikes and natural disasters, and railway officials were provided with firearms for their own protection. This book is a rather more personal account than Fawcett's, with less locomotive detail, though there are some spectacular crashes described. Happily Mr Hanson survived nationalisation and remained in railway service to see the introduction of diesel traction before retirement.

Looking back to another period is another book published in the same year (1989), again a very personal account covering many years of railway service in South America (and other parts of the world). This is *"David Angus (the life and adventures of a Victorian Railway Engineer)"* by Craig Mair, and recounts experiences in Brazil, Uruguay, Paraguay, Chile and Argentina from 1882 to the 1920's. These books are mentioned as they give some insight into the hard life of those who spent long periods far from home building and operating railways in a totally alien environment, not even part of the British Empire, and suffering constraints from sometimes despotic and often inefficient local and National Government. Fawcett's book steers clear of these aspects, and devotes itself to railways alone, although it does range somewhat beyond the confines of the line on which he worked.

Until the first publication of *"South American Steam"* by Roy Christian and Ken Mills in 1970, and a much more comprehensive sequel *"World of South American Steam"* in 1974, little was known about the motive power stock of South American railways, or where the surviving steam was to be found. Visiting Brazil for the first time in 1966 I was unaware that a place called Tubarao existed, much less that it was a steam paradise which was to become almost a place of pilgrimage for later generations of British and US enthusiasts!

Fawcett hints at the possibly bleak future facing rail transport – at least as far as passenger travel was concerned in his final Chapter. This turned out to be perceptive although the decline was perhaps less rapid than he might, privately, have felt was likely. Three years after publication of *"Railways of the Andes"* in 1963, *"Jane's World Railways"* records goods traffic on the Southern of Peru having increased from 243,070,000 ton/km in 1962/63 to 265,593,000 ton/km in 1965/66. Passenger traffic however showed a slight decline, and this trend was to accelerate throughout South America, as air services cut into the long-distance traffic, and increasing car ownership provided an alternative to the railway in the more prosperous republics, such as Chile and Argentina. One by one the South American railroads contracted, closed altogether, or just abandoned passenger services.

An early major casualty was the Transandine route, which suffered the additional drawback of being owned by two separate Governments, Chile and Argentina. Fawcett's own Central of Peru was still apparently prospering in the 1980's, with a through passenger service from Lima to Huancayo and return each day, carrying respectable loads and still providing a free service of oxygen to travellers. But the railway became progressively more starved of investment, and services on the whole route were suspended in mid 1992, though the 1996 *"Cook's International Timetable"* shows one train a day as far as San Bartolomé. Huancayo is therefore unreachable by rail, but oddly enough services on the metre gauge Huancayo-Huancavelica railway have increased since the 1970's, two return services a day being advertised.

Elsewhere the situation on the railways in and around the Andes is bleak. A rudimentary service on the surviving section of the Southern of Peru was reported to be in existence in 1995, though taking twice the advertised eight hours for the journey. Tourist trains still run between Cuzco and Macchu Pichu, and another less likely survivor is the 'international' route between Tacna and Arica, with a twice weekly railcar. Whether any of these railways will survive until the millenium is questionable.

Reverting to literature, the 1980's and 1990's have seen a relative avalanche of books on South American railway topics. Subjects covered include the Brazilian coal line at Tubarao, and the Buenos Aires Great Southern Railway. Out in 1996 is a bound list of Argentinian steam stock. There is a good deal of historical (non-locomotive) information in *"Peruvian Trams and Railways"* by T. H. Stephenson (Minerva Press, 1995) and Trackside Publications have issued two books "The Central Railway of Peru and the Cerro de Pasco Railway" and *"The Anglo Chilean Nitrate Railway Company"*. the latter greatly expanding Fawcett's 'Nitrate Road' chapter. Many issues of *"Locomotives International"* magazine have covered South America, and a South America Railway Circle has recently been formed, to collect and disseminate information on the area. For many years I have been working on coverage of the whole of South American railways in one book and it is hoped that this will be published in 1997.

The relative abundance of literature may provide those of us who missed the days of long distance steam travel, Buenos Aires to La Paz or Asuncion, Antofagasta to La Paz or the Transandine route between Buenos Aires and Santiago with some consolation. It is perhaps fitting that, with the end of regular operations on the Paraguay State Railways and the Guayaquil & Quito marking the virtual extinction of 'working' steam in the continent, steps are at last being taken to research and document what has existed. Some massive locomotives have been used in South America, often on less than standard gauge, but the Central of Peru found that the Andes type was the best, and stuck to it to the end of steam traction!

THE CENTRAL RAILWAY OF PERU IN THE 1920's. FIRST SECTION OUT OF OROYA WITH THE SANDCAR ON A FROSTY MORNING

Christmas card designed and drawn by Brian Fawcett, with printed greeting inside. The locomotive is one of the Central Railway's North British 2-6-0's.

(Collection – Alistair Goldie)

Chapter 1

THE BACKDROP

BUT for a disastrous civil war, Peru might have followed hard upon England's heels into the Railway Age. The necessary inventiveness and experience were in the country, in the person of Richard Trevithick, and the drive was not lacking. The Cornishman's schemes were supported by Francisco Quiroz, John Begg, the Liberator Simón Bolivar and others, all of whom strove to establish rail transport. But the Wars of Independence, between the first smoulderings in 1810 and the final collapse of Spanish Colonial power at Ayacucho in 1824, left a number of newly-born republics wavering uncertainly upon weak limbs, shaken by repeated internal upheavals, and barely able to subsist.

Peru had natural resources of incalculable value without the means of exploiting them. Perhaps that statement should be modified. The means of developing those resources were latent there before the war for independence had engulfed the country; for foreign commerce had commenced, first illegally and then legally, and Lima had its first foreign merchants even during the war. But the great European financial houses were chary of granting loans. Security was uncertain. Political tranquillity had not begun to exist – nor had ministerial integrity! Without foreign credit, Peru could not finance the ambitious schemes of Trevithick and his fellow enthusiasts which might otherwise have brought about an early development of her natural wealth.

Chile and Peru – including 'Upper Peru', which after the war became Bolivia, named in honour of the Liberator – shared the high Andean *Cordillera* with its great store of minerals. Ecuador and Colombia are also Andean countries; but by far the greater part of the towering mountain range running down the Pacific coast of South America from the Isthmus of Panama to Cape Horn comes within the boundaries of the two first-named republics. As far as the Spaniards were concerned, the Andes meant precious metals. The *Conquistadores* of the early sixteenth century found mining already established by the Incas, the people of the Old Empire seeking gold and silver because it looked pretty and was easy to work. The inordinate value put on these metals by the European conquerors at first amazed the natives; but once it was realized they did their utmost to hide as many of their own sources as possible. The Spaniards themselves were not slow in finding out that the *Cordillera* was full of gold, silver, copper and other non ferrous metals. Very soon, mines were being intensively worked wherever the white man had penetrated.

The 'Silver Curtain' was drawn about Spain's possessions in the New World to keep other envious nations out, and it endured for nearly 300 years. But the popular idea that incredible treasure was shipped from Peru to Spain is not confirmed by history. Once the supplies of gold and silver melted down from Incan artifacts had ceased and the colonists were relying only on the output of mines for their shipments of treasure to the Old World, overhead costs began to be felt keenly. To keep large labour forces at the richest mines, which were well above the timber line required careful organization for the transport of all necessary supplies. Timber – charcoal – foodstuffs – clothing – all had to be brought from distant sources on the backs of Indians, llamas or mules. Only silver and gold mattered to the miners. Less precious metals could not be produced economically.

As a lucky strike, Potosi was never equalled; though the tale is almost certainly exaggerated that silver to the value of over one hundred million pounds sterling formed the 'Royal Fifth' paid in the course of a single century. In any case, the *Cerro Rico* of Potosi was easy mining. Elsewhere it was; more difficult – and more expensive. Himself a mining man, John Miers, writing of the Cerro de Pasco mines in 1826, says:

'The books of the provincial treasury of Pasco prove that, in the year 1796, the produce of these mines, including those of Huallanca, was 227,514 marcs of silver;[1] and that, in the ten years ending in 1801, the average annual produce was 247,014 marcs. Looking at this produce, our attention is naturally excited to admiration at the riches which the immense profit of these mines must have yielded to the persons engaged in them. But, on more minute investigation, we shall find that mining speculations have never been profitable in Pasco… The expenses attending the working of the mines, and freeing them from water, by means of pumps, worked by men, was so great, that the charges incurred by the proprietors of one mine alone were a thousand dollars a week. Let us assume the average expenses of the whole 78 mines in work at one third of the estimate; their total expenditure in the course of the year will amount

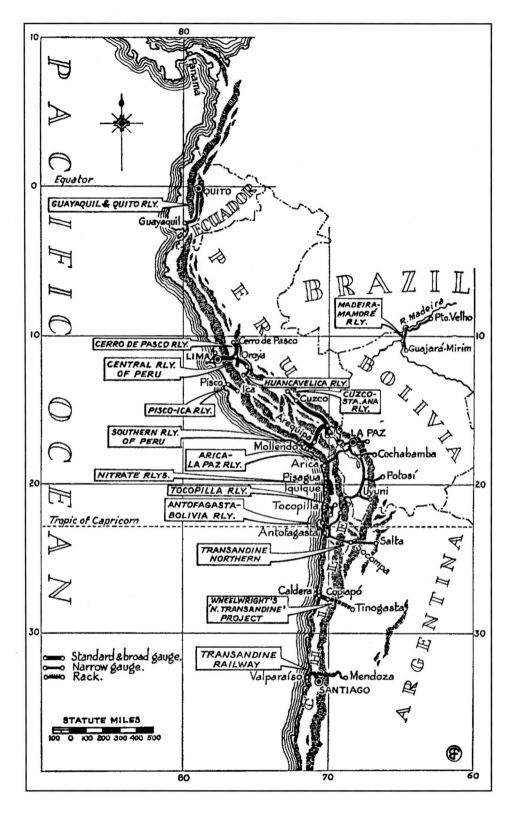

to 1,351,974 dollars... Estimating, therefore, the 247,014 marcs of silver at $6^{1}/_{4}$ dollars, it amounts to the sum of 1,549,381 dollars, which, after deducting the charges above stated, leaves 197,407 dollars; taking from this the expense of carriage, the profit yields but a small interest for the capital embarked in these undertakings...'

To some extent this may be one reason why Spain was bankrupt in 1696; though official corruption at the American end of the funnel had much to do with it. There is no doubt that large quantities of silver were being produced in Andean mines, but by the mid-eighteenth century less than one fifth of the revenue collected in the New World was reaching Spain. High administrative posts in the Americas were sold by the Crown and the Council of the Indies. Viceroys came to the New World, not to govern wisely and well, but to make all they could out of it. In consequence, the colonies suffered from mal-administration – and in particular, from enforced isolation – until the cauldron of discontent began to boil over in 1810.

Until 1810, foreigners were not allowed to visit the Spanish possessions in South America, nor were the inhabitants of those countries permitted to trade with foreigners, on pain of death. Even Spaniards might not set foot in the New World without special permission. Inter-provincial communication was discouraged, lest the knowledge of the inhabitants be increased by intercourse with others, and the spirit of rebellion fostered. No South American might own a ship, and none might have a cargo consigned to him. No foreigner, unless born in Spain, was allowed to reside in the country. No capital in any form, other than Spanish, might be employed in the colonies. Should any foreign vessel, even in distress, enter a South American port, it was seized as a prize and the crew imprisoned. That's why I call it the 'Silver Curtain'; Andean silver was certainly the reason for the restrictions – and it was also what finally cracked it.

The Spanish Colonial policy of forbidding intercourse with other countries was followed by stringent laws regarding the disposal of processed silver from the mines. The masses of porous, semi-refined silver after the mercury used in the amalgamation process had been roasted out were delivered to the *Callana*, or Royal Office, where they were melted, the Royal Fifth paid, and the bars marked with the treasurer's initials, the date and the weight. These bars were sold by the miner to a purchaser known as a *Rescatador*, who was required to register the deal at once with the President Agent of the Mining Intendency. An order was then granted to deliver them to the mint where a price was paid for them as low as might be without discouraging the mining industry altogether.

Meanwhile, foreign vessels had discovered that the Spanish coastguards were quite incapable of protecting a Pacific coastline thousands of miles in extent. Following the birth of the United States many small, swift ships began to creep round Cape Horn into the Pacific, their skippers following noses twitching with the glorious smell of money. They brought with them goods from Europe, such as the people of the West Coast countries had never possessed. The infant United States having as yet no industries of her own, her adventurous sea-faring sons from Down East came swarming round Cape Horn with cargoes of British goods picked up in Jamaica and Barbados. But the vast majority of the illicit visitors were Britons. Up and down the coast from Panama to Chile they found certain quiet anchorages where a vessel might without being disturbed unload its cargo of the textiles and the fancy goods in ever-growing demand as they became more widely known. But it all had to be paid for, and the currency used to purchase these goods was the *plata piña*, or masses of silver that should have gone to the *Callana*. Thus the old trade of piracy along the Pacific coast gave way to a more lucrative trade of smuggling. It could never have thrived as it did had not officialdom from top to bottom participated in the profits. Everyone concerned with the trade waxed prosperous but Spain herself.

If he proceeded legally, the *rescatador* who bought silver from the miner was forced to sacrifice very nearly 27 per cent of its value in duties, and the official price was pegged at a figure that rendered him no more than a tolerable profit. But if instead of taking his silver to the Royal Office in the first place, the *rescatador* bartered it to a smuggler in exchange for goods that were sold at huge profit to the clamouring people of the country, he came out of the deal, even after payment of a considerable proportion in graft, in very much better case.

Fully aware of the writing on the wall, Viceroy Abascal issued a decree in 1810 that British goods might be brought across the Isthmus of Panama and shipped to the Peruvian port of Callao on payment of a $37^{1}/_{2}$ per cent duty called the *Derecho de Circuito,* in addition to other taxes. By that time the local demand for imported goods was overwhelming. Thus was the age-old 'Silver Curtain' cracked. Hard upon the heels of that decree, British merchants began to infiltrate into Peru. Even at the crippling rate of duties and taxes they could make their fortunes. Shaken by troubles within, Spain lost her grip on the New World possessions. The foreign merchants now on South American soil were digging their heels in ever more firmly as their numbers increased. The captains and owners of trading vessels were doing so well that the British Navy took notice. British merchants and British ships in the Pacific required protection. More and more frequent became the visits of British warships. Traders found that consignments of silver bullion to England could be sent in safety by shipping them home in the holds of warships. Insurance rates were lower when they did so; for piracy was less of a risk. They paid handsomely for the privilege, and naval commanders clamoured for the West Indies station with the chance of a Pacific assignment. Humble merchant skippers could compete only by building up a reputation for meticulous honesty, speed and punctuality. As the sole medium of currency in these transactions, silver – *plata piña* – became so scarce at Peruvian mints that a crisis was only averted by the progress of the militant unrest spreading through the American colonies.

As they gained their independence, the new American states one by one opened their doors wide to unrestricted foreign trade. Even before the collapse of the Spanish regime in Peru the liberally-minded viceroy, ceding to the pressure from powerful business interests, had allowed a representative to go to England with the object of purchasing some of the steam pumping engines now engaging the attention of mining men everywhere. The only engines not affected by the reduced atmospheric pressure at extremely high altitudes were those of Richard Trevithick, father of 'strong steam'.

Trevithick had succeeded in conquering almost overwhelming prejudice against the use of high-pressure steam, and in doing so had developed not only boilers capable of generating the pressures, but engines of far greater efficiency than the Watt behemoths, while only a fraction of their size. His road carriage of 1801 was not the first of its kind but it was a huge stride forwards. In 1802 he was careering along the Tottenham Court Road in another steam carriage, knocking down garden fences and frightening pedestrians almost out of their wits. In the same year he built his first steam rail locomotive, with the blast turned up the chimney and a feed-water heater to boot. He was the first man – and only one – to insist that traction on smooth rails could be effected by adhesion alone. In 1804 he operated the first steam train ever to run on rails, a feat commemorated by the inscription to he seen on a plinth at Penydarren, Glamorganshire, at the site of the tramway on which it took place.

Payment not being forthcoming on the pumping engines for Peru, Trevithick accepted instead a partnership in the mine drainage project they were destined for, and arrived in that country at the beginning of 1817. It was hopefully believed that pumping the Cerro de Pasco mines dry would provide the tottering finances of the colony with another Potosi. The consummation of this dream was frustrated, firstly by the unreliability of the new engines, secondly by the fierce opposition to them on the part of the miners – who saw in them a threat to their livelihood – and thirdly by the breaking out of civil war. But in losing no opportunity to air his views on 'strong steam' and in particular its application to rail transport, Trevithick won his converts and sowed seeds that were to flower long after his departure from the country in 1824.

The historical backdrop now sketched in, it is desirable at this point to give some idea of Andean topography. Imagine a coastline 4,000 miles long backed by a towering range of mountains reaching nearly 23,000 feet in height, and with at least eight known summits of over 20,000 feet – a range running like a spine the length of South America. From the half-way line northwards a widening strip about 30 miles across separates the Pacific shore from the mountains proper. South of this half-way line, and well down through Chile, a 3,000-foot scarp rises from the shore to a *tablazo* or table-land at the foot of the main range. East of the *Cordillera* of the Andes, some 200 miles in width, lie the Argentine *pampas* and the forests of tropical South America stretching to the Atlantic seaboard.

Now imagine the Andes like the wall of a fortification, its western side precipitous, its eastern side a glacis sloping less steeply. The top, broad here and narrow there, is protected by breastworks with a comfortably wide passage between them. The mountain summits represent these breastworks; the passage along the top is the *Altiplano* or *Puna* (local names vary) – the high Andean plain running approximately north and south at anything between 10,000 and 14,000 feet above sea level. This is the home of the mountain Indian, the region of pastures, lakes and villages. Mining activities take place in the mountain ramparts walling it in. The passes giving off from the *puna* through the peaks on either side run from 10,000 feet in the south to nearly 16,000 feet in Central Peru.

The toughest railroading conditions imposed by the Andes are encountered in the climbing of the steep western rampart, where a great height must be gained within a short distance. Once over the summit of the first *Cordillera* – that on the Pacific side – the systems either drop to the *puna* and run along it, or penetrate fertile valleys below its general level. Some that cross over altogether and descend the easier eastern slopes will be described in the appropriate place. Snow is a problem only in Southern Chile. The perpetual snowline is receding. In Central Peru it was at about 16,000 feet only fifty years ago. Today it is found at 17,000 feet. Snowplows once used frequently during the wet season, when snowfall on the summits is heaviest, have now rusted away for lack of use.

The rainy season in the mountains, from November to May, brings repeated troubles in the shape of landslides, washouts, cloudbursts, flash floods and thunderstorms of almost unbelievable ferocity. Many of us who have lived years in the Andes have undergone the experience of being caught in a thunderstorm, with lightning hitting the ground all round, throwing up explosions of dust like shellbursts, and with noise enough to split the eardrums. The vicious sizzle of a lightning bolt within a yard or two of one is not easily forgotten!

Temperatures in the Central Andes at this time of year approximate those of an English March or November. Nights are raw but not freezing. On the other hand, during the dry season, from May to October, night temperatures drop below freezing point – sometimes below zero in the heights – while by day the thermometer may read over 100°F in the sunshine. At this time of year frost is the enemy of the railroads, forming during the hours of darkness what are known in the vernacular as 'whiskers on the rail', one of the greatest threats to adhesion.

The rainy season in the mountains extends downwards to about 5,000 feet above sea level on the western side, and below that level it is the swollen torrents that are likely to be dangerous. The Pacific littoral meanwhile basks in the warmth of a summer sun, under clear skies. But when the heights are enjoying their dry season, the littoral – throughout most of Chile and all of Peru – is enveloped in damp cloud, precipitating a light drizzle, or 'Scotch mist', known in Chile as the *Camanchaca* and in Peru as *Garúa*, hiding the sun and holding temperatures down to a level that can become uncomfortably raw, even within the Tropic of Capricorn. This phenomenon is caused by the off-shore upwellings of icy water from the deeps, misnamed the Humboldt Current. Southerly winds prevail all along the Humboldt. Aircraft landing strips need lie in one direction only. However, it creates problems in the cooling of internal combustion engines of road and rail vehicles climbing the western scarps of the *Cordillera;* since the breeze moves in the same direction and at more or less the same speed.

The eastern slopes of the Andes, and the mass of tropical South America on the Atlantic side of the continental divide, share the rainy season with the heights. On this side there is none of the aridity so characteristic of the Pacific shore strip, where real rain seldom falls. The less precipitous eastern slopes are green with pasture from the *puna* down to the tree line, and the rain forests of the interior creep up high into the foothills.

Where mountain and forest join is scenery of extraordinary loveliness, the more fascinating because of its wildness, and the knowledge that 2,500 miles of wilderness lie between the viewer and the Atlantic shores.

At Cabo Blanco, northernmost corner of Peru, the Humboldt Current turns westwards away from the Pacific coast and makes a big sweep out to the Galapagos Islands. Between the point of its departure from the littoral and the Panamanian isthmus the shore takes on quite a different character. The arid coastal desert gives way to tropical forest, clothing the lower slopes of the Andes and shrouding the rivers, possessing everything that is expected of equatorial jungle, including the plagues.

Travel in the Andean region was facilitated in the days of the Old Empire by a surprisingly good system of roads, provided at convenient stages with rest-houses. According to present-day ideas, these roads were narrow, having been built for Indian runners and freight transport on the backs of llamas – animals that refuse to carry more than 120 pounds in weight. The runners, called *Chasquis* by the Incas, worked in relays, achieving wonders in the speed of delivery of light assignments over remarkable distances. The Incas discouraged travel except on business. Their noble administrators and officials travelled in litters. Incan bridges were usually catwalks suspended from cables of twisted vegetable fibre. The sure-footed llamas were used to them; to the people who built them they no doubt appeared safe; but Europeans invariably thought otherwise! Where highways and railways have not introduced modern requirements, the same kind of bridge is in use today; but they are probably far more perilous now than in the days before the Conquest when they were maintained under the meticulous laws of the Incas, a people far more civilized than the Europeans who conquered them.

The horse and mule were introduced by the Spanish, who hewed their own trails in the walls of the mountains, barely wide enough for a laden animal, and proceeded to exploit their new possessions by means of them. These trails were of course inadequate. The high cost of freighting supplies to the mining districts and transporting the product of those mines to the coast swallowed up much of the profit to be made in the ventures. The slowness of that transport was another obstacle. Readers of books such as Prescott's *Conquest of Peru* are left with a quite wrong impression of Andean travel; for in the histories the gallant *Conquistadores* and their victims move about the country with an ease and dispatch out of all keeping with fact. To give you an idea of the true speed of animal travel in the mountains, take the Lima to Cerro de Pasco route, an actual travelling distance of 183 miles. This was covered by mule trains in nine to ten days, the maximum cargo for an animal being 400 pounds. Riders did it fairly comfortably in four days, without disastrous results to their mounts. Mountain Indians on foot could do it in under 50 hours! However, they were able to take short cuts impossible for a mule. This was in the days immediately preceding the railroad era; but it is doubtful whether it had improved at all during the three centuries since the Conquest.

Travellers carried their own blankets and as much of their own victuals as they could. On the road, they lodged in resthouses, literally crawling with lice; or in Indian hovels shared with – besides the lice – sheep, pigs, guinea-pigs, poultry and the host's family. It was sometimes necessary to camp in the open – cleaner, perhaps, but attended by some risk of being frozen to death. The daily stages were entirely dependent upon available supplies of fodder for the animals. Some stages were very short; others uncomfortably long. Infesting as they did the most frequented trails, bandits were always a hazard to be faced. Surprisingly enough, these hordes left the silver trains severely alone. They might even leave unmolested travellers of the humbler sort; but any foreigner was marked down as the most desirable prey. Murders were common.

Mule and horse traffic to some sort of itinerary was not unknown in the Andes just prior to the dawn of the railroad era. Diligences called *birloches* ran regular services over the 90 miles separating Santiago, the Chilean capital, and Valparaiso, its port. Omnibuses ran between Lima and the port of Callao, nine miles distant, taking an hour and a half for the journey and leaving from each terminus at 8 a.m. and 4 p.m. every day. Incidentally, shortly after his arrival in Peru in 1817, Trevithick learned of the existence of a horse tramway between Lima and Callao, no longer in use. The difficulty he himself experienced in freighting all his mining machinery up from the port in slow, unwieldy ox-wains filled him with the determination to institute steam traction on this abandoned tram route.

Writing in 1838, J. J. von Tschudi describes how every fortnight mail was dispatched from Lima to Tarma, Jauja, Huancavelica, Ayacucho, Cuzco and into Bolivia; while another went to the northern provinces, and a third to Arequipa and the south. Another travelled weekly between Lima and Cerro de Pasco by the trail euphemistically named the *Camino Real*, or 'Royal Road'. The mail was carried in relays, in charge of an Indian mounted on a mule, the stages being from six to twelve miles. As soon as the mail arrived at a station a flag was hoisted, and anyone who expected a letter might then come and collect it. Tschudi remarks that the Peruvian post was as tardy as it was ill-regulated. It might seem surprising that anything of the sort even existed in the interior of a country so sparsely inhabited and still virtually lawless!

The pattern of mule travel was much the same everywhere in the Andes, and it is still unchanged where highways and railways have not yet penetrated. That is the reason for the remarkable importance that air travel has achieved there. Back in the early 1930s freight-carrying aircraft were delivering heavy mining machinery to remotely situated mountain destinations which otherwise could have been reached only with the greatest difficulty. But air travel is for those who can pay for it, and the majority must move from place to place by land. When the smallholding on which he depends for his subsistence is not claiming his attention, the mountain Indian with a little silver in his pocket is overwhelmed with a desire to travel. Where there are roads and motor vehicles he may travel for a pittance on top of the cargo; where there are rails, he rides the train; where there are neither roads nor rails, he walks or rides.

It was inevitable that Tevithick, pioneer of railways, should have appreciated the crying need of the Andes for a form of transport capable of meeting the demands of the miners. On his arrival in the mining territory of Pasco, where some of his Cornish pumping engines were at work clearing the mines of water, he was horrified to see what rich ore was being thrown aside as useless –'attle', as he called it. Copper was of little or no interest. Lead was not mined in Peru until 1840. Only silver and gold could repay the 'adventurer' the huge costs involved in mining and processing the ore, and render him a reasonable profit. And the reason for these huge costs was lack of adequate transport. Railway communication with the coast would permit unparalleled development of the mining industry and win fortunes for those who provided it. Trevithick saw at once, and schemed accordingly; but war came to the country before his schemes could mature.

In 1798 a boy was born in Newburyport, Massachusetts, who played a major part in transport on the West Coast. William Wheelwright was scoffed at as a dreamer, but his dreams brought about the start of regular steam navigation in the Pacific. Among his many projects was a canal across the Panamanian isthmus. Trevithick had projected the same thing some years before. Bolivar was similarly interested in 1825. Actually, a canal had existed since 1788 – how many people realize that? – and by way of it canoes loaded with cacao crossed from ocean to ocean. This was the small canal of Raspadura. A note in the *London Shipping and Mercantile Gazette* of June 5, 1873, gives an account of it by Edwin S. Roberts.

Railroads to bring the minerals to the coast would require to be complemented by adequate ocean transport in order to place the wealth of the Andes in the markets of Europe and North America. Wheelwright never lost sight of the transport picture as an integrated whole – his view of the wood was never obscured by the trees. Coming first upon the scene as United States Consul at Guayaquil, Wheelwright's chief interest lay in steam-driven ships, the new-fangled 'insults to wind and water' that he had known since his childhood. His campaigns in favour of their use began in 1833, and the founding of the Pacific Steam Navigation Company of Liverpool in 1839 was a direct result of his efforts – a company, by the way, still flourishing under its original name; though now affiliated with Royal Mail Lines.

Wheelwright envisaged a rail link from a Chilean port on the Pacific, across the high Andes to the River Plate. This, bear in mind, was in the days of sail, when the passage from the Antipodes to Europe was a long and painful one, and every completed voyage an epic. His idea was to provide a quicker, more reliable route. The distance to Europe from New Zealand *across* lower South America was less than by the Isthmus of Panama.

Vessels sailing for Australasia could reach the heart of the trade winds not far north of Caldera, in Chile; while those leaving Australasian ports could easily pick up the S.W. winds to carry them right across the Pacific to Chile, making the passage in five or six weeks. On the Atlantic side, vessels of fourteen feet draught could sail well into the South American mainland, up the River Plate to Rosario, most of the year; and those of twelve feet draught had no difficulty in reaching Rosario at any time. It was about thirty days' sailing from there to England. The rail link across the continent should therefore be between Caldera and Rosario. The unloading and reloading of freight involved in his plan was considered to be justified by the time saved on the total voyage. After all, the same operation was necessary up on the Isthmus, and the newly fledged Panama Rail Road was coining money hand over fist.

Wheelwright may have known Trevithick, first of the great trio of Andean railroad giants. It is possible that Wheelwright was in Guayaquil when the disillusioned Cornishman arrived there in 1824 from Peru, fuming over the confiscation by Bolivar of all his hard-won assets. If they did meet, one can be sure that the similarity of their ideas produced some interesting conversation, which would have given a fillip to Wheelwright's embryo schemes. Trevithick had already been active, if unsuccessful, in the matter of iron ships driven by steam and screw propellers.

The third giant of the trio, Henry Meiggs, arrived in Chile at the close of Wheelwright's career. The three could therefore have linked hands across a period dating from 1817 to 1877. Meiggs was born in New York State in 1811, and made his way westwards to California with the 'Forty-Niners'. Very much concerned with civic matters in the infant but lusty city of San Francisco, Meiggs was involved in some shady deals that culminated in an embezzlement, with effects that obliged him to get out from under – pronto! There were warrants out against him when with his wife and children he crept out of fog-bound San Francisco bay aboard the barque America, his creditors in armed pursuit on a small steamer that, fortunately for Meiggs, broke down. He was forty-three years old at the time.

1. *A general view of Callao, the port for Lima, around the turn of the century. Extensive rail trackage along the wharves is evident.* (Collection – Keith Taylorson)

2. *Peru, original 'Oroya Railway'. A passenger train of the early 1870's headed by a typical Rogers 2-6-0, first mainline locomotive on what later became the Central Railway of Peru.* (Author's collection)

March 1855 saw the arrival of the Meiggs family at Talcahuano, in southern Chile, after a voyage by devious Pacific byways lasting five or six months. He had with him capital enough to start life anew in a country where opportunities for the not too scrupulous were beginning to appear, and it was not long before the business acumen that had made his name a byword in San Francisco began to render results.

The United States clamoured to Chile for the return of her erring son, but no extradition agreements existed at the time between the two countries. Diplomatic considerations becoming impossible to ignore, Chile was obliged to profess sympathy with the U.S. arguments, but apparently arranged matters so that when the U.S. representative, the extradition order in his pocket, sought Meiggs, that astute man was not to be found.

Meiggs seems to have had two distinct sides to his character. On the one side he was an upright, square-dealing man who honoured his agreements to the letter and was so considerate of each of the thousands of people working directly and indirectly under him that he won their sincere affection and unswerving loyalty. On the other side, he was a man who never scrupled to bend circumstances to his own advantage, whatever the effects upon others. He 'tamed' the Chilean *Roto*, which no one had succeeded in doing until then, and he did it by fair treatment and consideration of every one of them as an individual. The *roto* was notorious for his hardihood, his skill in the handling of the razor-sharp, curved disembowelling knife that all his tribe carried, his hatred of any sort of discipline, his love of cane alcohol as a beverage and his addiction to gambling.

At the time of Henry Meigg's coming, Chile was beginning the construction of a national railway network, and the North American fitted into the picture perfectly. He established a reputation by completing a contract for the building of the Maipo bridge, a particularly tough assignment in the construction of the southern lines. He then contracted to build the line on for 90 miles from Maipo to San Fernando, and completed this in under the stipulated time. The door was then open to him to commence the railroad construction exploits that will be related in subsequent chapters, and which set him up as king of all the Andean railroad builders.

On June 23, 1860, when William Wheelwright was reading to the Royal Geographical Society in London his paper, *A Proposed Railway Route Across the Andes From Caldera to Rosario*, his first steps in bridging the Andes by rail had already been made with a 50-mile line from Caldera to the copper and silver mining region of Copiapó, at an altitude of 1,200 feet. This line was begun in April 1850, and opened to traffic on December 28, 1851. Its coming created a forward surge in mining operations at railhead, and during 1853 ten million dollars' worth of metal was shipped out from Copiapó. All the copper was taken from ores yielding not less than 25 per cent! A desert region was thus enriched, a flourishing railway built, and a considerable source of freight provided for the Pacific Steam Navigation Company. A 28-mile extension was then projected to the silver mines of Chañarcillo for half a million dollars, and another to the Tres Puntos mining district.

It was Wheelwright's intention to take his transandine line across the *Cordillera* by way of a pass believed to be always free of snow. The Uspallata pass, east from Valparaiso, at 11,000 feet above sea level, was snowed up for three or four months in the year. Another convenient pass at nearly 14,000 feet was also subject to snow blockage. A good pass, away to the south near Concepción, was impracticable not only on account of snow, but also because of the danger from Araucanian Indians, a fighting tribe never dominated by the Spaniards. The route as projected by way of the San Francisco pass would have a summit of over 16,000 feet, and maximum grades on the western scarp of one in thirty.

In 1860 adhesion grades of this severity were considered excessively steep by the conservative, but not out of the question by the venturesome. Coplapó engineers – and they were the men on the spot – thought them practicable. To American railroaders they were not frightening. Worse grades already existed, and ten-wheelers worked over them without lying down. But the necessary financing of Wheelwright's ambitious railway was never successfully negotiated, and the whole project was shelved. The route surveyed is today a highway. As a railway it would have been the highest in the world.

Often claimed as the first railway in South America, the Caldera-Copiapó was actually put into service after the opening of the Lima-Callao Railway on May 17, 1851. The Lima Railways Company is not in any sense an Andean line, but it was first schemed by Richard Trevithick and was therefore a pioneer project of its kind. An enterprising Englishman in Lima, John Begg, had listened to the great Cornishman's arguments for a steam-operated rail link between Lima and its port, Callao. Begg was an enthusiastic supporter of the idea, in which he was joined by a Cerro de Pasco mining man named Francisco Quiroz, who saw in it what Trevithick insisted it could become – a link in rail connection between the mines of Pasco and the ocean, allowing these mines to be exploited to the full. As Prefect of Junín in 1833, Quiroz was still saying:

'No one is ignorant that the richest fountain of our national wealth this day is concentrated in the immense treasures of the mineral of Pasco. Its works, conducted with intelligence and managed with economy, would be more than enough to spread abroad abundance in all the republic, enough to draw towards us the productions of the whole universe, and to increase incalculably the delights and comforts of life... '[2]

Fulsome no doubt – in those days it was expected of an orator that he should be – but it shows how important railways were considered for the expansion of the mining industry in the Andes. It also explains why Quiroz himself was so interested in the Lima Railway. His own investments in Cerro de Pasco loomed in the background.

On May 13, 1826, Begg and Quiroz presented to the Supreme Government of Peru a request for permission to build a railway from Lima to Callao, and tenders were invited. Eighteen months later, Begg was out of the picture, and Quiroz, William Cochrane and Joseph A. Fletcher were the only ones to tender. Certain easy conditions were laid down by the Government, but there the matter rested. Money for the project was not forthcoming in the upheavals following on the close of the wars, with Peru bled white by San Martin and his relentless minister Monteagudo, and then again by Bolivar. William Wheelwright came on the scene in 1847 with a proposal for the construction, but was unable to pay the sum demanded as guarantee of good faith. Finally, in March 1848, Pedro Gonzales de Candamo and Manuel Vicente Oyague were granted the concession, and the work commenced, much of the grading being done by a labour force of several hundred convicts. Local opposition to the building of the line occasioned considerable delay, until the Government clamped down with heavy fines upon all who hindered the work of the engineers.

Lines connecting other suburbs of Lima in a rail network were subsequently laid. D.C. electrification came along early in this century in line with the Lima streetcar system, itself largely in the possession of Italian interests. The last steam locomotive, a 0-6-2 Kitson tank, was supplied in 1925. Competition with the Central of Peru between Lima and Callao, and of the streetcars on its other routes, finally killed the Lima Railways Company, which was taken over by the Central in 1934 for the sake of getting access to a number of industrial plants, and the old main line was abandoned. With its going there vanished a little realized link with Trevithick and the very birth of railways.

The Lima Railway was not the first in South America. Arguments between Peru and Chile about which country can claim that distinction take no account of the fact that British Guiana had beaten both of them to the post with a small railway working out of Georgetown, opened to traffic in 1848.

By the foregoing preamble you will realize that Andean railways were born of the mining industry, in countries with the linings of their pockets hanging out, where monetary resources were dangerously depleted by the struggle for independence from Spain. Now in the aftermath of the struggle-newly won independence inevitably leading into the 'shake-down' period, while power-hungry *caudillos* (political bosses) were blowing off the excess pressure of personal ambitions – attention turned towards the enormous potential mineral wealth locked up in the Andes. The key to that wealth was rail transport, the cheapest, most efficient means of moving freight in bulk ever devised by man. That claim is as true today as it was in the 1860s, when the 'railway fever', the germ of which had been injected by Trevithick, swept over Chile and Peru in the wake of the tempestuous William Wheelwright, and was brought to a head by that most daring of railrajahs, Henry Meiggs.

From an operational point of view, no railroads could pose such problems as those of the Andes. None climb so high. Himalayan summits may tower over Andean heights, but the loftiest of Himalayan rails would be considered middle-strata stuff by the Andean railroader. Conditions are tough in the Rockies of North America, but the length and severity of grades and curvature there are not to be compared with the high Andean systems. There is good reason to claim, then, that the railways of the Andes are the most interesting in the world.

[1] *The marc weighed 7 oz., 7 dwt., 22 grains.*
[2] *Peru As It Is. Archibald Smith. Richard Bentley, London, 1839.*

3. Henry Meiggs, 1877, the year of his death.
(from a painting by Brian Fawcett)

4. *Central Railway of Peru: the old Verrugas viaduct of 1890, 6,000ft above sea level, height 252ft, length 575ft, photographed 1906. Engine No. 44 is crossing with a special. This bridge was replaced in 1938.* (P. H. Fawcett)

Chapter 2

THE PROBLEMS

THE difficulties in the way of railroad construction in the Andes were basically the same as those anywhere else. It was in their complexity that they differed. Placing them under the five headings of (1) Topography, (2) Finance, (3) Labour, (4) Construction, and (5) Operation, it can be said that each of these created problems enough to daunt any promoters and 'adventurers' not driven onwards by a reckless enthusiasm. But for these enthusiasts, no Andean railroads would have been built!

The preceding chapter will give you an idea of the topographical difficulties. With absolutely no precedent to act as guide, perhaps these appeared less formidable than they do to us now. Trevithick and his contemporaries had no way of knowing what troubles can beset rail transport in the Andes. We who have experienced these troubles look back at the pioneers and wonder at their daring; but this daring was largely the outcome of ignorance. In any case, the schemes of the 1820s were never put to the test. Thirty years later, when rail transport actually commenced in South America, there was enough experience available in the world to enable basic problems to be overcome and to act as a guide in facing up to other and more difficult ones. With its national aptitude for converting the ideas of others into practical form, the United States, in the persons of Wheelwright and Henry Meiggs with a number of unsung but equally ingenious compatriots, dominated the Andean picture. Given the means and the circumstances, Trevithick would certainly have led the field. The Cornishman was no mere dreamer. His work up to the time of the Peruvian mining venture was ample proof of his ability to produce the fruits of his ideas as working appliances. It was no fault of his that the world's first steam operated public railway was not in Peru. As the apostle of high pressure steam, he fought and won a grim battle against intense opposition, and in doing so hastened the coming of the Industrial Age. His prototype locomotives served as a sound foundation for the development work carried out by those who followed in his footsteps. Posterity has unjustly relegated him to partial obscurity, while extolling others who reaped fame from the seeds he sowed.

The saying, 'What is humanly possible can be made financially possible', is true, no doubt, but its implementation in the face of reluctance on the part of the financial powers-that-be is, at best, exceedingly difficult. No sooner had they gained their independence from Spain than the new West Coast republics found themselves up to the ears in political upheavals, which caused the great banking houses of Europe to regard them with suspicion – just at a time when fat loans were sorely needed. When in spite of this a loan was raised, interest rates were fantastically high. In the 1820s, Hullett Bros. of London granted a loan to Chile of one million pounds, raised by the sale of 10,000 bonds, payable to bearer, at six per cent per annum. Converted into Chilean currency, the interest worked out at fifty per cent on the money actually received. Inasmuch as it was intended that Chile should get the million in paper, representing an actual £500,000, it was calculated that in nineteen years it would cost Chile £2,280,000 for interest and principal. The loan of half a million was apparently made – in cash – but some time afterwards, when the condition of the treasury was being checked, it was discovered that only £6,000 could be accounted for. The rest had gone, with absolutely nothing to indicate where![1]

Chile could raise loans only on the security of her mining – silver at first, copper later. At the time of the War of Independence she was the least known and most backward of South American countries. But the virility of her people raised her before long to the position of 'top dog', and her single-track economy was doubled with the wresting from Bolivia and Peru in the Pacific War of 1879 1882 of the nitrate deposits in the Atacama desert and Tarapacá.

Peru, on the other hand, could claim a firmer economic footing, backed not only by minerals, but by guano and sugar also. Guano had been used in the country as a fertilizer since the days of the Incas. Thanks to the teeming bird life along the fish-infested Humboldt Current, and the rainless climate of the coast, there were islands and headlands where the valuable commodity had accumulated so thickly as to seem limitless. In 1836 the brig *Heroine* arrived in Liverpool with thirty bags of it as a sample, and these were given away to any who might be interested in experimenting its properties. By 1841 Peru was marketing it abroad in ever increasing quantities. Europe's exhausted soil howled for more and more; Europe's eager farmers turned out their pockets to buy up all that came to her ports. With the mistaken idea that the horn of plenty was now inverted over them for keeps, Peruvians abolished all taxation and went on a spending spree. The only fly in the ointment was the awkward shortage of labour, of which more in a minute.

As deposit after deposit of guano was worked out, Peruvian faces began to fall. So there was a limit to it after all! But those faces brightened again when it was recalled that nitrate of soda was also a valuable fertilizer, and there were vast quantities of this in the south worked since 1830. Prosperity brought a clamour for improvements – for irrigation of the coastal desert strip, amazingly productive of sugar and cotton wherever a drop of water moistened it – for adequate port works to handle growing exports and imports – for modern transport. Railroads were what the country needed. The object lesson of the United States was close enough to arrest attention. What railroads were doing for that young nation, they could do for Peru. In 1862 there was a resurgence of the old Trevithick scheme for linking the mines of Pasco to the coast by rail. A complete national rail network was envisaged, such as neighbour Chile had actually commenced to build. On the crest of this wave of railroad fever came Henry Meiggs to Lima, preceded by the fame of his exploits in Chile.

Meanwhile, Peru was already in debt abroad. In 1849 the then President, Ramon Castilla – during whose term of office the Lima-Callao Railway was built – began paying interest on the foreign debt, for the first time in twenty-four years. He capitalized the arrears to the tune of £2,615,000, and issued new bonds at four per cent increasing annually by one half per cent to six per cent. That was fine. The value of guano, sugar and cotton exports was rising during the term of his office, which ended in 1862. Then came six years of the by this time familiar political strife while *caudillos* fought and killed each other, and – in 1868 – the accession of José Balta as President.

Cleverly urged on by the ambitious Meiggs, Balta began to spend right and left on public works, with unwarranted abandon. The country wanted railroads above anything else, and Meiggs was there to build them. A loan of £11,920,000 at six per cent was raised in 1870; another of £36,800,000 – to cover the 1870 one and provide still more funds – followed in 1872. Soon the country owed £49,010,000 abroad and £4,000,000 internally, with no hope of being able to pay even the interest. No more credit could be raised on guano; it was already in pawn to the last bag! Bankruptcy was inevitable. And then war with Chile brought an end to Peru's golden years. Invaded, occupied and ravished, it took over a generation for her to rise to her feet again and regain her still shaky legs.

After riding the crest of prosperity's wave almost to the beach, Meiggs died in 1877. This man, whose family roots stretched back through time to remote Dorset, had made himself the power behind the throne in Peru. In the fever of his ambitions, Balta ate out of Meiggs's hands. There was nothing reprehensible in Balta's aims. He wanted money – ever more money – but it was all for the development of the country. He would shape Peru into a storehouse of prime materials for the world's industries and agriculture; but the foundation for future prosperity must be a rail network. The sugar regions of the north would be linked to seaports where vessels could tie up to load and unload their cargoes, instead of lying off-shore in the mountainous Pacific swells amid a huddle of lighters. Arequipa, white city of the south, with its seaport at Islay, would be the focal point for traffic to and from Bolivia and from the rich Cuzco valley. Lima, the capital, would have its rail link with the fabulously rich mining territories of Cerro de Pasco, with the agriculturally productive Jauja valley, and with the untapped wealth of the *Montaña* east of the *Cordilleras* – the warm, fertile valleys where coca was grown, and forests were thick with valuable timber. Those tropic regions at present occupied by painted savages would be opened to civilization with the coming of railways; colonists would swarm there, the forests and their fierce inhabitants would be pushed back, the cleared lands would quickly produce crops for the world's markets. The soil there, with that climate and that rainfall, would grow anything!

Despite his money-making instincts, Henry Meiggs gave a fair return for what he took. The Government knew, at all events, what a railroad would cost to build, and they knew it would be built before the stipulated time, the construction well and honestly done, the *matériel* the best available. What they could not calculate in advance was just how much they would have to pay the astute Don Enrique Meiggs in the way of bonuses for every month gained on the contract time for the work. This Yankee with the Dorset ancestry had a genius for making flash estimates that appeared impossible of fulfilment, yet always turned out to favour him remarkably. Let me illustrate his methods with a little anecdote from the start of his career in Chile.

In the latter part of 1861 the new railway from Valparaiso to the capital, Santiago, 55 miles distant on an airline but 90 miles by the road over which the *birloches* or diligences ran, was bogged down at Quillota, less than a third of the 115 miles that would be the length of the completed line. Ahead was a formidable mountain barrier.

Wheelwright had urged the building of this line in 1842 so lustily that at length he was listened to. It was begun on October 1, 1852, with Wheelwright's own Caldera-Copiapó Railway a year old and doing nicely not so far to the north. In September 1855 four miles had been built, and the line was at Viña del Mar. The snag had been the tunnel at Punta Gruesa, and the almost complete lack of up-to-date equipment for boring it. Official inauguration took place, and people flocked in from all over that part of the country solely for the purpose of experiencing the thrill (plus cinders) of a ride by train through the tunnel in the dark. An English engineer named Campbell built the line on to Limache in 1856, and by June 1857 trains were running as far as Quillota. Then the money gave out.

It had cost a million pesos to construct the first four miles. A projected route by way of Concon was begun and then abandoned, at a complete loss of 327,383 pesos; to say nothing of a sum of 250,000 pesos loaned by the Government.

Successful wheedling backed by the substantial argument of Chile's mineral potential brought a loan of seven million pesos from Baring Bros. of London – on condition that it was all employed in continuing rail construction to Santiago. Those mountains in the way were a serious obstacle. A certain Monsieur Salles was brought from France at a salary of 20,000 pesos to advise. He plumped for the pass of El Tabón, thus justifying his presence with a wise decision. Ovalle Hermanos undertook the construction from Quillota onwards, found their profit smaller than had been anticipated, and backed out. The project came to a standstill, and ministerial hair was pulled out in handfuls at the hopelessness of the situation.

Enter Don Enrique Meiggs, the go-getter always on the spot at the right time. Minister of the Interior Varas invited Meiggs to have a little talk, spread the plans of the railroad out on the table, and said:

'If you are interested, Don Enrique; how much would you complete the line for – six million pesos, perhaps – or seven – or shall we say eight?'

Nobody ever caught Meiggs with his pants down. He had ridden over the route on muleback and his eye was uncannily accurate. A brief estimate pencilled on his shirt cuff was sufficient.

'Mr. Minister,' he replied, 'here's my offer: I'll do it in three years for six million pesos; but if I finish before that, you give me a bonus of half a million plus ten thousand for every month gained. How about it?'

'*Agreed!*' shouted the Minister, throwing the plans under the table. '*It's a deal* – and the italics are mine!' Hands shaking with excitement, he fumbled a contract from his breast pocket, held his breath as Meiggs scanned it, and sighed with relief when the Yankee took up the pen to sign.

Within fifteen days 4,000 men were at work. Dirt was flying, steel was moving, and the loud voice of Don Enrique Meiggs was heard on every hand. The obstacle of El Tabón was tackled with a force of 10,000 men under little Tom Braniff, later Chief Engineer of the line from Vera Cruz to Mexico City. In exactly two years and three days from the date of signing the contract, completion of the railroad was being celebrated in Santiago, and the 'vivas!' in his honour had Meiggs weeping with emotion as he totted up the bonuses owing to him.[2]

The popular notion that the Spanish in Colonial America had an unlimited supply of slave labour to draw upon does not accord with fact. The conquest of Peru was barely over before the King of Spain was ruling that Indians must not be enslaved. The *Conquistadores* and the settlers in their wake rebelled against this outrageous suppression of their rights, and Peru being at a vast distance from Spain there was no way of controlling them successfully. In the early days of the colony, therefore, the Indians suffered abuses enough to unfairly blacken the character of the very people who strove to protect them by wise and just legislation. In 1568, the Viceroy Francisco de Toledo established in Peru a system called the Mita, whereby one seventh of the adult male population in every Indian village was liable for forced labour, within a limited distance of their homes, and in return for a specified pittance. This opened the way to endless abuses. It developed into another system, called the *Repartimiento,* intended for the distribution to the Indians of European goods, but actually a means of enslaving them with debts they were never allowed to work off. In spite of this, the supply of labour on the coast was so scarce that other sources had to be found. The answer was, the importation of African slaves, a trade in which Britain took a leading part.

Nowhere else were African slaves treated with such indulgence as in Spanish America. Writing in 1825, Proctor talks of the happy life they led in Lima – never whipped – never punished.[3] He was speaking of the domestic slaves, who worked no more than they felt inclined to, became autocratic in the homes of their *patrones,* and in many cases were idle, pampered and useless. On the great estates of the littoral their lot was less of a sinecure; but, nevertheless, they were given land to work for their own sustenance and profit, with ample time for labour in their own interests. In 1823, a good African slave cost from £80 to £120. Negro females were more expensive than the males, being in great demand for the care of young children, a chore that Latin American mothers prefer to delegate until their own turn comes with the arrival of grandchildren. Negresses were frequently required as wetnurses, Peruvian women customarily marrying so young that they were often incapable of nursing their own babies.

When a black slave could not be purchased, it was possible to hire one. A negress was paid 15 dollars a month, four of which she handed over to her owner. All slaves were permitted to work for themselves during five or six hours daily. It was easy for one wishing to purchase his freedom to do so. They might sell themselves to another master, and their owners could not prevent the deal. The new master paid the cost to the old one.

Domestic slaves became very attached to the families of their owners. Basil Hall, writing in 1825, says: '… a degree of familiarity is allowed (in all these countries) between the servants and their superiors, of which in England there is no example in any rank of life'. Though in Brazil under Portuguese rule the whip was used much more freely than in Spanish America, the position of the domestic black slave was similarly assured. It is this tolerance that has resulted today in a complete absence of a colour bar in these countries.

Emancipation of the 17,000 African slaves in Peru by Castilla in 1856 was to most of them no less than a tragedy. The blacks turned out to be physically unsuited to work in the high altitudes. Bereft of the protection of their *patrones,* many starved to death, while hordes of negro men took to banditry in order to survive. Regarding the Indians of the mountains, the old *mita,* which had become a poll tax, had also been abolished. This had served to keep the mines provided with labour; and as soon as it was removed the Indians returned to their communities, to which they are by nature attached as closely as bees to the hive. The Government lost not only two million dollars a year in revenue deriving from the poll tax, but also the services of an indigenous population it had depended upon. The labour situation became desperate, particularly on the coast. The African element available for recruitment was small, and not in any case disposed to work hard. The only solution was to attract labour from abroad.

Colonists from Europe were welcomed, but they were not what Peru really wanted. The need was for hands – for labour, and cheap labour at that. The wealthy Peruvians were not industrialists. Their traditions and upbringing prohibited any form of manual work as demeaning. But to own property was to achieve status; and to command labour was lauded in proportion to the size of the forces attached to the estates. Peru lived by virtue of her mines and her agriculture, and these depended upon hired or enforced labour – the cheaper the better. European immigrants were not amenable to this kind of work, even if they could be attracted. But there was a source of cheap labour on the other side of the Pacific – a land of human ants, hardy, industrious, anxious to escape from an uncertain tenure of life occasioned by recurring famines and civil war – the Chinese coolies, in fact.

An immigration law was passed in 1849 which conceded to persons bringing foreign 'colonists' (a euphemism) into Peru thirty pesos per head. These might be of either sex, between ten and forty years old, but must number not less than fifty in each lot. With this incentive began the importation of Chinese coolie labour, a racket that soon became as profitable as slaving had been. There was, of course, the incentive to the Chinaman to leave his own country, or otherwise the trade would not have been possible. Watt Stewart sums up these incentives as follows:

'Every human migratory movement is due, of course, not only to the attractions, real or supposed, in the country of destination, but also to the propulsive forces in the country of origin. In China – in the southern region in particular – strong motives for an outward movement of population existed in the middle years of the nineteenth century. The multiplied millions of the Chinese have for centuries pressed upon the resources of their land. Let the normal pressure be but slightly increased or the normal condition of society be but a little disturbed, and the impulse towards migration is great. The conditions of life in South China at the time mentioned were decidedly abnormal. The chief cause of this abnormality was the Taiping Rebellion, a civil war of great magnitude which began in 1849 and was not ended until 1864. Historians have described it as the most devastating civil war in all history, since they estimate that it caused the death of twenty million persons.... The southern and south-western provinces of China were especially affected. A constant series of petty feuds and local insurrections occurred from 1848 in Kwangtung and Kwangsi. Armed bands of men wandered from village to village, plundering private houses and robbing public granaries. Under these conditions hundreds and thousands of the labouring class found themselves in extreme misery and sought a place – any place – where a living might be gained.[4]

Since 1847 Chinese 'colonists' were being shipped across the Pacific to the New World. The movement began in Amoy, but the Portuguese colony of Macao later proved the most convenient place of shipment – where contract labour could easily be recruited, signed up and shipped to the Americas with the fewest questions asked about the trade by nosy powers such as the British. By 1850 the trickle had become a stream! The conditions under which these wretched coolies made the voyage were comparable to those in the blackest days of the African slave trade. The mortality during the passage was appalling – sometimes as high as thirty per cent. To the speculator engaged in the traffic the value of each coolie landed in Peru was not less than £69 15s. 0d.; so that for economic if not for humanitarian reasons the lack of consideration for the human cargoes was bad policy. It also roused world opinion – led by the British – to the extent that the trade was finally suppressed; though not before a veritable flood of the cheap labour Peru clamoured for had been poured into the country. Some of this clamour had come from Henry Meiggs, who at one time was using more than 5,000 Chinese in his various railroad contracts.

The treatment accorded the coolies by Meiggs excited eulogies from Hutchinson in 1873,[5] who described seeing some five hundred of them in San Bartolomé construction camp on the Oroya Railroad (now the Central of Peru), and noted that some were fat – the only fat Chinese in the country! Meiggs fed them well on rice and beef in plenty, and a good breakfast of bread and tea before starting the day's work. Elsewhere in Peru they were treated like dangerous animals – in marked contrast to the African slaves – and kept in a state bordering on semi-starvation. But Meiggs was noted for his fair treatment of labour. Humanity was part of his character. His men adored him and gave him of their best. It was not mere business astuteness that guided his relations with the labourers in his pay. Humble *peones* who had been indiscreet enough to run themselves into debt and could see only calamity hanging over them would suddenly find their financial troubles alleviated. Young engineers cleaned out of everything they possessed in murderous construction camp crap games and poker sessions found salvation in a fatherly gesture of the sentimentally generous Henry Meiggs, who in all these cases endeavoured to keep his aid secret. Whatever this man's past record – whatever the historians say about his shady deals – I believe that in his human dealings he was a great and benevolent man. I have talked frequently with two men who worked very close to him. Their first-hand accounts mean more to me than sheets of the printed word by writers who judge him by the official records!

Meiggs achieved his remarkable railroad constructional feats by means of vast labour forces, well treated and well paid. But he and his brother John were continually on the lookout for more men. For them, even Chinese were in short supply. The native Peruvians, who might have been expected to form the pool from which all labour requirements could be recruited, preferred abject poverty on the brink of starvation to hard work. Industrious if unintelligent, the Mountain Indian would not willingly leave the region he belonged to, except for local excursions. He was a member of a *comunidad* – a village or commune in which every man, woman and child worked and lived for the community as a whole. Physically adapted to life in the rarefied atmosphere of extreme altitudes, his over-developed lungs had not work enough to do at low altitudes to keep healthy, and disease quickly carried him off. The Negroes were useful labourers at sea level, when they chose to be, but their numbers were comparatively few, and they could not stand the mountains.

The scarcity of labour for his first big Peruvian contract, the Arequipa Railway (now part of the Southern of Peru), caused Henry Meiggs to turn towards Chile, where his conquest of the *roto* – the

Chilean labourer – had put him on the road to success. The *roto* was a good worker if treated right, but about the toughest creature on two legs. Meiggs was probably the first – certainly the first foreigner – to learn the trick of handling him successfully. He was adored by the roughneck labour force of the Valparaiso-Santiago construction, and when notices began to appear in Chilean newspapers inviting recruitment for work in Peru, his men of former days crowded to sign up anew with their beloved Don Enrique.

The Arequipa line completed and the Oroya line begun, a large force of *rotos* moved up to Central Peru where they mixed – not always peacefully – with forces of Chinese and native Peruvians. But Meiggs's difficulties were not thus resolved. He needed more, and still more, men – and he needed more competent engineers. These, too, were hard to get. Peru and Chile could not supply them. It was necessary to bring foreigners in for the technical jobs. Even in the United States the supply was scant. North American promoters were scouring the engineering schools of Europe for young men to carry off for the far-flung railroad projects reaching across their continent. South America could offer little to attract these youngsters while competition for their services was so keen north of the Mexican border. However loudly the Meiggs brothers jingled their money bags, this difficulty of finding engineers remained a major one.

The constructional problems in the Andes were many, but less difficult of solution, perhaps, than those of finance and labour. Trevithick, in 1820, confident in the versatility of 'strong steam', insisted that where mules could go steam trains could be made to follow. On his first journey up the tortuous trails of the Central *Cordillera* from Lima to the pass of Antaranga, and down the other side of the western rampart to Oroya, it is probable that he envisaged rope inclines operated by hydraulic engines developed from the famous pole engines he had put to work in the Duchy in previous years. But before long he was certainly advocating a mountain railway worked by adhesion steam locomotives running on iron edge rails.

By the time he arrived in Peru, Trevithick had abandoned the idea of tram roads with flanged cast-iron trams on which plain tyred vehicles might run. Breakages and derailments were too common. Cast-iron edge rails were better. The adhesion of flanged wheels was vastly superior to plain tyres, but rail breakages were no less frequent than on a tram road. The alternative was wrought-iron, vastly expensive, frustratingly scarce. Spain and Sweden were the main sources of iron bar stock, and with the primitive tooling of those days the forging of rails for an extensive railway was a staggering task.

Given the men, the means, and the freedom from civil strife, it is possible that Trevithick might have taken steam traction up into the mountains; though it is difficult to imagine his ever winning to the summits. Had he made the attempt, the evolution of the locomotive might have been considerably accelerated; for the single-cylinder, fixed cut-off engines of the type he had built up till then would certainly have proved themselves incapable of starting a train on the unavoidably steep grades. The equally knotty problem of bringing a loaded train down these grades may not have occurred to him.

The grading and tunnelling of the line would not have overtaxed a miner of his calibre – provided the necessary man-power had been available. But the question of rails would have snagged him. Wooden rails and cast-iron rails were obviously unsuitable; wrought-iron rails were prohibitively costly as yet; steel rails did not appear until Robert Forester Mushet found a way of producing them in 1857.

It is my opinion that Trevithick was too early for successful steam traction in the Andes. He would have had too many difficulties to contend with. Boilers of the required horsepower for grade operation of that extent were not yet possible to construct for lack of adequate tools and materials. Steam losses were too high. A far greater precision in manufacture was called for than could then be provided. In northern Chile and southern Peru there was a perennial scarcity of water, if not a complete lack of it. Fuel was also a problem, overcome in later years by the costly importation of coal from South Wales. Wood fuel could only be brought at great expense from the eastern slopes of the Andes. It is true that useful coal deposits were discovered near Cerro de Pasco shortly after Trevithick's first pumping engines were installed there, but only limited quantities could be taken from these, and only one mine provided coal of steam quality. Once the guano industry was developed, ships from England brought coal out and returned with guano, but this was some time after Trevithick had left the country. In his day, freight to the West Coast was carried in whalers which might or might not make a call there, or in the vessels engaged in the smuggling trade and dedicated to the carriage of manufactured goods to be disposed of at huge profits in South America. No one was interested in bulk cargoes such as coal.

By the 1850s, when William Wheelwright's ambitions were turned towards a rail conquest of the Andes, the form of the steam locomotive was well established; pistons were more or less steam-tight, multitubular boilers of adequate horsepower existed, and the metallic brake shoe was in use. Trains could now be operated down as well as up long, steep gradients. Three and even four pairs of coupled wheels had been used, fireboxes could be tailored to meet the requirements of the available fuel, the properties of steam were understood and valve events calculated accordingly, thanks to Mr. Stephenson's link motion. Rolling stock, too, had developed enormously in America. The four-wheel pivoted truck was standard there, allowing for greater flexibility and safety in curving. Spring suspension was general. Headlights were powerful enough to illumine the track a reasonable distance ahead of the moving train. Iron bridges were now in use. This was an important point, particularly in narrow gorges with walls so precipitous that bridge builders had to be swayed down in cradles from above to prepare the abutments and anchorages.

The steepness of the western scarp of the *Cordillera* posed grade problems that took remarkable ingenuity to overcome. Rails had to gain tremendous height within a comparatively short distance. The valleys cutting into the main range narrowed very quickly, leaving no room for tracks to turn and twist about between the two sides while gaining height on reasonable grades; and their floors, occupied by mountain torrents, rose too steeply to permit of through tracks unless ropes or racks were used. David Simson, who had worked on the Chilean Transandine and Antofagasta-Bolivia Railway construction, voiced his opinion in 1913 to the Institution of Civil Engineers in London, that getting through mountains was far more a question of curvature than grades – that where curves could be made sharp enough, the line could be taken anywhere. This may have been true enough in some parts of the Andes, but in others there was not room for curves to double a line back on itself where it could no longer advance forwards. That was one of the problems Meiggs and his engineers faced in the building of the Oroya line.

The route decided upon for this line had to tackle a succession of funnel-shaped valleys, one above the other, their wide mouths at the bottom of a steep slope and their very restricted throats ending in a high step below the mouth of the next. Within the confines of each of these valleys tracks could be laid on ledges along one of the walls, well above the River Rimac, whose course the line would follow. But how could those steps at the throat of the valleys be climbed? There was not room for hairpin curves, and even if there had been, it would have entailed the construction of viaducts to bring the track across the valley again. Grades could not be made steeper than was planned, or train ratings would be too low for economic operation. Racks were undesirable from the point of view of complexity, expense and speed limitations. Nowhere had a line so physically exacting been attempted – there was no precedent.

Beside the Central of Peru, all other Andean systems are child's play! The Southern of Peru has its difficult bit, but the Central from the bottom to the top of the western scarp is as bad as the Quebrada de Carhuintala. The Chilean Transandine is topographically simple in comparison, its worst enemy being snow. The Antofagasta-Bolivia Railway has the same altitude, but gained over far more open mountain slopes, on much easier grades. The Guayaquil and Quito has worse grades and curves, in terrain possibly equally difficult, but is nothing like so high. H. T. Booker, ex-General Manager of the Central, whose engineering experience of high-altitude railroads in Peru and Chile is profound, insists that: 'No other line in the world can compare with the Central of Peru. The Chilean section of the Antofagasta-Bolivia was "duck soup" in comparison!'

Henry Meiggs tackled this monumental task at a time when the difficulties of its construction were far more formidable than would be the case today. Behind him was the experience of the comparatively easy Valparaiso-Santiago line – by this time part of the newly fledged Chilean State system – and the more difficult Arequipa line. Apart from those, there were on the West Coast only Wheelright's Caldera a Copiapó, the Arica a Tacna – a thirty-seven-mile standard-gauge road of little importance – and the Lima Railways Company, none of them of the slightest use as a guide to what might be expected in the high *Cordilleras*. But lack of a precedent could not daunt Meiggs; he set to and created one.

English rolling stock – certainly that of the period – was unsuitable for Andean service. The exceptionally easy conditions on British railways failed to show up weak spots in design. Moreover, the accent was on speed, which was contrary to mountain requirements. British practice did not allow for poor track; wheelbase was too rigid, independent suspension unsatisfactory; engines were under-boilered, built up of far too many bits and pieces liable to shake loose or fracture in really hard service, too complex, too awkward to maintain.

John G. Meiggs had some bitter things to say about an English bridge costing when in position a total of £3,350. It weighed 127 tons and took eight weeks to erect, shortly after which it failed. To replace it, an American bridge was purchased, which in position cost a total of £1,956, weighed 61 tons, took only eight days to erect, and rendered excellent service. That's how it was all the time. Under really punishing conditions the American material stood up much better than the European, because it was designed by practical men who had gained their experience in actual operation. European drawing offices were more concerned with pretty working drawings. British designers went out of their way to give their engines a 'clean' look by putting piping and auxiliary equipment out of sight, where it couldn't be got at to maintain or replace! They would cast cylinders and valve chests apart from the saddles and bolt them together, where an American cast saddle, cylinders and valve chests all in one. The result was that the British engines worked their cylinders loose as soon as they were flogged, causing frame breakages behind the saddle. Bar frames – an English invention at once seized on by the Americans – proved in every way superior to plate frames. American design, scoffed at by the British, produced a simpler, more reliable engine, cheaper to buy, far cheaper to maintain than anything from Europe, and able to withstand a continuous walloping, of a sort that soon put European engines in the back shop.

British design began to achieve success only when British practice was forgotten and ideas were radically modified to suit the peculiar operating conditions in the Andes; but the specifications were by then largely guided by American practice. The early Andean systems for which Meiggs was responsible were American-equipped from the start.

So rigorous were the demands exacted by these mountain roads that not even wholly American rolling stock proved ideal. Little by little the Andes evolved its own types. In what way these differed from those elsewhere will be the main theme of the next chapter.

[1] *Mier's* Travels in Chile and La Plata *(1826), Vol. II, App. B.*

[2] *The episode is related in* Los Ferrocarriles de Chile, Historia y Organización, *Editorial 'Rumbo', Santiago, 1943.*

[3] Narrative of a Journey Across the Cordillera of the Andes and a Residence in Lima and Other Parts of Peru in the Years 1823 and 1824. *Robert Proctor, one vol., Constable, Edinburgh, 1825.*

[4] Chinese Bondage in Peru. *Watt Stewart, Duke University Press (N. Carolina), 1951.*

[5] Two Years in Peru. *Thomas J. Hutchinson, 2 vols., Sampson Low, London, 1873.*

Chapter 3

THE SOLUTIONS

Most locomotive engineers, being staunch conservatives, firmly rooted in opinions based on their training, will doubtless find some of my statements controversial. But it must be understood that much of what is recorded here is based on the practice of the toughest of all Andean systems, the Peruvian mountain roads. There can be no standard. Conditions in Peru are not the same as in Chile, Bolivia or Argentina. Not even the gauges are the same. Traffic differs too. The Southern of Peru resembles neither the Central nor the Cerro de Pasco Railway. The Central of Peru, as the highest in the world and regarded by many as the hardest to build and operate, qualifies, I think, as the most interesting. What successful equipment it has evolved would be successful on any of the other railways; but what may have proved successful on the others would not necessarily succeed on the Central.

Generally known as a zig-zag, the Meiggs double-V switch is not original, but his use of it on the Oroya line shaped a pattern for the Americas. His previous work on the Arequipa Railway had not called for the use of this aid to the gaining of height where a horseshoe curve can't be located. His engineers probably lifted the idea from the Ghâts on the Great Indian Peninsular Railway where it had been in operation for some twenty years. Original or not, it was the answer to the problem of how to surmount those awkward steps where the even upward climb of the tracks was obstructed. One single and three double V-switches were required between Chosica (milepost 34), where the mountains proper begin, and Chicla (milepost 87½), railhead at the time of Meiggs's death. Seven more doubles were included in the rest of the line, built some years later.

These zig-zags have been a constant thorn in the flesh of the operating departments, limiting train lengths and losing running time. A train too long to be contained in the dead-end track beyond the switch where converging lines unite, must 'saw' through, a laborious operation, even with the addition of a parallel siding and 'scissors' crossover. For instance, a long train coming down the hill must stop before reaching the switch; the engine cuts off, goes through alone and waits outside, on the lower main track. The train is split, one half is run by gravity into the dead-end track, is picked up by the engine on the lower end and pulled out on the lower main, freeing the switch for the other half, which is then run in by gravity. The engine pushes the first cut up to couple with the other; brake pipes are joined, brakes tested, and the train goes off, the engine running tender first, but leading the consist, until at the lower zig-zag of the double V-switch the same operation has to be repeated. with a parallel sidetrack and scissors crossover two movements; are saved, but the train still has to 'saw' through, and this means considerable time lost. Trains working up the hill will not be similarly delayed, their lengths being less by reason of the limited tonnage rating. At the Central's only single V-switch there is a yard and a turntable, and ample room for trains as long as the system can handle; but single-ended engines are turned, and markers have to be shifted from one end of the consist to the other.

Lengthening of the dead-end tracks in these zig-zags would be a very costly and difficult process, and in some places would call for extensive tunnelling. In one place, the top leg of a zig-zag, now eliminated, was taken out on a trestle extension overhanging a deep gorge – and believe me, train crews brought their trains down into this dead-end with meticulous care; for a not too robust rail stop was the only thing to keep the engine from taking off into space at the end of the trestle in the event of poor judgment in stopping a train that could only just be contained beyond the switch. As far as I know, no fatal accident ever took place here.

Rack sections could have eliminated the need for reversing switches, but their cost and the complexity involved were obviously not worth it. A single rack section, or at most two, might have been preferred, had the conditions to be dealt with allowed of this – as on the Chilean and Argentine Transandine Railways. But on the Central it was obviously out of the question. A large number of widely-spaced rack sections would have been needed. Their cost was against the idea. It would have entailed complicated rack-adhesion locomotives, costly to buy and expensive to maintain. Flexibility in operating speeds would have been prevented, and a ceiling in tonnage ratings imposed. Rather than be tied to the rigid limitations of a rack it was better to sacrifice running time and use zig-zags. When Meiggs built the Middle Section of the Central, the zig-zags were long enough to contain in one piece anything that could be tied on to the tail of the little Rogers *Moguls,* and time lost in switching through a 'double' was not much more than would be required for engaging with a rack and negotiating the section at a speed somewhat under the usual speed with adhesion alone. Moreover, in Meiggs's day rack-adhesion operation was a novelty to be found only on one or two toy mountain railways in Europe.

Much of the track being supported on ledges cut in almost perpendicular rock faces, walled on the outside, the question of concentrated load and gross train weight was very important. The normal American practice of operating tonnage trains to the limit of drawgear capacity with as many locomotives as might be required to keep them moving was not for the Andes. Gross train weight was against it, even if zig-zags had not ruled it out. It was quicker to handle trains cut into sections, each with its own engine and crew. Wages of trainmen were not of the same consideration as in the United States.

The first bridges were of iron, changed to steel after some thirty years of service. Loftiest and longest of all on the Central was the Verrugas Viaduct, 575 feet long and 252 feet in height, the third largest in the world when built in 1870. A cloudburst and rock slide in the gorge it spanned carried it away in 1889 and tied up the railway's mountain traffic until the new steel viaduct was erected by the American Bridge Company and put into service on January 3, 1891. This in turn was replaced by another in 1937 by the Cleveland Bridge and Engineering Company of England. The second one was quite a lively dancer just

5. Central Railway of Peru: train No. 2 backs down the Viso zig-zag en route to Lima. The course of the upper main line can just be discerned on the mountainside above. *(Author)*

before its removal. When riding a Garratt across the long deck span, it was amusing to watch the water slopping out of the fire barrels set here and there on brackets projecting out from the side – amusing, that is, when imagination could be kept in check! Passengers riding over all the Central's bigger bridges get an impression from the coach windows of flying through the air, the unrailed bridge decks being little wider than the track ties, an exciting sense of insecurity not in any way actual.

One major problem to beset Meiggs's construction gangs in the vicinity of the Verrugas Viaduct was a disease of this name that played havoc, particularly among the Chilean rotos. One contemporary writer – Thomas Hutchinson – alleges that 'Oroya fever' (so called because of its prevalence on the Oroya line) and *verrugas* were distinct diseases. Oroya fever, he says, attacked the liver, and the Chileans predisposed themselves to its ravages by spending the nights drinking and gambling instead of resting. For a long time *verrugas* was thought to be fatal if not arrested in the early stages. Likened to a foul venereal disease, it

6. *Central of Peru Andes type 2-8-0 No. 218 roars out of a tunnel and crosses Copa Bridge, at a height of 12,000ft., with a freight of Oroya.*   *(Author)*

was considered that if sores erupted on the skin of the victim it was a hopeful sign. It was believed to be caused by drinking the water here, or in one or two other valleys in the Central Andes where it occurs. Much careful study of it was made; one doctor named Daniel Carrión actually infected himself with blood from a verrugas patient in order to study its effects. He died very quickly from Oroya fever; and the third viaduct over the Verrugas gorge is named *Puente Carrión* in his honour. We know now that the virus is carried and transmitted by a mosquito, in the same way as malaria.

The total death-roll figure of 10,000 during the construction of the Middle Section is probably an exaggeration, but all the same the death rate was alarmingly high – higher than it need have been. *Verrugas* – Oroya fever if you prefer – is confined to a belt at an altitude of approximately 3,000 to 7,000 feet, and within this belt Chilean labourers considerably outnumbered the others. The Chileans were physically unsuited to work in the higher altitudes.

It is interesting to note that diamond drills were used by Meiggs in rock drilling, even at that early date. He hurried tunnelling along by working from both ends at once, sometimes from the middle also by means of an opening in the wall. These side openings in some of the longer bores serve today as a welcome aid to their ventilation. The maximum error in alignment was never in excess of five inches, most creditable for the time.

A malicious slander is the tale that in his hurry to complete the single-track line ahead of time to win bonuses Meiggs spiked the rails to the solid rock in places without the formality of ties. Whoever invented the story was no railroad man. As it happens, Meiggs was surprisingly conscientious in carrying out the conditions of his agreements concerning the provision of sound work and optimum equipment. Any operating man knows that train services would be impossible on track composed of rails spiked to solid rock. However, it was originally dirt-ballasted. When I first knew the road in 1924, most of it was still that way.

An official 4.4 per cent (1 in 22.7) uncompensated for curvature is given as the maximum grade, but in fact this is exceeded in a few places, and reaches 4.9 per cent (nearly 1 in 20). The maximum curvature of 17.5° (radius of 328 feet) applies to the main line. Some sidings and turnouts are sharper. The figures refer to today's track. They may originally have been slightly different. What has altered is the loading gauge. The maximum width of 10ft 6in is still the same, but maximum height above rail level has gradually been reduced to today's figure of 14 feet. In 1926 locomotives were operating that stood 14ft 5in from rail to top of stack. Rock ballasting has raised the track slightly – whereby hangs a tale that shall be told in another chapter. Super-elevation on curves has to be kept down to a maximum of four inches, because of the relatively slow climbing speeds.

Safety switches are a typical feature, these being normally set for the turnout by means of counterweights. Trains coming down grade must stop while a brakeman runs ahead to hold down the switch lever until the train has passed over the blades. Originally, the escape tracks were mere stubs, often ending abruptly against a vertical wall of rock – a convenient if disastrous stop for a runaway – but some have now been lengthened into sand-drags, where space permits. There is one just below Galera Tunnel, where the line crosses the Continental Divide, which in its time has caught runaways in plenty coming down out of the tunnel. I went through it once myself. The effect is a cushioned stop within a matter of yards that would scarcely incommode a sleeping baby! But I may have been overappreciative, since a few moments before reaching it, I and my companions on the engine had been thinking of the many spectacular ways in which our mad career might come to a sudden end.

Certainly, the Middle Section of the Central was the toughest bit of railroad construction of the whole line – a very bold venture indeed. The story goes that at its start a young graduate engineer who thought he knew a thing or two remarked to Henry Meiggs that to lay a track on those tremendous mountain slopes was more than could be done. Meiggs replied: 'So we can't do it, huh! Well, let me tell you, young man, it's just precisely what we aim to do, and if you can't find anywhere to lay the track on, you'll have to hang it on balloons, see!' Perhaps the real aspect of his success was the gift he had for picking his officers – the engineers whose know-how and flexibility of mind could match up to the daring of his projects.

One-spot of the Central was a Rogers *Mogul*, weighing with tender 52 tons, carrying 140 pounds boiler pressure, and named *Oroya* – with an eye, no doubt, to the line's intended destination. The date of its entering service was 1869, and for some time to come it was the pattern for main-line power.

7. *This Baldwin Mogul was typical of Central Railway of Peru motive power at the turn of the century.*

(Author)

8. *Rogers 4-6-0 No. 78, as rebuilt at the FCC's Guadalupe shops between 1924 and 1925. The clean 'English' look of these rebuilds is pleasing to the eye, but made the locos highly inconvenient to service, and resulted in the Locomotive Superintendent's dismissal.*

(Author)

9. *Typical of mixed traffic power immediately pre-dating the Andes type, FCC No. 53 was a rebuilt Rogers of 1906, with a Hunslet boiler, Arequipa piston valves, and a North British tender.*

(Author)

Danforth and Cooke chipped in with four of the same. These little engines were coal burners. I came to the railway just in time to see the last of them. They were an object lesson in the elimination of all but the essential, except in the matter of décor. In a distant land where skilled labour was very scarce, where spares could only be procured from abroad after a considerable delay – there was no Panama Canal in those days, and the regular route to the West Coast was round the Horn – this mechanical simplicity was of enormous importance.

No. 2, *Lima* – another Rogers, dated 1871 – had cylinders 17 x 22in, 49-inch drivers, and a tractive effort at 85 per cent of 15,440 pounds, which would have given her a freight rating over the Middle Section of 85 tons in less than six cars. She was probably considered rather small for the job; for a slightly larger type was ordered from Rogers, this time with cylinders 18 x 24in, and drivers of 45 1/2 inches. The tractive force of 20,337 pounds allowed a rating of 114 tons in less than six, which meant another load. A steam brake was fitted on this and subsequent engines, whereas Nos. 1 and 2 had only handbrakes on the tender. The Danforth and Cooke engines fell between the 2 and the 4 in power, with cylinders 18 x 22, 45-inch drivers, and 18,849 pounds of tractive force. All these engines had steel fireboxes and tubes, and all were *Moguls* with the middle pair of driving tyres blind (without flanges) to reduce curve resistance.

The *Mogul* ruled the Central until 1906. The last batch were Baldwins, one of which – No. 44, *Verrugas* – was in active service until 1925, as a regular yard engine plus stand-in power for the Chosica *Rapido*, a fast passenger run she could handle as capably as a much larger ten-wheeler. Having ridden this engine frequently I can say that on heavy grades the *Mogul* type was not unduly slippery – less so than the ten-wheeler – but their comparatively low tonnage rating was against them. When all was well they steamed freely, but when all was not well the boilers felt their limited size at once. Coal was replaced by oil fuel in the first years of the century, and with the advent of oil boiler troubles began to show up in the way of cracked tube plates and leaking flues.

The *Consolidation* type 2 8 0 first came to the Central in 1906, also built by Rogers, a firm that had been absorbed into the American Locomotive Company. These were similar to engines already at work on the Cerro de Pasco Railway out of Oroya, much bigger than anything the Central had used up till then, totalling 110 tons in working order, with cylinders 20 x 28, a boiler pressure of 180 pounds, and drivers of 52 inches, giving a tractive force of 32,953 pounds at 85 per cent. Their rating of 155 tons in up to five cars over the Middle Section was a considerable improvement on the performance of the *Moguls*, the biggest of which was shy of this figure by 25 tons.

Nothing has been said of passenger engines for two reasons. Firstly, the same power is used on the mountain for passenger and freight; and, secondly, passenger service on Andean lines is financially of little importance in comparison with freight – in fact, passenger traffic is an evil largely forced on the railways by Government legislation. In England, for instance, passenger revenue is roughly 47 per cent of the sum of passenger and freight; on Andean lines it is not much more than 6 per cent.

Passenger traffic requires heavier and more expensive equipment, much of which is only indirectly productive of revenue. Gross weight, always of prime importance in the Andes, is thus increased disproportionately to the revenue deriving from the service. To give you an idea: the tare weight of rolling equipment required to move a 160-pound passenger is 1,232 pounds; while to move 160 pounds of freight, only 160 pounds of equipment are necessary. Passenger trains must be given rights over everything else, often at the expense of freight movement. A mishap with a passenger train is likely to prove far more costly to the company than an accident with a freight. It is no wonder, then, that pasenger services are not looked on with favour by the managements. I want to get this point straight before continuing, since the layman is inclined to regard passenger service as the be-all and end-all of railroading. In the Andes it is an unavoidable evil, and losses with passenger trains must be made good by freight traffic. Fortunately, conditions make special passenger engines unnecessary, and – except on the *Transandino* – train heating is not called for.

The remarkable success of the *Consolidation* type on the Central, Southern of Peru and Cerro de Pasco Railways pointed the way towards a standard type for general service on these lines; but other types were tried. The *Mikado* proved successful, but the addition of an engine truck tended to make them more slippery than the 2-8-0; moreover, the wide-grate, roundtopped firebox and long-barrelled boiler that is characteristic of the conventional U.S. *Mikado* was not the most suitable for oil fuel or for the pronounced tilt on heavy grades.

10. *The FCC's class of Yorkshire Engine Co. 4-8-2's were not a success, the 'Mountain' wheel arrangement being unsuitable for Andean conditions. This is No. 114 of the class in its original form.* (Author)

11. *Performance of the class was greatly improved by cutting a section out of the boiler, and removing the engine truck, turning them into 4-8-0's. No. 112 of this class was a maverick – a 'hoodoo' man-killer feared and hated by all drivers!* (Author)

In 1925 the Central experimented with some English Mountain-type engines which were almost if not quite a failure – an excessive amount of engine with no more tractive effort than the *Consolidators*. Copper tubes and fireboxes gave constant trouble, until after a year or two the whole lot had to be changed for steel. In spite of the equalized suspension, adhesive weight on the drivers tended to 'bridge' between the four-wheeled leading truck and the engine truck, making the locomotives so slippery that they could hardly get up the mountain at all if there were any damp or frost about! All of these engines were finally converted to 4-8-0s by cutting a course out of the boilers, and the change improved their performance somewhat.

Another experiment that failed were some British 2-8-0s of 1908, smaller than the Rogers engines of the same classification. These misfits had four-foot drivers, cylinders 19³/₄ x 24, and a tractive force of 29,836 pounds, being rated for 135 tons as against 155 tons for the American jobs. When received, they were so under-boilered that, before they could go into mountain service, *bigger boilers had to be fitted!* A man with a reputation as an 'expert' in Andean railroading was responsible for their design. How this man won his reputation is beyond me. He was also responsible for some hopper cars we were inflicted with, which were wrong from start to finish! A few of the engines had three cylinders. One of this lot dropped overboard in the Caribbean on the way out, and it was a pity the others didn't follow it! The boilers were unable to provide enough steam for two cylinders, let alone three. When tried on the mountain the centre cranks twisted on the axles, and the middle engines were at once condemned and stripped, which meant new saddles. Finally at work with large boilers and balance completely upset, the class remained a pain in the neck to everyone who had anything to do with them, 27 years passing before they went to the torch, an object lesson in what a locomotive should not be!

I shall pass over Garratts lightly. They were popular with the accountants for economies resulting from their rating of 340 tons and thus their ability to handle two ordinary trains with a single crew; but Traffic

12. An example of the classic Andes type, *which gave sterling service on the Southern, Central and Cerro de Pasco Railways. Southern's No. 102 is one of a series supplied before 1946, after which date domes and sandboxes were put under a single housing.* (Author)

objected to them for the delays they caused in service. They proved rather more costly to maintain than two single locomotives, while burning more fuel per gross ton mile. Moreover, they were confined to a single section of the line.

The *Andes* type evolved from the Rogers *Consolidation* – most successful power on both Central and Southern Railways – and the man responsible was the late Mr. Tom Jefferson, an engineer with many years of experience in Chile before he came to Peru. He was a Kitsons man, very hot on theory and design. A complete non-conservative, by which I mean that he did not cling obstinately to orthodox ideas absorbed in his youth, he sought the opinions of those among his subordinates who had the widest experience of locomotive operation on the line, and built up his specifications accordingly.

The bar frame was never questioned – its obvious superiority was fully recognized. The 20 x 28 cylinders and 52-inch drivers had proved ideal for the Central; but the Southern with its easier grades and faster running needed 56-inch drivers with another half inch on the cylinder bores. The Walschaerts valve gear departed from U.S. practice in being operated by a manual screw reverse. Valve lead in Peru must be much smaller than the usual figure in North America, or engines may not be able to re-start their trains if they stop on a heavy grade. This was a drawback with the U.S. Austerity locomotives produced during the last war – the 'Gypsy Rose Lees', as we called them. The Central had two and they were of little use, except on very easy grades.

The U.S. idea of using blind tyres on centre drivers to case engines in curving was proved wrong. It was not only unnecessary but it reduced adhesion. Flanges give tyres more gripping surface on the rails and must not be eliminated; but to case the rigid wheelbase on curves thinner flanges – known as 'half flanges' – can be used without undue sacrifice. The *Andes* type therefore has all its drivers flanged.

The 2-8-0 wheel arrangement is without question the best for the prevailing conditions. It puts a useful proportion of adhesive weight on the drivers while still allowing for an essential guiding element in the

13. *The Garratt type met with mixed success in the Andes. The Central Railway of Peru used them on one section of the line; No. 124 is seen resting between duties at Chosica.* (Author)

two-wheel leading truck. If the drawgear between engine and tender is well designed, the tender will guide the engine when running backwards. A trailing truck is not required, because on heavy grades, the shorter the boiler the better. In any case, trucks fore and aft tend to upset adhesion. When rounding the tight Andean curves the 'natural slip' of the inside wheels may cause a slippery engine to stall altogether.

When steam was still in use in the United States, boiler horsepower was considered more important than tractive force. In the Andes tractive force is more important than boiler horsepower. At the usual comparatively slow climbing speeds a boiler can be fitted that in North American eyes would be inadequate. A short barrel is desirable in order to reduce the differential in water level when heading up and then backing up four per cent grades, as on a zig-zag. The Belpaire firebox has proved to be the easiest and least costly to maintain, and a long narrow grate is the most suitable for oil fuel. The *Andes* type therefore incorporates these characteristics. The kind of burner is immaterial provided it does the job efficiently. The Central uses a round burner with spiral-jet nozzle, but the Southern has its own burner of a different type. The important thing is that the burner must be in an adjustable mount, at the front, so that it can be properly aligned, and inclined – otherwise steaming suffers. Oil heaters are unimportant with the relatively light crude oil supplied from the Peruvian oilfields in the north; but the fuel line is fitted with a steam-jacket heater, and a coil heater at the outlet in the tank, seldom if ever needed. During one happily brief period of burning the tar-like 'Bunker C', tank coils turned out to be useless, and to keep the sticky black mess moving in the fuel pipe live steam had to be blown into the tank. To clean them internally, fuel lines were provided with a steam blowback also.

Boiler tubes are welded at the bead after expanding in the firebox tube sheet, but 'prossering' has been found of no advantage. With oil fuel, less tube trouble results if the shape of the grate 'fits' the flame – as it does with a Belpaire box – thus reducing to a minimum the amount of cold air pulling in at the sides to impinge on the tube sheet. The Lemaitre multi-tubular blast nozzle and wide chimney were tried with good results on the Central, but are not a necessary part of the *Andes* type. Superheater dampers in the front end are not used.

The general practice is to lubricate driving journals with grease. Rods and motion are grease-gun lubricated. Oil to the valves and pistons is fed by hydrostatic lubricators – not by mechanical ones. This is another important characteristic of Andean locomotives. Lubrication to valve chests and cylinders must be generous when engines are working up grade at slow speeds with a long cut-off. Drifting down grade at higher speeds, very little oil is needed. The mechanical lubricator feeds in proportion to the speed, hence the use of the hydrostatic type that can be adjusted to actual requirements.

The exhaust-steam injector has been found most satisfactory and is adopted as standard in the *Andes* type. Live steam injectors must be non-lifting. Lifting injectors are the devil and all to start at high

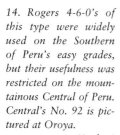

14. Rogers 4-6-0's of this type were widely used on the Southern of Peru's easy grades, but their usefulness was restricted on the mountainous Central of Peru. Central's No. 92 is pictured at Oroya.

(Author)

altitudes. Top-feed check valves towards the front of the barrel, and fitted with spreader plates, have the least ill-effects on the tube sheet. Feed heaters and feed pumps are excellent aids to steaming, but what with air brake equipment, sanding, lighting and other accessories hung on the short boilers, it would be marvellous if room were found for anything else and still leave firebox sides and washout plugs accessible.

There is only one power brake system for the Andes, and that is compressed air – automatic air with straight air control. Altitude alone rules the vacuum brake out; but its disadvantages are several. It consumes steam when steam can least be spared – its release after application on a climbing train sometimes calls for bleeding it off – its lack of a 'reserve' for emergencies makes it unacceptable. Peruvian law calls for three distinct brake systems on an engine. These are: power, hand and water. The latter is the 'repression brake', familar on the Chilean Transandine as a sort of steam counterpart of dynamic braking on a diesel-electric. In Peru the use of the water brake is not encouraged, since the damage it does to valve and piston rings is little, short of devastating. The equipment is fitted to accord with the law, but wary hogheads take up on the water valve stems with a Stillson wrench to make sure no water can leak past into the cylinders!

Sand is such an important adjunct to Andean operation that engine sandboxes cannot be too big. Air sanding is the only satisfactory system. Wet sanding proved bad, causing slipping rather than alleviating it. Gravity sanding defeats its own ends by feeding too much or too little. Air sanding blows a thin jet of dry sand under the tyre treads, where it is needed, in the right quantity, and its velocity is proof against side winds that otherwise might blow it clear of the track.

The importance of generous sand capacity on engines was instilled into me by years of service in the Mountain Section of the Central, where slipping is most frequently experienced. When our third batch of *Andes* type engines were ordered from England, the C.M.E. turned the new specifications over to me with the request to check them and suggest any further improvements. Many years before, I had spent a 'home leave' in the South of France and had been infected there with a great admiration for PLM power, among which were some big 4 8 4 tanks with dome and sandbox incorporated within a single casing – not, as a matter of fact, an unfamiliar practice on the Continent. The sandbox on our new engines was placed close to the dome casing, and it struck me that we might run them into one big casing *à la PLM*, thus increasing the sand capacity considerably, while at the same time providing a convenient 'dryer' in the shape of the dome itself. The builders were appalled, objecting that it spoilt the look of the engines. We held out for the change and it was incorporated. From that time on it became a fashion with British builders of overseas power to integrate sandbox and dome, and Tom Jefferson and I had our laughs together at the spreading popularity of what we considered to be our own idea of adopting a Continental 'kink'.

In contrast to the usual North American practice, Andean tenders had to be kept short. With a long tank on steep grades the injectors may be starved if water falls too low. At the same time, in the interests of visibility it is undesirable to make the tender too high. Fortunately, on the Central there is no shortage of water, and standpipes are conveniently spaced. This is not always the case elsewhere in the Andes.

A final point to mention in the evolution of the *Andes* type is the boiler pressure, which was raised from the old standard of 180 pounds to 200, thus increasing the tractive effort to 36,611 pounds, which allowed of a freight rating of 180 tons in five cars. Thus was the type evolved from the conventional American *Consolidation,* and it is likely to continue its successful career until bumped off the high iron by the diesel now beginning to take over. Peruvian systems are to be envied for possessing conditions which a single standard *bonne a tout faire* can meet, however tough these conditions may be.

The reader may be wondering why nothing has been said about electrification – that with so much water power in the mountains, the case for it must be overwhelming. Indeed, it has been considered repeatedly. But there are snags, and the greatest of these is undoubtedly the staggering cost. Private companies operating on a shoe-string, faced with perennial losses in exchange when buying *matériel* abroad – and it all has to be imported – cannot afford to gratify expensive tastes of that sort. Arrangements with another company to supply the power, rather than generate its own, may relieve the railway of some of the first cost, but it still leaves a formidable capital investment in power distribution and traction requirements, besides placing it in the position of being utterly dependent upon another company which, if unscrupulous enough, might then refute the agreements and proceed to dictate new terms in the knowledge that the railway must meet them or cease operation. Then again, the cost of the conversion is sure to be pared down to a minimum, thus preventing what the operating staff might consider a safe margin for future expansion of traffic capacity; and once a limit has been fixed nothing short of another expensive conversion can change it. The power conductor, be it overhead or third rail, is particularly vulnerable to falling rocks, landslides and washouts the three perils that beset Andean rails most if not all of the time – and such a mishap could paralyse half the system; whereas with steam or diesel traction it affects only a few trains. All in all, then, electrification offers as many disadvantages as it does advantages, and its expense cannot be economically justified unless traffic intensity permits of its being operated all the time at full, or nearly full, capacity.

There is little choice in the matter of diesel traction. Today's trend being in that direction, steam locomotives and their spare parts become increasingly difficult to obtain. Altitude is against the internal-combustion engine, in favour of steam. Diesel-electric maintenance calls for specialist personnel not easy to procure or train in Latin America. For all that, Andean roads are doing well in the matter. Asked if their 'World' units were being adequately maintained abroad, a U.S. builder of export diesel-electrics cited Peru as one of the places where this was best being carried out, a distinct pat on the back for locomotive staff on the Southern, at that time using them experimentally with a view to ultimate complete dieselization.

Just as the *Andes* type of engine was evolved, so have special freight cars been developed for the purpose of 'balancing' traffic, eliminating the movement of empties. On the Central, livestock moves coastwards from the mountains, merchandise in the opposite direction. It follows, then, that a car convertible from stock to box and vice versa could save empty mileage. This sounds simple enough; but a bigger problem was posed by the movement of petroleum to the mining industries in the mountains, and copper, zinc or lead ingots from mines to coast. On account of their concentrated weight, minerals are loaded over car trucks, never in the centre of the platform. The centre might therefore carry a 30-ton 'D'-shaped tank, leaving platform space over the trucks for loading ingots. A combined tank- and flat-car is now a feature of the Central, and considerable movement of empties is thus avoided.

So vitally important is the reduction of deadweight – of non revenue load in the consists – that cabooses are not used on the Central, and crews ride 'on deck'. This can be bad enough by day in the lashing mountain rainstorms, but in the bitter cold before dawn at nearly 16,000 feet it often becomes a real hardship, even for a Mountain Indian. Trains don't operate round the clock on this line, but they get off from their home stations at intervals from about 2.30 a.m. onwards, meeting a temperature at the summit that occasionally drops to zero F. In the old days of 'armstrong' brakes–not so long ago – brakemen had to warm their iron brake clubs in the firebox before they could bear to hold them!

The limitations of engine sandbox capacity brought about the introduction of sandcars in the Mountain Section. These little four-wheeled cars, carrying $2^1/_2$ tons of sand, were pushed ahead of the first southbound freight of the morning to sand the icy track for it and all the following sections. The brakemen detailed to ride them and keep the sand running down through the pipes faced the double ordeal of the cold, and the risk of being run down by the engine should the sandcar jump the track, as it not infrequently did. Needless to say, the chore was unpopular. The sandcars performed a service of doubtful value. An engine will slip on too much sand, or on wet sand, as readily as on none at all. In my day the use of sandcars was falling off, and I doubt if they exist now.

While in charge of motive power in the Mountain Section my eye was caught by the vast heaps of fine, powdery slag being jettisoned on the C de P's growing dump reaching down the valley from Oroya. It seemed to me that this slag didn't cake in the wet, as sand does, and I had the brilliant idea of using it as a substitute for sand on my engines. Why had no one thought of it before?

The Smelter Superintendent looked on anyone willing to remove that slag as a public benefactor, and into a hopper I had spotted down by the aerial tramway were dumped several loads of nice fresh slag, warm from the oven. Screened through fine mesh, this went day by day into the sandbox of a chosen freight engine for testing. We used gravity sanders at that time, and the slag came fully up to expectations in running freely down the pipes without any apparent tendency to cake – though it was far heavier than sand, and inclined to come through too fast. It also afforded a noticeably better grip on the rails. After the tests had been going on for a week or two, the roundhouse foreman asked me if I had examined the tyre treads of Engine 49. Immediate inspection showed that serious pitting was taking place, and the use of slag was at once stopped. Whether this pitting was the effect of chemical action or abrasion I don't know. I kept mum, hoping the District Engineer would not report similar signs on the rails, and fortunately he didn't.

Passenger stock is all of the open corridor type. The earliest coaches were some fifty feet long and tared at twenty tons. Their New Jersey builders included less 'gingerbread' in the construction than would have been demanded for home use, but the workmanship was superb. The Company built most of its own coach and baggage stock later, first of wood, then of wood and aluminium on steel frames. just under sixty feet over headstocks, the best coaches tared at twenty-seven tons. Second class seated 90, first class about 60. All these had open-ended platforms, in accordance with some archaic government ruling. Latest coaching stock on Central and Southern alike – built in England – is of lightweight construction, all metal, taring at about $18^{1}/_{2}$ tons, and seating 94 passengers in the second class. These coaches have closed vestibule ends.

All wheels on freight cars, coaches and tenders are of solid rolled steel, most of them with multiple-wear treads. Separate tyres cannot be used under existing conditions on the Central, the temperatures generated by brake shoe friction being so high that they quickly loosen on the rims. Brake shoes are of castiron to a special formula. In pre-airbrake days it was not uncommon for cars to require two changes of brake shoes from the summit to the coast; but with straight-air control wear has been reduced to the extent that shoes can easily do the whole trip before reaching scrapping limit. Brake shoe consumption is a matter of great moment, and dynamic braking with diesel-electrics will bring about an important saving in this respect.

Passenger train timings on the mountain have improved notably since the introduction of the lightweight stock. Fifty years ago it took nine hours for a passenger train to reach the summit of the line from Lima; at the close of steam's reign, with *Andes* type engines heading the new rakes, the same run was taking five hours. An average overall speed of 20 m.p.h., including stops, manoeuvres through zig-zags and so on, for 98 well-trafficked miles over those uncompensated grades means remarkably smart running and admirable train dispatching. It remains to be seen by how much diesels can better this.

Handling trains in the Andes is an altogether different technique to flat-road running. Starting full rated tonnage on the four-per-cent is an art in itself. The cranks must be positioned right – I'm talking of steam, of course – and you let the train drop back with a slightly cracked throttle until they 'catch'. Then you open up and there comes a surge forward, often followed by a grinding of driving tyre treads on the point of losing their grip. When you hear that, you throttle back a bit and sand, and if the rails are clean you keep going. As soon as she's in her stride you wind the valve gear up into the usual running position, which the dies will hunt for in the links, and find. Then you widen again on the throttle and relax. All this time the fireman will have been following your movements with the oil latch, and when you settle down he makes a final adjustment to the atomizer valve, cocks an eye at the haze over the stack, and climbs off his seatbox to 'sand her through'. If you are heading a varnish train the passengers may or may not have had a shaking – it all depends on your timing with the throttle. If yours is a freight, the drawbar reaction on the cars may have been fairly violent.

The fireman goes to the sandbox against the front of the oil tank, fills a funnel with sand, inserts the long throat of the funnel in the firedoor peep-hole, and shakes the sand through into the firebox. The roaring blast whips it straight into the tubes, and a black cloud belches up from the stack as the soot scoured out of them is blasted away. You cock an eye at the lubricator windows to check the feed, and perhaps you drain the reflex water gauge on your side to make sure it's showing a true level. The exhaust-steam injector is on the fireman's side – the left – and it's feeding steadily. Air pressures are right, steam is steady and all is as it should be. You may then look out of the window and enjoy the view, from time to time casting an eye back along the train, as specified in Rule 510, particularly when curving on your side, to see that nothing is amiss behind.

An old locomotive inspector, much respected over the whole line, once blotted his copybook on this very point. You'd think that the gentle-voiced old man, his face as serene as a Buddhist monk's, would be the last person to fall victim to the failings of lesser mortals; but the story goes that back in the days when Alfaro was a top freight runner, with the best engine in the section, he was afflicted with an overpowering pride, and on one occasion it ran him into trouble.

A visiting director of the Company was making a trip over the line with all the brass in a special that had stopped overnight at Chosica, the divisional point. Alfaro was put on the board to take the train up the mountain next morning, and he came to his engine wearing a top hat, frock coat and white kid gloves. As was the custom in those days, the first thing he did was to run his hand along the back of the main and side rods to see if any stain showed on his spotless glove. Its pristine whiteness remained unsullied. Alfaro's engine was, in fact, gleaming like an undertaker's Rolls-Royce, showing that the fireman and coalpasser hadn't wasted their rest hours on the previous night. Satisfied that all was worthy of the occasion, he backed his engine down on the special till the link-and-pin couplers kissed like thistledown.

As Alfaro, his gloves temporarily laid aside, went round the running gear with the oil can, the District Traffic Superintendent came up to request that he make the best time he could, as the GM and the Director were dining with the General Superintendent of the Cerro de Pasco Copper Corporation in Oroya at 7 p.m., and they wanted to make an inspection round first. The Conductor then brought the orders along, Alfaro signed them, took the clearance card, and handed the fireman's copy over. He noted that the dispatcher had 'given him the railroad' through half the section.

The Station Agent had shaken the moths out of his uniform cap and was out on the platform with all his staff to bow farewell to the distinguished visitor on the observation platform of the principal business car. The Conductor signalled a highball to the engine, the bell tolled solemnly, the whistle roared twice, and Alfaro cracked her open. Shouts went up as the engine moved gently forward. Alfaro smiled, thinking that they signified applause and admiration of his august self, by far the most distinguished figure of the whole select assembly. He widened on the throttle, hooked the valves up and felt a gratifying sense of satisfaction at the alacrity with which his engine left the yard. The steepening grade beyond the safety switch scarcely checked him. Never had he made a livelier start!

The two firemen seemed to be having an easier time than usual. The engine was steaming so well that they were actually able to do some brass polishing and floor waxing in the cab. The 'Crown Fuel' briquettes on the tender must be a particularly good lot, Alfaro reflected. The stack was almost clear, and the steam gauge needle held on the red line without a quiver. He sat there on his seat watching the mileposts flick by, bending the whistle cord meticulously at every tooting post, but afraid to put his head out of the window lest his top hat blow off.

Fifteen miles and half an hour later he blew for the first stop, a reversing station where the engine would take water and be turned. The station agent was out on the platform waving him in with a bunch of what looked like fresh orders in his hand, and the man's gestures were most peculiar – quite out of keeping with the solemnity of the occasion. Alfaro drew up at the platform, his face set in the most dignified expression he was capable of assuming as a mark of disapproval of the station agent's almost insolent attitude. But no sooner had the engine come to a stop than there was a chorus from station agent, yard pilot and peon, enquiring rudely where his train might be!

Alfaro deigned to look back prior to making a dignified but acid reply. Next moment his top hat fell off and rolled under the engine. Behind the tender was nothing but a boxcar and some fifty yards of bell cord stretched along the track like a thin and very elongated tail! At once he realised what had happened. Some wretched switchman in Chosica had forgotten to drop the pin through a coupler link when the train was made up. And the bell cord had not been tied on the end car. It had merely pulled through the hangers without sounding the gong in the cab.

With never a word he snatched the flimsies from the station agent, who explained that the dispatcher had ordered him back to Chosica at once to collect the special with its load of fuming brass. Retrieving his top hat, he took his engine to the table, and as soon as it was turned and the board was cleared for him, he set off back to Chosica with the boxcar, in charge of the coalpasser, to brake him. Yells and catcalls greeted him when the engine and its solitary consist at length rolled into the home yard. Leaving them at the tank, Alfaro collected his belongings, settled his top hat straight, and stalked majestically out of the yard, white gloves and all, to shut himself up in his home, where he remained obstinately *incomunicado* for three days, in the guilty knowledge that Rule 510 had been violated by him, as though he were no better than some beggarly passenger driver. The sacred writ burned before his eyes in the privacy of his house:

'Before leaving a station enginemen must look back to make sure that all the train is following, that no passengers are climbing on or off and that no one is in danger, and to observe any signal that may be given. While the train is running, engineers and firemen must look back frequently to see that all is well.' ...

While I have been telling you that little story, the train has passed through several tunnels. There will be a chapter devoted to tunnels; so we'll let them go now without further comment. However, there's another one coming. The whistling post plate, with *'Pito'* ('Whistle') in raised letters, has three smaller plates under it, one below the other, displaying respectively, 'T', 'P', 'T' (Tunnel – Bridge – Tunnel), but the one signal does for all, namely, two longs and two shorts-the same as the crossing signal. As you come through the exit of the first tunnel, and the smoke is clearing from the cab, you hear the metallic rumble under you that denotes a bridge. The bottom of the gorge is a hundred and twenty feet below, and the rock walls are perpendicular. Ahead, the slender bridge aims straight at the mouth of the next tunnel, its jagged entrance innocent of masonry, its top blackened with a wedge-shaped coating of soot, where the blast from countless engines has impinged. Beyond, you have half a mile of snaking track ending in the bottom 'V' of a zig-zag, where a southbound freight is waiting for a meet with you. Here's the whistling post with its *'Pito',* 'V'; and there's the train waiting, with the front-end brakeman at the switch to let you in on the main and out again up the reverse track before the freight can come out of the sidetrack and proceed down the mountain. You reach for the whistle, give the two longs and a short denoting the approach to a meeting point, and pinch down a bit on the throttle. The steady eighteen miles an hour holds till your engine is over the switch. You sign to your fireman, who reaches for the oil latch with one hand, opens the blower with the other and then fingers the atomizer valve. Throttle and oil latch move together. The blast dies away as a momentary haze over the stack clears. You know exactly how much trackage your train will occupy in the V-switch, and when the deadend is not more than some fifty yards ahead of the pilot-the newcomer to mountain operation finds this part of it nervewracking in the extreme – you twist the handle of the automatic brake to *Service Application* position, lapping it when the brakepipe gauge needle has dropped ten pounds. It's surprising how quickly that ten-pound reduction pulls you up. While still moving at better than a walking pace, the dead-end now only a few yards ahead, you push the brake valve handle back into *Holding* position, releasing the train brakes but holding the engine and tender brakes on. Thus you bunch the couplers for the reverse. As the engine comes to a grinding stop you twirl the screw reverse counter-clockwise into back gear and look out of the cab for the back-up signal. When it comes, almost at once, you blow three short toots on the whistle, put the automatic brake handle back into *Running Position* and crack her open. The bunched couplers allow of a smooth start; so that by the time you are clattering over the switch the train is moving at its usual running speed, the exhaust shouting *'Chaupichaca, chaupichaca!'* and the pistons answering with a contented, *'Fosdick, Fosdick, Postlethwaite and Fosdick!'* – the marching song of the mountain engine when all is going right. The tender is in front of you now, and the cars are above you on the steeply rising grade. Water has vanished below the bottom of the gauge glasses, but the lower test cock is safely 'wet'. The track you came up a few minutes ago is now far below, and the freight is out on the main with the air compressor exhaust showing a white plume above the water separator in front of the stack.

On the tail of your train, now in the lead, the First Brakeman stands in full view, signalling you on towards the top 'V'. When this is reached you push the train in more cautiously than in entering the lower switch; for there the engine was leading. Now you depend on signals, and the knowledge that your train will fit in the top dead-end track with a little to spare. A brakeman has dropped off at the switch, which is normally set for the down line. The moment the pony truck has cleared the blades, he lifts the handle on the stand, lining the iron for the up track, and gives you a highball. Two hoots, and you take the train out and up the main, stopping with the tail clear while the brakeman resets the switch for the down track, twists the 'bull ring' padlock over the handle to its locked position, whips his key out, and then comes sprinting up to climb aboard, while a highball is waved to you from the back. Then a fresh start, until the blast is again clapping out its steady theme – *'Chaupichaca, chaupichaca, chaupichaca!'*...

Bringing a train down is almost a relaxation. The fire is no more than a flame attached to the burner nozzle, and no further adjustment will be required. No blast now-only clatter, the rumble of wheels in tunnels, and a soft *'phut – phut – phut'* from the valve chest relief valves. Speed builds up quickly as you roll off the level on to the down grade, with a mixed freight consist behind you. With your arm on the padded rest along the window ledge, under your right hand is the handle of the straight-air brake control valve. You start building up the pressure in the control brakepipe at once; so that by the time you are up to the running speed of about twenty-five miles an hour you can feel that you have a firm hold on the train. If a sharp curve checks you, a touch of a finger lets a little air out to ease the brakes slightly; if too much speed is gained, a touch more of air brings it down. You find the pressure required for steady running, adjusting with a pound or two either way-the smoothest brake operation that can be imagined! Tunnels now feel cold as you clatter through them. The acrid, rather sweet tang of hot wheels and brake shoes wafts up into the cab; from a car behind comes the clink of a brake beam; in the darkness the sparks glow like catherine wheels about the car wheel treads.

A brakeman comes over the tank and stands in the gangway, ready to drop off and hold down an approaching safety switch. You blow a long toot at the whistling post and pack some more air into the control pipe, building the pressure up from thirty to fifty pounds. Shoes bite harder as the train pulls back on the engine. As you near the switch, if necessary – and only if necessary – you throw a hatful of air into the engine brake cylinders with the Independent Brake Valve. Engine brakes are used very sparingly, if you want to avoid a crop of loose driving tyres! With the speed at a walking pace the brakeman drops off the engine, runs ahead and pulls down the counterweighted safety switch lever to line up the main for you, seating himself on the now horizontal handle to keep it from lifting. Two toots of acknowledgment at his signal to come along, and you let air out of the control pipe till the train is rolling more freely, but checking as the last car clears the switchblades, so that the brakeman may climb aboard. Then, at a waved highball, you let her go once more.

Coming down into the top leg of a zig-zag, you stop before reaching the switch, for the brakeman to run ahead and line it up for you. Then you roll the train in, this time making the stop with the automatic brake. Full stops should always be made with the automatic. It serves as a check to ensure that should anything happen to the straight-air control – a burst hose, for example – the emergency brake is always there, charged and ready. On flatter parts of the line, where brakes are required only for full stops, the automatic brake is the only one used.

Down runs give you a better appreciation of the line and the amazing achievement of its construction. The difficulties you take in your stride with modern equipment evolved by years of operating experience were once considered insurmountable by all but a few eccentrics such as Wheelwright and Meiggs, who hold a high place in the forefront of the daring pioneers of a daring century – a century of tremendous inspiration, tremendous drive, and tremendous gambles!

Chapter 4

THE HUMAN ELEMENT

NEARLY all South American railroad enterprise was instituted by foreigners, and the lack of trained personnel in the countries concerned made it necessary to introduce a considerable foreign element to staff the new railways. National operatives replaced certain of these people as soon as training made them available. For instance, engineers and conductors – at the start of operations invariably foreigners – are now always nationals.

The imported skilled workers were not always easy to handle. Robert Stephenson had something to say on that point as far back as 1827. He was talking about English miners, but his words apply equally well to other trades – and to others besides the English:

'English workmen are not so manageable even in this country, and much less so in Spanish America, where they are apt to be spoiled by the simplicity and excessive indulgence even of the better classes, and where the high salaries they receive place them far above the country people of the same condition. All this tends to presumption and intolerance on their part, and ultimately to disputes and irreconcilable disgusts between them and the natives."[1]

The process of replacement was gradual, nationals taking over when the foreign incumbents retired, died or drank themselves out of a job. Even when the process had been completed in most places, there still remained one or two pockets of foreign monopoly; such as at the throttles of Cerro de Pasco engines, where American hogheads lingered on until quite recently. Once sacred to the imported specialist, the posts of roundhouse and shops foremen fell to national assistants; and so it went on, until virtually the only foreigners remaining were the officers. It stopped there. As long as British companies operated South American railroads they kept a majority of British officials. It still applies to the one or two companies surviving the wave of nationalism that swept control of the railroads out of the hands of one foreign company after another.

This foreign railroad enterprise has been cited as an example of 'exploitation' of the Latin American, as though it were something shameful. The various countries of South America began it themselves by howling for rail transport, which they were given – the Andes republics, at any rate – by one or two dynamic foreigners who happened to be gifted enough to transform dreams into reality. The companies formed to administer these railroads had perforce to make a financial showing to their shareholders, and to do this is no more 'exploitation' of a foreign country than it would be of their own. But for the incentive of possible gain the money would not have been forthcoming to build them, and the countries concerned would have been the poorer. So many people in all walks of life live directly or indirectly on the benefits deriving from the institution of rail transport that the foreign company is actually giving to the country far more than it takes. In most cases, the proportion of foreigners to nationals on these railways was controlled by law from the start.

Railroad men are cut of the same cloth everywhere. The calling moulds a type, just as the ocean does. In the subordinate categories the South American makes a fine railroader – industrious, keen and hardy. This is not always the case with the operating officers. There is a racial difference; and Hispanic tradition, still an influence to be reckoned with, militates against the donkey work that goes into the making of a good operating official. Speaking broadly, the young man of Spanish ancestry has no objection to an official position, provided he isn't required to dirty his hands getting it! This is the trend – not the rule. Unfortunately, know – how is a matter of *personal* experience where railroading is concerned. Second-hand knowledge won't fill the bill. Like seamanship, railroading is not learned from books – and this applies particularly to railroading in the Andes. Nor is it bestowed with a college degree. This is not to deny that the white-collar classes have produced some excellent executives, notably in Chile, where State railroad enterprise took its place early in the national way of life of a virile people. However, there remains the fact that a barrier has stood between the progressive operative of working-class origin and the administrative positions, albeit some of these men have possessed not only the experience but the intelligence for the posts; while the white-collar man, not obstructed by this same barrier, generally speaking prevented himself from qualifying for those positions in the foreign companies by a traditional reluctance to start at the bottom. Hence the reliance on foreign officials, amenable to training from the ground up, enterprising, and – if of the right sort – instinctively dedicating themselves to the work, making it the most important factor of their lives. The very fact of their 'foreignness' invests them with a certain authority, which would not be accorded by the subordinate grades to one of their own people until a footing had been gained over a considerable period of time.

The British official finds himself heir to a reputation for honesty and fair dealing, won in the past by the whole and still adhered to in the present by the majority; and to a great extent his natural inclination to associate in preference with his own kind removes from him the suspicion of bias or favouritism. The North American is not constituted in quite the same way, but by and large he too is inclined to associate with his own kind. The German is far more likely to become identified with the national life, marry a national and bring up his children as nationals; but he sacrifices his foreign 'authority' in doing so. The Italian, and to a less extent the Frenchman, are absorbed, and eventually lose all trace of foreign origin. Blame the English and the Americans for their obstinate insularity, if you like, but at the same time recognize this insularity as an advantage in the management of railroads in countries beset by all kinds of political intrigue, bribery, corruption and nepotism.

The lowliest of Andean railroad labours are carried out by that hardy individual the Mountain Indian, or his close relative of slightly mixed blood, the *Cholo*. His particular provinces are the track gangs, the freight sheds, the roundhouse pits – wherever the work may be hard, dirty and monotonous. The world he is born into confers no favours upon him. If dependent for his survival upon what he can produce from the Andean soil, life is an unrelenting battle with the forces of nature. In spite of that, the ties with his land and his community bind him so tightly that he never willingly relinquishes them, and even the comparative affluence of a modest pay packet in industry, with the unaccustomed security it bestows, cannot prevent the seasonal returns to his native soil. He is not cursed with intellect – coastal folk deride him as stupid and dirty – but he is inherently honest, and where fair treatment has been accorded him he is loyal.

These mountain peones are at their best under the toughest conditions of weather and altitude. With good supervision and direction, the labour they can perform is amazing, and so is their stamina. Given plenty of coca – the stimulating leaf chewed by them to allay fatigue and the pangs of hunger – they can labour forty-eight hours and even more without a rest. When a number of gangs are being used in all-out work on wrecks or landslides, wise superintendents provide generous quantities of raw alcohol, bread and steaming coffee, calling periodical breaks for refreshment. When this is done time out for sleep can be forgotten. Such luxury is a feast to a *cholo* labourer.

From these same people come youngsters more ambitious than their fathers, in proportion to the mixture of blood in them, who aspire to train service and roundhouse work. They may even win to the elevated ranks of roadmasters, conductors and enginemen. In the mountains they are what the *mestizo* is on the coast. This *mestizo* is a mixture of bloods which may include African, European and Chinese. He is astute, quick to learn, inclined to dishonesty; but his character really depends on the predominating blood in his veins. When this is African he may be unreliable; where the Indian is uppermost, he can be relied on more. Indian blood, you see, mixes better than African; and the Chinese additive is no disadvantage to either. This human cocktail is influenced by latitude. In Southern Peru and Northern Chile the *mestizo* is an excellent chap as far as work is concerned (though a political firebrand), but his character deteriorates as he approaches the equator. Mentally brighter than the *cholo* of the mountains, the *mestizo* of the coast is generally at the bottom of labour disputes.

There exists a social demarcation between *Obreros* and *Empleados* (literally, 'Workers' and 'Employees'), the difference being payment on a daily and monthly basis respectively. At the outer extremities of each class are complete racial differences, but in the middle both overlap. Speaking broadly, it might be said that the indigene predominates in the *obrero* and the Iberian in the *empleado*, and it is the latter class that mans the offices, the stations, the dispatchers' desks. A man capable of becoming a good train dispatcher is outstanding in any organization; one who can make a fine chief dispatcher is a superman! His knowledge of the whole system must be encyclopedic; he must know the traits of every engine, every engineer and every conductor; he must always be in complete control of himself, immune from panic, able to picture the whole without ever losing sight of the detail; he must be capable of concentrating for hours at a time on the trainsheets without letting his mind wander a degree off course; he must be a diplomat by nature; and, of course, he must be an authority on train movements and 'the book' in general. Day after day, night after night, he shoulders a crushing weight of responsibility – far more than anyone else on the system. No greater praise of the Latin American as a railroad man could be expressed than the assertion that he makes as good a train dispatcher as you would find anywhere.

Yardmasters are born, not raised from the ranks of conductors bumped off the main line. Personality counts for much in the formation of a good 'dinger'. Loud-hailers and walkie-talkies on the natural humps of Andean yards may make redundant the powerful voice of the old-time yardmaster, but the character that went with the voice is still required. Yardmasters are to Traffic what Roundhouse Foremen are to Traction, and in type they resemble each other. These posts, once the preserve of the foreigner, are well filled by nationals bred to the game.

One of the most important positions, which no foreigner can hold, is that of *Comisario*. This functionary is the 'chief of police', as it were, responsible for the safeguarding of property belonging to the company or entrusted to its care. He is a go-between in any matters in which the company must deal with the national police. He must know how to get things done in government offices; his contacts in the sphere of civil service must be influential. He is called upon to deal with situations as far removed as the nipping in the bud of trouble that might precipitate civil strife on the one hand, and bailing an official's automobile out of the deposit on the other. His methods are his own business: they are not questioned by wise management. He enjoys a large measure of independence, his official reward is good, and his unofficial rewards remain his own secret. He is worth it whatever they are, if he is the right man for the post. A South American is alone fitted to fulfil this duty. But good *comisarios* are rare, and when one does appear he is an asset indeed.

Being naturally skilful with their hands, South Americans make good machinists and blacksmiths. Fitters and their helpers on Andean systems need to be kept up to the mark, but in this respect they differ little from their colleagues elsewhere. From their ranks emerge outstanding men who in due course take over as chargehands and foremen, and in their turn hound the rank and file for such misdemeanours as using Stillson wrenches on hexagon nuts, knocking superfinished pins out with ball-peen hammers, or mixing fuel oil with the valve oil to make it go further.

I recall browsing through an old personal record file of a certain Andean road and being amused at the number of foreign enginemen whose careers with the company terminated abruptly with the words, 'dismissed for drunkenness'. These were not merely violations of Rule G in the broadest sense.[2] The offenders had repeatedly turned up for work dead drunk, or carried enough booze on their engines to get them into that condition, and warnings had failed to stop them doing it. Many of them were 'boomers', drifting from job to job, from country to country, 'pulling the pin' and clearing out whenever they ran themselves into serious trouble.

Not all were of this kind, of course. Without those who were not there could have been no Andean railroading in the first place. There were also the many steady foreigners in engine service and occupying the 'non-commissioned' ranks who helped train the personnel of the country for the jobs they later handed over. But drink was ever the weakness of the foreigner in South America. The South American himself is temperate in comparison; though I have known exceptions.

I well remember one such. As far as I knew he was an excellent engineman; but rumour had it that on occasions he hit the bottle hard. He spoke little, was conscientious in his duties and a great maker-up of lost time. One day I rode the engine of the principal passenger train with him down the mountain. Every manoeuvre through zig-zags and safety switches, every station stop, every start, was made meticulously. I had no occasion to talk with him, and he said nothing to me or the fireman. He just sat dead still on his seatbox, as erect as a wooden figure, leaving everything but the running of the engine to his fireman – even the oiling round. This struck me as odd, but it was my custom to avoid as much as possible any interference with crew regime on engines. After a fine run, dead on time, the bad grades behind us and the train standing at the last stop before its destination, this hoghead suddenly heaved himself up off his seatbox and fell unconscious on the deck. It was no stroke, as I at first imagined. He was dead drunk – paralytic! Peculiar clinking sounds heard in the darkness of tunnels must have been made by bottles being

15. *A Rogers 2-8-0 lost through a low-water boiler explosion at Naña, about 1920. Human error was to blame, and both enginemen were killed.* (Author)

16. *If left 'in gear' an engine will sometimes move itself, which is probably what has happened to FCC No. 81 at Oroya. If such an accident occurs when the roundhouse is full, it may cause a complete stoppage of traffic until the imprisoned engines are freed.* (Author)

taken from his seatbox and put back again. What was found in there proved to be cane alcohol. His dismissal was inevitable, a shock to me personally, and the loss to the company of a very good runner.

On relinquishing their throttles to nationals, some British and American engineers went up the ladder to become inspectors, or road foremen of engines. Where several of them worked in close proximity, none seemed able to speak a good word about the others. Rivalry and ill-feeling were apt to flare up into violence. My path once crossed those of two such men, whom I shall call Lancashire and Yorkshire. Lancashire was elderly, frail-looking, the possessor of a vitriolic tongue. It was his custom to carry with him a box camera wherever he went, and according to bulkier and more stolid Yorkshire this was for the purpose of snapping photos that might be used as evidence against anyone he disliked. Their enmity was implacable. One day, Yorkshire came into a coach of a passenger train to relax rather than ride the engine he should have been on, and found Lancashire seated therein. Lancashire spat some acid remark at his rival, and Yorkshire, picking him up by the scruff of his scrawny neck and the seat of his pants, threw him out of the window, camera and all. The train was moving at a smart pace at the time.

Not long afterwards, Lancs, sitting in the fireman's seat of a big freight engine, saw Yorks coming along the track on the same side of the engine, and opened the blow-off cock on him. Yorks was lucky enough to escape no more than slightly par-boiled in places, and when he looked into the cab to see who had done it, of course there was no one there.

A burst of labour unrest brought troubles to the railway, culminating in an enginemen's strike. Certain important train services had perforce to be run, and operating officials were called upon to keep them going. However, it was a blunder on someone's part to book the cantankerous Lancs as engineer of Train No. 1, the through passenger train up the mountain, with Yorks as his fireman. Originally an LNWR driver who had arrived at his present position via throttles in Africa and Bolivia, Lancs rated as the senior man, but Yorks – whose origin on the Great Central was probably confined to the scoop – was not the one to accept an inferior office without argument. Lancs took care to be on the engine in good time. It was American power with a firebox coming back almost to the rear of the cab and the decks three feet above the apron, making it possible for him to take up a position difficult to win by assault from below. The throttle lever was on top of the firebox, and of course was of the push-and-pull type.

When the Conductor took the train orders along to the engine he found a hot argument going on between Lancashire and Yorkshire about who was going to do the running. Lancs grabbed the flimsies, signed them without reading a word – never ceasing his lashing remarks to Yorks – and thrust them back into the Conductor's hands. Yorks then seized them, separated the copies, saw on them that he was named merely as fireman, and flung them all into the firebox. Lancs picked up a Stillson wrench and threatened to beat his rival's brains out. Yorks threw Lancashire's tea bottle at him, but it flew wide through the cab window. The Skipper fled.

What with the tight squeeze past the rear weather plate of the cab and the backhead, further obstructed by the steam-brake valve, Lancashire's stronghold was pretty secure; though if difficult to assail, it was also difficult to defend. Chattering and scolding like an excited monkey, Lancs brandished his Stillson, bent the whistle cord and cracked open the throttle, determined to show Yorkshire who was the hoghead of that mill. Yorks uttered a cry of baffled rage and dived at the thin legs of Lancs as the engine surged forward with a jerk that nearly stood the wretched passengers on their heads in the coaches behind. Lancs kicked out at his attacker's face, almost dislocating his toes on the vacuum brake air pipe. As Yorks grabbed one of his skinny ankles, Lancs smote downwards with the Stillson, but it struck the elbow of the steam-brake pipe and clattered to the cab floor. Yorks then reached for the other ankle, grasped it firmly, and pulled with all his might.

Determined not to be unhorsed, the champion of the Red Rose seized the throttle lever with both hands as his feet were snatched from the deck. There he hung suspended, screaming imprecations. Yorks tugged, Lancs gripped more firmly, and the throttle was perforce pulled more open. The train shot out of the yard like a scalded cat. Had there been the normal tally of switchmen and truckmen lazing about, it is not unlikely that some headless or limbless corpses might have strewn the tracks in the train's wake. There was no grade, and the consist being made up for the mountain, acceleration was comparable to that of an MU suburban rake. The passengers were by now on the coach floors with their luggage on top of them!

Yorks tugged again, swearing awful things if Lancs didn't immediately cede the position he had usurped. Lancs continued to scold in his high-pitched nasal scream, and held on. The throttle was back against the end of the sector by now, and the Johnson-bar being down in the corner, the roar of the blast was loud enough to crack the windows in the houses of the street alongside the tracks. Passers-by flattened themselves against walls and covered terrified faces as the train rocketed past with a din like an artillery barrage.

Half a mile up the track was the turnout from the main iron into the yard of the engine terminal. That particular switch had been carelessly left as it was after the engine was wheeled out earlier that morning, but neither of the two lunatics in the cab had eyes for the track and the switch targets. The train hit that open switch with an anguished scream from tortured flanges audible even above the thunder of the blast. By some miracle engine and tender kept upright, taking the switch without derailing. The rake then shot through the still open gate into the yard, and streaked towards the turntable.

The jerk on the turnout broke Lancashire's grip on the throttle and caused Yorkshire to drop the other's ankles, shoot across the gangway and all but tumble out. In passing the vacuum brake valve Lancs grasped it to save himself, pulling it into full application position before he fell to the deck. Fearing another assault, he picked himself up with alacrity, and suddenly became conscious that all was not as it should be with the train. A glance from the cab window disclosed to his horrified eyes, not the clear stretch of the main line's double iron, but the confines of the Locomotive Department's yard, and the dangerous proximity of the roundhouse. Slamming the throttle shut, he pulled the steam-brake handle over. His strength was not up to hossing the Johnson-bar into reverse, so he did the next best thing, and prayed. On the other side of the cab realization had dawned with equal suddenness on Yorkshire. He took off from the gangway like a fighter from an aircraft carrier's catapult, and crashlanded in the reeking drip-apron under the fuel oil tank.

Owing to the strike, no engines were standing on the lead track. Train No. 1 had a clear run to the turntable. The latter was of the balanced type, and when the engine ran over its deck it leapt so wildly that ball bearings were scattered about the pit! But the brakes had a good hold now – or maybe Lancashire's fervent prayers had been heard. On the other side of the table was the car wheel park, and the train came to a stop with the engine dammed up against a mound of wheels and axles.

Everyone was more frightened than hurt. The train was even able to disentangle itself from the wreckage in the wheel park, back out on the main once more and go on its rightful way, still in the charge of the two now thoroughly chastened knights of the Red and White Roses. But retribution descended upon them afterwards. Yorkshire found a job as boss of the municipal garbage incinerator. I never saw Lancashire again. Someone told me he went home.

The social laws affecting industry west of the Andes are not always observed to the letter except by the foreign companies. Trades union pressure and political expediency brought about the institution of social security and services before England had them, and at the same time laws were passed that placed on the shoulders of private enterprise a burden of expense enough to break the back of any organization whose finances were not healthy. This was a case of the pendulum swinging to the other extreme. In the past, the only security enjoyed by the worker and employee was the sense of fair play of their management, a virtue not by any means general in big business, but laudably possessed by some of the railroads.

Union differences, labour 'demarcation' arguments and restrictive practices have been a part of the way of things on the West Coast for some time, swelling or shrinking in accordance with the political colour of the government in office. Exaggerated pay increases are claimed with clockwork regularity in the assurance that if forced to arbitration a satisfactory proportion will be awarded in the interests of industrial peace. The pattern is familiar enough by now. Consideration of the lamentably low standard of living of West Coast labour until comparatively recently makes it difficult to condemn the trend. A track peon on the equivalent of 2/- a day (at par), albeit housed by the company, was able to feed and clothe his family only while working regularly, with absolutely no reserve to cushion non-working periods. Skilled men were of course on proportionately bigger wages, but ever on the fringe of poverty; and those employed in the railway departments based on cities were obliged to find their own housing.

Trades union pressure has brought about legislation enforcing notable improvements in the way of sick pay, dismissal compensation, paid holidays and pensions, but many foreign companies already had such arrangements in operation. Far from being soulless exploiters of cheap native labour, the foreign-administered railways were second to none in their considerate treatment of personnel. It is to be noted, too, that employment by these companies always has meant fair treatment, prompt and certain payment of wages, and in many cases excellent free housing. The provision of facilities for sport and culture, clubs and other amenities are ways in which foreign concerns 'pay' voluntarily for their right to 'exploit' the national. Their rates of pay, however low in the past, were usually better than the standard in national companies at the time, and still are.

Working hours and overtime have undergone the same improvements as pay scales. In the early days of Meiggs's railroads firemen slept on their engines, cleaned them and helped maintain them, putting in a 14- to 18-hour day in train service. Trainmen were similarly bound. Autocratic engineers and conductors 'lived ashore'; but, of course, their working day was much the same. Engine cleaning was a spare-time task, except for any that the extraordinarily hard job of firing permitted to be done on the road. Today, engine and train men are guaranteed 'on call' pay of 75 miles for 26 days a month, or mileage at ordinary and overtime rates; and if hours of duty amount to more than sixteen a man may not be called out again until he has had a full twelve hours' rest. The 'on call' rate is approximately three fifths of the average daily service mileage. Passenger trainmen earn less than in freight service, but their hours are generally shorter, their work easier, and a certain prestige accrues that must be taken into consideration. In a good freight section, at 'mountain' rates (higher than 'coast' rates), engineers and conductors may be earning more than yard-masters and roundhouse foremen.

The best enginemen in my day were those who had been brought up on coal firing. One outstanding example on the Central of Peru was Don Enrique Benavides, a passenger runner in the Huancayo district when I first knew him, and later an inspector. Don Enrique's engine was always a model of spit-and-polish and efficiency, as clean as he himself was dapper. With unfailing regularity he scooped in the monthly bonuses for the best fuel oil consumption. No one ever saw anything thicker than a light haze above the stack of his engine. The burner on that engine was a design of his own, built in his spare time. I knew that, but the Locomotive Superintendent did not, or there would have been trouble.

Locomotive Superintendents very rightly insist on standardization. At a time when burner performance is being watched in order to develop the most satisfactory type for the service, any private experimenting might cause confusion unless officially controlled. But Don Enrique was an exceptional man, and I felt it could be pardoned me if I turned a blind eye in order not to discourage his ability and interest in his work. Don Enrique's burner had been offered for consideration and had met with a peremptory refusal. How it would have shaped in general service I have no means of knowing, but under Don Enrique's own supervision it was more efficient than the one fitted as standard.

The extraordinarily tough conditions of Andean railroading do not favour the formality and rigid caste system in force among foreign staffs on many large British railways abroad. In the Andes the work is intensely personal. The systems have organizations of a size not too vast to be seen as a whole. The weight of each officer counts as surely as does each instrument in a chamber music ensemble. The result is a closely defined 'family feeling', and a pride in the importance of individual effort. The capability of every colleague is known to everyone. Under these circumstances it is inevitable that the rightly constituted official should place above everything else the interests of the system that he comes to regard as in part his personal property. It is thus a matter of course for him to meet emergency demands with all that is in him to give, without question; and as emergencies crop up frequently in the kind of railroading you find in the Andes, every occasion welds him more securely to the work. The more easily a railroad organization can be seen as a whole, the easier it is for a junior official to identify himself with it; thus is the interest in his work greater, and, as a corollary, the more comprehensive his experience, with a consequent growth of his value later as an executive.

The Departmental System of organization is the usual one. Departments are: Traffic (including Operation and the *Comisario's* section); Engineers (bridges, buildings and permanent way); Motive Power (divided into Shops and Traction); Electrical (telecommunications, installations and electrified track equipment); Stores; Accounts (including Train and Station Auditors). The Shops and Traction sections of the Motive Power Department will each have its own chief responsible directly to the Locomotive Superintendent or Chief Mechanical Engineer, as the case may be. There may also be a Chief Chemist, to control water treatment, and – as on the Central of Peru – to assay minerals for determining their appropriate freight tariff.

Foreign officials being few, and many of them having 'grown up' in Andean railroad service, their close contact with men of their own and other departments tends to foster sympathetic relations and mutual confidence. This was notable in the past, if less so in these days when dedicated trouble-makers find ears more conditioned to their diatribes.

There is apt to be a somewhat cosmopolitan colouring to any agglomeration of labour and administration on the West Coast. A British District Traffic Superintendent in the Peruvian Andes had in his section a Russian brakeman named Antipov, who was always in trouble. The man was a good brakeman, but when in liquor invariably made a nuisance of himself. His immense strength was most useful on certain way freights, or merchandise plugs, when particularly heavy weights were to be loaded or unloaded by hand, and Antipov was always ready to demonstrate his muscular power. When not busy he was mischievous. One day he set fire to the grass at a zig-zag out of sheer devilment, and burnt up the pasture belonging to an Indian homestead. It came as a climax in a series of petty misdeeds, and the Super called him on the carpet to mete out justice in the form of a fortnight's suspension. Antipov was outraged.

'Two weeks for *that, señor?* But it was only a bit of bunch grass. They always burn it at this time of year!' he objected.

'It was the pasture for the man's animals, and he was counting on it,' replied the Super. 'Why the devil did you have to set fire to it anyway? I'm sick and tired of your pranks, Antipov, and this time you're for it!'

'But señor – two weeks – it's excessive! A day or two perhaps; not two whole weeks. It won't happen again, I promise. You can trust me. Let me off this time and I'll prove it. You should give me that much consideration, señor. After all, we are of the same blood, you and I...'

---

[1] Life of Richard Trevithick. *Francis Trevithick, London (1872), Vol. II, P. 283*
[2] *Rule G insists that: 'The use of intoxicants while on duty, or the frequenting of places where they are sold, is prohibited'.*

17. *Last of the Central Railway of Peru's foreign drivers was David Ludwig, who came to Peru from the Midland Railway of Deely's day. For many years he ran Sentinel railcar No. 1 and the success of the unit was in no small part due to him.*

(Author)

Chapter 5

THE TRANSANDINE LINK

Darwin, in March 1835, left *Beagle* in Valparaiso and made an excursion over the *Cordillera* via the Portillo pass to Mendoza, on the Argentine side of the Andes.[1] Travellers between Argentina and Chile had a choice of two trails for the high Andean crossing. The less perilous and the lower one was by way of the Uspallata pass, under 23,380-foot Aconcagua, the giant peak that, by the way, is not unanimously regarded as the highest in the range. The other route, via the Portillo pass, was the higher, the windier, the most difficult. These trails raised the hair off many a European head by reason of their badness, narrowness and perilousness; but Darwin decided that the dangers of his return route from Mendoza, over the Uspallata pass, had been greatly exaggerated. The *cumbre*, or summit, of that trail was 12,454 feet high, the amount of snow lying about making this moderate altitude appear loftier than passes of 15,000 feet in the Central *Cordillera*. Both W. B. Stevenson and John Miers wrote vivid accounts of this mule journey from the Argentine *pampas* into Chile, some ten years before Darwin's visit, and their opinions of the trail were penned with considerably more emphasis than the great scientist's. By and large, it was much of a kind with mule travel anywhere along the length of the high Andes, but it happened to be a particularly important route – an international artery, for all its badness.

It was quite obvious that a rail link was called for to increase trade between the two countries and provide communication between Atlantic and Pacific ports quicker than the arduous sea passage round the Horn. As already mentioned, William Wheelwright had considered the practicability of a transandine railway here in 1854, shelving it in favour of his northerly San Francisco route on account of the snow problems involved. All the same, it offered the shortest distance, and the moderate altitude of the pass promised lower construction costs. Moreover, it was close to centres of population, and profitable volumes of traffic were envisaged.

It remained for the Clark brothers, Mateo and Juan, to arouse interest in a rail crossing of the *Cordillera* via Juncal and the Uspallata pass; and it was while they were engaged in the survey for an international telegraph line that the urge to organize such a project began to tickle them. As soon as the concession was in their hands they made a closer study of the route in company with certain engineers of repute – Figueroa, Warring Davis, Barker, Galloway, Pretot Freire, Duval and others. They came up with two proposals: one was to unite the towns of San Felipe and San Juan by way of Protozuelo de los Patos, some 30 miles to the north; the other was the good old route via Uspallata to Mendoza. As the shorter, the latter was chosen. At the time, there was no idea of a through line to Buenos Aires. A rail connection was contemplated only between the rich Mendoza valley and Valparaiso, and its object was to bring about a considerable increase in local trade by providing something better than the existing mule transport. That was in 1870. It was later on, when finances were obstructing the project, that the Argentine Government voiced a desire for the line to be taken across the *pampas* to Buenos Aires, by which time Juan Clark had a contract to build a metre-gauge line from the capital to San Juan via Mendoza, and another to extend it to the Chilean frontier either at the pass of Los Patos or at the Uspallata crossing. The Buenos Aires and Pacific Railway, formed in London in 1882, acquired the concession from the Clarks and began construction to a gauge of 66 inches. The first engine from B.A. arrived in Mendoza in 1887, concurrently with commencement of construction from Mendoza of the *Transandino's* Argentine section.

But the tough problems were mostly on the Chilean side of the pass. Completing their plans in 1875, the Clarks handed them to the Government, who approved them. The *Intendente* of Santiago, Benjamin Vicuña Mackenna, displayed them at the International Exhibition of that year. Long, easy adhesion grades characterized that first scheme, a hope that was killed by the low value put on construction costs by the Chilean and Argentine Governments when it came to guaranteeing the project. This cut out dreams of a tunnel under the summit, and made it necessary to reduce route length drastically in climbing to the pass. Thus it was decided to adopt the use of a rack, on the recommendation of an eminent engineer who had studied Abt's system at work in the Hartz mountains of Germany. There was a popular objection that the Uspallata pass was impossible of access to a railway, but a belated and careful survey brought a surprising fact to light: at the foot of the Las Cuevas valley, on the Argentine side, the *Cordillera* was less than two miles thick, and at its summit was only 40 to 50 yards in thickness. Dreams of a tunnel blossomed anew. It looked like the narrowest pass anywhere in the Andes, from Cape Horn to Panama!

The financing of the construction ran into difficulties. London bankers refused to accept the conditions laid down. The law of 1874 authorizing the work was replaced by another in 1887, guaranteeing Clark Bros. five per cent per annum on the cost of the Chilean section up to a limit of five million Chilean pesos, to commence on completion of the line and to endure for twenty years. In 1888 a new entity called *Clark's Transandine Railway Company* was formed, and work on the Chilean section finally started in Los Andes on April 5, 1889, the event being marked with a big celebration graced by President Balmaceda, who gave voice to a discourse well seasoned with patriotic allusions. It was unfortunate that little more than a year later revolution in Argentina and then in Chile caused all work to be suspended, with grading-done as far as Juncal – some thirty miles – at a cost of £550,000.

This hiatus in operations caught the Clarks in debt to the tune of £70,000 plus accrued interests, bringing the total up to nearly double that sum. An embargo was clapped on the work; but as some measure of normality returned, in spite of the embargo, they laid track for 17 1/2 miles, to the famous gully *Salto del Soldado,* at the cost of a further 300,000 pesos. Meanwhile, on the Argentine side where conditions were easier, new rails crept up to Punta de Vacas, which allowed of a semi-regular train service, the gap between railheads being bridged by mule-drawn coaches. Argentine rails continued to advance. In 1903 they reached Las Cuevas, 108 miles from Mendoza.

The Chilean section bogged down, Government promises unimplemented and embargoes heavy upon it. The Clarks, their losses estimated at £400,000, were shackled by the bankers, and requests to Congress in 1898 and 1900 for new financial arrangements achieved no useful results. Two more laws were passed, but these accomplished nothing.

Meanwhile, in 1896 the Bank of London, Mexico and South America and Messrs. Pearson & Son, the contractors, made an offer to the Clarks to subscribe 75 per cent of the capital required to complete the line on condition that other important firms subscribed the remainder. M. Grace, of New York, expressed his willingness to come in on condition that his firm might be allowed representation in Chile. To all of this Mateo Clark agreed, his condition being that it must be made quite plain that Clark Bros. were working in collaboration with the new contractors. Light began to show through the murk, but there still remained the question of Government guarantees to be hashed out.

The Transandine Construction Company was formed with Grace at its head, and with Clarendon Hyde representing Pearsons. A New York representative, Edwards Eyre, was detailed to go to Chile and get the work re-started. Eyre arrived in 1901 and, having taken a look at the 17 1/2 miles of railroad already operating, expressed his desire for a more favourable guarantee from the Government. The machinery began to move at last. A new law was passed in 1904 clearing up the troubles that had bedevilled the construction for 31 years, finally conceding just what the Clarks had originally asked for.

The Bank backed out, leaving Grace and the Clarks to carry on by themselves. A new agreement omitted the names of the Clarks, now no more than shareholders. The London house of Morgan subscribed half the necessary capital. Eyre, representing the *Transandine Construction Co.,* agreed to this, offering to carry on the construction for an increased cost totalling £1,485,000, including overheads and extras. Work recommenced with much celebration in 1903 after a lapse of twelve years. In 1904 it was similarly celebrated in London by a great banquet at which the Clarks were present. The political upheavals in Buenos Aires were blamed for having paralysed Argentine and Chilean credit in London. Fulsome speeches characterized the celebrations on both sides of the Atlantic. The Chilean Government voiced its determination to honour the long-suffering instigators by calling the new railway the 'Ferrocarril Transandino Clark', but forgot to do so!

A new study of the proposed route over the *Cordillera* was made by George Lyon, Henry Budge and others, out of which came the suggestion for a tremendous spiral tunnel near Juncal to avoid the worst summit snows. This idea was dropped in favour of another calling for a tunnel only slightly less than two miles long, just below the spot where the Clarks had originally intended to cross the summit of the pass.

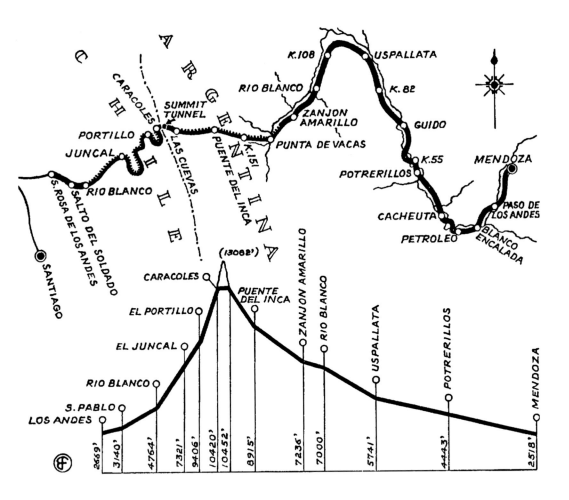

The new construction was in charge of Charles P. White. The first section, Los Andes to Juncal, was finished in February 1906; the second section, Juncal to Portillo, in 1908; the third, Portillo to the union with the Argentine section inside the Cumbre Tunnel, in 1910. With the whole railway now open to traffic, the optimistic estimates of the freight available turned out to be sadly exaggerated.

It would have been too much to expect that the incongruity of a metre-gauge bridge line, part adhesion and part rack, between two 66-inch gauge arteries, would pass unchallenged. But it was pointed out that the expense of building the *Transandino* to the broad gauge of Argentina and the Chilean State system, with adhesion grades only, would have been at least three times more than the line actually cost. It was also doubted if broad gauge curve limitations would have permitted the construction; and, if so, whether the far greater mileage of vulnerable high-altitude track exposed to snow risks would have justified the extra expense.

The doubts about the possibility of taking 66-inch gauge track over the mountains are not for those who are intimately familiar with Henry Meigg's standard gauge achievements. But by the time the *Transandino Chileno* was adequately financed the heroic days of the great railrajahs were done. The stuff of which these giants were made still existed – as witness the Clarks themselves – but the glamour was wearing off the venture of railroad construction; though foreign investment in South America was less difficult to obtain now than in earlier and more politically stormy days. With a rail-crazy President to fatten on, as Henry Meiggs fattened on Balta, the Clarks might have written a different story. The one they actually did write was an epic for all that.

18. *Cacheuta station, a view probably taken in construction days as one of the small tank engines is visible, as well as a crowd of onlookers.* (Collection – Keith Taylorson)

19. *Uspallata station, at a height of 5741ft, on the Argentine side of the border. The sturdy stone construction of the station building is shown to good advantage.* (Collection – Keith Taylorson)

Enemy Number One of the Chilean Transandine is snow. When preparing his plans for the project Mateo Clark was not troubled by fears of what snow might do. Wind would be a formidable ally for the railway in its fight against snowfall. The winds in that part of the *Cordillera* are tremendous, predominantly from south-west to west, and during a study of snow phenomena over a period of more than twenty years Clark knew that snowstorms were followed by winds that dispersed the accumulated snow from exposed surfaces. Thus, were cuttings avoided and the line built on fills and embankments it might be largely self-clearing. Snowfall ran to some 21 feet during a severe winter, as compared with the highest fall then recorded by the Canadian Pacific Railway of 45 feet. The danger was not in the actual snowfall, but from the avalanches roaring down the craggy slopes of the overhanging mountains.

During the preliminary surveys of the route it was necessary in many places to let engineers down on ropes from the cliffs above or suspend ladders for them in order to reach points where observations could be made. Work was not with level and theodolite only. Coming from all over Europe, the engineers used their own familiar instruments, frequently the tacheometer and plane-table with stadia telescope. This was before the tracks for supply mules had been scraped out of the mountain sides. There had been a great deal of the same sort of thing years before, during the construction of the Oroya line in Peru.

The biggest job of all was the Cumbre Tunnel under the divide, a bore 3,463$\frac{1}{2}$ yards long, with an approved section of 15.84 square metres on tangent and 18 on curve. This was bored from both ends, centrelines at the meet being only 2$\frac{3}{4}$ inches out, while level differed by only 0.67 of an inch. Natural ventilation in this tunnel, with its cross-section almost the same as that of the Simplon, was good, thanks to the aligning of the bore to take advantage of those prevailing winds. In service this worked out in such a way that had the volume of traffic called for it, trains hauled by coal-fired steam engines could have followed one another through at intervals of ten minutes in an entirely fresh atmosphere.

Before machines were received to speed the tunnelling, one metre a day was averaged by hand labour. Messrs. Walker, who subsequently took over the contract from Clark's firm, when three years' work on the Argentine side had resulted in only 327 metres being bored, speeded the operation from 9 metres a month to 45. Faster work was done on the Chilean side, thanks to the mettle of the Chilean miners and the fact that they were better equipped than their opposite numbers on the Argentine side. In 44 months the Chileans had bored 853 metres. Walkers increased this rate to 871 metres in twelve months. It was all rock except for 600 metres on the Argentine side. The tunnel was lined throughout with Portland cement concrete in mass.

At first the climate and the distance from supply bases made work on the summit tunnel difficult and slow. Everything had to be transported on muleback to the site on the Chilean side, but on the Argentine side the tracks had arrived before work began. The tunnel was isolated by snow for three or four months during the winter, and reliance rested entirely upon supplies previously laid in. When the machinery finally came, air compressors and lighting generators were worked by diesel engines of 80 and 120 horsepower. This, be it said, was prior to 1910; and the discovery that the engines developed only some 70 per cent of the nominal power at the altitude of 10,452 feet appears to have been surprising to some of the engineers.

The line from Mendoza, on the Argentine side, was difficult principally on account of the Mendoza River, a mountain torrent of considerable size given to the usual diabolical tricks that Andean streams play, such as rising enormously, in volume and in fury, minutes after a cloudburst, altering its course unpredictably, and so on. As the railroad tracks shared a narrow gorge with the river and followed it for about 65 miles, the only means of keeping out of the way of that wicked stream was to blast shelves in the precipitous rock faces at the sides and let the torrent have the valley floor to itself.

During construction work it was found that earthquake shocks did little damage to structures on the line. The devastating 'quake of 1906 that brought Valparaiso tumbling down in ruins did so little damage on the Chilean section of the *Transandino*, severe though the shock was, that engineers began to look on railroads as immune from earthquakes. The author's experience is that Andean railroads are decidedly not immune. Dislodged sections of overhanging mountains and cracked bridge abutments are to be expected of a really bad 'quake, and these can knock out operation for some time.

There was some ingenious bridge-building work. Original proposals called for a bridge near Mendoza with a span of 196 feet. But so tremendous were floods in the river that by the time the span was built it was nearly double that length. The Mendoza River was bridged in ten places within nineteen miles, spans

20. On the Chilean side of the border, a one coach working hurries across the Rio Blanco bridge around 1915, the tiny train dwarfed by the Andean mountains looming in the background. *(Collection – Keith Taylorson)*

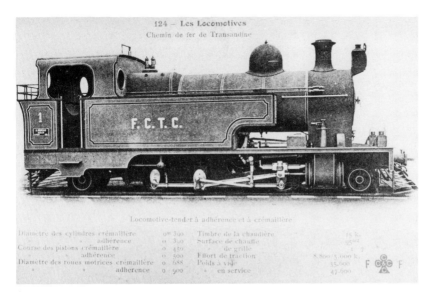

124 – Les Locomotives
Chemin de fer de Transandine

F.C.T.C.

Locomotive-tender à adhérence et à crémaillère

Diamètre des cylindres crémaillère	0ᵐ 390	Timbre de la chaudière	15 k.
adhérence	0 390	Surface de chauffe	95ᵐ²
Course des pistons crémaillère	0 450	de grille	2
adhérence	0 500	Effort de traction	8.800/5.000 k.
Diamètre des roues motrices crémaillère	0 688	Poids à vide	35.000
adhérence	0 900	en service	47.500

21. This locomotive, numbered '1' in the builder's official photo, actually became FCTC No. 4 and was one of two 2-6-2T delivered by Borsig in 1905. The rack engine frame was located between the first and second coupled axles and had two sets of rack pinions.

(Collection – Keith Taylorson)

59

being from 147 to 246 feet. None of these could be eliminated – in fact, as work progressed, their length had to be increased. Owing to the scarcity of timber for staging, it was necessary to evolve some other means of positioning the long bridge girders. In the case of the 246-foot span, this was done in the dry season by erecting the structure on an earth fill when hardly any water was flowing in the river. When the rains came, bringing floods, the waters washed the earth fill away, and there was the completed bridge standing four-square!

Apart from the summit tunnel, and not counting snow galleries, the line was provided with nine tunnels on the Argentine section, with a total length of 575 yards; and 26 tunnels on the Chilean section, their total length being 3,481 yards. This gave a grand total, counting the summit bore, of 7,519½ yards of rat-holes in a route length of 155 miles – about 2.7 per cent. A figure for the Central of Peru, based on the route mileage of the section where the tunnels occur, is over six per cent. This may not be a truly comparative figure; it is mentioned only to show that, as the Andes go, the *Transandino* came out of it quite well. Tunnels are such an unpleasant adjunct of heavy grades and tight curves that they shall have a chapter to themselves farther on.

Fifty-pound rail on wooden ties was laid for the adhesion trackage, and 55-pound rail on steel ties for the rack sections, the heavier rail being considered necessary in view of the heavy braking that was called for on the steeper rack gradients. That the rail in both cases was far too light was not questioned. Cheese-paring finances were the cause of that; not the engineers' choice. The track was indeed designed for loads and stresses far lighter than it was ultimately called upon to take. Expert criticism sparked for many a year on that very point. Today, 70 pound rail is in use.

The rack sections lie between Rio Blanco, on the Chilean side, and Punta de Vacas, on the Argentine side. There are six in Chile and seven in Argentina, with an aggregate length of 13.2 miles and 8.7 miles respectively. The Pacific side of the *Cordillera* is the steeper, as you find all along the Andes, and rack grades on the Chilean section are 8 per cent, as against 6.1 per cent on the Argentine section. The adhesion sections in both cases are limited to an easy 2.5 per cent; but curves are tight – 17° 32' (328 feet radius). On the rack sections curves are eased to 9° 40' (590 feet radius).

The three-bar Abt system of rack was chosen on the recommendation of Enrique Budge, the Chilean Government Engineer, after a prolonged study of all the systems then in use on mountain railways. The Fell system (centre-rail gripped by wheels on vertical axles) was considered, but dropped because it depended upon adhesion. At the time the line was projected, little engines of only 40 tons were contemplated, pulling trains of 70 tons at 5 m.p.h. For these, the three-bar rack was suitable, providing, as it did, a minimum of backlash. But for trains of 140 tons, behind 90-ton engines, at an operating climbing speed of 6.2 m.p.h., and a speed down of 9.3 m.p.h. (with some of the braking force coming on the rack) the two-bar system – more robust in section – would have been preferable. Dr. Abt himself had said in no uncertain way that in future the three-bar rack should not be used. In the case of the other Chilean rack-adhesion railway – the Arica-La Paz – two-bar rack was laid.

Each rack section was equipped with an entrance piece 10ft 9in long, with specially-shaped teeth, the rack bars being mounted on elliptical leaf springs which allowed of vertical flexibility to facilitate engagement of the engine pinions. Entering a rack is a tricky matter. Rarely do the teeth mesh at once. It is usually necessary to slip the pinions backwards or forwards until they engage, this always being done on the hinged entrance piece. Locomotives enter with rack engines turning slowly, these having their own speed indicators in the cabs. Direct-driven rack pinions on the steam locomotives proved easier to control when engaging than gear-driven pinions, and this was of consideration in view of the fact that any careless handling or faulty judgment by the enginemen could do serious damage to the entrance pieces and rack teeth. There were no switches in the rack sections; so that once engaged, rack engines were in mesh from end to end.

The Chilean Transandine may not have been unduly burdened with tunnels (whatever they may claim), but there is plenty of snowshed and avalanche shed in the higher reaches. Snowslides, like landslides, have a way of hitting the unprotected spots. Every season of operation from the opening of the line brought the need for more, and unforeseen, cover. Snowsheds are of timber and sheet iron. Avalanche sheds have masonry walls on the assault side with timber supports on the lower side, and roofs of timber and sheet iron. Snow and wind have occasionally played havoc even with these. Though no more than 33° south of the line here, temperatures at the *Cumbre* have been known to drop as low as 20° below zero (F), with a usual minimum of minus seven degrees. This calls for train heating, a little cross that more northerly Andean roads are not called upon to bear, and it was done with independent boilers and hot-water systems to the tune of nearly 900 pounds of equipment in each coach, in need of constant attention and each a source of undesirable smoke.

With its assorted mixture of British and German steam power, and a Shay thrown in for good measure, the Chilean Transandine must have been a storekeeper's headache before electrification, however interesting from the engineer's point of view. The Argentine section power was scarcely less varied in type. Hawthorn Leslie of Newcastle supplied the first two engines for the Chilean section. They were small 0-6-0 side tanks weighing 62,720 pounds, and they worked only on adhesion trackage between Los Andes, the railhead, and Rio Blanco. Along came the Shay in 1904, built of course by Lima of Ohio, holders of the Shay patent, a 138,880-pound job that was able to work up and down the rack sections by adhesion only, thus proving itself to be a useful member of the stable.

Shays are shaft-driven geared locomotives with characteristic three-cylinder vertical engines on the right-hand side, just forward of the cab. They have offset boilers, and the whole superstructure is mounted on two or more four-wheel trucks. Logging roads in the U.S.A. took to the Shay as a cat takes to liver. Where hundred-per-cent adhesion and great flexibility of wheelbase are required it would be hard to beat them; but one thing that is quite beyond them is anything approaching speed, and their drive usually announces its presence to all who have ears to hear. The *Transandino's* Shay had three 12 x 15-in. cylinders driving three trucks, two under the engine chassis and one beneath what passed for a tender. In common with many of its tribe in the logging trade, it could suck up water into the tank from beside the track, a useful accomplishment during construction days when its versatile services were in constant demand. It could not be induced to run at more than nine miles an hour; but except for a weekly visit to the shed for boiler washing it spent its time out on the line in service and gave remarkably little trouble.

The first two rack-adhesion locomotives were supplied in 1905 by Borsig of Berlin. These were 2-6-2 side tanks with outside cylinders, quite conventional in appearance, but actually fitted with an inside rack engine driving two sets of pinions. Both engines used the joy valve gear, the motion which belies its name. They carried a working pressure of 215 pounds, and in working order weighed 106,624 pounds. These were followed in 1906 by a larger sister, with a four-wheel truck under the cab to help carry a bigger boiler. This boiler drooped towards the front end at a cant of 1 in 25, that the change in water level between flat track and 8 per cent might be less pronounced. She weighed 127,680 pounds. Both these types were fitted with repression brakes, a system whereby the cylinders were turned into air compressors, cooled with water fed in from the tank. With throttle closed, steampipes and valve chests acted as a reservoir, and brake power could be controlled by an adjustable exhaust valve.

By 1906 it had become evident that heavier trains were called for, and the Consulting Engineers, Messrs. Livesey, Son and Henderson, were asked to work out power capable of taking 120-ton trains to the summit and coming down safely with the same rating. Dr. Roman Abt of Lucerne, whose advice was requested, went into a huddle with the German firm of Esslingen, and made the pronouncement that it couldn't be done. Any attempts to haul such loads, he insisted, would end in disaster! At that, the Consulting Engineers themselves produced a design for a rack-adhesion locomotive to do the job by handling trains of 120 tons on the 8 per cent rack sections at 6.2 m.p.h., and the same rating up the 2.5 per cent adhesion grades at the same speed, while able to take curves of 17° 32', and with a maximum axle loading of no more than 26,880 pounds. Kitsons, the Leeds locomotive builders, expressed their willingness to undertake their manufacture, since it had been agreed that the Kitson-Meyer type appeared to possess the required characteristics. This type, Chile's own articulated (I shall be mentioning the prototype in Chapter 7), had already been developed and proved during twelve years of service on the 42-inch gauge Tocopilla Railway with adhesion grades and curves more severe than those of the *Transandino*. The locomotive as projected would be carried on two steam-driven pivoted engine trucks, the one at the smokebox end having four pairs of drivers connected to two cylinders 16½ x 19in; and the other with three pairs of carrying wheels and two sets of rack pinions rigidly mounted on their shafts, driven by two outside 18 x 19-in. cylinders. This arrangement was classed as 0-8-6, but it might as accurately have been termed 0-8 + 6-0. At any rate, it was all engine-there was no tender. The boiler was shrouded with long side tanks, their neatness no doubt a delight to the draughtsman who designed them, but unpractical for the boilermaker whose job it was to change broken stays in the firebox sides. To further complicate an already too complicated design, the railway took it into its head to demand a second rack engine, this to be mounted on the adhesion engine unit, and using 13 x 14-in. cylinders. Someone had dropped a clanger! The completed engine weighed 200,032 pounds, and was a nut-splitter's nightmare!

In service, the boiler proved unable to supply steam to the four rack-engine cylinders, and the front engine was subsequently removed as useless. Two of these locomotives were built, the first going into service in 1907 and the second in 1908. They did the job; in fact they could handle 140-ton trains. Dr. Abt – was his face slightly red? – asserted that he had condemned the idea of working 150-ton trains on 8 per cent grades because he considered that the high tractive force might cause frame distortion of the rolling stock and bring about derailments. As it was, he said, some months after the Kitson-Meyers went into service displaced track cropped up and ties were frequently broken, a statement refuted by one of the *Transandino's* most distinguished engineers, who did however admit that some ties were found cracked.

The year 1908 also saw the arrival of a 6-8-0 rack-adhesion locomotive from the Esslingen Machine Works, a firm that had previously backed Abt in condemning the proposed use of more powerful engines. This weighed 190,400 pounds in working order. It had an articulated six-wheeled truck at the smokebox end with three sets of rack pinions driven by cylinders $21^3/4$in bore by $17^3/4$in stroke. Under the firebox and cab were four pairs of $35^3/4$in adhesion driving wheels, with forward-facing cylinders $15^3/8$in bore by $19^3/4$in stroke, carried on the main frame. The boiler rested upon flexible mounting arrangements, similar to the original Meyer idea. Boiler pressure was 210 pounds as compared with 200 pounds on the Kitsons. No. 11 on the roster was equipped to condense her exhaust steam and feed the boiler through a direct-connected pump, but the apparatus was later removed.

In 1909 there came another Kitson, with a larger fuel bunker. Esslingen supplied a sister for No. 11 in 1911, with different flexible steampipe arrangements.

'Special' steam locomotives invariably meant trouble. It has been so throughout the history of steam traction on railways. Special types have been accepted where their characteristics were essential for the service, but elsewhere the conventional has always returned to displace them. On the *Transandino* they were a necessity, and therefore their bad traits had perforce to be accepted until steam went by the board in favour of electricity.

The Shay with its geared transmission of 1 : 2.21 and its maximum speed of 9 m.p.h. was too slow for the adhesion sections. It could handle 80-ton trains up the 8 per cent rack sections by adhesion only, but bringing the same load down was risky. A repression brake was later fitted; but the Shay system is best suited for industrial or construction work, and not for mainline service on common-carrier railroads. The Borsigs did good work with trains up to 80 tons, their chief defects originating from the narrow journals due to the space restrictions of the metre-gauge. It was very difficult to get at the two sets of rack pinions between the frames. The narrow gauge ruled out Mallets by reason of the restricted fireboxes and ashpans that would have been unavoidable. This, at any rate, is the contention. But the author is convinced that had Mallet specifications been laid out on the drawing board, the snag would have shown up rather in the extreme length of boiler necessary to obtain adequate horsepower for the gradients, the 'run-out' of this boiler beyond clearances on tight curves, and the great concentrated weight of the locomotive. These are the defects that made the Mallet design unsuitable for the Andes. Garratts were also considered, but they were turned down as not robust enough for the tough chore of bucking twenty-foot snowdrifts with a wedge plow. Actually, Garratts were supplied to the Argentine section in 1929, but they were for adhesion only, and that side of the *Cordillera* does not present snow troubles as serious as those on the Chilean side.

The Kitson-Meyers beat the Esslingens on the score of snowplowing and the natural concomitant of putting the engine back on the track after derailment. The point can well be appreciated by those of us who have sweated and slaved to re-rail articulated engines, and therefore know how the brutes can spread themselves across the track and 'dig in'! They curved better than the Esslingens, and were less costly to maintain. Kitson-Meyer engine trucks could be disconnected and run out from under in three hours whereas the same operation with their rivals took two days. As so little work could be done on the engine units when in place under the boilers on account of the space restrictions, this was a considerable advantage. Esslingen steampipes were at first given to fracturing, in spite of ball and expansion joints. It

22. *Borsig 2-6-4T No. 6 awaits departure from Los Andes with a passenger train around 1910. This locomotive was a rack/adhesion type and was employed on working light trains from Los Andes through to summit, without changing engines at Rio Blanco.* (Collection – Keith Taylorson)

23. *For the International expresses larger motive power was needed. No. 9 was one of three Kitson-Meyer 0-8+6-0T which along with the Esslingen locos handled all the prestige traffic until electrification.* (Author)

was necessary to replace them with 'walking' joints, having a knuckle-joint in the centre and ball joints top and bottom. One cannot refrain from remarking that under Andean conditions flexible steampipe joints are the major curse of articulated engines, be what they may the manufacturers' claims for the excellence of their products!

Electrification of the 44 miles of Chilean section dates from 1927. It was completed in 1942. In 1926 three 1,060 h.p. rack-adhesion articulated I-C-C-I jackshaft locomotives were supplied from Switzerland – one from SLM and two from Brown-Boveri. These are of 85 tons, operate on D.C. at 3,000 volts and have six motors each. Adhesion tractive force is 23,100 pounds, but no less than 49,500 pounds for rack operation. Current is taken from overhead conductor by two pantographs. Hydroelectric plant in the vicinity of Santiago was arranged to supply three-phase, 50-cycle power at 44,000 volts to an automatic substation at Juncal erected by British Thomson-Houston, and two 1,500 kw motor-generators fed the catenary. Two more electrics were delivered from Brown-Boveri in 1961. These step up speeds on the rack sections with 150-ton trains to 18.6 m.p.h., doubling the speed of the first series, and on the adhesion trackage to 37.2 m.p.h. as against the previous 24.8 m.p.h.

Still in existence are the three Kitson-Meyers and one of the Esslingens. There is also a Borsig, a 1923 Baldwin, and the one-spot – the Hawthorn Leslie tank. Four Schindler 40-passenger diesel railcars are on the roster, of which two are in regular service. There is no talk of diesel-electrics on this line, nor is there likely to be any. The Chilean Transandine Railway possesses electric power enough and to spare for what traffic is to be picked up today.

Electrification of the rack section between Rio Blanco and Caracoles was a condition under which financial aid was given to the company by the Chilean Government in 1923. The State took over the £1,485,000 bond debt. It had guaranteed the interest on this for 20 years, and now guaranteed the interest on another half-million for line improvements, in return for which the Chilean Transandine Railway Co. Ltd. handed over 70 per cent of the share capital. Within fifty years of its inauguration the undertaking went into voluntary liquidation and the property passed into the hands of the Chilean State Railways.

The locomotive history of the Argentine section starts with six 2-6-2 tanks by Dubs of Glasgow in 1887. These weighed 72,240 pounds. Dubs supplied two larger ones of the same type in 1901, this time weighing 94,000 pounds. In both cases driving wheels were 39 inches and cylinders 14$\frac{1}{2}$ x 20in, but the original 140 pounds boiler pressure was increased in the later ones to 170 pounds. Between 1890 and 1899 there came a series of rack-adhesion 0-6-2 tanks by Beyer, Peacock. These had 14 x 20in outside cylinders connected to the adhesion drivers, and immediately below them two 13 x 18in cylinders for the rack pinion drive. They weighed 100,800 pounds, and did well until the international traffic, growing progressively heavier, called for through trains of 120 tons or more, a requirement that as already explained resulted in the advent of the Kitson-Meyers of the Chilean section. Three identical engines were supplied to the Argentine section in 1909, another of the same following in 1911. A repeat order in 1912 was filled with a couple supplied without the small rack engine on the adhesion unit. They weighed in working order 216,608 pounds, of which 120,960 pounds were on the adhesion drivers. Later in their existence all the Kitsons in both sections had their water capacity increased from 1,800 to 2,100 imperial gallons. They shared a somewhat distinguishing feature in the form of an 'umbrella' roof on the cab – a wide-eaved canopy well over windows and doors all round. Later, also, a 50-gallon tank was placed on the boiler top, fed by injectors, to give a suitable head for the water feed to the repression brake.

In 1909 the first of three 2-8-4 tank locomotives was received from the Vulcan Foundry, Lancashire, with 42in drivers, and weighing 162,400 pounds. Like their smaller Dubs brethren, these were for adhesion only, and working either alone or in couples they were able to face up to growing traffic demands for some time. But the day came when it was decided that Garratts might cut the consumption of Welsh coal to half that of the Dubs and Vulcan tanks for the same tonnage moved over the eighty miles of adhesion trackage between Mendoza and Zanjón Amarillo, where the Kitson rack engines took over for the last leg of the climb to the summit. Four Beyer-Garratts were delivered in 1929, with 36,060 pounds of tractive effort at 85 per cent of the 180 pounds boiler pressure, four 15 x 22in cylinders, and 42-inch drivers. They were reported as doing well; but five years after their advent the section was knocked out by floods and two of them were imprisoned in the Zanjón Amarillo shed until rail traffic was re-established. The others were temporarily removed elsewhere. For a time they worked on the

Railway Electrification

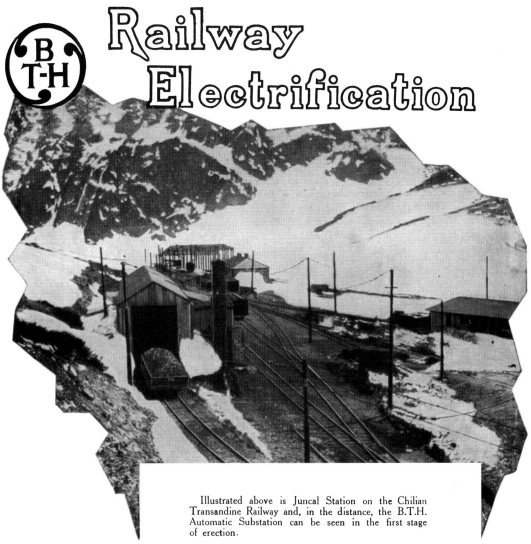

Chilian Transandine Railway

Illustrated above is Juncal Station on the Chilian Transandine Railway and, in the distance, the B.T.H. Automatic Substation can be seen in the first stage of erection.

This Substation will contain two 1,500 Kw. motor-generators, 44,000 volt transformers and switchgear 3,000 volt D.C. switchgear, high speed circuit breakers and automatic control and protective gear.

In addition to all plant necessary for power generation, conversion and transmission, this Company can supply electric locomotives and train equipments, and a notable example of such B.T.H. Railway Electrification in South America is that of the Suburban Sections of the Central Argentine Railway.

The British Thomson-Houston Co., Ltd.

ELECTRICAL ENGINEERS AND MANUFACTURERS

Head Office: Rugby, England. London Office: "Crown House," Aldwych.

Works: Rugby, Birmingham, Willesden, Coventry and Chesterfield.

Argentine State system, double-heading rack engines between Guemes and La Quiaca, their aid enabling train ratings on the 6.8 miles of rack section graded at 7.1 per cent to be increased from 180 to 380 tons. They returned to the *Transandino* in due course and were converted to burn oil instead of coal.

The Chilean section, incidentally, burned 'Crown Patent Fuel' briquettes in the early days, and was still on coal when electrification was completed. With average loads of 100 tons up and 140 tons down, the Kitsons used 162.87 pounds per mile, including lighting-up. The imported fuels in both sections were exceedingly costly when placed on engines – hardly surprising if you consider that besides the cost at the British port of embarkation there were ocean freight charges for over 7,000 miles, and then transport charges from the port of unloading to the railroad.

In its heyday, when the international rail route was the only practical means of making the land journey from Buenos Aires to Valparaiso or Santiago – let's say, in the '20s – you left Retiro Station of the 66-inch gauge Buenos Aires and Pacific Railway on Thursdays and Sundays at 9.15 a.m., and arrived at Mendoza, 651 miles distant, on the following morning at 6.10, an average of 31 m.p.h. There were two *Transandino* trains to choose from. The 'Ordinary' took off from Mendoza at 7.0, and the 'Pullman' International train at 7.30. The latter customarily had six cars in the consist: three chair cars, a diner, a kitchen car and a baggage car. With a permitted width of some 10ft 6in and a height of 13ft (as against 9ft and 12ft 10in respectively for British Railways passenger stock) these metre-gauge cars are roomy enough for comfort, and Pullman passengers had no reason to complain of poor value for their £3 6s. 8d. fare over the Andes. The 155 scenic miles of the narrow gauge link were covered in a little over twelve hours. The Kitson at the head end handed the consist over to a Chilean motor at Las Cuevas. The bell of this electric clanged as the train passed the international frontier in the middle of the Cumbre Tunnel, some 2,000 feet below the new motor road over the pass which was not yet teeming with trucks skimming the cream off the railroad's L.C.L. traffic. At 20.9 hrs., Argentine time – 19.25 Chilean time – the varnish rolled into Los Andes. At 20.45 hrs. Chilean time the 66-inch gauge Chilean State train left Los Andes for Llai-Llai and Santiago or Valparaiso, under catenaries all the way, arriving at either destination at 23.30 hrs., a journey of 38 hrs. 30 mins. overall time for a basic fare of £10 7s. 9d. ordinary, and £11 10s. 0d. Pullman.

In the opposite direction, passengers left Santiago or Valpo on Thursday or Sunday at 7.0 a.m., arriving at Los Andes at 9.50. An hour's wait, and then off in the *Transandino* Pullman International, arriving at Mendoza at 21.50 hrs. Argentine time. The broad-gauge BAP International departed at 23 hrs., arriving Buenos Aires at 19.0 hrs. on the following evening. There was a free baggage allowance of 110 pounds, and all could be checked right through.

Today's tale is a sad one in comparison. The year 1960, for example, saw only 27,314 passengers and 401 metric tons of baggage pass over the line. This works out at about 75 passengers a day. There are two air lines to compete with, these days, and fares by air in South America are highly competitive. Freight moved in the same year was a mere 23,232 tons (or less than 64 tons a day) to which must be added 133,804 head of cattle. Road competition is active from November to April. For the rest of the time snow is a main factor in curbing it.

Flangers, wedge plows and one Leslie rotary, a 104-ton job supplied by the American Locomotive Co., make up the railway's snow-fighting equipment. The chief trouble with the rotary arises from the damage so frequently done to the plow's blades by stones and rocks mixed with the snow. Since 1922 there has been a considerable increase in snow protection, with the Norwegian type of snow gallery in wide use.

The system's 13 passenger and baggage cars, and 111 freight cars, are braked with automatic air and straight-air control. Besides the Westinghouse, steam locomotives were equipped with repression brakes on both adhesion and rack engines, with handbrakes, and with band brakes on rack pinion axles. The operating rule called for running the train with the repression brake, using the straight air for checking, and holding the automatic air charged in readiness for an emergency. The Kitsons and Esslingens climbed bunker first, tunnels thus being less of an ordeal for enginemen – and in the case of the Kitsons, at all events, this made it easier for the engineers to engage the pinions of the rack engines gently with the racks. The Kitsons later had cowls fitted on the stack to deflect the blast rearwards in tunnels, or otherwise the smoke had a way of catching up with the cab, depositing ash on running gear at the same time.

With the object of making the setting of repression brakes easier, rack and adhesion engines could be reversed independently of each other – in fact, there were two separate lots of controls on these locomotives. Oxygen cylinders were put in cabs in case of emergency stops inside tunnels, a refinement certainly not copied by the Central of Peru, in spite of the latter's more numerous tunnels and their far greater altitude. On the Chilean side, a set of engine rack pinions with solid keys had a life of 31,000 miles. Spring pinions lasted only 12,000 miles; but they caused less damage to the racks than the solid ones.

The ratio of tare weight to pay load is of enormous importance on this line, as indeed it is on most high-altitude Andean systems. Seats on international trains of the heyday had to be booked in advance in order that no more cars might be in the consist than were absolutely necessary. The trips across were made only during daylight hours; so that sleeping cars might be avoided, with their tremendous tare and small passenger-carrying capacity. Coaches on the *Transandino* tare at about one quarter of those on the broad-gauge systems it bridges. For years, acetylene lighting was used in the coaches. The low operating speeds made battery charging by axle-driven dynamos a doubtful matter, but in any case the equipment for independent lighting would have weighed about one ton per vehicle, and tare considerations therefore ruled it out.

Rolling stock used wheel centres of the open spoke type to dissipate braking heat. At first, braking caused tyres to slacken off, but this was corrected by increasing shrinkage to 1/500 of the internal diameter. The experience is quite different to that of the Central of Peru, where braking temperatures must have been far higher than any known on the *Transandino*. The Central could use only solid rolled car and coach wheels. Separate tyres stood no chance at all of staying put!

The use of rack pinion shaft brakes was discouraged as far as safety would allow: for it was found that careless or sudden braking could not only damage the racks, but might even cause a derailment. Racks were found to stand up in service remarkably well, though occasionally broken by rock falls. Rack tooth

24. No. 101, the Transandine's first electric locomotive, built by SLM in 1926, is an articulated rack/adhesion 1-C-C-1, supply to its six motors being 3000v DC. It is seen here on a ballast working at Los Andes

(Richard Pelham)

wear was negligible; not to be wondered at perhaps, since engine pinions were providing the lubrication and taking the wear themselves. The Argentine section limited train tonnage exclusive of the engine to 120 tons or six vehicles, both up and down. The Chilean section rated up trains at 120 tons in six accordingly. This limitation provided a desirable factor of safety to prevent undue strain on racks and engine gear. On the Chilean side 140-ton trains were permitted to descend.

It was argued at first that in the interests of train safety, engines should push their trains up; but experience soon made it clear that it was far safer for engines to be in front. Running in the adhesion sections was fast enough to make good visibility from the cab necessary; moreover, when bucking snowdrifts the weight of the engine in the lead was called for to keep the wheels down on the track where they belonged. Pushing these light cars into thick snow would have spread the train all over the scenery!

Train operation is by means of the 'via libre' system, very common in Chile, and quite adequate for lightly trafficked single line. This entails station to station telephone, and a card or tablet to take the train from one station to the next.

Administration of the Argentine section had a career very much more chequered than its opposite number beyond the Summit Tunnel. The anomaly of a railway only a little over 150 miles long with two distinct administrations will not have escaped the reader. That these two bodies were of different nationalities, subject to different financial and political considerations, aggravated the situation. For all the protestations of eternal friendship on the plaque beneath the 'Christ of the Andes' over the pass, at the frontier line, there was not always agreement on operational policy.

This bronze effigy of Christ, by the way, marked the settlement of a border dispute between Argentina and Chile that but for the moving pleas of two bishops on either side of the *Cordillera* might have exploded into a war. Chile's fighting qualities and Argentina's size would have ensured that such a conflagration would have been far from a joke. The crisis came in 1900 after years of bickering. Popular pressure forced the matter to arbitration by an independent power. Britain's help was invoked, and a treaty was signed between the two countries in 1902. The guns of the frontier fortresses were dismantled and thrown into the melting pot, and of their metal was cast the effigy set up and dedicated in 1904. That brass or bronze guns were still guarding frontiers in 20th-century America may be surprising; but it has little to do with the Transandine Railway, and the 'Christ of the Andes' is mentioned principally because it is as well known as the line crossing the divide 2,000 feet below its plinth.

The Chilean Transandine Railway Co. operated the Chilean section until 1934, when it handed its administration over to the Chilean State Railways. In construction days the Argentine section was administered by the Argentine Great Western Railway until control of this entity was taken over by the Buenos Aires and Pacific Railway in 1907. When through traffic commenced in 1910 trouble arose from BAP tariff policies which prevented full economic exploitation of the line. Over the years there was a great deal of diplomatic wrangling, ending in cancellation of the BAP's contract. This done, in May 1923 the two sections were united under a single administration. The Chilean Government extended financial aid to the Chilean section, and the Argentine Government did likewise to the line on its side of the frontier, putting up bonds guaranteeing interest on debenture stock to provide the Argentine Transandine Co. with the means of carrying out certain improvements.

But there was no living happily ever afterwards for the Argentine section. The line slid back into control by the BAP, and matters grew steadily worse until all operation was suspended from April 20 to Dec. 5, 1932, while fresh diplomatic talks were in progress on the vital matter of raising traffic.

And then, on January 10, 1934, Nature stepped in to deal the adhesion section of the Argentine side a crippling blow. Up the valley from Mendoza, near Cacheuta, a large lake had been formed in the mountains by a dam of glacial ice. The ice wall suddenly gave way, and the contents of the lake rushed down the gullies to the Mendoza river, swelling it to devastating size and force. The railroad track was obliterated for miles, and rail traffic from Chile could only be operated as far as Punta de Vacas, whence connection with Mendoza was made by road. Eastbound passengers were now obliged to face the ordeal of a long journey over a poor highway in 'pick-ups' of uncertain age driven at headlong speed by daredevils who appeared never to doubt that divine protection was theirs. This state of affairs lasted until 1944, when rail traffic was restored over a roadbed laboriously reconstructed on the ruins of the one carried away by the flood.

The Argentine Government purchased the Argentine section of the Transandine Railway in 1939 and made it part of the Argentine State Railways. World War II created demands that brought about

25. *The 1926 Cummins engined General Motors railcar known as the Gondola being turned by driver and conductor outside the shed at Rio Blanco.* (Richard Pelham)

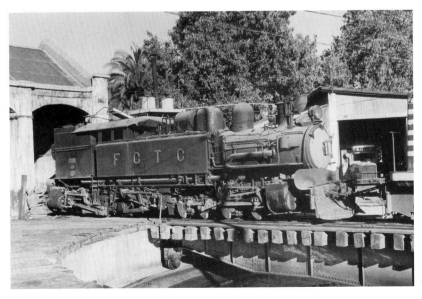

26. Although ousted from passenger duties after electrification in 1928, the Kitson-Meyers remained in service and one was retained at Los Andes, for snow-clearance duties, until 1977.
(Richard Pelham)

completion of the work still undone since 1934, and the railway was reborn into an era in which competitive forms of transport were beginning to predominate. In 1947, backdated to July 1, 1946, the Argentine State system, of which the *Transandino* was now a part, became the *Ferrocarril Nacional General Belgrano*.

It may reasonably be supposed that this, the youngest of the great Andean railways, has nothing to look forward to but a heavily subsidized existence and an early demise. Grandiose schemes for a new tunnel between Juncal and Puente del Inca, cutting out much of the present rack mileage and most of the part subject to snow troubles, have been in the wind for many years, but are unlikely to mature with the railway depreciating in value. All the same, reasons of prestige and international policy may well ensure the line's preservation for some time to come. It would not be the only Andean road to enjoy that privilege.

State administration of railways in South America creates one undesirable condition that can be the cause of their downfall. A perennial shortage of purchasing power brings about requests for loans from the highly industrialized nations. This credit is used for the purchase from these nations of the means of developing the national economy, and railway rolling stock is usually a big item. All too frequently it is insisted that this must be in line with the most advanced practices extant, however unsuitable for the needs of the railways to be supplied. The consequence is that the railways are cluttered up with a medley of impressive-looking N. American, British, French, German, Czech, Italian, Japanese, and what-you-will rolling stock, bought at huge cost, where under private enterprise standardization had been a fetish. Credit exhausted, nothing remains for the purchase of spare parts for these. Lack of specialized experience occasions operational troubles, breakages cannot be made good, units must be 'cannibalized' to keep others in service, and the end is that whole classes finish up prematurely on the rip track.

Not even the ablest railroad managements can hope to combat the dire results of direction by politicians!

---

[1] Journal of Researches During the Voyage of H.M.S. 'Beagle'. *Charles Darwin. See Chap. 15, 'Passage of the Cordillera'.*

Chapter 6

GOOD ANGEL OF THE ALTIPLANO

THE Antofagasta (Chili) and Bolivia Railway Co. Ltd. – to give this British company its anglicized title in full (I shall be referring to it as the FCAB) – began as a 30-inch gauge nitrate carrier in the bleak coastal deserts of what was then part of Bolivia. The ambition to become an international rail route came later, once its growth had made a good start as one member after another joined the expanding parent stem. By that time Chile had annexed all the nitrate territories in the Pacific War, and cut off from Bolivia its land outlet to the ocean with the ports of Antofagasta and Cobija. There was then no rail link with the Andean highlands from Chile. Cobija exists today only as a crumbling pattern of almost obliterated ruins through which the Antofagasta-Tocopilla highway passes, but these ruins were caused by earthquake and not by war.

The system which ultimately leased and operated a total of 1,821 miles of track began as a 22-mile stretch opened for nitrate traffic in 1873 between the busy nitrate port of Antofagasta and Salar del Carmen. It was built by the Antofagasta Nitrate and Railway Company under a concession obtained from the Bolivian Government, and in 1877 was extended to Carmen Alto. In 1879 – the year the Pacific War broke out – it reached Salinas, north-east of Antofagasta, and was in Central by 1882, the year the war finished. The following year railhead was in Pampa Alta, at milepost 94.

Chile's victory over Peru and Bolivia cut the Andean republic completely off from the ocean, pushing the frontier back safely beyond the profitable nitrate sources. That the Company was granted a concession by the Chilean Government to push the line on to Ollagüe, on the new frontier of Bolivia, 274 miles from Antofagasta and 12,100 feet above sea level, indicates that there was a keen eye on the possibilities of international traffic.

Bolivia at that time possessed no railways. Now landlocked, her only practical outlet for the remarkable mineral wealth that was hers, other than what funnelled into railhead at Ollagüe, lying in the copper belt, was by way of Lake Titicaca, where steam navigation had been in existence since 1861, and the Puno-Arequipa-Mollendo railways of what is now the Southern of Peru. The first rail construction concession in Bolivia was given to a N. American company in 1863 by the government of President Achá for a line to open up rich agricultural districts north-east of Cochabamba. But this project came to nothing. Achá was keenly alive to the need for developing transport in the country, but he was overthrown in 1864 by the megalomaniac Melgarejo, whose presidency from that year until 1871 was marked by unceasing civil strife and acts of crazy savagery. It was this lunatic Melgarejo who at a state banquet ordered all the ambassadors present to kiss the naked posterior of his favourite prostitute, an honour that Queen Victoria's representative declined with some heat. In reprisal, Melgarejo had this grave diplomat tied face to tail on a donkey and paraded thus through La Paz streets before a jeering multitude. On hearing of this insult, Queen Victoria called for an atlas and a blue pencil and struck Bolivia off the map, an act that was quickly communicated to Melgarejo, who then mobilized his troops and ordered them to march to England and conquer it! This episode may appear irrelevant in a review of Bolivia's railroad history, but it underlines, I think, the backwardness and ignorance that existed at the time in the Land of Tin.

During the Morales administration that followed that of Melgarejo there was an attempt to build a railway from Mejillones, now the site of the FCAB's workshops, to Caracoles, but nothing came of this either; and the first Bolivian railway actually to be built and go into traffic was the Antofagasta to Salinas line. The Pacific War and its effects put a stop to any more railroad enterprise within Bolivia's restricted bounds till the progressive government of Doctor Anicete Arce granted a concession to the Huanchaca Mining Company to prolong the Antofagasta line from Ollagüe to Uyuni, a route length of 110 miles. President Arce had a hand well immersed in the financial undertaking of the Huanchaca Company, hence his personal interest in the line which was acquired in 1887 from the old company.

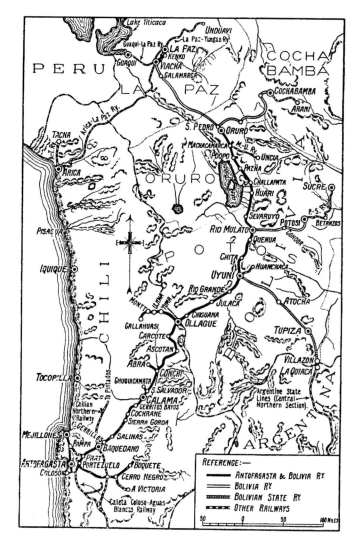

REFERENCE:—
- —— ANTOFAGASTA & BOLIVIA RY
- ═══ BOLIVIA RY
- ▨▨▨ BOLIVIAN STATE RY
- ◼◼◼ OTHER RAILWAYS

It was in the following year that the Antofagasta (Chili) and Bolivia Railway Co. Ltd. was founded in London to purchase the railway and the concession from the Huanchaca Company, extending the line to Oruro under further concessions from the Bolivian Government. The sale was completed in November of that year, and the Huanchaca Company was then granted a lease of the railway for fifteen years as from January 1, 1889. The State had guaranteed Huanchaca six per cent interest on capital invested in the extension of the line from Uyuni to Oruro, which shows how useful it can be when a president is one of the most influential shareholders. Moreover, Huanchaca possessed valuable mines at Pulacayo, not far from Uyuni, and rail communication with a Pacific port enhanced their value considerably.

The line was through to Uyuni by 1889, and reached Oruro in 1892. At first there was stiff opposition to the railway from certain factions in the Government, who tended to regard the enterprise as Chilean encroachment – and war wounds were still raw! But the President smoothed out the misunderstandings, and the undeniable advantages it brought to the country caused Bolivian eyes to focus in a more kindly manner on the British company in the background. The line continued to be operated by Huanchaca until expiration of the lease at the end of 1903, when the owners took it over once more and operated it themselves.

Bolivian railroad construction was given a fillip – strangely enough – by the so-called 'War of the Acre' in 1900-1903. The rubber pickers of the area, mostly Brazilians, rose in arms against the Bolivians, and the Brazilian Government morally supported them. There were not enough people involved for the 'war' to be a notably bloody one, but national prestige plus valuable rubber country were at stake, and the first of these ingredients is in itself enough to cause a conflagration. But the flare-up served to draw official attention to the extreme difficulties of communication in the region of the Acre. Brazil envisaged a railway to eliminate the appalling risks to river traffic in a series of rapids on the Madeira River, and thus connect Amazon navigation with some 2,000 navigable miles beyond, giving Bolivia an Atlantic outlet in the process.[1] For building this line – the 226-mile Madeira-Mamoré Railway (appropriately called the 'Mad Mary') – Brazil needed certain tracts of Bolivian country in the lower Acre, which under the terms of the Treaty of Petropolis of 1903 Bolivia ceded in exchange for an indemnity of £2m.

This tidy little windfall neatly served as a basis for a contract with the National City Bank of New York and Speyer & Co. for railroad construction to the value of £5¹⁄₂m, including 126 miles from Oruro to

Viacha, 132 miles from Oruro to Cochabamba, 109 miles from Rio Mulato to Potosí, and 56 miles from Uyuni to Atocha. All to be laid to a gauge of one metre, the work would be done under the name of *The Bolivia Railway Company*. Actually, their cost exceeded the estimates, for the country traversed by the lines was in many places very hard going, and a further loan of £2m. was raised, this being financed by the FCAB itself. In 1908 an agreement was made for the FCAB to take over the operation of these lines on a 99-year lease, with rentals on a sliding percentage of the gross receipts, starting at 25 and rising to 40 per cent.

Founded in 1606 as the Royal City of San Felipe of Austria (in honour of the reigning Spanish monarch), Oruro is the centre of Bolivian tin mining. Its native name, adopted after the breakaway from Spanish rule, derives from the Uri-Uris, an Indian tribe whose remnants are to be found only on the Island of Panza in nearby Lake Poopó. The importance of this town in the scheme of things Bolivian was paramount in the silver era, after which it lapsed until the growth of the tin industry in this century gave it a new lease of life. Originally 30-inch track as far as Oruro, where metre-gauge leased track carried on to Viacha, FCAB found it expedient to widen the gauge to suit the Bolivian standard, and converted the section between Oruro and Uyuni to metre in 1916.

Since 1908 the Company had been operating its trains into La Paz from Viacha over the tracks of the Guaqui-La Paz Railway, but in 1917 its own line was completed, without any guarantee or financial help from the State. The London company in fact brought nothing but good to Bolivia without ever being a financial burden, and meticulously fulfilled all its agreements and obligations to the country. That it was entirely beneficial to Chile also will be pointed out in a minute. A claim such as that can't be made for every railroad. The Viacha-La Paz connection, incidentally, was relocated in 1924 between Kenko and Chijini, La Paz, the first line having proved very costly to maintain on account of slides and washouts. The new one, with maximum grades of three per cent, was longer but less troublesome to operate. These two constructional feats really constitute the most difficult section of the whole system, which otherwise faced lesser problems than the high-altitude Peruvian lines.

Another FCAB section to cause operating headaches in the way of slides and washouts is the Cochabamba branch built by The Bolivia Railway Company. Cochabamba is linked to the rich food producing region of Santa Cruz at the edge of the wilds to the east by a highway just under 370 miles

27. Antofagasta port in the early years of this century. A Baldwin 0-6-2ST of 1892 shunts a train of open wagons, conveying sacks and boxes, along one of the moles. *(Collection – Keith Taylorson)*

long built by Macco Panpacific together with the *Corporación Boliviano de Fomento* and opened in 1954. There had been talk for a long time of taking rails down to Santa Cruz from Cochabamba, but one abortive attempt to do so ended at Vila Vila where the railroad idea was abandoned. This immensely important link, which might eventually make Bolivia entirely self-supporting in foodstuffs, was originally projected in 1913 by my father, P. H. Fawcett, who prepared the surveys for a highway – in preference to a railroad in order to avoid more easily the dangerous parts – and submitted the whole scheme to an enthusiastic Government, who assured him that there would be no difficulty about concessions once the company had been formed with British capital for the construction. The Madeira-Mamoré pricked up its ears at once. Santa Cruz de la Sierra was close to fluvial navigation, you see, and an outlet for Bolivia to the east by way of the river would be sure to bring streams of freight for the 'Mad Mary', that nowhere-to-nowhere railway in the very heart of South America's wildest jungle. But for World War I it is possible that the Fawcett Highway between Santa Cruz and Cochabamba would have become a reality. As it was, four years of disruption ending in 'tight' money upset the apple cart.

But Bolivia eventually got its eastern outlet, when the Santa Cruz-Puerto Suarez railway was opened in 1954; though this 'prestige' road, built largely by Brazilian enterprise westwards from a point eleven miles away from Corumbá, on the Bolivian frontier, may never shine as an international artery. However, it had the distinction at the start of its career of being perhaps the only 20th-century rail system to have its trains shot up with arrows by wild Indians as a mark of disapproval at its intrusion upon their preserves.

Completion by the Government of the Atocha-Villazon Railway in 1925, a 127-mile line connecting The Bolivia Railway Company's Uyuni-Atocha stretch with the Argentine frontier at La Quiaca, gave Bolivia a southern outlet and a rail link with Buenos Aires. Short though it is, this line was a tough construction job, the whole of its length lying between 9,500 and 14,000 feet, replete with the usual Andean concomitant of tracks winding along mountain ledges above giddy depths, and so on. In 1912 a million-pound loan was raised in France for its construction, but World War I put a halt to the work with only thirty miles of grading done. The Ulen Corporation of New York was given the contract in 1920 and finished the work five years later, the final cost of this rail link amounting to £2,400,000.

Completion of the Guaqui-La Paz in 1906 and the Arica-La Paz in 1913 gave Bolivia a choice of three outlets to the Pacific, rather in the form of a three-pronged fork with La Paz at the converging point. The longest prong was the FCAB, 729 miles, with an awkward change of gauges at Uyuni necessitating transhipment of freight and passengers. The prong to the north – the route via Lake Titicaca and the Southern of Peru to Mollendo – required two transhipments, but totalled only 527 miles in length. The shortest prong was the middle one, the Arica-La Paz, with no breaks of gauge or transhipments, and only slightly over 291 miles to the ocean; but Arica's inadequate port facilities prevented this railway from carrying off the prize. Had all Bolivian exports originated in and around La Paz, the FCAB would have won little of it; but fortunately for them they had the rich mining centres within their zone of operations.

The Bolivia Railway Co.'s line from Rio Mulato to Potosí imposed constructional difficulties in plenty, the terrain being rugged in the extreme and much of it often snow-covered. At Condor station the tracks reach an altitude of 15,705 feet above sea level. At Agua de Castilla, on this branch, are the Porco silver mines, which were producing before the Potosí deposits were discovered. Potosí was founded in 1546, and by 1573 could boast a population of 120,000. The silver mountain of Potosí, 15,900 feet high, is pierced by some 6,000 to 8,000 shafts or adits, and has produced silver to the value of over £350m! From Potosí a Government railway extension runs eastwards to the legal capital of Bolivia, Sucre.

When the Antofagasta (Chili) and Bolivia Railway Co. Ltd. took over operation of its lines on expiration of the lease to the Huanchaca Company, only one nitrate *oficina* (plant) existed in the neighbourhood of Antofagasta. That was in 1903, when the nitrate boom in that area was commencing, and by 1908 twenty plants were in operation or being built. The traffic in nitrate grew to such volume that the port of Antofagasta was unable to cope, and the Company was granted a concession to lay tracks to Mejillones, 37$^{1}/_{2}$ miles to the north, claimed to possess the finest harbour on the West Coast. The locomotive and car shops of the railway's Chilean section are located here. In 1908 the purchase was made of the 30-inch Aguas Blancas Railway, which served the Aguas Blancas nitrate district and the port of Coloso, 6$^{1}/_{2}$ miles south of Antofagasta. From the main stem broke away the Boquete and Augusta Victoria branches. Inasmuch as the nitrate-carrying sections of the railway are at comparatively low altitudes I shall avoid going into details of these. Suffice it to say, firstly, that the Chilean Government built a line between Augusta Victoria and Socompa, on the Argentine frontier, to link up with the Transandine Northern line of the Argentine State railways connecting Buenos Aires and Antofagasta via Salta, this being put into service in 1948 and handed to the FCAB to operate; and, secondly, that the 441-mile Chilean Northern Longitudinal metre-gauge between Pueblo Hundido (where it connected with the State system) and Pintados was handed to the FCAB to operate in 1919. The Longitudinal was completed in 1914.

The discovery of methods whereby nitrate could be processed *in situ* removed the need for *caliche* to be taken to the coast for treatment and gave a tremendous boost to the nitrate industry. Between mileposts 73 and 107 on the Chilean section there were some 38 miles of spurs serving the many *oficinas*. Where nitrate ended the copper belt began. A branch ran up to Chuquicamata at 8,846 feet, where the Anaconda Copper Company had an output of 600 tons of pure copper a day. From Ollagüe the 60-mile Collahuasi branch was built in 1907 to serve what were among the richest known copper mines in the world. This branch reached 15,835 feet at Punto Alto, between Montt and Collahuasi, until recently the highest rail summit in the world. Due to lack of traffic, tracks have now been lifted at the top of this branch, and the present summit height stands at 14,440 feet.

When the system was in its heyday nitrate constituted the most important traffic in the Chilean section, and as much as a million tons of it were hauled in a year. There were also copper ingots and ore, borax from Cebollar, beyond the highest Chilean mainline point at Ascotán (12,976ft), and a stream of tin shipments from Bolivia. In the other direction foodstuffs, mining equipment and fuel moved up from Antofagasta to the many *oficinas*, mining concerns and towns along the line. All this on a gauge of no more than thirty inches, little over half the width of the familiar standard gauge! But if the track width was of toylike proportions the stock rolling on it certainly wasn't. It was as wide as standard British rolling stock, and as high. Trains moved surprisingly fast on the 65- and 75-pound iron, for all the tremendous overhang outside the wheels, and the standard of comfort in the passenger stock was as high if not higher than anywhere else in the Andes.

In spite of the rugged country covered by the railway, and the great altitudes reached in places, mainline grades were kept down to three per cent or less, and there were no tunnels or switchbacks. In fact, the line was unspectacular in comparison with the Peruvian railways or the Chilean Transandine. However, some of the branches could show grades considerably more severe. The Chuquicamata branch, for example, had a maximum of 4.62 per cent; though this was relocated in 1953 with a two per cent compensated grade. The chief maintenance troubles as far as track and structures were concerned arose from the very concentrated weight of rolling stock due to the ultra-narrow gauge. But the Collahuasi branch suffered from heavy snowfalls in winter, and a snowplow was kept there. In the Bolivian section there were parts that, as already mentioned, were subject to landslides and washouts, and it is principally for this reason that the FCAB served as a 'cradle' for a peerless breed of Andean railroad engineers.

Two gauges and two administrations. Each section was in itself a complete, independently managed railway. Each had its own locomotive and car shops. In Bolivia, these were located at Uyuni. To avoid transhipment of freight at the frontier, equipment was installed at Uyuni for switching freight car trucks from the 30-inch to metre-gauge and vice versa, the narrower gauge car bodies being mostly of 20 tons capacity and of much the same size as those of the Bolivian section. But delay was entailed in doing this. The transhipment of passengers and baggage also caused inevitable delays. Traffic was building up to such volumes that the Board of Directors decided to take the big step and widen the gauge of the Chilean section to one metre, in line with the Bolivian gauge and Chilean Government policy. The outbreak of war in 1914 postponed the conversion, but after the war it continued to become increasingly obvious that the step must be taken.

To convert the gauge of an international main line of 384 route miles (discounting branches) without disrupting traffic is a major triumph of engineering, both civil and mechanical, and if the financing of British railroad construction in South America has restricted the ambition of the builders, the capacity of the operating men when put to the test has not been found inferior to any. Running a railroad on a shoestring becomes second nature to the Andean executive. Conversion of the Antofagasta's main stem was taken by the official staff in their stride, with no song and dance. I venture to believe that if such a feat had been carried out as expeditiously in England or the U.S.A., the Press would have spread the story over the pages of their Sunday supplements. We in Peru, not only next door to them, but a company of similar character whose lines actually met theirs at one point – even we rank-and-filers heard little or nothing about it.

A change of gauge is not merely a matter of moving one rail in or out a few inches. If it were, there would be nothing much to it. True enough, FCAB's clearances were already of such generous proportions on the 30-inch that the change entailed no expansion in dimensions of car and coach bodies; but apart from the track with its switches and crossings, there were 61 locomotives, 103 coaches and 2,140 assorted cars to be converted in Mejillones shops, plus the erection of a large number of new metre-gauge locomotives and cars. The shops were tooled purely for maintenance, not for constructional work. The Company, unlike the Peruvian Corporation roads, did not build its own cars and coaches.

Advantage was taken of the fact that a fair proportion of the rolling stock was nearing the end of its useful life and in any case required to be replaced; so, too, in the track there was much re-railing needed with new and heavier iron. By 1926 it was plainly to be seen that the conversion, if done at all, must he tackled at once. The interchange facilities, increased operating speeds and greater capacity of metre-gauge locomotives and cars persuaded the Company to go ahead with it. At the same time, it was necessary to plan the work in such a way that there was always on hand sufficient rolling stock of each gauge. Some sections of the track could be third-railed at once, and left thus until the remaining trackage, where third-railing was impracticable, had been spread. The work commenced in 1926. Meanwhile, new metre-gauge rolling stock was ordered, together with the material required for converting the old. The new cars would tare at 10 tons and carry 30, and the new 2-8-4 tank engines would pull double the rating of the old 30-inch gauge eight-coupled tender engines.

The CME in Mejillones, H. R. Hood, began by outshopping one or two converted old engines a month together with two new engines and up to thirty cars. Towards the end, 250 to 300 cars per month were going out converted, which entailed dismantling and alteration of 500 to 600 trucks, and pressing wheels on to 1,000 to 1,200 new axles. This may not sound impressive in terms of Swindon or Crewe, but for small shops with some 600 men, and regular maintenance to be attended – albeit reduced – at the same time, it is a tremendous task.

The number of bridges between Ollagüe and Uyuni ruled out third-railing, in the interests of preserving alignment, and both rails were therefore spread. Only one bridge in the Chilean section needed to be altered, but there were a number of important stations to do, some of them with sizeable yards. The preliminary work progressed well, and the time drew near for the final big show. Of a total of 236 miles of track to be widened, 56 miles had been third-railed, leaving 180 to be spread – 106 in Bolivia and 74 in Chile. It was decided to close down the line between Calama and Uyuni for six days to carry out the work, and permission was obtained from the two Governments to do this. The dates decided upon were July 5-10, 1928. Storms could be bad in the mountains here, and if one came while the work was in progress it might cause a serious hold-up, but that was a chance that could not be avoided. Labour was a problem. The region between 10,000 and 13,000 feet was very sparsely inhabited. Gangs must be made up, camps pitched at strategic points and well provisioned, new ties prepared and positioned beside the track, new rails distributed, screw spikes provided. Thirty-five gangs were formed, each with its camp and provisions for ten days. The men were recruited from all over the country, and two days before the count-down special trains deposited them in their sections, enormously enthusiastic, each gang determined on being the first to finish its respective task. No doubt pay packets were wagered freely. These were the grandsons of the men who helped build the Meiggs roads, to whom gambling was the breath of life.

A. G. Hunt, General Manager of the Chilean section, his departmental chiefs and their officers had carried out a marvel of organization. The start was delayed on July 5, but husky Chilean arms swung to such good effect that by noon of the 9th the job was all but done. Fine weather held, though the cold in those heights was bitter. On that very day the first through work train nosed down from Uyuni to Ollagüe, and next day it returned, picking up all the gangs that had finished. On the 11th the fine weather broke and for several days tremendous gales lashed the bleak terrain, piling mountains of sand on the track and delaying the first metre-gauge train on its run from Bolivia through to Chile. The first international train out of Antofagasta on July 10 was given an official send-off. The station was bedecked with the flags of Chile, Bolivia and Great Britain, and the Provincial Governor spoke of the great contribution to the prosperity of Northern Chile made by the Company.

The whole of the work was not yet finished, however. There still remained a network of nitrate and copper feeder lines to convert, and trackage in yards and in docks. The Aguas Blancas section was left at its original 30-inch gauge; but the 70-mile Boquete branch was changed as far back as the end of 1926, and the following year the Mejillones branch was third-railed to handle both gauges. The Collahuasi branch was done in August 1928, and the Chuquicamata line in October of the same year. The former had third rail laid over the part subject to snowstorms, to avoid the chance of the line's being blocked while the rest was spread. The work took a week; that of the Chuquicamata branch a mere week-end. By December meter-gauge operation was in full gear.

The journey from Antofagasta to La Paz could now be done by passengers in thirty-one hours, whereas formerly it had taken forty-two, with the need for changing trains at Uyuni. There was also a through connection northwards from Baquedano to Iquique by rail, and southwards to Santiago, as well as through Uyuni to Buenos Aires. As far as freight was concerned, there was no longer that awkward changing of car trucks at the gauge break.

The FCAB's office of 'good angel' was not enjoyed only by Bolivia. In the matter of water, Antofagasta also had reason to bless the Company's name. Where nitrate is, water – by nature – is not. It is the waterless character of the region that is responsible for the presence of the nitrate of soda; and as the nitrate industry built up large concentrations of population, the water problem had to he overcome.

At San Pedro, 197 miles up the line from Antofagasta, the FCAB blasted a great reservoir out of solid rock, filled it with water taken from the melting snows of San Pedro Volcano and the Siloli spring, at 14,500 feet, 38 miles distant from the line. An 11 inch pipeline carried this water from the reservoir to the coast, supplying besides the railway Antofagasta city and the nitrate *oficinas* at the rate of some 7,500 tons a day. A special Water Department of the FCAB handled this work under a Hydraulic Engineer, with assistants on the line to control the supply. The steady drop in the pipeline made pumping stations unnecessary, and the flow was recorded automatically on charts by a series of venturi meters. Pressure build-up in the pipeline was checked by exhausting to the atmosphere in special 'relief tanks'. A sea-water evaporating and condensing plant was installed at Mejillones to supply the workshops with fresh water, in the manner familiar in the nitrate ports along that parched coast.

Antofagasta, then, was blessed with the inestimable gift of pure water in plenty – water so good, indeed, that the railway required no softening plants; though two 'zerolit' water treating plants were in use on the Longitudinal when under FCAB administration (the Chilean Northern is now operated by the State Railways), one at Aguas Blancas and the other at Catalina.

Coal was originally the fuel used by the railway's locomotives, but in due course a change was made to oil. This was generally the same as on other Andean lines, imported fuel from Europe giving way to national coal as deposits in the country were found and developed, and finally conversion to oil, existing in reasonably large quantities in several South American countries.

What disconcerted me the first time I climbed into the cab of the chunky 4-8-2 Hawthorn Leslie (1928) tank on the head-end of the *International*, as it awaited departure hour one morning in Antofagasta, was the discovery that what from outside looked like a cab with plenty of headroom for a tall man was actually so restricted in height that I had to fold up in the middle to stand on the deck in front of the backhead. The reason was that the oil-fuel tank was housed in the cab roof. Every square inch of space on these engines is occupied, and so shrouded with side tanks are they, so hung-out by domes, sandboxes, throttle stop-valves and headers, feed-water heaters, air compressors, turbo-generators, tool boxes, jacks and what not, that it is a problem to find the boiler!

The 182, with her 21 x 24in cylinders and 51in drivers, could churn out 31,752 pounds of tractive force at 85 per cent. She looked small, but really would have more than filled the British loading gauge. Nearby was No. 38, a North British 2-8-4 tank, only slightly less powerful, one of the stud bought in 1927 for the metre-gauge. It is these that were moving the freight in the Chilean section.

The roominess of the *International Limited's* coaches made it hard to believe one was not in standard gauge stock. The Gloucester dining car in particular was superbly appointed. Sleepers had berths running fore-and-aft instead of across. Day coach seats were well-upholstered and comfortable, which cannot be claimed for those of all Andean railways. This stock was in fact better than anything we had in Peru and I was duly impressed. Couplers are of the MCB type and air brakes are the English Westinghouse. All freight stock is on bogies, of course.

28. *Brian Fawcett's classic view of Antofagasta station in 1939, with Hawthorn Leslie 4-8-2T Np. 182 awaiting departure with the Internacional for La Paz. The train consists of a baggage car followed by a Day Coach and three sleepers.* (*Author*)

29. *Around 1940 the Hunslet Engine Company supplied a diesel locomotive on test for the FC Guaqui-La Paz railway. It was shipped via Antofagasta and made its way under its own power over FCAB tracks to Viacha, and eventually Guaqui. Locomotora Diesel No. 1 is pictured here at Antofagasta station.*

(*Hunslet collection – Andrew Neale*)

The International tilts upwards on the double-tracked section immediately upon leaving Antofagasta; for there is two and three per cent grade between the terminal and Portezuela, eighteen miles away and 1,820 feet up. Trains are handled on the staff system in this section. The staff is divisible into three. Throughout the line, some of the staff instruments are automatic, others are semi-automatic, and where the staff is not in use, trains are controlled by the *'via libre'* station-to-station card system.

Double track extends only to Portezuela. Beyond that it is single track. The Boquete branch leaves the main line at O'Higgins; and at the junction of Baquedano, So miles from Antofagasta, the tracks cross those of the Chilean Northern. The train is now running through the nitrate district, where in its day there was an industrial activity reminiscent of the English midlands. The bleakness of the *pampa* is pronounced-no vegetation relieves it until Calama is reached, 149 miles inland and 7,450 feet up, where irrigation from the River Loa has produced a refreshing belt of verdure. Passengers nervous about mountain sickness may be tempted to stop over here with the idea of escaping unpleasant effects higher up. But mountain sickness is like seasickness – if you are subject to it you get it; if you are not it doesn't worry you!

The nitrate *pampa* is behind, the high Andes are close, and you are now in the copper belt. From San Salvador, a few miles on from Calama, the branch line 6.2 miles long runs up to Chuquicamata. From Conchi another branch leads up to the 11,453-feet-high Conchi Viejo mines. It is near Conchi, 188 miles from Antofagasta, that the main iron crosses the River Loa again, on a fill and culvert, detouring $7^1/_2$ miles to avoid the two old wrought-iron lattice viaducts that previously carried the track across a dry river bed and the river proper. The old bridges belong to the era of the 30-inch gauge, when the little 2-8-0 outside-framed 'cabbage cutters' flailed the crank counterweights of their $37^1/_2$in drivers with enormous loads of minerals or empties on their tails, and perhaps a veteran English or N. American hoghead in the bouncing cab eager to pour into any receptive ear tall tales of handbraked runaways or snowbucking exploits on the grades of the Collahuasi line. The Antofagasta enginemen of my acquaintance have all been grand story-tellers.

More than one veteran has recounted to me tales of the Kitson-Meyer that graced the Chilean section back in 1908. As a whole the system has seen a heterogeneous collection of locomotives in its lifetime, but this Kitson must have been the queerest of the lot. It was both tank and tender engine, 2-6 + 6-4, with 14 x 18in cylinders and $37^1/_2$in drivers. At the smokebox end the engine was mounted on a pivoted frame as in the ordinary Kitson-Meyer, but the cab end of the superstructure carrying the boiler was also pivoted and rested on the front end of the tender frame, beneath which was the rear engine guided by a four-wheeled truck – a sort of 'steam tender' carrying a goodly portion of water and coal. Long side tanks fenced in the boiler, and the engine stood only 11ft 6in above the rail. judging from the accounts, one would be forced to conclude that it spent more time on the ballast than on the rails. There were certainly some daring locomotive superintendents in those days, and a good bit more financial freedom than is customary now, so it would seem!

With the snowy cones of San Pedro and San Pablo volcanoes lit by the sinking sun, the train skirts the great reservoir of the Company's two-million-pound water scheme. The easy climb through the bleak, open highlands continues, the heights painted with those pastel shades of orange and purple against the darkening blue of the sky that the miraculous Chilean evenings in these treeless regions provide as a contrast to the drab tints of daytime. *The International* breasts the summit of 12,976 feet at Ascotan, 239 miles from Antofagasta, and begins the slight descent to Cebollar, six miles beyond, where the line runs beside a borax lake 24 miles long, reputed to be the largest single deposit of borax in the world. At one time the trains from the Borax Consolidated Company's workings here constituted an important factor in the line's freight movement; but this has now ceased. Not long after leaving the lake, the engineer is making a brake pipe reduction and the air brakes slap on for Ollagüe, junction with the Collahuasi line, an important yard, milepost 274 and 12,100 feet up.

From Ollagüe the Collahuasi branch runs off in a northwesterly direction into the mountains. The new diesel-electrics have been tried out up to the summit in order to test their high-altitude performance, and results have been satisfactory.

Until 1914 the railway was running heavy freights of up to a thousand tons with link-and-pin couplers and 'armstrong' brakes. There were some mean accidents, and the clamour for automatic couplers and air brakes was loud. One of their ex-air brake inspectors, whom I knew very well back in the '20's, used to insist that the automatic air with straight-air control on the train was originally developed by the FCAB. This is a statement difficult to accept.

From Ascotan right through to La Paz the main line runs fairly level, at rather over 12,000 feet, rising to over 13,000 feet at Kenko and El Alto and then dropping down the mountain side to Chijini Station, La Paz. The really high spots are off the main stem-Collahuasi and Condor. The *International* runs over an unspectacular route from the Pacific, its best scenic offering being the short last leg of the trip from Viacha into La Paz.

Inasmuch as at the time of writing this the FCAB is not operating in Bolivia for reasons that shall be explained in a moment, one must turn the clock back to follow the *International* to Uyuni, milepost 384, where it sighs to a halt in the wee hours of the morning. From here, the train continues on to Rio Mulato and points north, while passengers for Argentina go south-east to Atocha, and then over the Atocha-Villazon Railway to the frontier. Three main lines thus converge and join in Uyuni, and there is a fourth line – a branch to Huanchaca, which has already been mentioned as the primary reason for the FCAB's Bolivian operations.

The Bolivia Railway Company has had an even more varied collection of steam locomotives than the Chilean section, including six Kitson-Meyers, two lots of Henschel tender engines and a number of examples from the U.S.A. The 351, a Baldwin 2-4-2 of 1886, appears to be the oldest on the roster. The Kitsons, bigger than the one in the Chilean section, had units arranged à la Mogul turned the wrong way round, if you consider the smokebox as the conventional leading end. However, if you accept the cab as leading – and Kitsons obviously had this idea in mind – the engines can be classified as 2-6 + 2-6. Tunnels are less unpleasant when the boiler follows along behind. These engines, like the Tocopilla prototypes, had two stacks, one rising through the bunker abaft the cab to exhaust the cylinders of the engine unit at that end.

Like the Mejillones shops of the Chilean section, Uyuni shops were equipped for maintenance of the Bolivian stock and not for construction. The creative urge was never considered a part of the FCAB's mechanical policy. They had enough on their plate as it was.

The Kitsons of 1913 were not the Bolivian section's only incursion into the realms of the articulated locomotive. in 1928 three 4 8 2 + 2 8 4 Beyer-Garratts appeared on the scene and were put into service on the Potosí branch. They were almost giants for the metre-gauge, showing up 55,190 pounds of tractive force, and weighing on the hoof 373,230 pounds. They proceeded to move 424-ton trains over the three-per-cent where previously the ticket had been 234 tons. When the Company's traffic in Bolivia shot up on account of World War II, three more Garratts were hired from the Argentine State system (the erstwhile Central Cordoba was metre-gauge) to help out on the Potosí line. Another was borrowed from the Buenos Aires Midland for work between Uyuni and Oruro. With these extra units in service, the home team of Garratts moved to the Oruro-Cochabamba branch. Their 48-inch drivers gave them a speed of $7^1/_2$ m.p.h. with full rated tonnage on the maximum grades, which seems an overly modest pace even for the narrow gauge. The Company liked their Garratts enough to order two lots of them.

New locomotives of the '50's were conventional, but big. As elsewhere, a few bites of the astringent fruit of articulation sufficed to turn attention back to the good old reliable work-horse of everyday, whose long-term operating economies showed up in general and light repairs rather than in spectacular paper savings in the way of double trains with no crew increase. But the FCAB's impressive Vulcan Foundry 4 8 2 tender engines closed the steam chapter, and with the coming of the '60s came also the diesel-electric, in the shape of six C+ C, 1,425 h.p. hood units from General Motors, since May 1961 in service between Antofagasta and Calama. Chilean section CME Mr P. J. Dawes now has a diesel shop at Antofagasta, and – so I am told – enginemen are taking to the growlers without difficulty.

But let's get on with the *International*. Passengers for Potosí and Sucre changed at Uyuni to a direct train via Rio Mulato, which is 446 miles from Antofagasta and 280 from La Paz. Beyond that point, at Huari, Lake Poopó appears on the left of the train, an extensive body of water fed from larger Lake Titicaca by way of the Desaguadero River. It presents a fascinating mystery in that, though its level remains constant, considerably more water flows into it than is known to flow out. The train then passes through Bolivia's richest mining territory, with the ex-Patiño interests much to the fore – Colquechaca silver mines – Pazña – San José – Poopó smelters. Then Machacamarca, junction of a 56-mile private feeder line from the Uncía, Huanuni and Llallagua mines. Tin – lead – silver – more tin – and with it all

30. *A Hudswell Clarke 'cabbage cutter' 2-8-0, typical of road power on the FCAB in 2ft 6in gauge days.*

(Author)

31. *The metre gauge 2-8-4T road freight locomotives built by North British in 1927 in preparation for the gauge conversion had everything hung on them bar the kitchen sink! The oil fuel tank was contained in the cab roof.*

(Author)

an inhospitable monotonous landscape of rocks, saltpans and pampa – the Bolivian Altiplano, rich with minerals that were locked up there till the FCAB provided a key for Bolivia to open them with.

Centre of this mining industry is Oruro, 145½ miles from La Paz, junction of the 132-mile Cochabamba branch. Where that line wends its way through the mountains there is rugged going and little monotony, though the summit, 37½ miles distant, reaches a mere 13,573 feet before the line plunges to 7,800 feet and rises gently to Cochabamba, at 8,370. But the main stem continues over the *Altiplano* and The Bolivia Railway Company's iron for another 127 miles to Viacha, where the rails of two other systems converge – the Guaqui-La Paz and the Arica-La Paz. From there over the remaining 18½ miles into Chijini the expectant passengers of the *International* were given the *pièce de resistance* in the way of scenery before being decanted from the train into the 12,000-foot Bolivian capital at the bottom of a basin with a 1,500 foot wall on one side and on the other a snow-covered massif 75 miles long dominated by 21,200 foot Illimani. FCAB timed their crack train to arrive at its destination at the evening hour when the most impressive view was to be had. In the matter of view, the relocated *'bajada'* from El Alto was no less impressive than the original one of 1917.

The FCAB came up against competition principally in Bolivia, where roads had been built parallel with the railway – a somewhat wasteful procedure where financial resources are tight and unserved areas of potential value remain without any transportation. Cheap motor fuel aggravated the situation. As in so many other places, this meant that the highways skimmed off from the railroad the cream of the high-class freight and a considerable amount of passengers. Air competition made itself felt mostly in the through passenger traffic. The business man and traveller of means were bound to be attracted by a flying time of two or three hours as against the thirty-one hours which was the best the railroad could offer from Antofagasta to La Paz. But it was on the Cochabamba branch that competition was keenest.

Political unrest in Bolivia during the latter half of the '50's brought about a crisis in the Company's operations there. Throughout its history the country has been stormy in that respect. The conditions under which the railway was operating grew progressively more difficult. An estimated loss of half a million pounds in 1958 was followed in 1959 by the prospect of an even greater loss. Traffic was down forty per cent, inflation was rampant, Bolivian currency was depreciated, and attempts on the Company's part to economize in working expenses were prevented by the Government, which compelled it to hold on its payrolls thirty per cent more men than were actually required for the reduced services. Railway tariffs were frozen, or even reduced, while operating costs soared. The rail unions interfered in management and even used physical violence. They countermanded official orders and opposed all efforts to economize.

It was no longer possible for a private concern to continue operating under such intolerable conditions. The Company offered to sell its railways to the Bolivian Government, even dangling the bait of a bargain price of £4,650,000 payable over 25 years – it offered to run them at Government expense while the matter was being considered – but the outcome was that in February 1959 the FCAB was obliged to suspend its Bolivian operations entirely. The Government decreed that the railways should be run by the State Railway *Directiva*, and a Commission was appointed to study the whole railway question.

This once superbly run, well equipped and beautifully maintained railway undertaking, reft from its owners and lessees by the Revolutionary Government and handed over to a national management quite unfit to operate it, then began to deteriorate fast. Maintenance went by the board. Passenger services became but a skeleton of what they had been. Of the 65 locomotives on the Bolivian roster only 13 were still working in late 1961, and these were so run down that they couldn't handle their tonnage ratings. No less than heartbreaking is the picture of these wrecks dragging their infrequent and random-run trains over trackage and bridges no longer safe – taking nearly a month to get from the Argentine frontier to La Paz – and turning in a monthly deficit of £85,000 in the process, Property and stock previously valued at £16m was being imperilled. The result was that a new President saw the imminent collapse of even this remnant of rail service and with it the complete financial collapse of his country. The workers themselves clamoured for a renewal of British control before it was too late. The Company was invited to take over its lines once more, but understandably declined. A managerial agency contract was then offered by the Government to run them for two years pending a study and decision by the World Bank on their rehabilitation. The FCAB agreed in the meantime to undertake the onerous task of managing the system for the two-year period for account of the Bolivian State, and the latter professed its willingness to purchase the properties, on terms yet to be arranged, the ownership passing to the State at the end of March 1962. To provide funds to cover some items of railway operating expenses, Bolivia obtained loans from certain European Governments.

In Chile, meanwhile, operations have continued. Business as usual, and a reasonably steady movement of copper serving as backbone of the traffic. In addition, the port of Antofagasta retains its importance, as it still handles Bolivian imports and mineral exports.

International traffic over the Transandine Northern and the link between Augusta Victoria and Socompa operated by the FCAB for the Chilean Government is not of much consideration – mostly cattle, and very few passengers. The Argentine State road from Salta to the border is interesting, however, not only as a comparatively recent construction, but also for its height, reaching as it does 14,682 feet above sea level at the Chorrillos pass.

In 1925 the Company's total passenger movement amounted to 663,787; in 1960 it was 96,496. The 1960 figure lacks the Bolivian traffic; but even if there had been that to double the total it would still represent little more than the ghost of what it was in the fat years of the '20's. This is of course the general trend with long-haul passenger services and is a reflection of the times. But in the FCAB's case, it also reflects the fact that the fortunes of such a system are always bound up primarily with the haulage of freight.

The farther north and west one moved away from the giants of the Golden Age of Argentine rails, the less protocol one was likely to encounter. But the FCAB was a true if distant echo of traditional procedure, judging by the accounts of those who had worked on its lines, reflecting a formality of departmental etiquette beyond that usually found in the organizations of the British-owned Peruvian roads with their N. American background. The Antofagasta docket bestowed status as well as prestige. It denoted experience and correctness. The FCAB was a gentlemanly company, never mixed up in financial shenanigans or double-dealings, a bringer of nothing but good wherever it went. Together with its neighbour, the Peruvian Corporation, it is one of the two last remaining strongholds of major British railway enterprise in South America. Those whom it moulded were shaped to fit the exigencies of Andean railroading anywhere along its length, from shore to sky.

What the future holds for the Company remains to be seen, but whatever it be there will remain in the hearts of many in the regions it has served a genuine feeling of goodwill; for the presents it has bestowed are greater than all it has taken.

---

[1] *Mention is made of this in* Exploration Fawcett *(Hutchinson, 1953), the author of which, Col. P. H. Fawcett, was commissioned by Bolivia in 1906 to 'rearrange' the frontier in this region.*

32. *A general view of Iquique, terminus of the Ferrocarril Saltiero. Various unconnected lines, shunted by steam cranes, also served the port area.* (Collection – Keith Taylorson)

33. *No. 104, one of the chunky 2-8-2's of the Nitrate Railways, pictured at Iquique shed. Note the small driving wheels, required for heavy hauling on the steep grades. Built during the Great Depression of 1929, these Baldwins were delivered within 90 days from receipt of order!* (Author)

Chapter 7

NITRATE ROAD

NORTHWARDS from Antofagasta to the Peruvian border stretches the Nitrate *Pampa*, bleak as a lunar landscape, but rich in a commodity that before the Great War of 1914-18 filled the northern Chilean ports with windjammers loading for Europe and Australia. At that time Chile was meeting over ninety per cent of the world's demand for nitrate of soda as a fertilizer and for high explosives. The industry came into being with the decline of Peru's guano exports – and the Tarapacá deposits were, in fact, part of Peru's mineral wealth until Chile appropriated them as spoils of the Pacific War.

The nitrate industry received a knockout blow with the development of synthetic processes that could undercut natural nitrate in cost, and while *caliche* is still quarried and processed in the *oficinas*, as the plants on the nitrate *pampas* are called, output is now only about a tenth of the synthetic nitrates produced. Where once a hundred *oficinas* flourished, today twenty are in operation. But well over half the world's production of iodine, a by-product of nitrate processing methods, comes from Northern Chile.

Nitrate of soda exists in quantity by virtue of the rainless climate of that inhospitable desert. Peruvian governmental eyes turned towards it in 1873, when President Manuel Pardo decided to make the Tarapacá nitrate deposits a Government monopoly. The Minister of Finance said to the Minister of Foreign Affairs:

'However long the guano deposits may last, Peru always possesses the nitrate deposits of Tarapacá to replace them. Foreseeing the possibility of the former becoming exhausted, the Government has adopted measures by which it may secure a new source of income, in order that on the termination of the guano the Republic may be able to continue to meet the obligations it is under to its foreign creditors.' [1]

A law of 1875 authorized the Government purchase of all the nitrate *oficinas*. In 1863 the amount of nitrate sold was 74,400 long tons. By 1873 the figure had increased to 291,500 tons, with the Government pocketing the handsome sum of 2,250,000 dollars in export duties. The Tarapacá deposits of 150 square miles in extent, at 3,000 feet above sea level, were calculated to yield seventy million tons of nitrate, and the current market value was £12 10s. a ton. Private enterprise, largely British and Chilean, was doing so well that the State was assured of a regular source of revenue from it. Yet the temptation to cut open the goose that was laying the golden eggs was too much for the *politicos*. Shortly after the law was passed fifty-one nitrate companies were bludgeoned into agreeing to sell their properties to the Government for 18m. dollars; but resentment was boiling up in them.

The doubling or trebling of the export charges would have served Peru's purpose far better than nationalization, and the booming industry could have stood it. As it was, Peru lost it all within a few years, when victorious Chile removed the old national boundary from south of Antofagasta and placed it above the northern limit of the nitrate deposits. The Chilean Minister of Foreign Affairs declared quite frankly in 1881: 'The nitrate territory of Tarapacá was the real and direct cause of the war'.[2]

The chief port serving the Tarapacá region is Iquique. First of the nitrate carriers was the *Ferrocarril Salitrero* (Nitrate Railways Co. Ltd.), a standard gauge line climbing up the coastal scarp out of Iquique with fearsome grades and curves to the 3,000-foot pampa. It dates from 1865, and like the Antofagasta Railway has been a cradle for British mountain railroaders on the West Coast. Its steam locomotives were among the most powerful in South America. Some 2-8-2 + 2-8-2 Garratts built in 1926 were at that time the largest of their species in the world. Tom Jefferson, originator of the *Andes* type 2-8-0, was an Iquique man, and his design included a number of Nitrate Railways' ideas.

The northern end of this railway is at Pisagua, another nitrate port. In their heyday, with sixty or more big sailing ships moored inshore to load nitrate, with hordes of thirsty, hard-fisted sailormen roaming the streets in search of women, liquor and battle, the nitrate ports of Taltal, Antofagasta, Tocopilla, Iquique and Pisagua had all the makings of terrestrial infernos, but for the presence of the equally tough Chilean *Carabineros*, who were free enough with their carbines to ensure at least some respect for law and order.

But another nitrate carrier is to be described here, a highly efficient 42-inch gauge system located half way between the Antofagasta Railway and the *Ferrocarril Salitrero*. The *Ferrocarril Tocopilla al Toco* (it will be referred to from now on by its initials, FCTT) is not an Andean railway in the manner of the FCAB and the Chilean Transandine, but it qualifies for mention rather than the Nitrate Railways by virtue of its electric operation on the steep seaboard scarp, with a conveyer-belt efficiency of freight movement little troubled by passenger obligations.

The railway belongs to the Anglo Lautaro Nitrate Corporation. It was opened to traffic in 1890; was taken over by the Anglo-Chilean Consolidated Nitrate Corporation in 1925; and was headed by the name *Compañia Salitrera Anglo Chilena* in 1931. Its total trackage is a moderate 184 miles, which includes 21 miles of track meandering over the nitrate pampa where *caliche* is quarried. The altitude it reaches today is a mere 4,570 feet above the Pacific. But the line is historically interesting, and its efficient freight movement over the 24 miles of four-per-cent combined with very tight curvature connecting the pampa with the port of Tocopilla is a model that any Andean road might envy.

The gauge of 42 inches has always been a thorn in the flesh of the Chilean communications authorities, who desired standardization to the metre and 66-inch gauges throughout the national network. It irks them the more that the FCTT connects with the Chilean Northern – the old 'Longitudinal' – at El Toco, kilometre 539 of the State-owned metre-gauge system. An eye accustomed to a healthy 4 feet 8½ inches between rails finds that the 42-inch gauge has a remarkable way of widening to standard gauge proportions with growing familiarity; yet the metre-gauge never loses its narrow look!

The whole line lies in a waterless desert. Until fresh water was piped down from the main *Cordillera* in Bolivia, every drop for the town of Tocopilla, its vast power house and plant of the Chile Exploration Company, besides the railway itself, had to be distilled from sea water in a mighty system of evaporators. Water, then, was a powerful argument in favour of electrification, if not throughout, at least on the 'Bank section'; and this was completed in 1927.

Electrolytic copper is shipped out from the port, but the be-all and end-all

Map of the Nitrate Railways, showing 397 route-miles of line.

86

of its existence is nitrate. The railway was built to move nitrate, and nothing else mattered. It was born of the nitrate boom, and the growing demand for nitrate soon created a howling need for heavier trains than the road's original engines could handle. Locomotive Superintendent Robert Stirling was obsessed with the idea of articulation. He was familiar with the Meyer project of 1862, and the French and Belgian materializations of the Meyer system of articulation in 1869 and 1873 respectively. There is every reason to believe that he knew about, and may even have personally inspected, an interesting design produced by Baldwin in 1892 for the Sinnemahoning Valley Railroad in the U.S.A.

The Baldwin 'Edward T. Johnson' had its boiler, cab and side tanks mounted on a girder frame supported by two six-wheeled articulated engine trucks with Vauclain compound cylinders facing aft. There were no idle axles. Built by Kitsons of Leeds in 1894, Stirling's design resembled it so closely that its inspiration can scarcely be doubted. Lieut.-Col. E. Kitson Clark stated categorically in 1920 that: 'In 1894 Mr. Robert Stirling, of the Anglo-Chilean Nitrate and Railway Co., having to deal with a line 17 miles long of 1 in 25 gradient, 75 per cent of which was combined with curves 181ft radius, suggested to Messrs. Kitson a design on the lines of that made by Meyer. The principals of the firm had already noted the type on the Continental railways, and it has since been developed in many various designs'. To this is appended the footnote: 'It was subsequently found that an engine of this type had been made two years before by the Baldwin Co. It was compounded on the Vauclain system, but beyond general dimensions, no particulars were available'.

Apart from the compounding there were slight differences. The Kitsons carried the drawgear on the engine trucks; Sinnemahoning No. 3's link-and-pin couplers were on the girder frame. Also, the Kitsons had the exhaust from the rear unit turned straight up through a stack on the bunker behind the cab. But otherwise the extraordinary similarity makes it appear that, if Kitsons knew nothing of the Baldwin, Stirling certainly did; and that Stirling's part in the development of the KitsonMeyer design was therefore far greater than Kitsons gave him credit for. The point is of interest inasmuch as the design provided certain attractions for special conditions that gave it a world-wide vogue until the unquestionable

34. *Although primarily a nitrate carrier, the FC Saltiero operated a few passenger services. A train from Pisagua trundles into Iquique behind Baldwin 2-8-2 No. 108.* *(Author)*

35. No. 105 is one of (possibly) four Baldwin-built 0-6-6-0 Mallet Compounds, originally built for Russia in 1917, but diverted to other customers due to the Russian Revolution.
The FCTT used them between the nitrate ofici-nas of Maria Elena and Pedro de valdiva, on the pampa.

(Author)

36. No. 10 (Kitson 3532 of 1894) was the proto-type Kitson-Meyer, the forerunner of many of its type supplied to the FCTT and other Chilean railroads. By 1939, when this photo was taken, the loco had been sig-nificantly modified, al-terations including side tanks cut back, and the addition of Westing-house brake gear.

(Author)

37. No. 29 was the first Kitson-Meyer 2-6+6-2T supplied to the FCTT. Like No. 10, she was later modified with the addition of Westinghouse gear, electric headlights and generator. The earlier open cab has been replaced by a closed-in version.

(Author)

superiority of the Garratt system killed it. But the Kitson-Meyer is as inextricably bound up with Chile and the nitrate boom as is the Beyer-Garratt with South Africa. Its intimate association with the Andes may not have been pronouncedly happy, but it cannot be overlooked.

The considerable overhang of side tanks on narrow-gauge Kitson-Meyers made stability on curves hazardous, if one may judge from the candid remarks of Andean locomotive inspectors of experience with this type. Such a statement was made to me when a sharp curve on the steep seaboard grade of the Tocopilla Railway was pointed out as the place where one of the KM's had rolled over and gone down the mountain in the bad old days before electrification. The maker's claim that the boilers were easily washed out and examined was not corroborated by the men on the job. I have already described the *Transandino's* Kitson-Meyers as a boilermaker's nightmare, and the characteristics that made it so were common to all.

Stirling's Tocopilla KM's carried 160 pounds pressure in the boilers, and their two engine units, each of only $74\frac{1}{2}$in wheelbase, churned out a modest 24,000 pounds of tractive effort. A total weight in working order of 123,984 pounds rested on the $34\frac{3}{4}$in wheels. Their Walschaerts valve gear was something of a novelty in British design of the period.

A further order was supplied by Kitsons in 1905, this time with rather more power. These had outward-facing cylinders, and pony trucks on each unit. When I was on the FCTT in 1939 this latter class was at work on the *pampa* between Tigre and Maria Elena *oficina;* while traffic between Maria Elena and the farther *oficina* of Pedro de Valdivia was worked by 0-6-6-0 Mallet compounds originally built for Russia. The tonnage rating of the Kitsons was 480, and of the Mallets 380. The Mallets advertised their projected Russian destination with characteristic handrails along the outside of the running boards. They rode like wheelbarrows on a cobbled street, with a racket that drowned out every other sound. In comparison, the Kitsons were quiet and well behaved. When I knew her, prototype No. 10, still in switching duty at Tocopilla, snaked about the yards as silently as a ghost.

There is room between the ocean and the flank of the mountains for Tocopilla to sprawl without any pronounced tilt. The line from the nitrate pampa comes twisting in behind and above the town, to join the yard in the equivalent of a reversing switch. Vessels anchor out in the bay and load nitrate from lighters.

The electric locomotive depot services seven B-B, 1,500 volt, D.C., General Electric units, each powered by four 150 h.p. motors. Let's take one of these chunky box-cab motors for a run up to the end of the electrified section and down again, just to take a peep at some straightforward mountain operation. Apart from an elevated panorama of Tocopilla, and the bay from a shoulder near Carmelita there's nothing scenically inspiring – merely the slag-grey scarp innocent of vegetation rising to the monotonously dismal and bleak plain where Northern Chile's golden harvest was reaped in the latter quarter of the last century.

The cabs at either end of No. 605 are surprising for their immaculate condition, particularly if you are from a steam road where press of business forces wipers into a multiplicity of shed chores to the exclusion of wiping. Here the enginemen do the polishing of metal fittings and the waxing of wooden decks, till reflections bounce off everything in sight. Beyond the cabs, the passage and gratings around the electro-pneumatic control equipment and blowers are as spotless as sustained effort can make them. About the engineer's position on the right side of the cab are clustered the controls in the typically American layout which places everything where the hand can reach it easily, an object lesson to a Europe woefully backward in this respect. Meters and gauges are on a panel beneath the front window, in direct line with the eye. To their right, the whistle cord and, above, a push/pull-button switch-box for pantographs raise and lower, blowers, air compressor stop/start, and so on. The K-14-a automatic and independent air brake valves stand slightly out from the side sheet. To the left is the master controller pedestal, field controller above – for regenerative braking on the down run – and the current controller beneath. Attached to the pedestal are the S-3 straight air control valve, and the air sanding valves.

The youthfulness of the engine crew may surprise you. New men were trained for the electrics, and the Chief of Electric Traction chose footballers as prime material in the conviction that the snap-speed of their reflexes in an emergency was greater than that of the older steam men. This unorthodox policy has paid off on several occasions. Moreover, these youngsters have brought into their work a fresh keenness demanding and obtaining an excellent working knowledge of electrical and air brake fundamentals, where an old-timer set in his ways would have been inclined to take everything for granted.

LOCOMOTIVES & WAGONS

Metre gauge 2-6-2 type tank engine, with 12in. by 18in. cylinders for Chilian Nitrate Oficinas. Weight 28 tons.

W. G. BAGNALL LTD.

ARE BUILDERS OF

LOCOMOTIVES

of highest class work-manship and materials
FOR ANY GAUGE OF RAILWAY.

2ft. 6in. gauge Caliche wagon with carrying capacity of 5 tons, for Nitrate Oficinas.

2ft. 0in. gsuge 2-6-2 type locomotive weighing 48 tons, and fitted with 13in. by 16in. cylinders, built for service in India.

ALSO MAKERS OF
TIPPING TRUCKS, SUGAR CANE, NITRATE AND OTHER SPECIAL WAGONS.

W. G. BAGNALL LTD.

Castle Engine Works, Stafford.

From the point of view of age it is hard to tell at sight which is the engineer and which the assistant, till they move to their respective positions in order to roll the 605 out of the shed, along the house track and over to the consist of empty 20-ton gondolas for the pampa. Pulling a polished button in the switchbox above his seat, the juice-jerker raises one of the two pantographs, and the air compressor commences its chatter back in the belly of the unit as he follows his first action by pulling another button in the same box. With main reservoirs pumped up, switches in and independent air brake tested by gauge, he flicks back the reverser, toots the air horn and notches the master controller into the first series transition contact. Her bell tolling solemnly, the 605 whines gently out into the blinding sunshine, accelerating as the controller moves up the sector to full series position, or half speed. Each of its movements from notch to notch is accompanied by the slam and hiss of the electro-pneumatic relays of the main controller beyond the cab bulkhead.

The snag about switching with road electrics is the fact that you daren't dwell on transition notches more than a minute or two. With big motors a heavy current is passing through the grid resistances, and overheating takes place rapidly. Even with 'K' controllers such as are used on small industrial electrics and street-cars you must get through the transition notches to full series and full series-parallel as soon as you can without overloading the motors and possibly burning one. Large road electrics call for even greater care; but one soon gets used to it and acquires a knack.

As the master controller cuts out, the main controller relays open contact with a loud bang, and the 605, checked with a whiff of independent air, fists her MCB coupler into the grip of an open knuckle on the consist of 170 metric tons in 14 cars. Made up by the almost uncannily quiet Kitson-Meyer No. 10, this train stands ready, and while the brakeman twists air hoses together the conductor hands up a crossed 'via libre' card for a meet with descending motors at Reverso, first stop up the line. The standing automatic and straight air brake tests are made, and before getting the signal to back the consist on to the reversing switch and highball out of town, the engineer reaches for the buttons and starts the blowers for cooling traction motors and grid resistors. These whoosh into action with a crescendo ending in a sustained roar. To any who may imagine that electric locomotives are quiet in operation, let me say that many of the species make more noise than steam – but it is quite a different kind of noise. However, neither can compare in this respect with the deafening racket in the engine room of a diesel-electric cab unit!

With the switch of the main iron cleared, No. 605 lunges up to the collar and whines off with her load, almost at once tilting her footboards upwards on the four-per-cent. By the time the controller is in full series she is rumbling over the bridge spanning the Antofagasta highway. With the controller moving through the transitions towards full series-parallel she heels slightly to the left on the curve rounding the *Casa Verde*, residence of several knights-bachelor of the railroad's staff, and then Tocopilla shows spread out below, backed by the still bay with lighters clustering about the anchored ocean freighters. Over yonder, on the point, sprawls the big power station, its output 103,000 KVA with steam and 90,000 KVA through transformers.

Once the singing motors are 'on the power house' and speed has reached its unvarying up and down figure of 16 m.p.h. the engineer can relax, while his assistant takes a look inside and perhaps does a few chores. The modest speed seems a veritable crawl after standard gauge alacrity with steam in the Peruvian Andes, and this impression is even more pronounced during the descent. Here there are no tunnels, no rainstorms, no 'whiskers' on the rail through frost. Traction wheels are unlikely to lose their grip under the smooth torque of the electric motors; though it could happen if oil had dripped on the rail from a tankcar, or during the winter months when the coast is enveloped in the dank *Camanchaca*, the low-hung mist created by the cold Humboldt Current.

Leaving Tocopilla below, the track winds up to Reverso, hugging the contours at the base of the scarp. A *quebrada*, or narrow valley, opens up on the right just beyond the town. To reach the *pampa* the line climbs up through this, but here at the bottom it crosses the mouth to the farther slopes, rising steadily to the reversing station of Reverso, which can now be seen as the top of a double zig-zag with its foot in Tocopilla itself. The 605 changes ends here, and there is the meet with the two descending motors, coupled together, without a train. These come down quite safely with the regenerative braking, their tyres cool to the touch. Oh marvels! what an enviable condition to a steam man used to blue wheel treads and melting brake shoes!

38. *In 1939, after electrification of the bank section,* No. 606 *pulls out of Tocopilla and crosses the Antofagasta highway with a train of empties.* (Author)

39. *On the open cast mining tracks at Maria Elena, the* caliche *is moved in by battery/catenary electrics.* (Author)

Brake tests again; another crossed *'via libre'* card, this time for a meet in Quillagua; highball, and again the careful urging of the master controller up the sector to final safety in series-parallel. The *'via libre'* cards, by the way, are plain for a clear line and crossed for a meet. All is single track, of course. You don't find double trackage on Andean grades.

Some of these curves are terrific, and all are fitted with guard-rails. When the train rounds the shoulder of mountain and enters the *quebrada* a panorama of Tocopilla Bay opens up that is the one scenic thrill on the line, as already mentioned. For the rest, the arid slopes, grey and forbidding, are depressingly monotonous. Up on the *pampa*, or from the ocean this drabness is painted out as the evening sun drops towards the horizon, and it is then that the golden light tints the bleak contours with delicate pastel shades, creating moments of indescribable beauty before the Pacific swallows the light of day and darkness settles.

Quillagua appears, balanced on a ledge where a curve swings round another shoulder of the mountain. Here we go in the hole for the 602, heading a train of 21 loads in 672 tons, which halts on the main to spoon up a clear card before rolling off again under the obstinate resistance of the four motors. This was a tank stop in steam days. The tank is still here, and the water pipe feeding it follows the track all along. Where there has been any leakage from this pipe plant life has quickly taken advantage of it. A few stunted shrubs have rooted here and there in its immediate vicinity, enhancing rather than alleviating the desolate aspect.

The 605's engineer edges out on the main with a clear card, and soon has the train creeping up the mountain at the customary 16 m.p.h. His assistant takes another look over the equipment in the belly of the electric. The tropic sun is near the zenith and the temperature within the motor's Brunswick-green body is almost painful. The cabs are cool enough, but here in the middle there is the heat from blower motors, the controller and the motor-generator producing low-tension current for control and lighting. The rear cab is empty. There one can lean out of the window to enjoy the relief of whatever zephyrs may be playing among the contours of the hills.

After an hour's climbing from Tocopilla we are approaching the top of the Bank section. The next stop is Barriles, and we may be sent back from there to the port with a train. Away down below us, on the floor of the *quebrada*, is the highway from Tocopilla to Maria Elena. Except for occasional pick-up cars of advanced age, handling passengers that the FCTT doesn't cater for, there's little traffic on it. In any case, a bulk nitrate carrier is not much concerned with road competition and the skimming off of high-class freight.

Barriles sends us on to El Tigre, end of the catenary, where steam takes over. I am evoking a day before World War 11, when steam was working the *pampa* sections. Today, the same electrics I knew are meeting diesel-electrics; for the last steamer went to the torch in 1959. Another difference between then and now is the closing down of the Toco branch, which takes off from Tigre, over the Ojeda Ridge, in my day the highest point of the system at 4,785 feet. All the nitrate plants there have ceased operation. No longer do the Kitson-Meyers fuss in and out of the Tigre yard from the Toco line and Maria Elena. Today the pampa is worked by four 100-ton D-E's and eight 65-ton road-switchers, based on Maria Elena, whose performance is stated to be most satisfactory.

In the old days there was a condenser plant at El Toco taking brackish water from the Loa River to help the Tocopilla plant provide water for the railroad. The tanks at El Tigre still remained as a landmark when I was there, and were in fact used by the Kitsons. It is here that the line turns south from its generally west-east direction up the scarp. The 80-pound iron runs straight across the *pampa* – in marked contrast to its tortured gyrations up the mountain – through Colupito (now the highest point), Carrillos and Tupiza to the great plant at Maria Elena, which comes into view from a distance as a cluster of tall stacks and iron roofs amidst a cloud of white dust rising like smoke from the parched ground. The railroad shops are located here. Tocopilla is tolerable – even pleasant – because it lies beside the ocean; but Maria Elena and more distant Pedro de Valdivia lack this saving grace. He who is not bound to them by the ties of his work counts the hours to his departure.

The Mining Department moves some six million tons of ore annually over the double-tracked Vergara-María Elena section with its own electrics. Out on the *pampa*, where the *caliche* is scooped up by huge excavators creeping and crawling hither and yon, wobbly feeder lines reach in to the sites of operation, and a number of battered looking 40-ton steeple-cab C.E. battery-pantograph motors muscle the gons

40. *Two more GE box-cab electrics meet at Quillaga in 1939. This was a watering station in steam days and the tank can be seen (left).*   *(Author)*

41. *FCTT coach, built Metropolitan Carriage and Wagon Co., 1903.*
(Richard Pelham)

within reach of the clamshells to receive the discharge of rocks for the processing plant. The noon light is blinding out here, and the summer heat stifling. These electrics operate under catenaries on the permanent trackage, but much of their movement is over temporary tracks under battery power alone. It is the same at Pedro de Valdivia, the Company's other great plant.

From El Tigre to Pedro de Valdivia the FCTT tracks are not too far distant from those of the Longitudinal Railway, and there is an annual transfer of traffic to the tune of some 2,000 passengers and 10,000 tons of freight. The occasional passenger cars are hitched to the end of freights – there are no purely passenger trains. Passengers are no more than an inconvenience, since the FCTT exists specifically to meet the requirements of the two *oficinas*, Maria Elena and Pedro de Valdivia.

The railway originally ran between Tocopilla and El Toco, hence its name. When the Maria Elena plant was under construction in 1926 the successors to the Anglo-Chilean Nitrate and Railway Corporation asked for a Government concession to link it up by rail with El Tigre, and this was granted on condition that by 1936 the whole system should be converted to metre gauge in order to facilitate interchange with the Longitudinal. A request for a postponement was granted with an extension to1946, at which time another extension was granted, to 1966. Inasmuch as traffic interchange with the Longitudinal is now so reduced, it is hoped and expected that the FCTT's decidedly foreign gauge of 42 inches will be allowed to remain unaltered when the next deadline comes.

Traffic is unbalanced, present approximate annual volumes being 190,000 tons of petroleum, general supplies and construction materials up from the port to the *oficinas*, and 1,004,000 tons down, almost all of it nitrate. This means a considerable movement of empties, a condition that in the case of an ordinary common carrier would be financially most embarrassing. But the FCTT is not ordinary; it is ancillary to an undertaking engaged in the production of a commodity – in much the same way as the Cerro de Pasco Railway in Peru, to be described later.

On the Tocopilla section, one of the seven electrics is usually stopped while the remaining six make a total of some 24 round trips daily between Tocopilla and the top, either to Barriles or Tigre. The whole service enjoys a stability – a sameness – that by the very nature of their lines is denied to the high Andean systems, where the unexpected invariably crops up. In the one case, you always know where you are; in the other, monotony has no place whatever.

No. 605 is at the west end of Tigre yard, at the head of 21 cars each loaded with about 20 tons of gleaming white granulated nitrate, and the engineer is engaged in making the standing brake tests. The FCTT is most meticulous in observing air brake codes and rules. All their brake material is maintained according to the book. Some years before my visit they had shaken free of the vacuum brake, replacing it with the Westinghouse automatic empty and load air brake with straight air control. This fact explained my presence. I was in Tocopilla to drink at the fount of their experience, my own railway being on the eve of adopting the same air brake equipment.

The independent brake sighs off at the conductor's highball, and with a crossed card for a meet at Barriles we take up the slack in the 670-ton train and tool it to the edge where the four-per-cent drops down to the coast. Skill and judgment is called for at this point; for the engineer must cut motor current and switch to regeneration before the grade causes speed to build up. Then, as the train begins to push forward against the motor, he notches the field controller gently up the sector, an eye glued to the ammeter on the instrument panel in front of him to ensure that amps don't exceed 300. He must coordinate amps and speed carefully, and once established hold the balance with touches of straight air in the train brakes. Accustomed as I was to charging down four-per-cent with freight trains at up to 30 m.p.h., the modest crawl here seemed slow enough to threaten the long train with a complete stall from flange resistance on sharp curves. My temptation was to cut back the field controller and head faster into a curve to get round it without having to feed her current. But, while curves unquestion ably did slow us up, we kept going, and the needle of the ammeter held fairly steady. These 60-ton electrics regenerate about 36 per cent of the total current required for a round trip up the hill and back. This in itself is a remarkable economy, but to it must be added the saving in brake shoes and wear and tear of the foundation rigging. When bringing a train down with regenerative braking the engineer's hand must never be far from the automatic brake valve; for if a contact should burn out or the motors suddenly unload for any other reason, the train would be off like a bullet.

On one of these trips down the hill to Tocopilla, a locomotive inspector recalled the training of enginemen in air brake operation on the Antofagasta Railway. A brake inspector asked of one driver –

'What would you do if your train started running too fast on the grade?'

'I'd make a service application with the automatic,' was the reply.

'And if the train continued to run too fast?'

'I'd make a heavier application.'

'S'pose nothing happened and speed was increasing – what would you do?'

The driver pondered a bit and said: 'Why, darn it, I'd make an emergency application!'

'And s'pose nothing happened?'

'For the love of Pete, man, I'd hoss that Johnson bar back! Then I'd slam the brake valve into full release and charge up again, and then I'd big-hole her and wipe the clock!'

'And s'posing she kept right on running – what would you do?'

'I'll tell you what I'd do,' observed the driver with great deliberation. 'I'd take all them damn Westinghouse instruction books out of my seat box and throw the whole bloody lot into the firebox!'...

The 601 with empties for El Tigre is in the hole for us at Barriles. By the time we are in the yard the regenerative braking has been cut out completely and the motors switched to current. Air rushes out of the automatic brake valve to a seven-pound reduction, which pulls us up positioned to collect another crossed card for a meet at Quillagua. The moment release is complete we're off again, notching in the regeneration as the train bends downwards on the grade at the far end of the yard. The amount of straight air required to steady the train when speed tends to pick up is scarcely enough to warm the wheel treads. But handling these electrics down hill calls for more attention than the climb up. There's no relaxing with your feet on the window-sill as on a steam locomotive, with the brakemen doing all the work, clubbing up brake wheels and watching for flats!

The 603 with twelve empties and a meat car is waiting for us at Quillagua. We grab another crossed card here for Carmelita. That will be for the 606, which we met in Reverso as we were on the way up. Her crew will have taken time out in Tocopilla for lunch, and now she's back on the old rock pile for the after-noon's work.

Ah! there's the sea again; and now Tocopilla and the spread of the bay are beneath us as we trundle round the shoulder of the mountain where the *quebrada* ends. Next stop is Reverso, where we have to change ends for the drop down into town. It will be our turn to put the nosebag on when we get in. What a relief it will be to escape from the heat and glare for an hour!...

The last leg of the trip is almost over. Here we are skirting the town at the steady gait that seems so slow. Sometimes one almost wishes a contact would burn and let the train get moving! There'd be no harm done; the air would hold it easily. Now the *Casa Verde* is on our right and we're tilting on the curve leading to the bridge over the Antofagasta road. The engineer is cutting out regeneration and building up straight air to hold us steady till the automatic air halts us at the foot of the main. It was just three hours ago that we started out on the round trip.

The Chief of Electric Traction asks me how I like regenerative braking. 'You ought to see what the difference is when a train comes down with air only,' he remarks. 'Tell you what; you might go up to Reverso after lunch and bring a train down from there on automatic air, with 20-pound retainers turned up... Electrification is the poetry of railroading, I tell you. Can't think why you people in Peru don't go in for it, what with all that water-power you have up there!...'

---

[1] Peru in the Guano Age, A. J. Duffield. *Richard Bentley & Son, London, 1877.*

[2] The War Between Peru and Chile, Clements R. Markham. *Sampson Low, London.*

Chapter 8

'WONDER RAILWAY OF THE WORLD'

MOLLENDO, one of the two Pacific ports served by the Southern Railway of Peru, is not inspiring as a town, but the station has atmosphere. There is no train shed. Under a rocky bluff, the platform gives out at one end through a gate to the dock, at the other to a long curve through the yard towards the shore where the Pacific swells break with ceaseless thunder, and a mist of spray carries in over the tracks.

The roundhouse is under the cliffs on the outside of that curve. A couple of fat-bellied 0-6-0 saddle-tanks will probably be muscling cars about the yard, if you happen to visit it during working hours. Both are numbered in the 40's but one is obviously British and the other just as obviously from a U.S. builder. The British look is out of place here; for the Southern – first of Henry Meiggs's Peruvian roads – is, for all its British ownership, predominantly American.

No. 1, three day coaches and baggage car, is behind the 65, an Alco *Ten-wheeler*, awaiting the highball at 1.45 p.m. for Arequipa, 107 miles away. The 65 is tall, black-painted, has two single-stage air compressors bracketed on the fireman's side, is oil-fired, with drivers 58 inches in diameter (a big wheel for the high Andes!), cylinders 19 x 26in, and carries 180 pounds of steam in her wagon-top boiler. Her engineer – he will inevitably he called 'Don José' – is conscious of the great dignity surrounding a senior engineman in South America, and being an *Arequipeño* he possesses a twinkling eye, a keen sense of humour, an enviable record of good service, and violently expressed political views. His fireman, not yet beyond a nickname, will in due course become just such another 'Don José'. At the moment he's busy taking up a turn or two on the rod cups to get the hard grease well in over the crankpins, while his lord and master is leisurely doing the round with the oil can, engaging freely in conversation with the conductor who has brought along the clearance card.

Before air services throughout South America became what they are, Mollendo was at the northern end of the *Diagonal de Hierro* (the 'Iron Diagonal'), with Buenos Aires at the other end, the lines between being the Central Argentine, the Atocha-Villazon Railway and the FCAB in Bolivia, the Guaqui-La Paz and – via the Lake steamers – the Southern of Peru. This railroad chain was advertised with a view to the international passenger and freight traffic. The international side of the Southern's business is the principal one in any event; for it is the main gateway of Bolivia.

The FCS (*Ferrocarriles del Sur del Peru* is the pike's proper title) is no museum of ancient rolling stock. It is a modern standard gauge transportation system with 535 scrupulously maintained route miles of track, by 10ft 6in in width of rolling stock and 15ft in height of the same – in other words, a man-sized system.

When the station bell announces the proximity of train-time, engineer and fireman climb into the 65's high cab, and the fireman 'rolls' the engine bell to hurry along any laggards. Following the conductor's highball, Don José bends the whistle cord in two prolonged whoops, cracks the throttle slightly, and lets the 65 take up the slack in the automatic couplers as gently as possible. Then, when the train is taut, he widens on her. The engine cants on the curve as the barking exhaust increases its tempo, and the station buildings rattle to the drumming of the oil fire. Switcher crews lift a hand in farewell as No. 1 trundles through the yard. Then the train is out on the main, the 65's Johnson bar up near mid-gear, and the blast a soft accompaniment to the flailing rods. Here along the shore it's easy going on the flat – not enough blast up the stack for the fireboy to sand her through.

At Mejía, nine miles south along the shore, the single track cants to the left towards the piled foothills away from the ocean. At Ensenada, the second stop, the flat ends and grades begin. The beat of the 65's exhaust is slower and louder now, and the sand funnel goes into the firebox here. A black cloud of sooty smoke wafts away, leaving the stack clear of all but a light haze.

Don José' hooks the motion up but slightly after leaving Tambo; for No. 1 has her feet on four-per-cent from here up to the La Joya *pampa* – sixteen miles of collar work hard enough for a *Consolidator*, let alone a *Ten-wheeler*. It was here, where the tracks wind up twisting and turning through the gorge of

Cahuintala, that construction of the old Arequipa line posed its stiffest problems. It was, in fact, this foothill barrier between the sandy La Joya plain and the ocean shore that all but prevented this railroad venture in the first place.

The original idea of a railway linking Arequipa with the coast at Islay, a village only a few miles north of Mollendo where in the Bay of Matarani there was some shelter from the tremendous surf, brought about a survey in 1856 by an engineer named Van Hippel. However, the history proper of the line begins with the decree of 1860 calling for its construction, which resulted in two other engineers, Frederic Blume and Manuel Echegaray, making a new survey to check that of Van Hippel. The knotty problems were in getting a line up to the pampa from Islay, and then taking it through the next mountain barrier to Arequipa, second city of Peru, at 7,550 feet above sea level. To give you an idea of how the work was handled; Echegaray knew nothing about railroad surveying but he happened to possess an old and very inaccurate theodolite, which was the party's sole instrumental equipment. Blume, for his part, was presumably gifted in some subtle way – not that it mattered; the Government knew nothing of surveys and in any case were not willing to spend any money on it!

These two ingenious 'engineers' succeeded in borrowing money enough to make their 'survey' from Arequipa, down through the Huasamayo gorge, across the *Pampa* of Islay (as it was then called) and by way of the *Quebrada* of Cahuintala to Mejía. Then they came up with a scheme calling optimistically for maximum grades of three per cent and a total construction cost of two million pounds plus. The Government offered guarantees to any daring company ready to undertake the construction. One expressed some interest, and had its engineer, Oswald Younghusband, make studies of the project. He upped the estimate to £3m,[1] and when later this was somewhat reduced, funds were authorized guaranteeing seven per cent on it.

At the time, there was no real justification for the railway; but it happened that Arequipa was strongly represented in the Government, and local prestige was at stake. Dr. Polar, of Arequipa, was particularly interested in getting the line built – and in 1868 he became leader of the Cabinet. Meanwhile, the achievements of Don Enrique Meiggs in Chile had won the admiration of the Peruvian Minister in Santiago, who insisted to the powers-that-were in his own country that consummation of Peru's rail-building dreams would be more certain were the Yankee genius persuaded to come north. That was ten years ago, and Meiggs, when approached, had at first displayed no great enthusiasm. However, continued persuasion at length prevailed and he came to Peru in 1868, with a staff of specialist assistants, to declare that he could build the Arequipa line for £2,400,000. A concession had been given to Patrick Gibson and D. J. Pickering, but was later cancelled. The field was open. Meiggs beat out of hand four other competitors and landed the contract. The rail-crazy Balta was nominated President, and Don Enrique astutely turned to his own advantage a national disaster in the shape of a devastating earthquake on August 16, 1868, which laid Arequipa flat, shook the coast from north of Callao to Mejillones, and caused a tidal wave that came in right over Arica, wrecking the town. While the whole country was weeping and wringing its hands at the appalling loss of life and property, Henry Meiggs donated fifty thousand dollars to the Government (in the person of Balta) for relief work in Arequipa, Arica and Iquique. Whether this was bribery and corruption, or a timely charity of which the beneficent Meiggs was fully capable, I leave to the reader's decision. Suffice it to say that it certainly weighted the scales in his favour with Balta when it came to the subsequent contracts. It seems pretty certain that well-placed bribes won him the Arequipa job; and it is said that he allowed for these, including them in his estimates. Meiggs knew all there was to know of how to succeed in business. It was the romantic age of the great American transcontinentals, and Peru's desire to be up-to-date in the matter of railways played right into his hands.

Despite their wobbly theodolite, Blume and Echegaray's survey was accepted by Meiggs, who followed the same route; but he decided on Mollendo as the ocean terminal, considering it more convenient than Islay. The contract price he stipulated of twelve million *soles* (say £2,400,000) was for the fully equipped line, ready for service, to be completed in three years from a date forty days after signing agreements. Should he take longer, he would pay the Government a penalty of £4,000 a month until the work was completed. Should he finish in less than the contract time, the Government would pay him a bonus to the same value for every month gained on the deadline. What could be fairer than that? The railway's rolling stock was specified by F. Blume, Alex E. Prentice and Gerrit S. Backus on behalf of the *Comisión*

Central de Ingenieros for the Ministry of Public Works. There would be ten first-class American locomotives to burn bituminous coal, equipped with Bissel's safety trucks and all modern developments, designed to haul a net payload of 50 tons on four per cent grades and 352-foot curves at ten miles an hour. All cars and coaches were to be mounted on four-wheeled bogies, and each coach must seat sixty passengers.

There were murmurs that Meiggs was demanding too high a price and offering inadequate guarantees in return. But it was pointed out that he was no ordinary contractor. He had been persuaded to come to Peru – begged, almost, to undertake the construction of Peru's rail system. In actual fact, Meiggs needed no begging. He was out to get the contracts by every means known to him, and he knew exactly what he was doing, which was more than the Peruvian Government were aware of. *They* considered his demands reasonable. The cost of the line in service would be a quarter of a million pounds less than Younghusband had estimated. Meiggs was exigent, but he was never greedy. His vast profits were won by sheer ability to do a better job than was thought possible. That's how it was in Chile, and that's how it was with the Arequipa line. He wasted no time. Idle talk was not for him. The contract was signed on May 4, 1868, and work began on the 27th of the same month. In June, work had started near Arequipa; in July at Mollendo.

Late in 1869 Henry Meiggs was joined by his brother, John G., who took over management of the Meiggs enterprises. They were similarly dynamic, those two, and of similarly impressive figure, but John G. lacked his brother's personality. John L. Thorndike was the Chief Engineer of the Arequipa line, having the same status as the Superintendent, Joseph B. Hill, also an American.

Requests for employment came to Henry Meiggs from all over the world, but his policy was to avoid as far as possible the use of foreign assistants, even though competent engineers were in seriously short supply. When it came to labour, he was forced to import foreigners. The Peruvian labourers were mostly mountain Indians, reluctant to go too far from their home acres. Chinese were being brought in, but not in sufficient numbers for the Meiggs's needs. When recruitment was initiated in Chile, hordes of the old gang came pouring up into Peru, the *rotos* eager to work with 'Don Enrique' once more. Bolivians, too, were brought in, principally for work at the Arequipa end. Of the total forces of 12,000 men, some 10,000 were non-Peruvians. Chilean *rotos*, Bolivian yanaconas and Peruvian serranos formed a dangerously explosive mixture, and merry hell popped in the construction camps. Drink, gambling, fighting, whoring and disease ran riot. Two thousand men died during the two construction years; but apart from that, the work was reasonably free of disasters. A work train with 250 barrels of blasting powder was blown up on the La Joya pampa; and one of the American engineers fell down a thousand-foot precipice – that was about the sum of it.

Train No. 1, with Eng. 65 talking it up loudly on the heavy grade to the accompaniment of squealing flanges as the coaches lean into the tight curves, covers in some thirty minutes what constituted the worst part of the construction and took a year to build – the development in the *Quebrada* of Cahuintala. This part cost £600,000 and required 19,000 barrels of blasting powder. Moreover, the three per cent maximum grades envisaged optimistically by Blume and Echegaray had to be upped to four per cent when the grading was actually tackled. The Government wanted the line to start from Islay; Meiggs wanted it to start from Mollendo. There was argument, but Meiggs prevailed, and Mollendo came into being. We know now that it was a boner on Meiggs's part, as far as service requirements are concerned; for Mollendo is an open roadstead frequently so bedevilled by heavy seas that vessels cannot load or discharge, and in any case there is no dock for them. At Matarani, round the corner from Islay, they now tie up alongside and the railroad tracks snake up from the port works to La Joya, where they tie in with the Mollendo-Arequipa main iron.

The railway was in sight of completion when in mid-1870 came a spate of labour troubles with the makings of a really serious revolution in Arequipa. But in spite of that, on December 24, 1870, the first train came through. As in Chile, so it was in Peru. Henry Meiggs had done it again. He'd beaten the contract deadline by over six months, and there would be a tidy little sum in bonuses to collect. The job was well and truly done, the equipment sound. British rails and bridges, American rolling stock, and a fine railway ready to operate. True enough; it had cost the Government an extra £200,000 to have Meiggs provide piped water supplies over the bone-dry La Joya *pampa*, but enthusiasm was such that an official publication of 1871 hailed him as one who, 'without profaning the word, may be called the

42. Mollendo yard in 1935. Later, following the shift in much of the shipping traffic to the new port of Matarani, this complex was superceded by a new yard at Matarani.   (Author)

43. No. 49, a powerful Rogers 0-6-0 switcher used in Mollendo yard.
(Author)

Messiah of railways'. This water main, by the way, was required to supply Mollendo as well as the railroad. Eighty-five miles long, with a flow of 433,000 gallons a day, it was at the time the largest iron pipeline in the world.

Train No. 1 breasts the top of the bank at Cachendo, 3,250 feet above the sea, and pulls up to a five-pound brakepipe reduction by Don José, who spots the tank of No. 65 at the water plug for a drink and climbs down from the cab to oil round the running gear. The principal feature of the flat, dry *pampa* are the *medanos,* or moving sand dunes that are scattered over the plain in the vicinity of La Joya – perfectly formed crescents of light toned sand contrasting sharply with the darker volcanic surface of the ground. Impelled by winds blowing always in the same direction, these dunes 'walk' across the *pampa,* at the rate of some fifty feet a year, watched carefully by roadmasters and section foremen anxious about their track. When a *medano* threatens to cross the rails, they guide it safely by placing rocks on one of the horns of the crescent. Years of experience have made them adept in the guiding of these wandering dunes.

Misti, a snow-capped extinct volcano, rears its white top against the blue sky immediately behind Arequipa, and from the cab of the 65 can be had glimpses of the distinctive cone, together with other even more impressive snow peaks above the summits of the next range of hills – Chachani, Pichu Pichu, 21,723-foot Coropuna and 21,000-foot Ampato – an unforgettable Andean panorama. Huagri past, the train pulls up in La Joya, 55 miles from Mollendo.

The Matarani cut-off was completed in August, 1952. The FCS built it for the Government to serve the new Matarani port, and have since been operating it on contract; but the idea is nothing new – the drawbacks of Mollendo appeared very soon after the Meiggs line went into operation, and a safe port where ships could tie up alongside became a crying need for the Bolivian international traffic, which is the Southern's bread and butter. This cut-off is 39 miles long, with a stiffly graded and twisting climb up the *Quebrada de Guerreros,* through six short tunnels, to the *pampa,* where the track straightens out on a long and fairly flat tangent across the plain to La Joya. It cuts sixteen miles off the rail route length from Arequipa to dockside. While 95 per cent of the railroad's import/export tonnage, including bulk petroleum products, passes through Matarani, Mollendo is still called upon to handle the overspill when, rather than wait for a berth at Matarani, vessels choose to load or unload there.

Whooping twice, the 65 leans into the collar and walks away from La Joya with No. 1. This and other way stations are no more than small yards with a passing loop, a siding or two, a tank and a station building with the traditional bay window on the low platform, housing the station agent-operator's office with the usual table in the bay complete with telegraph instruments, sounders, telephones and so on. The N. American stamp is upon it all, giving the line a flavour completely different to that of the Chilean systems that have been described. Nowhere on the Southern – not even in Arequipa – is there a train shed. Stations are naked, open to the Andean skies, sometimes divorced from any visible settlement to justify their existence.

Station agents are enjoined to wear their uniform caps when passenger trains are present. In the larger places, where a station staff exists, they often obey this rule; but out in the sticks the agent-operators prefer to ignore it, unless they are tipped off that brass is on the prowl. The peoples of Spanish origin, however mixed the blood, rarely take kindly to non-military uniforms, considering them menial and therefore degrading. Dignity is everything. Station agents are persons of great esteem in their communities. On the trains, conductors are men of enormous importance. They are the skippers – chiefs of their trains – but their dignity is if anything less overpowering than that of the regal beings at the throttles of the engines, who while relegated legally to a position of secondary authority, consider themselves by virtue of their long training, skill and specialized knowledge actually of a higher social status than a mere 'big ox'.

Galloping across the *pampa* for another seventeen miles, through San José and on to Ramal, No. 1 comes to the second difficult section of the Mollendo Division and is swallowed by a succession of deep gorges where the grade stiffens and the track twists and turns crazily. After the stop at Vitor the direction of travel changes from north to east. Don José has the Johnson bar well forward, and a thunderous blast from the stack is accompanied by the heavy drumming of the fire as tongues of white flame lick out from the firedoor peep-hole. From the gangway there are views to be caught that nowhere on the line can be surpassed. It may be the distant glimpse of a silvery Pacific in the late sunset from an opening in the surrounding hills, or it may be the gorge of the Chili River backed by a tumbled country rising to the

44. No. 65, a Rogers 4-6-0 of 1907, rebuilt in Arequipa shops, heads Train No. 1 from Mollendo to Arequipa.
(Author)

45. Built by Arequipa shops for special use in 1882, No. 30 La Joya shows signs of Belgian influence. Arequipa assembled in all 32 of its locomotivies, mostly using parts supplied by Rogers.

(Author)

46. *As passenger traffic was of little importance in Peru, even the major stations have relatively modest facilities, and are not roofed. Arequipa station stands at a height of 7550ft. and is the headquarters of the Southern Railway.*

(Author)

47. *A typical Arequipa-built sleeping car at Juliaca, after arrival on the night train from Arequipa.* *(Author)*

great cone of Misti, its bare flanks rosy in the last glow of the dying sun, and every fold and crevice a streak of deep purple shadow.

Quishuarani – Uchumayo – Huaico – Tiabaya – how the Quechua names ring! It's dark now and there's not far to go; in fact, the twinkling lights of Arequipa are in sight from time to time. The approaches are no longer bleak, and the villages cluster more thickly. Past Tingo, where the two enginemen begin preparations for arrival. The evening peace is shattered by a prolonged yell from the whistle, a cry that will roll on over that vast plain for an incredible distance, in spite of the thinning atmosphere. The throttle goes back at the yard limit board and Don José drops the reverse lever into full gear as the fireman reaches for the bell rope and the Alco bell on the boiler top begins its solemn, ecclesiastical tolling (churchmen covet these bells, and many an American church or chapel summons its worshippers with such a relic from a scrapped engine). No.1 is in. This is Arequipa, and were it daylight you would see a city built of gleaming white volcanic blocks, full of the baroque architecture of the Colonial era, trees and gardens mingling with the buildings in the manner in which the Hispanic races have always excelled.

Just now, at train time, Arequipa is ablaze with lights; for it is 7.15 p.m., five hours and a half out of Mollendo. The platform is crowded with people, most of whom are there merely to see who arrives; but small *cholo* boys swarm about the first-class cars in the hope of carrying passengers' baggage, struggling and yelling in their efforts to win patronage. Up by the engine are one or two obscure figures under the cab. Don José is handing down some mysterious packages to members of his family. Don't be inquisitive about them – Don José is an old-timer and has earned the blind eye. Look rather at the dancing torch as the fireman goes round the engine feeling the journals, and listen to the sing-song whine of the turbo-generator and the soft, lazy chuff of the air compressor.

The FCS has always been a tightly-knit, patriarchal administration, self-sufficient to a far greater degree than the Central; though less of a money spinner. L. S. Blaisdell's tenure of office as General Manager was such that in the first half of this century the Southern became identified with him, and he with the Southern. As an American, he conserved the original American traditions of the road and kept them very much alive throughout the greater part of those fifty years.

When I say that the Southern was more self-sufficient than the Central, I'm thinking of the remarkably ambitious output of the Locomotive Department's shops in Arequipa, where not only did they build freight and passenger cars – sleepers, chair cars, day coaches and baggage cars – but for many years locomotives as well. Out of a total of 46 engines in a roster of 1908, no less than 32 were Arequipa-built, ranging from a 4 8 0 to a 2-2-0. Incidentally, every engine on this roster was named as well as numbered – 'Stephenson', 'Trevithick', 'Don Quijote', 'Sancho Panza', 'Conquistador', 'Economista', to mention a few.

The original Arequipa line was powered with *Moguls*, some by Danforth & Cooke but most by Rogers, similar to those that worked the early Oroya line, and equipped with the huge balloon stacks associated with wood burning. Actually, they burned coal, imported from South Wales at enormous cost. Southern locomotive practice departed from the Central's in several ways, but both systems belonging to the Peruvian Corporation Ltd. of London (now of Toronto), the Southern, greater in mileage but smaller in revenue, from time to time received Central reach-me-downs. Easier grades and faster running brought the 4-6-0 into a prominence in Arequipa that it never knew on the up-and-down Central. There were also the Rogers 4-8-0 compounds of the 50-class, carrying 185 pounds boiler pressure, with cylinders 20 and 31 inches by 28-in. stroke, driving 52-inch wheels. Until comparatively recently the imported engines were all of somewhat ancient vintage, rebuilt with modern fittings such as superheaters and feed-water heaters. The Arequipa-built engines were strictly speaking assembled from imported parts,. For instance, Arequipa shops did not cast driving wheel centres and bar frames, forge main and side rods, or roll boiler plate. They were not tooled for it; and the term 'Arequipa built', in the case of locomotives, must be accepted with reservations.

Developed on the Central, the *Andes* type 2-8-0 found its footing in Arequipa in 1937, originally their 80-class and now renumbered in the 100's. The difference was the larger Southern driving wheels, of 56 inches, with an extra half-inch on the cylinder bores to compensate. A power shortage in 1952 resulted in the Central's shipping down to Arequipa two of the 2-8-2 + 2-8-2 Beyer-Garratts, but these were a flop on the Southern. Fuel tanks were too small for the longer runs, and axle loadings being already up

48. At Crucero Alto, 14,668ft highest point on the southern, the terrain is bleak and inhospitable, but the skies are an ever-changing wonder. Distance posts are marked in kilometres from Arequipa. *(Author)*

49. The Puno-Cuzco train arrives at Juliaca on a May morning in 1946 behind Rogers 4-6-0 No. 85. No. 85 of the same class waits to make up her train for Arequipa. *(Author)*

to the limit it was not possible to enlarge them. Wheels were too small for the faster FCS timings, and hammer blow was so pronounced that it caused excessive wear and tear. Fuel costs and maintenance per gross ton-kilometre were higher than with the *Andes* type – as indeed was the case on the Central also.

And then, in 1956, the Southern, under the managership of P. B. C. Robinson, with N. C. W. Bellerby as CME, departed from the traditional paths of steam and began a comprehensive programme of dieselization. Six Alco 'World' type diesel-electrics, derated to 1,300 h.p. from 1,800 h.p. for high-altitude operation, proved successful, and running costs per ton-mile plummeted. Scrupulously observed preventive maintenance helped them give very little trouble. The ratio of steam locomotive fuel costs to those of the new diesels worked out at about 3 to 1; while overall operating costs, including maintenance, crews' wages, etc., showed up in the ratio of $2^{1}/_{4}$ to 1.

These were followed by two types of Alco C-C hood units. There was one DL-53 I, rated at 975 h.p. and numbered 300, which gave excellent results. The latest DL-543 hoods, also Alco-built, have the low-nose profile, use the Alco 12-Cyl. 251-C diesel engine, are equipped with six traction motors, and are rated at 2,150/2,000 h.p. at 1,025 r.p.m. at sea level. A special arrangement for controlling fuel and turbo-charger speed automatically according to the altitude is designed to cut the power loss throughout the altitude range to less than 15 per cent. All the DE's have dynamic braking, Westinghouse automatic air brakes schedule 26 L and straight-air control for the train, as on the Central. The latest hoods carry three headlights, the centre one fixed and the outer ones angled to illuminate the track when rounding sharp curves. It is probable that the DL-543s will spell the policy for dieselizing the Central's main line. Hitherto it has been the Central that has led; now it may be the Southern's turn to show the way.

Besides the railway rolling stock, FCS shops must maintain the five Titicaca lake ships, about which I shall have something to say when we get up to the port of Puno. The Locomotive Superintendent over a period of many years during the Blaisdell regime was a marine engineer, whose heart was principally with the ships, and it was his assistant who was concerned with matters appertaining to the high iron.

While in numerical strength Arequipa shops may not be large, the fact is that the Southern Peruvian is the best worker in the country, and that is what counts. It is in the layout and appointments of the first-class day coaches, buffet cars and sleepers that the travelling public is most likely to see and appreciate his skill in the matter of coach building and cabinet work. On their wooden seats without upholstery, second-class passengers are less likely to cast appreciative eyes about them. Even as the Central, the Southern within recent years has had rakes of lightweight coaching stock from Cravens of Manchester; but a traveller on the *International* night train from Arequipa to Puno will still find Arequipa-built, nine-compartment *Dormitorios* in the consist. Berths are arranged transversally in these, two to a compartment, with the fittings usual in the familiar European sleeping cars. Water tanks are carried under the floors, and the water is lifted by an air pressure of 25 pounds.

One may board the *International* after dinner, turn in to bed shortly after leaving Arequipa at 10 p.m. and get up at the lake port of Puno, 12,500 feet above the ocean. But sleeping car passengers for Cuzco rise in the morning to find their car cut off in Juliaca, and before unloading to change into the Cuzco train may order breakfast in their compartments.

No. 11, the night *International* over the Puno Division, runs on Mondays; on Wednesdays and Fridays there are day trains, pulling out of Arequipa at 7.30 a.m. and arriving at Puno at 6.40 p.m. The night train gives a day crossing of the lake, and the day trains give a night journey along the lake to Guaqui, the port for La Paz, where a Guaqui-La Paz train connects for the trip to the Bolivian capital.

Although the name Arequipa means in Quechua 'remain here', it had been decided to take the iron on to Puno and Cuzco before construction of the Mollendo Division had reached Cachendo. In 1868 President Balta had authority from Congress to put through a comprehensive programme of rail construction in which these lines figured prominently. Needless to say, the contract plums went to the dynamic Meiggs. Had he not invested wisely and well with that very object?

John L. Thorndike made a study of the Puno line in the same year, reporting to Cerrit S. Backus, on behalf of the Peruvian Government, and Henry Meiggs's representative, the engineer Ernesto Malinowski. Thorndike – he hailed from the same part of the U.S. as Meiggs priced the job at £6,940,000. Backus insisted on reducing this to a round £6m, and Malinowski agreed. There was no question of whose tender would be accepted. Competitors were wasting their time in tendering. Having landed that one safely, Meiggs then claimed the right to quote for the line from Juliaca to Sicuani, and presented his figure of £5,192,800. Of course, he got it. As brother John G. sagely remarked, they had Peru bound hand and foot! In 1873, Hutchinson said:

'All these railroads of Mr. Meiggs, taking them in the order of their geographical position – first, from Ilo to Moquegua; second, from Mollendo to Arequipa, to Puno, and on to Cuzco; third, from Callao over the Andes to Oroya, and thence (as I hope it will extend) to the Ucayali, one of the important sources of the Amazon; fourth, from Chimbote to Huarez; fifth, from Pacasmayo to Guadalupe, and to Cajamarca – seem to me but the initiatory steps, or breaking of the ice, into Peru. I do not speak authoritatively – for I hold no claim to be in the confidence of Mr. Meiggs on the subject – but simply from my own observations of such of them as I have visited. The result of these makes me opposed to a belief I often hear expressed, – that the lines in question can never pay, or, in fact, never can be a commercial success. Admitted that they are not likely to do so for some time; but they lead to and connect with lines that must pay, because penetrating through the richest mineral districts of the world.'[2]

Balta's critics claimed that the railways in the process of being built in Peru (including what is now Northern Chile), in 1872 said to be 'South America's most extensive system', were mortgaged to the last spike without being economically justifiable. On the contrary, the Mollendo, Puno and Cuzco lines were the economic salvation of Southern Peru.

Apprehensive that Bolivia intended to build a railroad from La Paz to Tacna, where it would connect with the Arica-Tacna Railway, thus killing existing arrangements anent the Puno line, Meiggs rushed its construction, and work commenced on July 11, 1870. The Franco-Prussian War was making it difficult to get delivery of materials from Europe, for which reason smaller forces were employed than was the normal Meiggs practice. Bolivian workmen predominated in this section. There was nothing much in the way of constructional difficulties. The one tunnel, mentioned elsewhere, is not of any account, and of the five bridges, the largest is on the outskirts of Arequipa.

The first engine reached Puno on January 1, 1874, but owing to financial difficulties the line was not completed until 1876. Its 219 route miles opened up the desolate puna and brought rhyme and reason to the service of the little steamer that for fifteen years had been plying the waters of the world's highest navigable lake. Starting from Juliaca, the Cuzco line had been commenced in 1872 and grading was in progress along the puna, mostly with Bolivian labour. There was talk of brutality on the part of Government authorities in recruiting labour at the Cuzco end, the men virtually conscripted for the work being given an advance of forty cents, and being hunted down and jailed if they failed to report on the job within three days. Engineers of experience were in short supply – there were scarcely any doctors – skilled tradesmen were few. There was no lack of applications for the specialist positions by unskilled men, but that was not of much help! The line started off on the wrong foot. Physical difficulties in construction were of slight consideration, but the money bogy and political troubles brought the whole project to a standstill in 1875 with 130 miles of the 210 graded, but no rails laid. All the Meiggs railroad construction work was suspended. Balta had been assassinated in 1872. Manuel Pardo, his successor, found a debt of £60m. hung about the country's neck, requiring an annual interest of £4m. Guano just wasn't enough to meet the situation. Balta had wildly overspent, and all that Pardo could do now was to cut down expenditure in every way he could. The widespread Meiggs projects could not escape the pinch. A new contract to complete the line was made in 1877, but in September of that year Henry Meiggs died.

The Meiggs concessions and rights were managed by one Charles Watson and a directory until 1887, when the Government alleged that the obligations were not being carried out, and nominated its own commission to take over. In 1886 John L. Thorndike had acquired the contract rights from the Watson directory to continue building the line, but this too was stopped by the Government. Thorndike then fought the official commission tooth and nail to no avail. The country was broke – brought to the verge of ruin by the disastrous war with Chile.

Backed by the security of the Guano deposits, a total of £55,393,800 had been borrowed in England between 1849 and 1871. The £12m Railway Construction Loan of 1870 was oversubscribed five times in London; but the 1871 Public Works Loan of £23,215,000 was only nominally subscribed as confidence began to wane. During Balta's administration servicing of the foreign debt became more and more irregular. Revenues from guano having become barely enough to cover deficits in the budget, loans were now guaranteed by the nitrate deposits of Tarapacá. The Pacific War of 1879-82 ended with these in Chilean hands and Peru was left bankrupt.

Seeing no possibility of Peru's meeting her obligations in connection with those loans, the bondholders in London met in 1886 to elect a committee to protect their interests, and Lord Donoughmore, representing them, with the cooperation of Michael P. Grace (you may recall his name in connection with the financing of the Chilean Transandine), arranged with the Peruvian Government a contract whereby the bondholders waived their claims in exchange for the use of certain Peruvian railways for 66 years, the exclusive rights to navigate Lake Titicaca for the same period, an area of forest country totalling 5m. acres on the lower eastern slopes of the Andes, two million tons of guano increasing to three million when the Cuzco line was completed, and £80,000 a year for thirty years. A company named the Peruvian Corporation Ltd. was incorporated in London on March 20, 1890, to manage the interests of the bondholders, and this company completed the Cuzco line to Sicuani in 1893, still 87 miles short of Cuzco. Construction went on: traffic was inaugurated as far as Checacupe in 1907, 148 miles from Juliaca, and to Cuzco in the same year.

In 1928 a new contract was signed whereby the Peruvian Corporation received the railroads in perpetuity in exchange for the payment of £247,000 and the waiving of the annuity and the remaining guano rights. At the time there was much wagging of heads among the British staff on the railroads. The opinion was that the Government no longer having a proprietary interest in the railways would allow unbridled road competition which otherwise would have been curbed. Time and events proved that there was some justification for these fears; but it was undoubtedly this factor that preserved the Central and the Southern as two of the three major British railway enterprises to survive into the '60s in South America.

The rail journey from Arequipa to Juliaca is long and monotonous – eleven hours of rolling upland country, treeless, unexciting – relieved principally by the views of distant snowcovered summits. Misti, the perfect cone when seen from the west, loses its symmetry when its north side comes into full view. Trains pull out of Arequipa at a lively clip, swing round to the right, cross the long viaduct, and head upwards for Yura, eighteen miles away and twelve hundred feet higher.

The grade is steady, the line uninterrupted by the accidents of construct on that so beset the more rugged Central – no zigzags and only that one tunnel. The *Andes* type on the head end walks the train on and up with all the bark of a steam locomotive working heavily, but without being unduly thrashed. Forty-four miles from Arequipa the throttle lever is shoved forward, and a seven-pound reduction pulls up the day *International* in the station of Pampa de Arrieros, where two westbound freights are waiting the meet, both of them behind – shall we say – 50-class 4-8-0 cross-compounds. Then on again, with a burst of short, sharp toots from the Ashcroft as a herd of llamas appears on the track out beyond yard limits.

Cañaguas – Sumbay, and its bridge – Pillones – Vincocaya – the steady blast talking it up with unvarying beat, and coach wheels going 'a-chunk-a-chunk-a-chunk-a-chunk' in monotonously stable rhythm on the rail joints of the 80-pound iron, cushioned from the redwood ties by soleplates and held by screw-spikes. Well-ballasted, neat track this – permanent way that looks permanent – transition curves too, despite their tightness.[3] Upwards of 14,000 feet now, and the cloud effects overhead are characteristic of the high altitude. Cumulus cloud is as solid as dough against a sky blue strangely darkened from the reduced refraction in the crystalline atmosphere. Then the whistle yells triumphantly, the blast dies away as the throttle is closed, and with the clinking rattle of a juddering brake beam the train comes to a halt at Crucero Alto, 117 miles from Arequipa and 223 from the ocean, where the line crosses the Divide at the summit altitude of 14,666 feet above sea level. An *Andes*, westbound with freight, is waiting here for the meet displaying on the smokebox the white flags of an 'extra'. On the Southern, freights are not designated by timetable but run as extras, this allowing more flexibility in movement although calling for train orders.

There is a mixture of international freight from Bolivia and produce from the Cuzco Division on this drag – minerals from across the lake, vegetables and cattle from the other line. Locomotive ratings are up to 600 tons here, more than double the figure from Mollendo to Pillones; for the grade eases off to two per cent and less.

The 72 miles from the summit to Juliaca, divisional point where the Arequipa, Puno and Cuzco lines meet in the form of a 'T', are made more interesting by the lakes of Lagunillas and Saracocha on either side of the track, and the grazing herds of sheep, llamas and alpacas on the rolling hillsides. As the line drops through Santa Lucia, Maravillas and Cabanillas, the bleakness of the heights gradually gives way to signs of cultivation and settlement, increasing as Lake Titicaca draws nearer. Then Juliaca is reached, tucked in behind low hills, a wilderness of reeds between the town and the lake on the far side.

Arequipa, a city of Colonial charm and perennial sunshine, is a tourist attraction; but the uplands beyond Crucero Alto – the *puna*, Lake Titicaca, and the Cuzco valley teeming with picturesque Indian life – are the very seat and heart of the Inca Empire, and its cradle; and it is there that the visitor to Arequipa will sooner or later be heading. Airways and highways have broken what was once virtually the Southern's monopoly of this tourist movement, and the effect is felt most in first-class passenger traffic.

Thirty miles on from Juliaca the *International* pulls up at Puno, its destination, where passengers for Bolivia transfer to the waiting steamer. It may be the 850-ton oil-fired, twin-screw, 14½ knot *Ollanta*, of 2,000 i.h.p., built in 1929. She can accommodate 66 first-class passengers, and carry 750 tons of freight. If this, the flagship of the Southern's fleet of five vessels and one dredger, is stopped, her place will probably be taken by the 650-ton, 12-knot, twin-screw Inca, built in 1905. Then there is the *Coya*, of 450 tons, built in 1892, able to accommodate 74 first-class passengers. The *Yapurá*, built in 1871, is of 170 tons. But the most interesting from a historical point of view is the baby of the family and at the same time the grandmother of them all – the little 180-ton *Yavarí*, converted in 1953 to a tanker.

After being built, all these vessels were broken down for transport to lakeside and re-assembly on the Huaje Slipway at Puno, where the dry dock has a capacity of 1,000 tons deadweight. *Yavarí* is over a century old, which may well be a record for a merchant vessel still in regular service, and it speaks

50. On the Bolivian side of Lake Titicaca, at Guaqui docks, ENFFCC Baldwin 2-10-2 No. 704 shunts boxcars alongside the Peruvian Corporation's steamship Ollanta, *as Smiths Rodley steam cranes unload cargo from the ship.*
(Richard Pelham)

volumes for the work done on her before she was launched in 1861. She came up from the coast in pieces, on the backs of Indians and mules. The FCS has no details now of her original engines, but when she was handed over to the Peruvian Corporation in 1890 she was recorded as possessing a 45 i.h.p., 2-cyl. steam engine. Except for her hull there is little of the original in her now. Today she is driven at 10 knots by a 220 i.h.p. internal combustion engine.

The lake crossing of 120 miles takes 12 hours. At the Bolivian end is the port of Guaqui, and the metre-gauge line 60 miles long connecting it with La Paz. Traffic over the lake and the Guaqui-La Paz Railway is composed mostly of Bolivian imports – flour, sugar, wheat and general merchandise – while exports are mostly minerals from the La Paz area. Local traffic has increased considerably of late, but the Bolivian tonnage still represents some 22 per cent of the Southern's total.

On occasions the lake can kick up enough to make itself felt, albeit the normal condition is one of tranquillity. Southern Railway vessels share the waters with hundreds of reed *balsas* manned by the lacustrine Indians. A tribe of very primitive mountain people called the Uros (mention was made of relatives of theirs in Chapter 6 in connection with Oruro) dwell on floating islands of reeds in Titicaca, and form one of the attractions that bring foreign tourists to these parts. Guaqui, the port on the Bolivian side, is an ancient settlement mentioned in 1550 by Cieza de Leon in that most fascinating work, *The Chronicle of Peru*; and thirteen miles up the line of the Guaqui-La Paz Railway is the first station, Tiahuanaco, where lie the ruins of one of the greatest archaeological treasures in South America, a megalithic prehistoric city site built, according to Indian traditions of Cieza's day, by bearded white men.

The metre-gauge La Paz train from Guaqui may be headed by a Hunslet 2-8-0 tender engine of fairly recent vintage, and somewhere along the line it may pass a Hunslet 300 h.p. pressure-charged diesel-mechanical locomotive dating from 1939. A light grade of one half of one per cent leads to Quercata, milepost 23, where it steepens to not more than one per cent and then drops slightly to the junction of Viacha, 41 miles from Guaqui, where FCAB and Arica-La Paz lines converge for the entry into La Paz. Fourteen miles beyond brings the train to El Alto, at 13,396 feet above sea level, end of steam operation; and here 550 v., D.C. electrics take over for the 5½ miles of the 'Bajada' down the mountain to the terminus, last leg in the three-hour trip from the lake.

Now, this up-ended section of track linking El Alto with La Paz, 1,372 feet below, is interesting for two reasons. It was the first railroad electrification in South America; and it has one of the steepest adhesion grades in the Andes, reaching a maximum of *seven per cent* (1 in 14.3). A concession for the building of this railway was granted by the Bolivian Government in 1900, and in 1903 the line was at El Alto. It was completed in 1906, and four years later was sold by the Government to the Peruvian Corporation for £350,000. The climb out of La Paz was electrified in 1905, diesel-generated power being supplied from Purapura, half a mile out of the capital. Today the Purapura station no longer operates, and power is purchased from the City of La Paz.

The electrics creep up this truly formidable grade with 60 tons hooked to their automatic couplers. They bring their trains down on air brakes alone, but before tackling the descent all excess slack in the riggings is carefully taken up.

The Southern's *Ten-wheelers* can make surprisingly good time on the monotonous, easily-graded tangents along the *puna* between Juliaca and La Raya. We're on the Cuzco Division now, aboard the northbound passenger that took off from Juliaca at 8.45 a.m. of a crackling, frosty Titicaca morning behind Rogers 4-6-0 No. 81. The class she belongs to has handled passenger services all over the system from the time of their advent in 1907 without any trouble on the mainline grades.

The Central possessed three of the 81's sisters; the Cerro de Pasco, one. With saturated boilers and 'D' slide valves, these northern members of the clan were suitable only for work on the two-per-cent; but the Arequipa stud-most of 'em, at any rate-blossomed out with superheaters and piston valves, able to turn in a good enough performance on the limited stretches of FCS four-per-cent to qualify for the varnish ratings.

The consist of the Cuzco train is wooden stock with bench seating to handle the teeming second-class traffic, predominantly Indian – and mountain Indians, be it noted, invariably travel with as many cherished possessions as they can carry, from tin jerries to poultry, the latter tied by the feet in clusters and carried upside-down, protesting vociferously. They may even have sucking pigs with them also, in which case the piglets are often nursed in public during the journey by the goodwife, at the same fount and in company with any young children she may have that qualify for the privilege. A plentiful supply of domestic foodstuffs, replenished at each station stop, mixes its aroma with that of overripe fruit, llama-wool blankets and garments, and Indian bodies that have never known a bath, to create an overpowering, sour smell that characterizes second-class travel in the Andes. Ticket inspectors are not to be envied as they fight their way through the overcrowded aisles, and clamber over the mountains of bundles and packages filling every bit of space.

Ordinary first-class may be impregnated with a residue of odour from the adjacent second-class, but it is respectable, and the seats are comfortable. The elite among the passengers are likely to be found in the saloon car, which is a kind of super-first-class. There is a chair-car surcharge for the saloon, and the buffet at one end provides snacks, drinks, refreshments, and a lunch that would knock spots off what one generally pays far more for in European dining cars. The catering is done by a cook and his assistant. You may have seen the latter out on the back platform of the car before the train started from Juliaca, wringing the necks of half a dozen unfortunate chickens destined for the day's menu; later you would certainly meet him about the individual tables of the saloon passengers, clad in a white steward's jacket, very much the efficient waiter from the waist up, but unblushingly *cholo* in the way of trousers and shoes.

The first hundred miles of the journey is through some of the best sheep country in the Andes – and the physical resemblance to the Scottish Border is remarkable. At Chuquibambilla, 68 miles from Juliaca, there is in fact an experimental sheep farm where the Government has achieved magnificent results in the way of wool. Cattle are much in evidence too, giving the lie to assertions that cattle and sheep cannot live together.

On this stretch, more perhaps than on any other, the vast expanse and loneliness of the *puna* can be felt; but the run is monotonous only till the 81 breasts the 14,153-foot summit at La Raya. After that, the mountain valleys swallow the line and the scenery becomes more and more interesting as the train eats up the miles on the gentle falling grade into Sicuani, milepost 123. Snow-covered peaks are in sight much of the time now, peering down into the widening valley over the shoulders of the mountain walls on either side. The mellow cries of Eng. 81's Ashcroft bounce off the crags above the fields and cultivated terraces on the slopes; little villages appear as Indian life becomes more prolific. At Aguas Calientes the train halts beside bubbling springs of hot water, from which rise clouds of steam.

From Sicuani onwards the scenery is truly lovely. The train is now in traditional Inca country, approaching the very heart of the Old Empire, and remains of that remarkable culture appear. The huge megaliths of the Temple of Viracocha rise majestically amid a chaos of volcanic rock beside the Vilcanota River skirted by the track.

The 210-mile journey over the Cuzco Division is a long day's run at Andean train speeds, and darkness falls before the varnish reaches its destination. But ere nightfall blots out the valley there has been a chance for first-time visitors to see the increasing colourfulness of Indian life at trackside. The valley here is rich – rich in agriculture – and even possesses a few industries, such as the textile mills at Marangani. Because of its richness, the rural population is relatively thick.

At 6.40 p.m. Eng. 81's whistle announces the approach to Cuzco. Second-class passengers are jostling to collect their bits and pieces, livestock and progeny ready to disembark, jabbering away in Quechua to an accompaniment of cackles, squeals and bleats. First-class passengers get their luggage down from the overloaded racks, pull bags out from under and behind seats, push past one another and clutter up the aisles unnecessarily, as passengers invariably do, be it in England or Peru! With tolling bell the engine rolls up to the platform of the one-time golden capital of the Inca Empire. Air brakes sigh off to the clank of dropping yokes as the wheels that have rolled to an average of 21 m.p.h. for ten hours come to a standstill. Those saloon passengers who have booked accommodation in the Company's own Hotel Continental, over the station, are quickly and comfortably settled. The other passengers, plus the hordes that meet the train, debouch into the night and head up the hill towards the city centre, in taxis, buses and on foot. Those unable or unwilling to tote their own luggage for half a mile at an altitude of 11,007 feet have no difficulty in finding porters, with a multitude of men and small Indian boys clamouring vigorously for the office.

51. Cuzco station stands at a height of 11,007ft, and is the terminus of the line from Arequipa. The architectural style is markedly different from the same company's Arequipa station. The top floor of Cuzco's station building is used by the Railway Company as a Hotel.   *(Author)*

For track considerations, the diesels have not yet taken over from steam on the Cuzco Division, nor do the *Andes* type operate there. Freight traffic is principally petroleum products, gasoline, cement, cereals, flour, sugar, fruit and vegetables, cattle and general merchandise, as well as a limited amount of minerals. It is the extraordinary historical interest of the country served by the Southern that justifies its slogan 'Wonder Railway of the World' – not, as might be at first imagined, a vainglorious claim to unique operating efficiency and service to the public. Nevertheless, its efficient services are taken for granted in Southern Peru, and there can be no greater commendation than that!

1 *These sums are stated at the then exchange rate of 48d. to the Sol.*

2 *Two Years in Peru. See Bibliography.*

3 *Transition curves are spiralled to give a smoothly-graduated lead-in. They are laid by the conscientious engineers of responsible systems who take a proper pride in optimum track; but transitioning is not by any means a general practice on the West Coast of South America.*

52. The locomotive depot at Cerro de Pasco, at an altitude of 14,208ft, 82 miles from Oroya. This railroad was thoroughly North American in style and all equipment in this scene is from American builders.

(Author)

53. For a primarily mining line, the Cerro de Pasco's passenger train was an impressive sight that would have been the envy of many a main line railway. Train No. 2 leaves Oroya in 1960.

(Author)

Chapter 9

"A RAILWAY ON THE ROOF OF THE WORLD"

THE Cerro de Pasco Railway's slogan is an apt one, if somewhat trite; and no one could deny the right of using it to a system with a *lowest* point 12,272 feet above sea level. Moreover, the C de P is an honest-to-goodness, hard-working, standard gauge ore carrier and public servant, using conventional equipment, operated on the train-order system, under standard-code rules, and is traditionally U.S. in all but one item, to be explained at the end of the chapter. There are no tricks or frills about it – no rack sections or rope inclines – no spectacular grades or hair-raising curves – no bridge-spanned gorges or labyrinthine tunnels such as abound on the Central of Peru, to which it connects in Oroya. It's just plain railroad – the main line, that is – but its total of 170 miles includes the 50-mile branch from Pachacayo to Chaucha, separated from the parent system by 25 miles of Central trackage. This branch, the Yauricocha Railway, hits 15,500 feet in altitude, and 25 miles of it lies at over 15,000 feet, in terrain where snow and ice can be troublesome.

Its origin has much in common with that of the Central. Without doubt, the earliest schemes for providing Cerro de Pasco with a rail outlet burgeoned in the mind of Richard Trevithick during his first exhausting journey up there from Lima, over the old *Camino Real*, through Oroya to Tarma, and then across the bleak, inhospitable Junín *Pampa* to Cerro de Pasco. That was in 1817, and the Cornish engineer was accompanying the mule train freighting up the second batch of his steam pumps to the Mines of Pasco. Two were already in erratic operation there, one in the Santa Rosa mine and one at Yanacancha. A third, destined for the Caya Chica mines, was in course of erection under a particularly aggressive Cornish artisan named Tom Trevarthen, whom Trevithick had sent to Peru on the ship *Wildman*, which sailed from Portsmouth on Sept. 1, 1814, with the first ship-load of four complete pumping engines and four steam whims. The man responsible for Trevithick's presence in Peru, Francisco Uville, was with him during that crawling trek up the precipitous mountain trail and had explained clearly the exorbitant cost of freighting silver down to the capital on muleback. He had also pictured to Trevithick the difficulties of supplying a region destitute of timber with pit props and construction material from the forests low on the eastern slopes of the *Cordillera*. There was still another chronic problem: that of feeding the mining population and providing the bare necessities of life. Everything had to be freighted to the mines on the backs of men and animals, over appalling trails.

Mining activities in the Pasco region having hesitantly recommenced after the capitulation of the Spanish in 1825 – as far as the shattered equipment, widely dispersed labour, depleted funds, and the political upheavals of the early Republic permitted – there accompanied it a resurgence of the railway idea sown in Peruvian minds by the man who was the first ever to operate a steam train. And as an idea it remained until that colossus of railroad contracting, Henry Meiggs, thought he saw in it, and the properly organized exploitation of the mines it would serve, a 'safe' means of saving his own and a bankrupt Peruvian Government's financial skin. His fortune, you see, was bound up in the ambitious railroad construction schemes to pay for which Balta, goaded on by him, had pawned the guano deposits. The supposedly 'inexhaustible' supplies of guano had failed, and if he were not to go down in ruin, a more reliable security must be found on which Peru might raise further loans from Europe. The vast mineral potential of Cerro de Pasco was to Meiggs the logical answer, and he grasped it as eagerly as a drowning man seizes a lifebelt.

At the time engaged in building the Oroya railroad, Don Enrique proposed to the Government the formation, by himself, of a company to drain the mines, exploit them intensively, and build – at his own cost – a railway to open up the region, in exchange for concessions of all the mineral deposits not at the moment being worked there, and the whole of the machinery and equipment publicly owned in Cerro. The Government pulled a long face but finally agreed, realizing that the fabulous and somewhat exaggerated wealth of the Mines of Pasco could well become the carrot to be hung in front of the shy noses of European investors now that guano was no longer available for the purpose. This was in fact

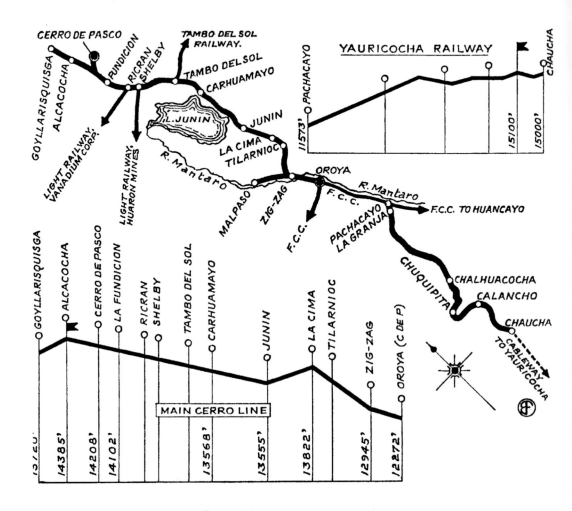

YAURICOCHA RAILWAY

CERRO DE PASCO
TAMBO DEL SOL RAILWAY.
GOYLLARISQUISGA
ALCACOCHA
FUNDICION
RICRAN
SHELBY
TAMBO DEL SOL
CARHUAMAYO
L. JUNIN
JUNIN
LA CIMA
TILARNIOC
R. Mantaro
MALPASO
ZIG-ZAG
OROYA
F. C. C.
R. Mantaro
F.C.C. TO HUANCAYO
F.C.C.
PACHACAYO LA GRANJA
CHUQUIPITA
CHALHUACOCHA
CALANCHO
CHAUCHA
CABLEWAY TO YAURICOCHA

PACHACAYO 11573'
CHAUCHA
15100'
15000'

LIGHT RAILWAY, VANADIUM CORP.
LIGHT RAILWAY, HUARON MINES

GOYLLARISQUISGA
ALCACOCHA
CERRO DE PASCO
LA FUNDICION
RICRAN
SHELBY
TAMBO DEL SOL
CARHUAMAYO
JUNIN
LA CIMA
TILARNIOC
ZIG-ZAG
OROYA (C DE P)
CHALHUACOCHA
CALANCHO
CHAUCHA

MAIN CERRO LINE

13'620
14385'
14208'
14102'
13568'
13555'
13822'
12945'
12272'

54. A scene from 1933: engineer Fitzgerald checks the running gear of oil-fired Alco-Rhode Island 2-6-0 No. 51, at the head of train No. 1 at Oroya, just arrived from Cerro. (Author)

what Don Enrique assured them. The mine owners in Cerro howled blue murder, but to no avail. Against the will of the power behind the throne they were as nought. Meiggs got the concession in 1877, subject to the condition, amongst others, that he must first complete the Oroya line, connecting his Cerro de Pasco iron to it, and but for his untimely death in September of that year, the Cerro de Pasco Railway would almost certainly have been seriously put in hand.

It is interesting to note that Viceroy Pezuela had granted a similar concession to Cap'n Dick Trevithick, but in that instance the pitch was queered by the outbreak of civil war. During the height of the railway fever of the 1860's, which ruined Peru, the idea was to build a line to link Cerro de Pasco with a rail artery from Lima to Jauja, a country town at the junction of two rich agricultural valleys. As a starter, the Government sanctioned a 66-inch gauge feeder line to carry ore from the Cerro mines to a smelting centre at Pasco, only a few miles distant. This precipitated a gauge battle. Government Engineer Joseph Hindle argued that a gauge of 42 inches was preferable, pointing out the advantage in cheapness of construction with an exactitude that included cents in the estimates; and in 1867 the Government agreed to this. The company to operate it would be called 'The Cerro de Pasco Railway Company', and its capital of some £650,000, in £10 shares at 7 per cent per annum, carried the State guarantee. The first contract, with Wyman & Co., lapsed. Other would-be concessionaires offered insufficient guarantees of their good faith. Arguments blew up again, this time by champions of metre-gauge. And so it went on until 1873, when the seven-mile narrow-gauge railway was at length built. Its name passed in due course to the line of today.

The mining company of Backus & Johnston in Casapalca offered in 1898 to build the railway from Cerro to Oroya, where the Central tracks had arrived in 1893, and also construct the Rumillana drainage tunnel in Cerro, projected by the late Don Enrique Meiggs. The Government insisted on a maximum grade of three per cent, standard-gauge track for a union with the Oroya line, and the best equipment obtainable. In return, the concessionaire would get the railroad in perpetuity together with free grants of land for its construction. Failure to offer sufficient assurances of meeting these conditions caused B & J to drop out, their place immediately being taken by Ernest Thorndike, who had carried Central tracks to Oroya from Chicla, where Meiggs left them. In 1899 the concession was his. In 1902 Thorndike turned it over to James B. Haggin's 'South American Development Co.' Suddenly the Government discovered errors in the survey for the proposed line. They gave Haggin ninety days to run a new one, which he did; and his 'Cerro de Pasco Railway Co.' was then approved. The green now showing for him, he opened the throttle and eased forward. In 1904 freight traffic between Oroya and the town of Pasco was provisionally allowed, and shortly afterwards passenger traffic similarly permitted. The immediate result was that freight charges over the route served by the railway dropped to less than one third of what they had been by pack trains of llamas.

Seventy-five miles of the main line's total of eighty-three were laid along the proposed route of a mythical 'Pan-American Railway' that never came to anything. In 1903, Haggin was granted a concession for a 23-mile branch off the main line to open up coal deposits at Goyllarisquisga, and another of 11 miles to the Quishuarcancha coal mines. This last branch was abandoned in 1929, all the rails and ties taken up from it being used in the construction of the Malpaso branch, a line to a big dam then under construction for increasing hydro-electric power in Oroya.

Operation began with six locomotives, four passenger coaches, a business car, and 145 assorted freight cars herded by three cabooses. Two of the locomotives, Nos. 8 and 9 – at the time of writing this still in yard service – dated from 1902, and were 2-8-0s with 20 x 24-inch cylinders, 52-inch drivers, and saturated boilers carrying 180 pounds pressure. These can safely be cited as the first engines of the type that inspired the highly successful *Andes* type subsequently to dominate the C de P, the Central and the Southern of Peru. Their four original stablemates, delivered in mid-1903, were the 50-53, *Moguls* with 57inch drivers. All were built by Rhode Island Works of the American Locomotive Co. New York Air Brake equipment predominated on coaches and cars, but there was some Westinghouse also, the two systems working satisfactorily together. The 20-ton wooden coaches, with open platforms at either end, remained in service as long as *Moguls* headed the passenger trains, in spite of the advent of a smart rake of all-steel vestibule stock for Nos. 1 and 2, 'The Flamingo'; and this was because the new 50-ton coaches were too much for them and could only be used when a 'Mike' or one of the later series of the big 2-8-0 freight engines was available to take over the run.

In 1915 the newly incorporated *Cerro de Pasco Copper Corporation* acquired all the mines and related plant from the Cerro de Pasco Investment Co. – an entity that included the holdings of the South American Development Co. – and also took over the railway; though the latter remained intact as a company separate from that exploiting the mines until January 1961. The mining properties included those in Morococha, a town until that time reached by a branch line on the Central from Ticlio, and in 1921 a new line eleven miles long was built by the C de P connecting with the Central at a place later known as Cut-Off . This entailed working C de P trains into Oroya over nine miles of Central trackage, and it was soon found convenient to sell the Morococha cut-off to the Central. The Yauricocha Railway, already mentioned, officially began operation in 1948. The highgrade copper ore deposits at Yauricocha were in fact part of the Backus & Johnston properties of which all capital stock had belonged to the C de P Copper Corp. since 1916. Diminishing ore bodies in the regions so far worked made it desirable to develop Yauricocha, difficult of access though it was, and in 1942 construction began on the railroad and the 9-mile aerial tramway linking the mines with railhead. The mining engineers had to carry out the construction themselves, World War II making it impossible to get railroad engineers for the task. The completed road was then rented to the C de P Railway Company and operated by them.

Up to comparatively recent times all C de P engines were fired with coal from the parent company's properties. Goyllarisquisga coal, with its 9,930 B.T.U.s and 32.5 per cent ash (Quishuarcancha coal wasn't much better), demanded two firemen per engine, whose labours when steam was being worked were nothing short of spectacular. This was particularly the case when big power began to come in, from 1907 onwards. Crews complained that in a strong cross-wind half the fuel blew off the tenders! Most of what went into the firebox carried right on through the flues and stack without landing anywhere inside. Much of the remainder promptly fused into mighty clinkers on hitting the fire, so that slicebars and rakes were in use whenever scoops were laid down and grates were not being shaken. C de P tracks were walled with slag and ballasted with ash and unburnt *pampa* coal, all of it representing the sweat, blood and tears of a generation of firemen and coalpassers. But it had the same result that was experienced in earlier days on the Central: enginemen pupped to scoop and slicebar made better engineers when they graduated to the right side of the cab than those brought up on the seats of their pants with an oil latch in their hands- much the same, I should say, as a seaman trained in sail aboard one of the old windjammers.

Highest point of the C de P proper is Alcacocha, on the Goyllarisquisga branch, 14,385 feet above sea level. Grades on this line are of no more than 2.5 per cent, with minimum curves of 16 degrees approximately 359 feet radius), but there is one curve of 24 degrees (240 feet radius). The branch joins the main line at Vista Alegre, near La Fundición, nine miles from Cerro de Pasco. It is a bleak region, this high Andean puna, devoid of trees and shrubs, but supporting enough *ichu* or bunch grass to feed numerous herds of llamas, and – in the C de P's ranches at Casaracra, Atocsaico and elsewhere on the properties – sheep and cattle in abundance.

Cerro de Pasco itself is a nondescript town at 14,208 feet, notable for its coldness, wetness and general unattractiveness. It is ancient, hollow underneath with a myriad old mine shafts, some dating back to the start of mining there in 1630, surrounded by the newer and organized workings of latter years. A writer of 1871 described it as a town of 10,000 people, lacking 'order and design in every part' – the streets crooked and uneven – the houses stuck about anywhere everything filthily dirty. The town, he asserted, looked as though it were built on the back of one huge lode – lode-stuff everywhere – what Cornish miners call an 'iron gossan'. Well, the town of today has obviously improved greatly, but the truth of the above description is still recognizable.

The many lakes in the mountains here appear vividly coloured, according to the mineral nature of their beds. Everywhere, outcroppings of rock break through the thin soil. It is a chill, inhospitable region of tremendous spaces, walled in by dark crags along the Continental Divide – dark, that is, where not covered by perpetual snow. Yet under certain conditions it all takes on an aspect of extraordinary beauty. The distant view from Carhuamayo of fantastically eroded rock a hundred square miles in area, known as the *Rock Forest,* would make anyone not in the know believe that the slopes under the mighty Viuda range were carpeted with redwood. Sights one can't forget are the enormous expanse of Lake Junín pink with the thousands of flamingoes spooning food in the shallows, and a multi-coloured surface rising into the air to disintegrate into the vibrating wings of hundreds of thousands of startled ducks as a passing locomotive whistle shouts. The incredibly squalid Indian huts with their reed-thatched roofs exuding

55. *Train No. 1 at La Cima, 13,822ft. The Cerro de Pasco's Andes locomotives were well maintained and very smart.*
(Author)

56. *Flexible as a weasel, this Alco 2-8-0 is not inconvenienced by the tight curve at Desvio Doble, 15,000ft up on the Yauricocha branch.*
(Author)

smoke from the llama-dung fires, their ragged inhabitants scratching a meagre living of potatoes and quinua from the reluctant, half-frozen ground, accentuate rather than relieve the loneliness of the scene. These are the people who not so long ago firmly believed that on moonlit nights strange monsters crept up through the reedy fringes of Lake Junín – formerly Chinchaycocha – to seize cattle grazing on the firmer ground and drag their prey back to the depths to devour it at leisure. One wonders if some 'Loch Ness Monster' did in fact once inhabit this great stretch of water. If so, Junín was but one of many lakes infested with living relics of past geological ages; for one comes across the tradition again and again in the Andes.

Familiarly known as La Fundición, the smelter at Tinyahuarco was blown in during 1906. It handled all the Cerro ore until the new smelter at Oroya was completed and began operation in 1922. At Ricrán, the next station down, a narrow-gauge feeder line belonging to the Vanadium Corporation of America comes in from Lake Punrun. A mile or-two farther on, at Shelby, there is another narrow-gauge line connecting with the French-owned Huarun mines which produce between 20,000 and 25,000 tons of lead-silver-zinc ore per month. At Tambo del Sol a metre-gauge Government road breaks off towards the east. About this small, incomplete streak of rust have been woven great dreams of its eventual development of the Pucallpa forest region. So far, however, the opening up of the eastern forests has been done by road and by air, and this ambitious rail project will probably never come to anything.

The C de P Railway runs down over easy grades not exceeding 1.5 per cent, skirting Lake Junín between Carhuamayo and the village of Junín. Here a battle was fought in 1824 between the patriot forces under Bolivar and the Spanish royalists of General Canterac. Canterac was defeated so decisively that the War of Independence in Peru needed only the final crushing victory at Ayacucho to be brought to a triumphant conclusion with the freedom of all Spanish South America assured. A monument close to the track commemorates the event. At La Cima, altitude 13,822 feet and 23.5 miles from Oroya, the line tilts downwards on a grade of 2.25 per cent, through rolling fell-like country greener and less unfriendly than the *puna* – very like the hills of the Scottish Border – through Tilarnioc to Zig-Zag, where the Malpaso branch peels off. This is the only zig-zag on the main line, and once past it there's an easy run down the Mantaro Valley into Oroya. Before construction of the big 500-foot stack in the Oroya smelter the surrounding country was scorched bare of vegetation by the sulphur smoke from the plant. Today much of the little green that these altitudes can claim has crept back. Chulec, the Oroya officials' residential district, shows up on the left, beyond the Mantaro River and the golf-course with its balding grass fairways and sand 'greens'.

The line curves round a shoulder of mountain where the valley narrows to a throat, and enters Oroya yard limits. The gorge widens rapidly. The engine terminal, scale house, wye and smelter line capture incoming freights here, but passenger trains pass through with the mellow cry of the chime whistles flung back by the rocky walls behind the Inca Club and the hydroelectric station, skim over the Yauli Bridge, tilt on the sharp curve rounding into the C de P Station (always known as that of '*la Railway*' to distinguish it from the Central's '*Estacion del Central*') and come to rest with sighing universal valves beside the grey stone structure forming the brain centre of the system, where the general offices, the train dispatcher and the Superintendent are housed.

The man responsible for running the C de P Railway carries no highfalutin' title. He is neither the President nor the General Manager. He is just the 'Superintendent', and as such he is inseparably wedded to the railway, living within knocking distance of the tracks where he can be got at instantly at any hour of the day or night.

No recollections of the C de P are possible that do not include A. T. Howard. For many years throughout the period of my acquaintance with the line and my tenure of office in the motive power department of the Central in Oroya, Howard as 'Super' was not only the living personification of the C de P Railway, but the Railway was in effect Howard. Originally from some small road in the western U.S.A., he was the *beau ideal* of the hard-boiled N. American railroad man, so surely born to the game that the idea of his ever doing anything else was utterly inconceivable. Like several others among the Corporation's officials on 'The Hill' (as the foreign staff liked to call the elevated regions of their mining camps in the aggregate) A.T.H. went out of his way to foster an impression of ruthless toughness entirely out of keeping with a kindliness and good nature that inevitably showed through as soon as his guard was down. The bullet head, the beetling brows, the aggressive chin, the ferocious mouth clamped on the end of a well-chewed cigar stump, all combined to create a frontwise aspect as daunting as a dreadnought's bow. But from the rear the effect was otherwise; for however pitiless the calculated frown on A.T.H.'s face, there was a crease behind, where his head joined his neck, that spread in a broad smile, as though to say: 'Don't take him at his face value – the last word is mine!'

One manifestation of A.T.H.'s toughness was a simulated scorn for all British institutions on the Central. British-built locomotives, for example, were 'no goddam' good', a condemnation not entirely unjustified in view of the fact that those most familiar to him were the swaybacked crocks relegated to my command in Oroya to get them out of sight and mind while waiting to be taken by the works for general repairs. These mechanical wrecks staggered and rattled in dreary procession past his office windows morning and evening, leaking steam from every joint, and generally advertising their presence with groaning slide valves and stifling clouds of dark-brown oil smoke wafted in upon him by the prevailing breezes. It was a commonplace thing when battling out of the Central yard, up the main past the C de P Station with a full rating on the tail of a belching 60-class, to see an enraged countenance appear suddenly under the eaves of the office building as A.T.H. sprang up from his desk and hurriedly slammed his windows shut to keep our smoke out. His own muzzle-loaders could themselves smoke the scenery up considerably, but he can't have been allergic to coal fumes.

Another reason why Howard disliked British locomotives is worth relating. Not all my engines were wrecks. There were some Alco 'Mikes' that A.T.H. swore, quite correctly, were the only good ones in my section. There were also some cumbersome English Mountain type engines, far larger than anything the C de P could show, but no more muscular, and given to a marked predilection for slipping. They were the most 'English'-looking engines we had, and this alone was enough to damn them in Howard's eyes.

It was at a time when the Central was changing over from one system of water treatment to another, the mixtures of feed waters bringing about an epidemic of chronic priming that enginemen endeavoured to check by feeding vast quantities of Dearborn boiler compound through the injectors and blowing down on every possible occasion. Outside our yard, at the south end, in front of the C de P Station, ran a street open on one side to the parallel tracks. Central enginemen pulling out with freight drags, and with the contents of the boiler pouring from the chimney, would open up their blow-off cocks here. Besides distracting A.T.H. in his office with the deafening roar, the blast across the street had almost brought one or two of the less robust adobe houses down in ruin, had wrecked stock in a few open shops and had scared numerous defenceless citizens clear out of the ponchos. The Chief of Police complained to the District Traffic Superintendent, though not before A.T.H. had voiced his displeasure, and as a result strict orders were issued that there must be no blowing down within yard limits anywhere, except at the places specially prescribed for it.

Now, Howard was experiencing the gratification of owning the smartest car in Oroya, a brand-new Buick sedan that was his pride and joy. So far, wealthier Smelter officials had not gone one better, and A.T.H. rammed home the superiority of his own luxurious conveyance by having a small army of station peones constantly at work Simonizing it into a state of almost unbelievable gloss. The rounds he had previously made daily on his two legs he now did, as far as he could, in his car, for the pleasure of showing it off to an envious public.

At that time the Railway had two yards in Oroya. There was the one mentioned formerly, and another beyond the station, running south beside Central tracks to a district called Huaymanta, where it ended in a ladder from a switch leading off the Central's main line. Incoming cars consigned to the C de P were cut off Central trains at Huaymanta and switched into this yard by gravity. Very close to this switch was an unprotected road crossing leading out of town.

Howard had occasion to pay a visit to the remote end of this Huaymanta yard and took advantage of it to drive there in his car. As he neared the grade crossing he was aware of a Central freight approaching up the grade from Oroya, making heavy weather of it with one of the big English 4-8-2s on the smoky end. He was too good a railroad man to cross over in front of an oncoming train. Instead, he halted close to the track to await the train's passing, settling himself back in the Buick's comfortable seat to inspect the rival stock in a spirit of good-natured criticism, doubtless hoping for a missing marker flag or unconnected bellcord so that he might twit Central brass at their next meeting. Behind him, an overloaded truck rattled up wheezing to a halt with its front bumper not a foot from the Buick's back one.

The morning was full of low-lying sulphur smoke from the smelter which combining with the damp from a recent rain storm formed a coating of soapy ice on the rails. Only too ready to slip her drivers even under ideal conditions, Engine 112 was rocking in flurry after flurry of madly spinning wheels, barely making headway except in the brief moments when the tyres bit on the sand cascading down from the sandboxes. She would lunge forward with a jerk sudden enough to pull the drawgears out of the banging cars, advancing only a few yards before the next flurry of slipping began. The engineer had his hands full trying to coax her along without 'burning' the rail tops or allowing the train to stall and slide backwards, and his fireman was occupied with the threefold task of synchronizing the firing latch with the restless throttle, keeping the injector from flying off, and whanging sandpipes with a hammer to prevent them from clogging. Neither man paid much attention to what might be on the grade crossing.

In addition to the slipping, the 112's boiler had been priming off and on since they left the Central yard, and this suddenly came to a head when the pilot was close to the crossing. Filthy water shot up through the stack as the roar of the blast became a whooshing cough. Howard winced as the moisture atomized in the air and fell over the shining finish of his car in a gentle, sooty drizzle. But worse was to come – much worse! The tiring engineer slammed the throttle home and reopened it, hoping that the contents of the boiler had settled. Again a Niagara belched up from the stack. He made the quick gesture to his fireman that meant 'blow her down'. The blow-off valve handle was on the fireman's side, just under the front door.

This class of engine had the blow-off valve exhaust set rather low, with an extension pipe facing outwards from the firebox mudring on the left-hand side. As the fireman, oblivious to what might be in the way of the blast, yanked the valve open, the drivers found their grip momentarily and the train surged forward until the crossing was completely blocked by the engine. Another flurry of the wildest slipping halted it there. Meanwhile, the blow-off valve let go with a roar. The 'spread' from the extension pipe whipped up assorted gravel from the dirt surface of the road, combined it with sludge, horse manure and partially dissolved Dearborn from the boiler and hurled the mixture against the cherished car of the horrified Super. As A.T.H. instinctively ducked, the windscreen starred above his cringing head and the car trembled and shook under the bombardment. His shouts of rage and alarm were unheard in the din of the escaping steam. He was imprisoned there. The car could not be backed, because of the truck behind; nor was there room to turn off the side of the road. There was nothing for him to do but remain where he was. Fortunately for him, previously closed windows prevented his being parboiled, but the agony at the thought of what his car was undergoing equalled any physical torture.

When Engine 112 finally managed to summon up enough adhesion to move on and the fireman considered the concentration of solids in the boiler sufficiently reduced to warrant his closing the blow-off cock, Howard's car was a sorry spectacle. There were no dents – if you discount a few dimples here and there – but the shot-blasting process had obliterated chrome and headlights, and besides leaving the body with something of the look of a mangy pariah dog, had then attempted to hide the ruinous condition of the cellulose under a jammy coating of nastiness! Howard's wail of anguish when he crawled out of the car and surveyed the damage was so heartrending that the driver and passengers of the truck behind gravely removed their hats, thinking they must be in the presence of a dying man.

A.T.H. was not one to lodge his complaint at district officer level. It went straight to the GM's office in Lima-by telephone. Of course, restitution was made, but the car never regained its pristine beauty, and I – as the one responsible for Engine 112 and her crew – never heard the end of it. He was too big a man to harbour personal grudges, but his loathing of the Central's 110 class engines never diminished one whit.

Howard's minions, the 'Hawgheads', were not all of them free from prejudice either. Having paid a visit to my roundhouse out of curiosity, one of them – fresh from California and the Southern Pacific – remarked on descending from the deck of the 110: 'That's the goddamnedest cab I ever seen. Everything's where you can't get a hold of it. I wouldn't take one of them mills as far as the end of the yard!'

Yet at that time the C de P was running its passenger trains in the tradition of the '90s in the Far West. That is to say, the rangy Moguls, or the single Rogers Ten-wheeler No. 20 (that was sister to three of a similar type on the Central), were pulling open-ended wooden passenger cars with pot-bellied stoves to warm them and with glass chandeliers originally intended for Pintsch gas lighting. The up-to-date steel coaches with combine, and observation car carrying the name Flamingo on the drumhead, came along

57. *Alco 2-8-2 No. 4 of 1927 halts on the Yauli bridge, Oroya, to pose with a complete crew in 1928. These big coal burners were hand fired and required two firemen. To the left of the buffer beam stands the train conductor, a man of some dignity in the Americas.* (Author)

58. *Known in Oroya as a 'dinky', a tiny Davenport-built 0-4-0ST belonging to the C de P smelter pays a visit to the Central roundhouse in Oroya, during switching operations in 1934.* (Author)

later. As already mentioned, these proved too much for the *Moguls* or the 20, and the varnish had therefore to be headed by one of the 10-class Baldwin *Mikados* of 1907, with 52-inch drivers, or an Alco 2-8-0. There were in due course eight of the latter, impressive engines with their high boilers, short stacks and big sandboxes. The first four of the series, Nos. 5-8, were delivered in 1916. In 1925 another couple, rather more up-to-date, were purchased; and in 1930 came Nos. 1 and 2, with Worthington feedwater heaters and all the fixin's. The last two were oil fired – all the others burned coal – and all had 52inch drivers. It was on these that C de P firemen really had to work. In the United States the Brotherhood would have insisted on stokers being fitted. In Peru it didn't matter. Labour was cheap, and human arms were more reliable than any mechanical stoker.

When the 1 and 2 were delivered, Howard promptly locked them away out of man's sight, like vestal virgins, in a shed built for two up in the Huaymanta yard. To the query of us all on the Central, 'When are you going to use those new engines of yours, A.T.H.?'he would reply,'Why should I burn up oil fuel just to provide traffic for you guys? The coal engines can keep all my cars movin' right now!' The oil fuel used by the Corporation had to be shipped up over the Central, you see. Alas; how time passes! The 'vestal virgins' are now dowagers of advanced age, due soon to be ousted by diesel-electrics.

Besides the 10-class *Mikes*, there were two of the same wheel arrangement built by Baldwin in 1913. These, numbered 40 and 41, possessed drivers only 42 inches in diameter, and they moved with a waddling gait, like overfed geese. Their tiny wheels made them remarkably slippery. Both were in Oroya yard duty in my day; though one was removed temporarily for the construction of the Malpaso branch.

Only light repairs were done on the Railway. General repairs were handled by the plant in the Smelter, thus eliminating the need for locomotive and car shops with their necessary equipment. Needless to say, the Railway found flies even where no flies existed. For their part, the Smelter complained that engines were customarily worked beyond all civilized ideas of standards between shoppings.

Throughout my time in Oroya it was C de P policy to have North American engineers running main line trains; though by the middle '30's some of the senior Peruvian firemen were taking over throttles. This brought a number of remarkable characters into our midst, preserving at the same time the U.S. flavour of the line. From the point of view of efficiency its effectiveness might be doubted – not, let me hasten to add, for the same reasons that had caused the Central to drop the policy many years before, but because the unaccustomed altitude took it out of men obliged to lead a physically active life in an atmosphere deficient in oxygen. On the whole they were good enginemen with plenty of experience; but in spite of some big talk, I can scarcely believe that all had come from the right-hand side of the cab on the railroads of their own country.

Dean of the 'Hawgheads' was old Fitzgerald, once upon a time of the Newfoundland Railways. It was he who ran trains 1 and 2, the passenger, down from Cerro in the morning to connect with the Central's No. 2 for Lima, and back to Cerro in the evening with passengers arriving from Lima on the Central's No. 1. His usual engine was No. 20, the Rogers *Ten-wheeler,* relieved at times by one of the 50-class *Moguls.* It was with No. 52 that Fitz had a narrow escape. He was involved in a bad accident at Casaracra, when the 52 turned over on him. The engine was stripped of cab, running boards, piping and almost every other fitting outside the boiler, yet Fitz lost only a few square inches of hide. He had as many lives as a cat, had that hoghead! On another occasion he arrived in Oroya with the passenger train, his head split open and his overalls soaked in blood. He had been running flat out, craning over the side of the cab to look backwards and see if any boxes were smoking, when he was hit by a water plug not properly swung away from the track. A lesser mortal would have been killed outright, but old Fitz brought his train in on time and laid off duty only for a few days.

Another veteran was Pike Penn, who in common with several of the others had come to the C de P from the Southern Pacific in California. Pike was well nourished, genial and considerate of his firemen, being on that account popular with them. He had a phobia against Japs, a not uncommon foible of the 'Native Son' at that time. Pike generally drew the 3 or the 4, then the best of the freight engines, and emassed a huge monthly pay packet in dollars gold moving ore and empties between Cerro and Oroya. He was an artist with the air, able to stop a tonnage train with a single automatic reduction and the tank manhole spotted right under the water plug he was aiming at, without touching the independent brake valve. It takes real 'brake pipe feel' to do that!

Gibbs and Williams, also Californians, were two more 'Hawgheads' of the same era as Pike Penn, to share in the lucrative pulling of C de P freight. The passenger train paid Fitzgerald nothing like as much

59. The railway at one time had four of these 1907-built Baldwins, with 52in drivers, they were accounted good engines. No. 12 is seen at Oroya in the 1930's.

(Author)

60. No. 41, one of another, less successful, class of Baldwin 2-8-2, supplied in 1913. The 42in driving wheels made the engines very 'slippery' and they were relegated to Yard service.

(Author)

as these freight engineers pocketed every month. Williams must have been older than he looked; for he had fought in the Boer War in a British line regiment – thirty years before the time I'm writing about. The tactics of the various battles in that war were his hobby. He possessed a comprehensive library on the subject, in which I found some interesting reading. Riding up to Cerro and back with him on the five-spot, just to keep moss from growing on the annual pass Howard courteously presented to me every year, I was treated to a running dissertation lasting the round trip on Spion Kop and other campaigns, broken only by an interjected invitation to 'take her over' as we came down from La Cima to Zig-Zag on the last leg into Oroya.

The contracts of these men expired and they had departed before huge Bill Williamson came on the scene. I probably got to know Bill Williamson better than any of them; and in fact we shared an adventure that shall be related when the subject of tunnels comes up. He hailed from the Illinois Central, inevitably claiming acquaintance with Sim Webb, the fireman whom Casey Jones told to jump on that fatal run in 1900 which added a leaf to the pages of American folklore. The last of the breed I knew before leaving 'The Hill' was Bedford, who later made a big effort to come over to the Central. Some of the 'Hawgheads' may have had more than a drop of restless boomer blood in their veins. To several, money was of less importance than mobility, I think, with the result that wistful glances were occasionally cast towards the broader horizons of the Central, a closed door to them for reasons of policy, had they but known it.

Norb Voerding was one of the first C de P runners I knew. We had two days together on a wreck down the Central's Huancayo line, when the C de P wrecking outfit was hired by us at a cost of some $200 (U.S.) an hour. Their 60-ton Brownhoist was far, far better than our own wrecking crane, and – as far as the Mountain Section was concerned – was available at much shorter notice. With the crane was a competent crew, a bunkcar, a kitchen and dining car, tool cars, et al. Before the Central took to air brakes, this outfit, equipped with air, had to be pulled by a C de P locomotive when on our line, hence the presence on the occasion of which I speak of Norb Voerding and the No. 10.

The C de P wrecker was hired on several occasions during my incumbency in Oroya. It always did the job competently and quickly. Being designed by practical engineers with personal experience of wrecking it could be run fast and could go through any switch, could be set up and brought into action with a minimum of delay and with the least amount of man-power. When making heavy lifts with the big hook, you could feel confident that it wasn't going to capsize. Our own hook in nowise compared with it. Ours was of too small a lifting capacity, was totally unsuitable, had a rigid wheelbase that made any running a perilous matter, was inaccessible, unstable and slow to manoeuvre. It was necessary only to look at this drawing office nightmare to know that cheeseparing of the estimates had saddled us with a misfit. It was an example of the usual skinflint British policy of boggling over a ha'p'orth of tar and losing the ship in consequence! Small wonder, then, that when faced with a wreck within range of Oroya demanding the services of a 'big hook', we made a strong case to the GM for authority to ring up the C de P Super and ask for the loan of his efficient wrecking outfit, and damn the expense! In parenthesis I shall add that Howard did things well on his wrecking train. Conforming to true U.S. style, the cook had genius, and one ate like a fighting cock in that dining car as long as the job lasted.

The use of U.S. engineers posed a language problem until such time as they had acquired enough Spanish to be understood by, and understand, their Peruvian conductors. But they overcame the difficulties, apparently without any fatal misunderstandings over train orders. The C de P operated cabooses on their freights, an amenity for brakemen and conductors not available to their colleagues of the Central on account of limited train lengths, deadweight, and so on. The 'status' conveyed by those waycars was considerable. Conductors in the Americas are in any case important men, and bear themselves with an appropriate dignity. They are the 'Skippers' of their trains, a fact often resented by the men at the throttle, who being up in front like to consider themselves No. 1 in the order of precedence.

The C de P Railway of A. T. Howard and the 'Hawgheads'was an efficient freight carrier, however 'traditional' the one passenger train may have been. Actually, the latter was quite up to the standard then demanded; and the steel stock of the *Flamingo* was a result of growing highway competition that called for something better than the old wooden coaches if the train were to be kept filled. Under conditions of today, the figure of 38,000 passengers a month is not bad, even though 1,500 of them are deadheads.

The Cerro Corporation's own traffic constitutes about 80 per cent of the total movement of freight on the railway, which cushions it well against the vagaries of public supply and demand, and competing forms of transport. Some 15,000 tons of freight move monthly on the Yauricocha Railway, of which over 85 per cent is Corporation traffic. This tonnage necessarily moves over Central iron lying between the Yauricocha line and the parent system, a satisfactory arrangement for the intervening road. There is in any case close cooperation between the two railways, with combined tariffs for through traffic, and so on. It was so in Howard's day. Now it is still more so; for Victor F. Sampson, who has been in the C de P Super's chair for a number of years, is the son of the late Traffic Manager of the Southern of Peru, and began on the Central as a traffic learner.

Of the 462 freight cars, 110 of the 50-tonners have roller bearings, and another series of 37-ton hoppers is being converted to use them. Besides these, there are nine special service cars and the wrecking crane, seven cabooses, four business cars and twelve coaches.

Of the 18 locomotives, 10 are in poor condition and there is great difficulty in getting spares for them. It is therefore the intention to bump these out of service on a unit for unit basis with seven 1,300-horsepower diesel-electrics and four 650 -horsepower switchers. This will leave the eight steam locomotives of the newest series, the purchase of which is really the climax of the story.

In the early 1950s Vic Sampson found the power situation on the C de P becoming critical. New locomotives were needed, but – and this was the rub – steam locomotives were no longer being built in the U.S.A. However, he was familiar with the highly successful *Andes* type engines operating in growing numbers on the Central and Southern, and came up with the proposal that some of the same be purchased from England for the C de P. The first five, oil fired, were delivered by Beyer Peacock in 1954, made their triumphant debut with tonnage ratings of 1,200 from Cerro to Oroya, 400 from Oroya to La Cima, and 800 from there to Cerro, and a repeat order for three more followed.

British engines invading the all-American sanctuary of the C de P Railway! That such a thing could happen on his beloved pike would have shocked Howard to the very core of his being. I can imagine him turning an outraged countenance towards his assistant, Bill Pride, and exclaiming: 'It can't be, Bill! They're no good, I tell you – *no goddam' good!*'

61. *Guadalupe shops, a mile from Callao, as they were in 1935, seen from the roof of the Locomotive Dept. office.*
(Author)

62. *Last days of the old Callao station, built in Meiggs' time. A Sentinel railcar in local Callao – Lima passenger service is at the plateform.*
(Author)

Chapter 10

HIGHEST AND HARDEST

THE Central Railway of Peru begins at Callao, which could more conveniently be termed 'at tidewater' had this part of the Pacific shore any appreciable tide. A mile up the line from the dead-end fronting the Plaza Grau is Guadalupe, headquarters of the Locomotive Department, where the workshops, stores and engine terminal for the Coast Section are located.

The only trains to make the run from one end of the line to the other, a distance of just over 216 miles, are Nos. 1 and 401 (and their corresponding southbound counterparts, Nos. 2 and 402), the 'Mountain Trains', top passenger rakes, which officially set out from Desamparados Station, Lima, in the early morning. But the engines derive from Guadalupe, and they run light to Monserrate carrying markers, thus qualifying technically as trains, albeit without cars or coaches.

The *Andes* type mixed traffic engine No. 226 is well groomed for the varnish run, her tender and cab middle-bronze-green picked out in black, the number and initials of the road in yellow – F.C.C., for *Ferrocaril Central* – the pilot beam red with polished brass numbers, and the boiler jacket planished Russian iron relieved by brass-lubricator and feed piping. She stands at the ramp near the gate to load enginemen's seatboxes, where we shall join her at 6 a.m. for the run 'up the hill'-and to ensure good weather in the mountains, with small chance of even 'dry' slides, we shall make the time of year between May and September, Lima's winter, with skies heavily overcast by low cloud and with a thin drizzle settling. The engineer is inevitably a 'Don Jose'; the fireman, also Jose, may be Quispe or Castro or what you will.

Back in the days when the Central ran a local passenger service of trains every half hour, worked by 2-6-2 tanks, Callao to Monserrate, seven miles, was double-tracked. This service, much liked by commuters, was shelved in agreement with the *Empresas Electricas*, operating the interurban streetcar line between the port and the capital, in exchange for the local freight traffic. No. 1, which formerly started out from Callao, was then terminalled in Lima instead.

Outside yard limits, Callao to Lima is today single track. Clanging through the Guadalupe gate out upon the main, the 226 picks up her heels as soon as the open cylinder cocks have blown the goo of sleep out of her valve chests, and sets off up the line at a smart clip, passing on her left the big electrified Central Yard serving the docks and the adjacent oil deposits. Miranaves ('Look at the ships') is a well-named location where the yard lead tracks closes up beneath the drivers. At no great distance beyond is Villegas. Watch out here from the engineer's side of the cab, and you'll see the overgrown ruins of Henry Meiggs's once imposing mansion.

When Meiggs began construction of the Oroya line from Lima, the old Lima Railway had the concession for all rail transport between the two cities. Don Enrique required his own rail link with the port for obvious reasons, but the Government was unable to concede him the right to build a public railway. He took the hint by buying up for his own account the necessary land for a right-of-way, and laid a private railway, a step not at all to the liking of the rival concessionaire, and one that might not have been permitted had his influence been less than it was.

The Villegas estate was part of the land he purchased. The lovely house in which Meiggs ended his days was burned down during the Pacific War, only a few years after his death from heart failure. No attempt was ever made to rebuild it. A few pinnacles of ruined wall and the remains of what was once a fine terrace, all of it overgrown, were to us rails who passed them day after day a reminder of an almost legendary figure now forgotten by all but the few. His original office in Monserrate was burned down by my own hand in 1924 as part of a clearance scheme in the old station during an epidemic of bubonic plague. At that time he was no more than a name to me, or I doubt if I could have brought myself to perform the act of destruction!

The Central itself is an enduring monument to the great man – the line he conceived as the Central Transandine, that became the Callao, Lima and Oroya Railway, and finally the Central Railway of Peru,

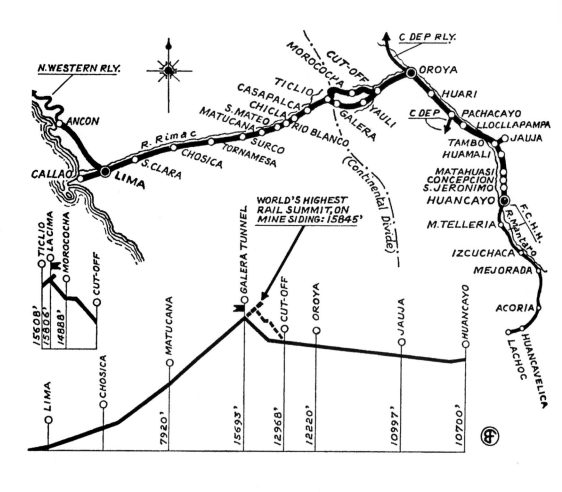

N. WESTERN RLY.

ANCON

CALLAO   LIMA

R. Rimac

S. CLARA

CHOSICA

TORNAMESA

SURCO

MATUCANA

S. MATEO

CHICLA

CASAPALCA

TICLIO

MOROCOCHA

CUT-OFF

GALERA

RIO BLANCO

YAULI

C DEP RLY.

OROYA

HUARI

C DEP

PACHACAYO

LLOCLLAPAMPA

JAUJA

TAMBO

HUAMALI

MATAHUASI

CONCEPCION

S. JERONIMO

HUANCAYO

F.C.H.H.

R. Mantaro

M. TELLERIA

IZCUCHACA

MEJORADA

ACORIA

HUANCAVELICA

LACHOC

(Continental Divide)

WORLD'S HIGHEST
RAIL SUMMIT, ON
MINE SIDING: 15845'

GALERA TUNNEL

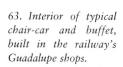

TICLIO 15608'
LACIMA 15808'
MOROCOCHA 14888'
CUT-OFF

LIMA

CHOSICA

MATUCANA 7920'

GALERA TUNNEL 15693'

CUT-OFF 12968'

OROYA 12220'

JAUJA 10997'

HUANCAYO 10700'

63. *Interior of typical chair-car and buffet, built in the railway's Guadalupe shops.*

(Author)

130

64. Much of the Callao and Guadalupe switching was done by handy little 0-4-0 well tanks of this type built by Beyer-Peacock in 1909. All the Central's engines were oil-fired.

(Author)

65. The newest engine on the Lima Railway, taken over by the Central in 1935, was this Kitson 0-6-2T of 1925; but it proved difficult to find a suitable service for her.

(Author)

66. The two best of the FCC's 80-class North British road engines of 1907 were saved when the class as a whole was scrapped, and converted for heavy switching (shunting) duties in Lima's new Union Yard which replaced the Callao yard.

(Author)

but which at the close of the last century was known to boomer rails in the U.S. simply as 'The Meiggs road in Peru'. By the time one has done with cogitations upon the forgotten Don Enrique the 226 is whistling for Monserrate, and the Municipal garbage incinerator is flashing by on the fireman's side. The River Rimac's adjacent pebbly margins in this vicinity are anything but edifying, themselves a depository for garbage and a perpetual attraction to the myriads of vultures that in their office of scavengers are protected by law.

The Union Yard and Monserrate are both electrified. Switching motors are General Electric and Breda-Brown Boveri, working on 550 V current purchased from Lima Light & Power. They are augmented by steam and diesel switchers – in fact it is really only the lighter shifts that are within the capacity of the little electrics.

Picking her consist off the coach tracks here, No. 226 takes it off to Desamparados Station, a mile up the line, beyond La Palma junction, where the Ancon branch takes off to the left of the main, crosses the river on a skew bridge and threads through the suburb of San Lazaro.

The 23½ mile branch to the seaside resort of Ancon, north of Callao, started out ambitiously as the broad-gauge Lima-Chancay Railway, and was opened as far as Ancon in 1870. The Chileans destroyed the line in 1880, during the Pacific War. The Ancon section was rebuilt and incorporated into the Central later; and the metre-gauge North Western of Peru was constructed from Ancon to Huacho and Sayan, northwards up the coast. The Central line has a stiff climb out of Ancon, through a wilderness of bare sand, and then levels off in what at one time was a rich sugar and cotton region giving the railway a not inconsiderable movement of freight. Today, railcar passenger services between Lima and Ancon are well patronized during the season, but freight movement on the branch is of little importance. As is generally the case, way-freight traffic was taken from the railway by a parallel highway.

Except for a scanty umbrella shed in the centre of the island platform on the far side of the footbridge, the tracks in Desamparados Station are open to the sky. No. 401 holes up on track No. 3, and the gates of the first- and second-class waiting rooms are thrown open to allow a torrent of vociferous humanity to swarm across the southbound platform, over tracks 1 and 2, to the waiting coaches. I shall quote a graphic account of the scene from a diary note made on the spot one January morning many years ago.

'Huge crowd travelling – crush, rush and pother! The Trainmaster stands in the doorway of the baggage room; airbrake and traffic inspectors fuss about; Don Juan Valdivia sits regally at the engine's throttle and Fireman Manuel Salas has the apron up oiling the rubbing block and wedge. The newly risen sun, the panting air pump, the green and gold coaches with the llama emblem on the sides, and the jostling throng struggling on the coach steps, hampered by their mountains of parcels and packages, make the scene typical. No. 44 cuts off and goes over to the baggage room to pull out the loaded baggage car and back it down on the head end of the consist. I climb to the engine's deck and lap the H-6 brake valve, watching the duplex gauge. Down drops the brakepipe needle as the shacks cut in the coaches, and I make a heavy charge of air with the handle held in release till the brakepipe pressure is almost up to the standard go pounds. With the main reservoirs recharged to 110 pounds, I then lap the brake valve and watch the brakepipe needle for leakage. Not a pound does it drop! A similar test with the straight-air discloses no perceptible leakage whatsoever – nor does the independent brake show any. This is the satisfactory result of good installation, and I hope to keep the high standard for some years yet. From the rear of the train comes the automatic brake test signal. I do the test application for Valdivia, who is oiling round. Then the straight-air test, by which time Salas has reached over to flick open the valve of the air-operated bell motor. Valdivia climbs up from the platform; I jump down as he takes his seat and the conductor hands over flimsies and clearance card. The bell clangs steadily as Don Juan releases the independent brake and cracks the throttle (there's no whistling in Desamparados, so the usual double toot is omitted). No. 1 creeps out with a discreetly moderate bark from the exhaust, and looking back from the cab, Don Juan Valdivia waves a farewell to me. My weekly inspection of the Mountain Train's brakes is done. It has just struck 7 a.m. by the 'Oxford Chimes' of the big clock over the front of the station, and I'm off to get some breakfast before going down to the office in Guadalupe to face the Saturday morning madhouse.'

In construction days Monserrate was the only station in Lima. Subsequently there were four – Monserrate, La Palma, Desamparados and Viterbo. The original Desamparados was destroyed by fire early in the century – and with it vanished a wealth of valuable records. The present earthquake-proof

67. *Desemperados station in Lima in 1924, as Rogers 4-6-0 No. 57 brings in a train from Ancón, a seaside resort north of Callao.* (Author)

68. *Desemperados was the location of the Central's administration offices, and in this later view the station looks considerably smarter. Andes No. 226 prepares to leave with train No. 1 for Huancayo* (C. Crofton Atkins)

edifice was then built, housing the administration offices of all but the mechanical department. The buildings stand on the city side of the tracks; on the other side is garden, well maintained and profusely stocked with sub-tropical flora.

Hutchinson describes the getaway of the Mountain Train in 1872 as an event – a ceremony, one might almost say-that over 90 years has varied little. It is Monserrate he is speaking of, however.

'Here all is life and activity – some stationary engines doing their work – a locomotive[1] roaring like a mammoth bull, enchained and goaded, as if it wanted to get off and tear its way without stop or hindrance through Cordilleras and over Andes; – passengers getting their tickets; – luggage and cargo arriving; and the general hubbub and fuss of a train about to start. For it is near to eight o'clock in the morning. The hour approaches; the fuss increases, but subsides as the outer door shuts; – the Conductor, Mr. H. 0. Denning, cries out interrogatively, "All Aboard?" and, looking up and down to see that everything is right, waves his hand to the engine-driver, and jumps up. The engine gives one great spasmodic roar, and – with the tolling of its bell – away we glide...'

Today there is no visible morning sunshine. Desamparados platforms are wet enough from the drizzle to reflect the columns supporting the overhanging administration offices. Engine 226, pulling No. 401, the *Rapido.*, with a consist of the new lightweight stock, whips the 125 tons on her coupler up to speed as though she were running light. Through Viterbo Station, under the Balta Bridge, past the Lima-Lurin Railway station, and she's out of Lima. Half an hour later No.1 will be following, with principally older and heavier stock, and a train of 160 tons on a slower schedule to handle the way traffic.

Lima to Chosica is twenty-five miles of easy running up the Rimac Valley, that gradually funnels into the foothills. Grades here nowhere exceed 2.75 per cent, and the average rise is only 93 feet per mile. In its lower reaches the valley is largely under cotton, but towards Chosica residential districts have grown up for the well-to-do of Lima who seek escape from the gloom and damp of the coastal winter. And you can see why; for No. 401 climbs swiftly up towards that low ceiling of heavy, reeking cloud, and at Moron bursts through it into brilliant sunshine. In 17 miles from Lima the train passes from winter into summer. It may be a little more or less, the actual distance varying from one day to another. The transition seems almost miraculous; but the explanation lies in the climatic peculiarities arising from the Humboldt Current. Conversely, when it is blazing summer in Lima, Chosica lies on the edge of the mountain cloud belt and the devastating rains; but the town itself enjoys perpetual summer. Chosica is the divisional point, end of the Coast Section and beginning of the Casapalca District. Until recently, a large hotel dating from construction days dominated the station, and when I first knew the Central it was patronized during the 'season' by members of influential Lima families in search of the sun. It was railway property, and a gallery overhanging the platform of No. 1 track ran the whole length of the upper storey, from which a magnificent view of activities in the station yard as far as the roundhouse could be enjoyed by any visitor who might be interested. It served us railway officials well.

One of my first assignments when acquiring traffic experience in early days on the Central was to investigate the truth of complaints communicated to the General Manager by hotel guests of substance, that at night the delicate ears of wives and daughters in the bedrooms opening upon that gallery were frequently offended by the colourful language of the yardmaster as he rawhided his crews. The GM passed the complaints to the Traffic Manager, who detailed me to spend a wakeful night in the hotel balcony and report if there were any justification for them. 'I hope not,' he remarked. 'C . . . is a damned good man and can get more work out of his crews in less time than any other yardmaster we have!'

It seemed to me rather like splitting hairs. The night freight from Monserrate, No. 201, arrived in Chosica between 11 p.m. and midnight, a customary 350 tons on her tail, rounding up into the station with a thunder that literally rocked the hotel. There ensued switching operations as the consist was broken up into sections for Train 203, due to start off up the mountain at 3 a.m., and these operations were not by any means noiseless. Then, at 2 a.m., engines began coming out of the roundhouse for the early sections, whining, thumping, hissing and tooting. Fuelled and ready, they backed down on their trains to await departure with roaring pops and drumming fires. Finally, at leaving time, there was a storm of whistling, echoing and reechoing from the rocky mountain scarps on either side of the town. Guests in the hotel might just as well have tried to sleep in the middle of the yard – yet they complained not of that, but of a little bad language overheard by some freak of acoustics above the general din!

69. Andes 2-8-0 No. 100, *the second bearer of that number, arrives at Desemperados with train No. 42 from 'the mountain', formed of Craven's lightweight stock.* (C. Crofton Atkins)

70. *Train No. 1 pulls up in Chosica in 1934, in front of the old hotel, later demolished. The engine is No. 47, a Rogers 4-6-0 rebuilt with a Hunslet boiler and partly 'Anglified' in 1925.* (Author)

F.C.C. DEL PERU

TRENES DE PASAJEROS AL INTERIOR

Con el objeto de dar facilidades al comercio y al público en general la Empresa tiene establecido actualmente un servicio rápido de trenes de pasajeros a Oroya y Huancayo, de acuerdo con el siguiente itinerario:

TRENES EXPRESOS, EN CADA DIRECCION:

Lunes y Sábados:

Sale de Lima (Desamparados).....................	8.50 a. m.
Llega a Oroya...	4.26 p. m.
Llega a Huancayo.......................................	8.07 p. m.
Sale de Huancayo.......................................	6.55 a. m.
Sale de Oroya...	10.30 a. m.
Llega a Lima (Desamparados).....................	4.53 p. m.

TRENES ACELERADOS, EN CADA DIRECCION:

Martes, Miércoles, Jueves y Viernes:

Sale de Lima (Desamparados).....................	8.05 a. m.
Llega a Oroya...	4.20 p. m.
Llega a Huancayo.......................................	8.20 p. m.
Sale de Huancayo.......................................	6.35 a. m.
Sale de Oroya...	10.30 a. m.
Llega a Lima (Desamparados).....................	5.20 p. m.

PRECIOS DE PASAJES

Lima a Oroya, 1a. Clase S/. 12.85 ida.	S/. 19.30 ida y vuelta
,, ,, ,, 2a. ,, ,, 6.20 ,,	,, 12.40 ,, ,, ,,
Lima a Huancayo 1a. ,, ,, 23.25 ,,	,, 34.90 ,, .. ,,
,, ,, ,, 2a. ,, ,, 11.40 ,,	,, 20.20 ,, ,, ,,

Utilice esta Vía por ser la más cómoda, segura y barata.

LA EMPRESA.

Old C . . ., the Yardmaster, possessed only one arm, but more than his fair share of lung power. He looked like a bulldog, roared like a lion, and could by voice alone from his office door flick a recalcitrant switchman at the far end of the yard as though with the lash of a whip. The old boy was pally with me, and I tipped him off about what I was sent to Chosica to do. When No. 201 arrived that night and was carved up for early northbound sections he kept such a check on his tongue that his hump riders and switchmen thought he must be ill.

All went well until 3.30 a.m., when the last section was being made up. A student brakeman running a boxcar down from the hump stalled before making a coupling, which meant that the switch engine had to go in and kick the car into the rest of the consist. Old C ... witnessed it all, and had yelled without effect for the man to ease off on the brakes. But when the car stopped short of the cut, C ... forgot everything and released his carefully pent-up vocabulary in a stream of the most expressive Spanish invective I had ever heard. It was unfortunate that there fell at that moment one of the rare lulls in the yard operations.

Lights flickered on and off as delicately nurtured ladies in the bedrooms along the front of the hotel checked the hour of the outrage. Another spate of complaints was bound to pour into the General Manager's office; C ... would be warned to pipe down of nights, and northbound sections would in consequence leave Chosica behind time because of delays in switching. When reporting to the T.M. next day, I said:

'From 11.30, when 201 arrived, until 3.30 he said nothing objectionable whatever, sir.'

'But what about after 3.30? What I want to know is: are the complaints justified or not?'

'Well, at 3.30 he did say something or other, sir; but my Spanish isn't all that good yet, and I don't know if it was bad language or not!'

'Great Scott; you don't know if – ! Oh well, I understand. just keep an ear open whenever you're overnight in Chosica, and I'll tell the Manager we are looking into the matter carefully.' As an afterthought, when I was about to leave, he added:

'By the way; cultivate C ... and I'm sure your Spanish will soon become usefully fluent!'...

If I linger in Chosica much longer, No. 401 will be late in getting away when the 226 has taken water! Chosica roundhouse has been my charge all too often. I switched my first engine there, worked my first night shift, smoked my first pipe by the turntable (and was miserably sick behind the pump house). The Central's two remaining Beyer-Garratts are stationed in Chosica, their services confined to the Casapalca District alone. Reminiscences galore clamour for out; but it's leaving time, Don José is reaching for the whistle cord – and the mountains proper are now ahead of us.

The first taste of heavy grade lies just north of Chosica yard limits.[2] Not that the 226 notices it: she talks it up just enough for the fireman to sand the flues, breasting the top after a steady acceleration as though no grade existed. The next bump at Ricardo Palma is taken with similar ease; but at Cupiche, $4^1/_2$ miles farther up the valley, there is a grade crossing, and beyond it commences a really formidable climb up to the Purhuay Tunnel, first bore encountered on this run, and second longest of the system. An official maximum of four per cent is an understatement. One knows that. The engines themselves don't lie, and to those who possess many years of experience on this line there are no secrets. That grade is nearer five per cent than four!

Freak flooding of the Rimac in 1925 carried away some three miles of the old track here, including two biggish bridges, one of them renewed only months before. The line followed the river in those days, on the valley floor. The old terraplane and the bridges were patched up to allow of traffic being resumed three months afterwards, but to avoid another similar *debacle* a new line taking off from Cupiche was built well up the mountain side out of reach of the highest floods, with a tunnel carrying it through a rocky promontory. The grade cases inside this tunnel, but it was always something of an ordeal for the Garratt crews on account of heat, a point to be enlarged on in Chapter 15.

The village of Cocachacra means nothing today, but in the pre-rail. era it was an important staging halt on the *Camino Real*, and a highwaymen's hang-out. In rail construction days it also loomed big. Fruit abounds in the neighbourhood. Straight up the mountain above the village is San Bartolome, where the train will be passing in due course, after leaving the next stop, Tornamesa (Turntable), the first reversing station. The grade as far as Tornamesa is now of little account – a scant two per cent – but watch that tunnel at Rio Seco when we go into it. There's nothing above it. It is, in fact, designed to carry flood

71. *All southbound trains were obliged to stop at the north end of Verrugas Bridge to register, as a precuation against excessive speed.* (Author)

water pouring down the mountain at this point safely over the track and into the river. I have personally never seen it other than bone dry; but when Chief Engineer Malinowski was building the line here in 1871 the hazard must have been pronounced.

Fruit sellers invade the train drawn up at the platform at Tornamesa while No. 226 cuts off, takes water, blows down her boiler and clumps on to the table to be turned in order to head No. 401 out of this dead-end stop. It is the only single 'V'; so from here through to Huancayo passengers who chose their seats in Lima to face the direction of travel are now stuck with their backs to the engine!

Coupled once more to her train and brake tests completed, No. 226 gives two long hoots and pulls out. At the end of the yard her boiler tilts upwards on four-per-cent. The grades proper begin here and never let up till the line crosses the divide under Mount Meiggs, 10,729 feet higher up. The 226 is really barking now. The tight curves combined with the grade make this a mean bit to get over. I have stalled here on several occasions with both steam and diesel railcars. In construction days there was a large camp on the hogback above us on the left, with powder magazine, workshops and all. The Chilean rotos whooped it up big here of nights, gambling, drinking and fighting – and dying like flies from *verrugas*.

The track swings round in a wide circle at San Bartolome village, immediately over Cocochacra and several hundred feet above it. The valley below and the vicinity of the track are well covered with shrubs and fruit trees, in contrast to the bleak, cactus-infested slopes above the green valley floor elsewhere. But this verdant oasis ceases as we round another wide curve, which brings the train out on a ledge cut in the contours of the slopes high above the river. One looks straight down on Tornamesa as though flying over it in an aircraft, for now the track is continuing its proper direction up the valley which down there sloped too steeply for adhesion rail grades. Not, however, for the Central Highway, that was opened in 1935 to provide damaging competition by paralleling the railroad's main stem, though nearly all the time at a lower level.

Carrion Bridge, third viaduct to span the Verrugas gorge, has already been mentioned. On the other side of it the train roars round a curve in a short cutting and comes out upon a ledge carved from the rock in the face of an absolutely sheer precipice. The place is called Cuesta Blanca. An imaginative passenger might well wonder what chances he'd have if a derailment took place here – on the outside. One Christmas Eve I had the job of rerailing a Garratt that hit a fallen rock and came off just a bit farther on, beyond the tunnels. The leading engine unit was completely derailed, on the outside, but the rear unit was on the track. As we tried to ramp the derailed unit on again, the other one came off and spread the whole engine across the track. It. was then necessary to lift her on with the traversing hydraulic and screw jacks that all Andean, and most overseas, engines carry as standard equipment. A slip while doing this could have tipped that engine over the edge into the abyss; but all went well and we did the job without any further mishaps. In such a position and in such a perilous place a wrecking crane could not have been used. Railroading in the Andes is an entirely specialized form of the calling!

Looking straight up at the masses of rock as big as a church apparently poised over the track, ready to shake loose from the vibration of the train and fall on one, imaginary speculation can almost create alarm. I was on the tank platform just outside a Garratt cab once when I saw one of these boulders coming! It wasn't as big as a church, but it was quite as big as a large garden tool-hut. Falling from some distance up, accompanied by a medley of 'satellite' rocks and stones, it bounded towards us in immense arcs. These falling rocks are known as 'galgas', or 'greyhounds', in Spanish, and the term is aptly chosen. I decided to stay where I was, being uncertain where the rock would hit, or whether it would bound right over us. The enginemen didn't see it coming, but the brakemen back on the train did – and they also saw from their angle of view that the engine was going to get it!

That wildly leaping rock hit the cab roof right over the engineer's head, and not three feet from me. It was on the descending arc of a tremendous jump that I thought would clear us, but it caught the roof a glancing blow – by some miracle of good fortune – leaving a deep dent in the plate before continuing its bounding course down the mountain to the narrow bottom of the valley. The other big stuff went over us harmlessly, but rip-rap broke the cab windows and left a bruise or two on me. The expression of shocked surprise on the unsuspecting hoghead's face after the appalling crash just over his head was worth the anxious moments to witness! Those unfeeling brakemen on the car tops behind were well-nigh helpless with laughter.

72. In 1938 the second Verrugas Bridge was replaced by a new bridge called Carrión, seen here in 1937 during erection.   *(Author)*

Surco station has a little yard on a back-up spur from the main, and here the wives and children of the village pile on to the train to hawk bunches of fragrant violets. In these verdant oases, amidst the rocks and huge cactus, flowers grow in profusion. At *Quita Sombrero* ('Take-off-your-hat') Bridge – properly named Ucuta, and site of another whopping construction camp that was railhead when Hutchinson came up here in 1872 – the line is again on the valley floor, which it follows up to San Juan, where it doubles back on itself on the opposite side of the river, and on the engine one is treated to an optical illusion. What now appears to be unvaryingly steep grade is actually almost level. The increasing speed of the train is as much a surprise as it would be to see water flowing uphill! Then the track rounds a shoulder of mountain in a full horseshoe bend to continue in the right direction once more, but by this time high above the valley floor. The equivalent of a zig-zag has been negotiated without the need for V-switches.

Rock ledges – curves and reverse curves – short tunnels – thunderous blast echoing from the precipitous walls – then out upon the spidery lattice span of the Challape Bridge, like Carrion on a rather smaller scale. The valley rises steeply towards the level of the track, and the river bursts downwards in a series of cascades. Then Don Jose is whistling for Matucana, 56 miles from Lima and 7,840 feet above sea level. With its gum trees and pastures Matucana is a pretty spot, but the straggling town has suffered severely from the fury of the flooded river on several occasions. Central tracks here are equally vulnerable. Cactus reaches its upper limit, and the bleakness of the rain shadow belt is much alleviated by the general appearance of bunch grass, shrubs and a few trees wherever roots can find a hold on the slopes. Many of these slopes are intricately terraced by the industrious farmers of ancient times who in that way managed to augment in good measure the very limited strips of highly productive soil bordering the twisting, turbulent river.

In a narrow gorge five miles up from Matucana is Viso, the first double zig-zag. Not far beyond that, the line, on a ledge high above the river, comes out from a tunnel upon the scene of one of the worst trouble spots of the whole line. Ocatara always has been a bad place. It began in construction days, when the Chilean rotos fought and won a bloody battle here against the Peruvians. The Chileans were by then disillusioned. They had come flocking to their beloved Don Enrique's banner satisfied with the terms of their contracts, only to find that the value of the wages that sounded so generous in Chile was in Peru very much less than expected on account of the rampant inflation brought about by the Government's spendthrift policies. At no time were the rotos amenable to discipline, law and order; when discontented they were dynamite!

Always a bad place for slides, some thirty years ago a whole mountain top broke away and swept down over the track, obliterating everything, filling the bottom of the gorge, damming the river, and knocking out all movement of traffic for weeks. Subsequent attempts to shore up the side of the mountain with plantations of spruce proved a failure. Slides have fallen regularly ever since.

Here the scenic aspect of the line is at its most spectacular. Chaupichaca and its grim relics are at a short distance beyond Ocatara, and from there the track creeps up the gorge to Tamboraque, foot of

73. Matucana station, at 9871ft, 103 kilometres from Callao. Matucana was at this time a centre for dairy produce.
(Author)

74. *A classic portrait of* Andes No. 48, *running as* Extra 48N *on the test of the Central's first air brake passenger rake, after replacement of vacuum brakes in 1940. The location is the Auri zig-zag, km. 123.* (Author)

another double zig-zag. Farther on, San Mateo appears below, its streets laid out on the river banks as on a map. The town's station balances on a ledge three hundred feet above, clinging precariously to the side of the mountain. Snaking along its perch on the mighty rock buttresses the line winds through tunnel after tunnel, comes out of the smoky darkness upon the bridge across the gorge of the Infiernillo, and on the other side dives into darkness once more. Thus the train arrives at the next zig-zag, Cacray. After that, more tunnels, another high bridge, and the approach to Rio Blanco, where Backus and Johnston once operated a sizeable copper smelter, now dismantled. Here you are 75 miles from Lima and 11,501 feet up, and passengers disposed to mountain sickness may now claim to feel the first effects of the altitude without being branded as over-imaginative.

Many ex-sailors from any of the large navies whose warships have visited Peruvian waters may recall Rio Blanco as the end of excursion train runs put on for their benefit. Running on a tight schedule, No. 401 does not tarry there, but hurries on, rounds a horseshoe curve inside a tunnel and across a bridge low above the seething Rimac, here white in colour, and then leaves the valley floor for more ledges on the heights – more bridges and more tunnels. The tightly crowding walls of the gorge fall away to let some welcome sky in. The slopes ease off somewhat on one side, if not on the other, and amid the bunch grass are frequent patches of purple vetch and other alpine flowers. The sunshine is brilliant and hot; but the deep shade where the sun cannot penetrate is cold with the bite of the high altitudes.

Chicla is at the foot of a zig-zag a mile and a half long, the top end, Saltacuna, overlooking the village and five layers of track beneath. There are two small yards at Chicla, the one at the station proper containing the first of the southbound freights for Chosica, waiting the meet with the Mountain Train. This was railhead for the Central in 1878, where the tracks arrived some months after Meiggs's death. The outbreak of the Pacific War in 1879 caused further construction work to be suspended, and it was not until 1890, after formation of the Peruvian Corporation, that John L. Thorndike took the rails on,

75. *Cacray double zig-zag, km 132. The lower end of the zig-zag can be seen at right (centre).* (Author)

reaching Casapalca in 1892 and Oroya in January 1893. The altitude here is 12,250 feet above sea level, and the distance from Lima 79 miles. Hardfought miles too, every one of them. A bald statement of distance covered cannot be compared with anything in normal railroading. Only by Andean standards can the performance be judged.

Time was when the engines of all trains were turned here in order to head their consists pilot first. Up at Saltacuna, at the top of the zig-zag, was another turntable. The double operation was a notable time-loser – so much so that the practice fell into disuse. But at a later date, prudence called for southbound engines to go to the lower end of their trains in Saltacuna and head them down the zig-zag, albeit tender first. The 226 pushes No. 401 Out of Chicla, the First Brakeman standing on the tail of the train – now in the lead – keeping the necessary lookout with the application valve of the back-up hose, connected to the final brakepipe hose coupling, within instant reach of his hand. With him is the Conductor, positioned to 'swing a washout'[3] from the car steps should occasion arise.

Some distance up the valley from Chicla the line doubles back on a tight horseshoe curve and climbs up the opposite side. just at the bend is Bellavista where the Casapalca organization of the Cerro de Pasco Corporation has a hydro-electric power station and a mine adit. From here through to Oroya mining is a prominent part of the scene.

Just below the top of the zig-zag, at Cuna, there's another southbound freight in the hole for a meet with us. A third stands sidetracked in Saltacuna. From here, as we back round the bend into the reversing station, passengers on the side of the train facing outwards from the mountain can look down on Chicla far below, with a panoramic view of several layers of railroad track, and the gorge of the Rimac, curving round in an 'S' bend. just where the lowest and most distant section of the track vanishes into a tunnel

143

76. *The lightweight stock of Train 401, the express version of Train No. 1, makes easy work for Andes No. 100. Here on Copa bridge the altitude is 12,000ft, and the mountains are moving back to let the sky in.*

(C. Crofton Atkins)

in the farthest curve of the bend is the place where old Roadmaster Ellis, a stalwart who had worked on the construction of the line under the Meiggs brothers – and the smartest man in cleaning up a wreck I ever knew – picked up the remains of the 100 when she took her fatal leap over the rail stop at the end of the Chicla yard.

Saltacuna to Casapalca is not far; but as we wind up the valley, now on a ledge far above its floor, you will see Bellavista laid out in plan underneath, and the freight extra that made the meet with us in Cuna rounding the horseshoe curve, for all the world like a toy train. First view of Casapalca is the tailings dump from the zinc concentrator plant of the C de P. Then we're blasting up through the yard on a natural hump of four per cent. In front of the station building the tracks are level. The bottom end of yard limits is protected by a safety switch – and its presence is certainly called for. Imagine, please, an important divisional point where freight trains were formerly exchanged by Chosica and Oroya engines *on a tilt of one in twenty-five.* All switching here was done by road engines.

Having run up past the 'gate' at the north end of the yard, No. 401 drops back down into No. 1 station track, and Don Jose spots the tender under the water tank standpipe. As soon as the tender is filled she'll be off again.

The Rapido's passage through the Chosica section has been too fast for me. While the 226 is taking water I should like to go back again and have a quick look at it from the freight angle. The varnish has covered the 62 miles of the section in not much more than three hours; while the several sections of

77. *A general view of Casapalca in 1930. The industrial buildings are the property of the Cerro de Pasco Copper Mining Corporation, producing mainly zinc concentrates.* (Author)

freight train No. 203 took nearly five hours to battle their way up from Chosica to an altitude of 13,632 feet at Casapalca.

The difficult conditions of the Central make round-the-clock operation undesirable, and running is arranged in such a way that trains are not called on to pass at night through those parts of the line where slides and washouts are most prevalent. For all that, freight extras out of Chosica and Oroya take off in the wee hours of the morning, long before daylight, generally from 4 a.m. onwards. Previously, 2.30 a.m. was the start of their day's work. By dawn they are at the beginning of the bad stretches, and there's time for them to do their full duty and depart usually before darkness falls, except when unforeseen delays crop up. That's not to say, though, that Central freights never have to work through the heart of the mountains with headlights on.

The first freight out of Chosica will be between Surco and Matucana when day dawns, if not actually beyond Matucana. That from Oroya will be in Galera or Ticlio. Trainmen are not in the habit of fasting. Follow a freight brakeman and you'll never go hungry! While the engine is watering and turning at Tornamesa prior to doing whatever switching may be required, brakemen pay a visit to a small shop in an adobe hut fronting the yard, where very strong, very good, and very hot black coffee is on tap, together with *butifarras* for their special benefit (rolls sliced in two to encompass pork, lettuce, goat's cheese and other ingredients). This is merely a stop-gap-not breakfast.

Breakfast proper is found at Matucana, where the brakemen know bakehouses with rolls fresh from the oven, and sources of more coffee, with or without the creamy Matucana milk. Time permitting, they can also get fried eggs and ham, as well as fresh bread with the incomparable butter of the region.

At Tamboraque, next station up the line, there is coffee available for the initiated in the backblocks of the station agent's house. Rio Blanco today has nothing; but Chicla station again provides refreshments.

78. *Andes No. 217 at the head of Train No. 1 – the stopping train to Huancayao – takes water at Casapalca while passengers and crew stretch their legs. The male nursing assistant, whose job is to administer oxygen to queasy passengers, is at the front of the picture.*
(Author)

Finally, at Casapalca the famished brakemen make a bee-line for a hash-house where a gigantic meal is forthcoming at infinitesimal cost, which a gourmet might relish so long as he kept his mind aloof from the lack of culinary hygiene. Foreign officials riding the freights, who hesitate to demean themselves by going where the brakemen go, are subject to the high cost and poor grub in the only two available hotels suitable for their status. For my part, I always preferred to follow the trainmen and feed fat – and to hell with hygiene!

Oroya crews have their corresponding beaneries all along; but in my opinion the Chosica Section does better in that respect. Enginemen, more closely tied to their engines than trainmen are to their trains, tend to carry their own supplies with them. Coffee in a well-stoppered bottle nesting among the pipes up on the steam header is always hot. Seatboxes contain plenty of room for supplies. Brakemen, too, keep a coffee bottle 'on the hob', as it were, on the boiler backhead, for the sake of emergency refreshments between eating houses.

I remember one Chosica freight engine crew who grilled cutlets on the top of the firedoor whenever the pangs of hunger were felt. An area on the flat top of the big, box-shaped door was kept free of plumbago for the purpose. Whether tunnel smoke affected the taste I couldn't say; but I do recall that the aroma, wafting back from the cab along the train, set every brakeman (four per train were carried in those days) to drooling at the mouth!

The early morning departures from Chosica leave in the mind vivid impressions of the great, tumbled boulders in the glare of the headlight, and the weird columns of the gigantic organ cactus – like Doré's 'Corpse Candles' – looming up in the beam stabbing the pitch darkness ahead. As an accompaniment to the thunderous crash of the blast, thrown back on one from the rocky walls above the engine, would be heard from time to time the penetrating sing-song of the turbo-generator, while in the cab every plate, every pipe, danced with a ring and clatter bordering on panic. Outside, the 'clonk, clank – clonk clank' of main and side rods, with perhaps more play in the bushes than should be, beat out the exhaust's rhythm; and, possibly, the 'dock, duck' of a loose driving box wedge added its sound to the general symphony.

Garratt cabs float serenely, regardless of what the engine units are doing. The Engineers' Department once complained bitterly of damaged track in the Casapalca District from unreported derailments. Ties were splintered and scarred; spikes were gouged, and rails marked. The signs were that some engine's pony truck was coming off repeatedly and climbing back on again. The Chief of Traction turned the mystery over to me, while the engineers continued to tear their hair over the damage that day after day was being reported by section foremen and roadmasters.

Hours in the pits beneath the Chosica freight engines focused my suspicions on one of the Garratts. Truck wheel flanges at the front end – the more remote from the cab – were, I thought, a trifle battered-looking. But if this truck were the culprit, I was at a loss to see why it should derail. The gauge was correct between tyres, boxes and suspension were normal, lateral movement appeared to be in order. And why did the engineers who had handled the engine say nothing – why, having derailed, did it rerail itself? There was only one way to find out something definite, and that was by watching the performance of the truck on the road.

Easier said than done. There wasn't much room on the buffer beams of our Garratts, as the tanks came almost up to the edge, leaving only a narrow foothold there. To see the pony truck in action, I had to lie over the coupler pocket, head down far enough to look in between the bars of the pilot. It was necessary to hang on with one hand in order the leave the other free to use the electric torch. Altogether a most uncomfortable position in which to spend an hour or two – mostly in the dark before dawn. True, one was far enough away from the stack to escape the searing heat of the exhaust in tunnels; but hanging down in front of 180 tons of thundering engine with one's face within inches of the ballast, the imagination is apt to picture fatal occurrences. It would be so easy to slip and fall on the track, under the pilot. I had once seen the bits of a brakeman to whom that very thing had happened! A rock on the line, or stray livestock, could bring one to a messy and certain end. But the contingency most probable was that the infernal truck would jump the track, and the consequent dancing of the front part of the engine unit might shake me off and under. The enginemen couldn't see me I was completely hidden from everybody.

With the Garratt running boiler first from Chosica to Tornamesa, and myself festooned in this uncomfortable position in front – in darkness relieved by the headlight and marker lights just above me – I reviled the need for such perilous acrobatics. However, the truck behaved in no way out of the

79. Garratt No. 124 takes water at Rio Blanco, on a grade of between four and five per cent.

(Author)

147

80. Spotting an engine at the water plug when dragging a freight up a four per cent grade calls for no little skill, especially when the locomotive is a giant Beyer-Garratt! (Author)

ordinary. At Tornamesa, the engine went to the other end of the train and coupled on cab first, which placed me next to the first car. This felt less uncomfortable, but the noise was worse. Here the really bad curves began. I watched the track flanges jump and fall – jump and fall – on some of these. A little more and the wheels will be off the track, I thought. Why were the flanges tending to climb like that? It could only be because side swing was in some way restricted – some defect that had not long existed – certainly not a fault in design. And then, suddenly, I spotted the trouble.

The truck centring spring assembly was carried in front of the frame cross-member, fortunately for me in full view. On sharp curves that coil spring was closing up solid, and when that happened further side swing was prevented. I recalled that the spring had been changed only a week or two ago. It must be one made in the shops, with a closed length greater than the original. Our day's trip was free from derailments, and on getting back to Chosica I had the spring removed and checked it. Sure enough, that was the trouble.

Andean curves are such that they give no tolerance. Andean grades are so steep that weight distribution is altered and leading wheels are left slightly loaded. All the derailments had taken place when the defective truck was leading, on heavily-graded zig-zags, and each time a convenient reverse curve ramped the wheels on again. In the darkness the enginemen couldn't see what was happening. On a single engine they would have felt it, but not necessarily on a Garratt. This defect might have brought about a very ugly accident indeed. By the grace of God, it didn't.

---

[1] *He has interpolated a footnote here: 'The American locomotives do not whistle; they may be said to roar, like the continuous bellow of a lion or a bull'.*

[2] *For the purposes of train classification and general convenience, the Central calls inland from Callao 'north' and towards Callao 'south'. True compass bearings may assert the very opposite, but no matter. Northbound trains have preference over southbound trains of the same class; which means that at a meet between two freight extras, it is the southbound train that goes in the hole.*

[3] *'Swinging a washout' is vernacular for the violent emergency signal to the engine demanding an immediate stop because of danger.*

Chapter 11

OVER THE TOP

HERE in Casapalca the most difficult part of the line is behind us. What lies ahead is in places tremendous, in terms of construction on other mountain railways, but judged by the standards of this unique line it is easier going than the stretch between here and Tornamesa.

There are no reliable figures extant showing the cost per mile to build the Central. Meiggs's contract of 1869 was for a cost from Callao to Oroya totalling 27,600,000 *soles,* which at that time was the equivalent of £5,520,000. But everything went haywire with the suspension of rail construction contracts, the death of Meiggs and the tragedy of the Pacific War. It took a year and seven months to build the first fifty-six miles from Callao; over six years to complete the next forty to Chicla.

The feats involved in building these Andean railroads tend to obscure the achievements of their operation. Relocations and additions, as well as upkeep, indicate that, discounting modern facilities, the engineers of today are man for man no less ingenious and daring than those of the pioneering era. They certainly possess a greater scientific knowledge of their calling, as well as the aggregate experience disseminated by a more comprehensive and far-reaching technical press. It isn't only engineers, civil and mechanical, who deserve the eulogies. Traffic men are to be equally lauded – and it is from the traffic side that General Managers usually emerge. The travelling public, who strain their vocabularies in marvelling at the triumph of the builders, fail to realize the headaches and heartaches imposed on the operating staff by the exigent conditions of the Central.

You have an example of modern ingenuity just north of Casapalca. Until a few years ago, the line climbed out of the yard on a grade like the side of a house, round two tortuous curves past the C de P plant, once a Backus and Johnston copper smelter, to a zig-zag named after these two enterprising men. It then continued forwards up the narrow defile to another zig-zag named Tingo, the top leg of which came to a dead-end on a stump trestle protruding from the side of the mountain at a dizzy height. From there the line pushed on and up into a more open valley at Chinchan, where it took a wide sweep round, over the infant Rimac, and up another mountain flank to a ledge overlooking Casapalca, far below.

The new relocation cuts out Tingo zig-zag altogether, thus eliminating a source of delay. The line from Johnston, top end of the lower zig-zag, is extended back to a new V-switch named G. W. Morkill in honour of a late much-beloved General Manager, and from there continues up the defile at a correspondingly higher level than the old line, and on a similar grade. This enables it to join the old main line again at the upper Tingo V-switch.

Another recent improvement has been the construction of an interchange yard in the valley at Chinchan, which has superseded Casapalca with its awkwardly steep through tracks. Not that Chosica and Oroya engine and crew interchange always takes place here. Chosica power often continues up to Galera, beyond the mainline summit. The two Garratts, Nos. 400 and 402, work through to Chinchan only. These engines are never turned; but of course the smaller engines are, and in Chinchan this is done on a wye in preference to a turntable.

No. 401 covers the twelve miles and two-thousand-foot differential between Casapalca and Ticlo in forty minutes, including a three-minute stop at Chinchan for a meet with No. 402, the southbound Rapido, and its protecting pilot handcar No. 132. In practically no time at all passengers on 401 are looking straight down upon Chinchan yard from a mountain ledge at a spot called Desgraciados. Just beyond that point, and immediately north of a passing loop called Meiggs, the upper Rimac valley comes into view, with Casapalca so minute in the distance far below that the rapidity of the climb causes passengers to marvel.

Martin Van Brocklin, one of Meiggs's engineers, gave his name to a bridge near here; but just before reaching this relatively small bridge, there is a spot where slides have been frequent in the wet season. These can be dangerous for southbound trains; because a blind curve prevents any obstruction being seen in time to stop. Trackwalkers continually patrol the whole line, however, and handcars preceding

81. *A southbound freight prepares to leave Ticlio for Casapalca in 1931. In the background the Morococha branch snakes uphill towards La Cima.* (*Author*)

82. *A La Cima, the highest rail summit in the world – 15,806ft (almost three miles) above sea level.* (*Author*)

passenger trains down the hill are an added precaution. But freights are not always so adequately safeguarded.

On one occasion, an Oroya engine – No. 59, a Rogers 2 8 0 – was belting down here with a heavy train, and on rounding the curve was confronted by a whopping rock slide covering the track. It had just fallen; in fact stones were still coming down. On the engine was an American locomotive inspector named Duffy, a man who had cut his mountain teeth on the Antofagasta road. The hoghead at once began doing things with brake and reverse lever; but Duffy saw that it was hopeless trying to check the speed to a safe figure before the engine plowed into the mess, and he had other ideas. He kicked the brake off, pushed the Johnson bar down forward as far as it would go, and hauled the throttle wide open. To do this, he had to shoulder the hogger out of the way, but in spite of the slight time lag in carrying out these operations, the 59 took off with a bellow and was really moving when she hit the slide. If you have ever tried the old, old trick of shooting a candle from a muzzle-loader through a one-inch board you will know just how that engine went through the rock slide!

Rocks and gravel exploded upwards and outwards as the 59's sharp-nosed pilot plunged into the debris. She came through to the other side still on the track, but with the pilot and beam crumpled to a ruin, headlight and markers smashed, cylinder lagging stripped, and the cab half-filled with dirt. The engineer and fireman were all a-tremble from shock, but old man Duffy was quite imperturbed, and merely remarked: 'There! I knew we could make it if we got runnin' fast enough!'

Van Brocklin bridge preludes eight tunnels within a mile along a ledge with a fearsome drop down hundreds of feet on the outside, and a view of the intricate twists of the Central Highway struggling up from below. Then the line sweeps round the head of the valley to Ticlio, at the foot of Mount Meiggs, a conical peak above the Divide where the 1,287-yard Galera Tunnel carries the main line through to the Atlantic side of the *Cordillera*. Ticlio is 98 miles from Lima and 15,610 feet above sea level, highest junction in the world; cold, dismal and lonesome. Pity the poor station agent condemned to exile in this miserable place – or, for that matter, in Galera at the other end of the tunnel! Traffic no doubt had trouble in finding men willing to accept the posts. I, too, found it difficult to provide truckmen in each of these places, and also to keep them there.

The summit – 15,806 feet – is a mile up the Morococha branch that starts from Ticlio. La Cima is the former highest point; but a few years ago a spur was built from La Cima to the Volcan Mine, overlooking Ticlio, and this, reaching 15,848 feet, is the world's highest railroad summit yet attained.

Snow was never a hazard up here in my time; though I recall an old wedge plow kept in Ticlio out of use – until 1926. The permanent snow line is at about 17,000 feet, which is well clear of the rail summit; but in the wet season there may be snowfalls even as far down as Oroya. These never amount to much.

A railbus connecting with the Mountain Trains for the nine- mile run to the mining centre of Morococha handles the branch passenger traffic. Built by the Central itself during the year 1902, this line is spectacular for the wide summit views it affords – the peaks, vividly – coloured lakes, glaciers and perpetual snows – but the three zig-zags of Anticona, Huacracocha and Churruca make for slow operation. Minerals, the bulk of freight traffic from Morococha, go down to Oroya by way of the line joining the main at Cut-Off station, ten miles south of Oroya.

There was some criticism of Meiggs's choice of a route to Oroya from Ticlio via Yauli – the existing main line – and Watt Stewart in his book on Henry Meiggs has a footnote to the effect that: 'A branch line has actually been built across the summit of the Andes at Morococha and the Galera tunnel has thus been proved to have been unnecessary. . .'The rail distance between Cut-Off and Ticlio is slightly shorter by way of Morococha than by the mainline route, but the Morococha route is without question slower for trains to operate over. Moreover, Morococha is a dead-end station, itself a cause of delay. In my opinion Meiggs was absolutely justified in planning the line via Yauli, and if it had originally been laid through Morococha, extensive and very costly relocations would have been required to speed up traffic and allow of higher train tonnage ratings.

Meiggs had gangs grading the Oroya section and boring the Galera Tunnel while track was being laid in the lower reaches at the start of construction. When the Peruvian Corporation continued the work after the hold-up at Chicla, Thorndike's relatively simple job was to lay the rails, and this was completed

83. Andes No. 207 *returns from Chinchan to Galera with a train of empty tank cars. The box on the buffer beam* contains trainmens' supplies, as cabooses were not used on the Central. (Author)

84. A Sentinel steam railcar heads back towards the coast after a spell of relief work in Huancayo. The results of mountain sickness among the passengers mar the customarily smart middle-bronze-green livery. (Author)

through to Oroya in January 1893. Beyond Galera the character of the mountain slopes presented few of the difficulties encountered on the Pacific side. It was all straightforward enough, except for the short Rumichaca zig-zag, and a very steep drop down the side of the Yauli valley. The steep part is only 15½ miles long, and of this the really difficult portion (for southbound freights on an icy morning) is not more than four miles in length.

Galera Tunnel being operated on the staff system, No. 401 halts in Galera station to deliver the staff before pulling out past the safety switch at the north end of the yard and tilting downwards where the grade begins. Water sinks to vanishing point in the gauge glasses, but it is still safely above the top of the crownsheet, as is shown by a glance at the indicator plate alongside the water column. The fireman adjusts the firepan doors and cuts down on fuel oil till no more than a flame blossoms from the burner nozzle. Engines use the merest whiff of fuel when running down grade. In spite of the increased speed, lubricator feeds are also reduced. With a drifting throttle, Don Jose holds the train comfortably with the straight-air brake. No. 401 runs fast. Anyone who has experienced the crawl down Andean grades on the Chilean systems will find Central passenger train speeds noticeably lively. The Central and Southern move the varnish up, as well as down, considerably faster today than their own officials of thirty years ago would have dreamed possible. But to accomplish this they must have plenty of steam, and that means heavy oil consumption when working uphill.

We ran some tests once between Oroya and Galera with one of the big Alco 2 8 0's of the C de P with an idea of hiring the coal-burner to tide us over a serious power shortage. Starting from Oroya with the tender piled high with 'pampa' coal (the powdery muck from Goyllarisquisga), we 'doubled' the hill from Mahr – at the foot of the steep part – to Galera, and after the second trip had only a few scoopfuls of slack left in the back corners of the bunker. I had been watching the diminishing pile anxiously as the fireman and coalpasser worked like fiends feeding that insatiable firebox on the last pull up to the top. There were no coal stocks on the line. If we cleared the bunker the engine would have to give up her train and return home under tow.

When we were ready to leave Galera for Oroya there were literally no more than half a dozen scoopfuls of dust left. Yet we made Oroya with our train; though with less than a hundred pounds of steam on arrival there! The capacity of the big boiler plus what was in the firebox served for an hour and a half of running, so light was the demand for steam on the down grade.

Passengers on 401 who have been feeling the effects of the high altitude breathe a little easier as we romp down through Viscas to Rumichaca. The Company is required by law to carry oxygen on these passenger trains, with an attendant to administer it, and a number of green-faced sufferers will have taken advantage of the supply. People subject to seasickness are generally prone to mountain sickness also. Imaginations stimulated by the exaggerated talk of others may in some measure aggravate the attacks. One wonders if the day may come when intense competition from local air services forces the Central to pressurize the Mountain rakes!

Air competition for the top-class Lima-Huancayo passenger traffic befell in the days prior to 1935, before the Central Highway was built. The railway won hands down – and it was a question of ceiling! Our trains ran with complete reliability, breasting the summit of the *Cordillera* in all weathers. But the air-liners, with their ceiling at that time limited to about 18,000 feet, could cross the divide only by the passes, and if visibility was poor (as was often the case), the risk was too great. A few months of trial air service choked them off, and the Central was not challenged again until the highway was opened. Not many railroads can boast of having beaten an air line on the score of altitude!

Train No. 2 is waiting at Viscas for a meet with us. There is no station here – only a siding. Below Rumichaca the valley is wide. On the opposite side are the C de P's San Cristóbal mines, with an aerial tramway to transport minerals farther down the valley to Mahr. Yauli hot springs and bath-house betoken an unsuccessful attempt to attract visitors to waters of reputed medicinal value. Yauli itself is a sprawling, semi-ruinous Indian village with nothing attractive about it. It had its day in the colonial epoch, and was a staging post on the *Camino Real*, which in Casapalca forked into two branches, one crossing the Divide by the same route now taken by the Central's Morococha branch, and the other cutting across to Viscas by way of a landmark called. the *Piedra Parada*, or 'Upright Rock'.

85. A superb panorama of Oroya, headquarters of the Mountain Section, and terminus of the Cerro de Pasco Railway. The important roundhouse at which Brian Fawcett spent the formative years of his career is at bottom right.
(Author)

At Mahr the line levels off on the floor of the valley with a nice long tangent ahead, and Don Jose lets the smoking brakeshoes fall free of the wheels altogether. Mahr Tunnel, just beyond, is named not for a railroad bore, but for a drainage tunnel opened in the early '30s by the C de P to drain Lake Morococha, the bed of which had on several occasions subsided, inundating the mine workings beneath with appalling loss of life. Mahr Tunnel, some five miles in length, passed through ground that Richard Trevithick would have described as 'orey'. The gleaming grey-white stone brought out of the diggings at the lower end, at Mahr, was perfect for ballast, and Tom Crawford, at that time District Engineer of the F.C.C. in Oroya, was told to help himself to all he wanted. The result was that the whole of the Mountain Section was in time ballasted with it. When that was completed the track was a picture to look at – and the glistening ballast contained something like six per cent of silver!

C de P properties abound now. Next along the tangent is the Pachachaca hydro-electric station. Then 401 pulls up at Cut-Off, where, on the train's left side, the line from Morococha comes in. From here to Oroya grades are two-per-centish and curves are easy, allowing the *Rapido* to cover the ten miles in eighteen minutes. The 226's 52-inch drivers rotate in a haze at that speed! Oroya, 130 miles from Lima and 12,220 feet high, announces its proximity at Huaymanta with a hospital, new C de P plant buildings, and working people's houses. The 226's whistle shouts loud and long, awakening echoes from the rocky sides of the gorge behind the town; the drivers crash over the switch frog of the turnout into the C de P's yard; Don José reaches for the automatic brake valve to make a ten-pound split reduction; and No. 401 draws up in the C de P station, where a sister engine in black with white trimmings and lettering stands

86. The smelters of the Cerro de Pasco Corporation, a vital source of traffic for the Central, dominate Oroya. The Central's main line for Oroya (the track in the centre) in fact threads through the smelter, on its way north to Huancayo. (Author)

at the headend of the connecting C de P train for Cerro de Pasco. The hour is 1.01 p.m. The other Mountain train, No. 1, will be arriving from Lima at 2.26.

No. 401 stays here for only twelve minutes. The 226 cuts off and rolls down into the Central yard, to the fuel and water tanks and the roundhouse, her day's work finished after achieving an overall average speed of nearly 22 m.p.h. from Lima. This sounds laughable to a flat-road man, but in the Andes it represents a remarkably fine performance. Another 200-class engine is ready to take the *Rapido* on to Huancayo, and at her throttle is another Don José. No time is lost in coupling up and making the brake tests. The Oroya sub-dispatcher has orders ready; the C de P 'high-line' crossing is clear, and the semaphore protecting it is 'off'. The ringing double toot of the whistle sounds throughout Oroya, and with bell tolling the train sneaks down through the Central yard, past the station building, over the C de P crossing, and through the heart of the great smelter plant, where masked and goggled workers in the roasters congregate in the lofty steel galleries above the track to watch the train pass. Towering above everything but the crowding flanks of the gorge is the 'Big Stack', a 500-foot concrete monster, one of the tallest of its kind when it was built in 1935 to lift the sulphurous smelter fumes clear of the canyon.

The policy in my day of powering the Oroya section with crocks and leaving the inhospitable Andean heights as much out of sight and out of mind as possible is well-nigh incomprehensible when it is recalled that something like seventy per cent of the railroad's traffic originated with the Cerro de Pasco Copper Corporation, centred in Oroya. There would have been more sense in locating the locomotive shops there, if not the whole of the railroad administration, but for the fact that 'phantom freight' in the shape

87. *Train No. 2 romps past the loop at Huanchan, Km 231.* (Author)

88. *Train No. 2 behind engine No. 90, halts for a red train order flag at Pachacayo and a meet with a track inspection car. The date is 1930.* (Author)

89. *A North British 2-8-0 of the 60 class on Train 207, the way-freight for Huancayo, at Tambo in 1930. The Jauja branch leaves the main line here.* (*Author*)

90. *Further on, Train No. 2 halts for No. 90 to take water at Rocroa. All the coaches of this rake were built at Guadalupe.* (*Author*)

of material and supplies – particularly petroleum – would have been considerable. But one must allow for the deterrent to the higher brass of Oroya's lack of amenities, the unpleasant effects of high altitude, and virtual 'exile' from the social attractions of Lima. If not in Oroya, the works could have been in Chosica, in perpetual sunshine, within easy reach of Lima, yet at the very doorstep of mountain operations. The existing site at Guadalupe is wrong from a practical point of view, and the space occupied by the shops could be usefully employed as a freight yard immediately adjacent to the docks.

The Oroya section is harder on motive power than the Chosica section. The latter admittedly includes the physically most difficult parts of the line, but the work is straightforward. Oroya engines are subject to the rough treatment of heavy road work plus switching operations in a number of places where wickedly tight turnouts and fixed structures are in the nature of obstacles. There is far more movement of minerals in the Oroya section than in the Chosica section, and mineral traffic is tougher on all the rolling stock concerned than is petroleum or general merchandise.

The Huancayo line, beyond Oroya, has its share of minerals originating from the C de P's Yauricocha mine branch, but eucalyptus pit props for the C de P mines on 'The Hill', livestock for Lima and agricultural produce, make up most of the freight from the Huancayo Valley.

This extension of 78 miles from Oroya to the Huancayo railhead was built between 1905 and 1908, following the Mantaro River all the way. Twelve miles down the line is Huari, where coal deposits once of some value called for a rail connection; but the rich Huancayo Valley was the main attraction for the extension. At the head of this valley is the town of Jauja, which even before Meiggs's time had been earmarked for connection with Lima by rail. At the other end of the valley is Huancayo, now of far more commercial importance than Jauja. Continuing down the Mantaro Valley from Huancayo is a Government owned and operated metre-gauge line, the Huancayo-Huancavelica Railway, that has a potential strategic importance in the way of freight were it exploited to the full.

Besides freight, the Huancayo line enjoys a lively passenger movement, principally of second-class traffic between Huancayo and Jauja, worked extensively by diesel-mechanical railcars powered with Saurer 180-h.p. BXD engines. The Central's first railcar was a Sentinel-Cammell 6-cylinder steamer put in service in 1929. This unit worked the Huancayo-Jauja run, a distance of 28 miles, in a daily shuttle service, year in and year out, and paid off its original cost over and over again.

Oroya to Jauja is all good sheep and cattle country; thereafter, one finds cereals, timber and quaint Indian villages in irresistibly attractive settings. From one end to the other, the line is 'green', in marked contrast to the slag-like bleakness of the lower Pacific slopes. Rainfall is heavy between November and April. The 'dry' season is characterized by sparkling, frosty nights, intensely cold, and by hot sunshine at midday. So dry is the air at this height that extremes of heat and cold are not felt as on the humid coast.

To us rails, riding the Huancayo line was always a pleasure, whereas the other direction was all too frequently a penance. No. 401 quickly leaves behind the smoke-seared environs of Oroya. For a time the slag dumps fed by aerial tramway from the smelter continue down the valley on the other side of the river, but the monotonous procession of buckets ends in the tall structure of a U turn tower, and clean rock and green bunch grass are left unsullied from there on. There are no trees here. You won't see many trees till we approach the junction of this valley and the Huancayo Valley at Tambo. The valley here is narrow, walled in by rolling fell-like hills. There are no visible crags or peaks – no glimpses yet of distant perpetual snow. It would take little effort to imagine oneself on the Scottish Border, in the vicinity of Beattock for example.

Grades never exceed a gentlemanly 1½ per cent. Flanges squeal a bit on the curves, but when the going is easy this is of no account. Andes engines have a passenger tonnage rating of 350 and a freight rating of 650 up this line from Jauja, but the sky is the limit for the down run. There are no zig-zags, few bridges, and only four tunnels in all. A few bad spots do exist where slides and washouts are likely during the rainy season; and there is one place where the track crosses a stretch of ground ever on the move, like a glacier, slowly but inexorably towards the river.

At one time in my day we had an epidemic of cattle and sheep rustling by our train crews, that brought the most fantastic claims against the Company. A freight would run down a few animals on a blind curve and strew the sides of the terraplane with carcasses. Having stopped as promptly as he could, the hoghead and his fireman would get down from the engine, choose a carcass, heave it up into the cab with the help of the trainmen, and butcher it there. Each man got his share, the larger quarters being surreptitiously off-loaded short of the yard on return home, to be collected later. Hide and head went out of the side somewhere along the line where the river ran close. A conscientious report of the mishap was passed in, as regulations demanded; but it was the gory evidence discovered by the road-master at trackside that drew attention to what was taking place after the accident. In the roundhouse we were not without suspicions. However carefully decks were hosed down by the criminals, certain ugly blotches were overlooked! The owners of the stricken animals naturally valued them at an exaggeratedly high figure.

Worst of the culprits were Driver L – – , the Federation's 'griever' in Oroya (equivalent of a union shop steward), and his permanent fireman, a fat young man of the mountains named Crispin. L – – was the bane of my existence. He was always up to mischief, and at the first hint of retribution would threaten to bring out the enginemen on strike and tie up the section. Crispin was of a milder nature than the turbulent L – – , tainted more by the bad company he was obliged to keep than from innate sin; but between the two of them there was never a dull moment for me.

L – – 's engine killed some bullocks on the Huancayo line. L – – and his minion, Crispin, carved up one of the carcasses in the cab, and were caught literally red-handed by me. L – – tried to bribe his way out of it by offering me a quarter, but it didn't work. He and Crispin both drew a substantial holiday without pay – and since the justice was administered by the CME himself, beyond L – – 's union jurisdiction, no threats of strike action were availing.

L – – wisely decided that the game was not worth the candle, but Crispin had acquired the habit, and couldn't keep his thieving hands off any sheep that strayed into the proximity of his engine at a halt where supervision was lax. Jumping the engine at a meet one day I found a miserable ewe huddled up in the corner of the cab on the fireman's side, against the firebox, and Crispin had the nerve to claim that he put it there because the poor thing looked so cold! I warned him seriously that any further kindness of this sort to animals would find him back wiping in the shed, off the board for keeps.

Not long afterwards I happened to go down to Llocllapampa, thirty-three miles from Oroya, to check up on certain repairs we had done to the Sentinel railcar, now on the way back to its regular beat in Huancayo. We had a meet in Llocllapampa with 208, the freight from Huancayo, and I decided to return to Oroya on its engine, with L – – and Crispin.

The old 67 was holding the main when the Sentinel arrived and turned into the loop. I climbed to the engine's deck on the far side. There was no one in the cab. The two enginemen were down on the platform oiling round the motion. But no sooner was I in the gangway than the bearded face of a billygoat appeared from behind the backhead on the fireman's side and glared at me with red eyes full of hate. Round its neck was the end of a frayed rope. The creature had apparently been tied to the injector pipe and had chewed itself free. Besides that, it had eaten most of the upholstery off the top of Crispin's seatbox. At sight of me it began to fidget and dance, lowering its head with wicked intent. I left the cab hurriedly the way I had come, and not an instant too soon. Luckily for me, the goat decided that the cab was its castle. Instead of pursuing me to the ground, it stood in the gangway nickering awful threats.

At that moment L – – climbed into the cab on the other side, slamming his oil can on the apron with a loud clatter before mounting the steps. The goat instantly swung round on the defensive, and L – – , standing in the gangway, was confronted with this horror poised for violent action. He turned to jump down, and the billygoat's horned head caught him at the moment of take-off, with the result that L – – flew through the air, cleared the end of the platform and rolled head over heels down the ballast into a ditch not entirely free of prickly pears. His Federation dignity was torn to shreds.

For the first time in my experience, L – – supported me when I lit into Crispin and told him to get that wild beast out of the cab, and fast! Easier said than done. Crispin's half-hearted attempts to board were unsuccessful. However, while he was thus engaged, L – – and I, accompanied by the intensely interested brakemen, climbed over the back of the tender to the top of the tank with the intention of entering the cab that way. But the goat was permitting no invasion from either below or above. Crispin was quickly routed and forced to join us on the tank top. Fear of possible casualties discouraged a mass assault. What then was to be done? The Sentinel had pulled out for Tambo long ago. We should have been taking water in Rocroa by now, miles up the line. Yet here we were, spiked in Llocllapampa by a goat, of all things, while water dropped lower and lower in the gauge glass and the roar of escaping steam from the pops was less and less interrupted by intervening periods of quiet.

It was decided to lasso the goat with the bellcord. The gong wire was detached and festoons of cord pulled in over the car tops, until enough was to hand for action. There was not much room between the cab roof and the tank top on that engine. The rope artist had to get down on his knees and endeavour to drop the noose over the goat's head. The goat contemptuously tossed the noose aside each time, until at length he grew tired of it and retreated to Crispin's seatbox for the remains of the straw upholstery. He watched us intently as he ate, ready for instant action should we make an attempt to descend to the deck.

We were saved by the station peon. This worthy Indian, belying the reputation for extreme simplicity that coastal *cholos* like to hang on their mountain brethren, sized up the situation and attacked from the rear, creeping along the running board from the pilot beam. To aid him, we held the goat's attention by feints in his direction with the noose.

All our cabs had ample front doors giving out upon the running boards, and these doors were almost always kept wide open. The peon crept up to the cab, reached in through the door, and seized both the goat's hind legs. At the same instant we dropped down from the tank to the deck and flung ourselves on the frantic beast. Unable to defend itself, the goat was overwhelmed, its legs tied with the bellcord. Blatting with frustrated rage it was lifted down to the ballast, untied and sent packing with a few kicks on the rump.

L – – 's wounded dignity kept him from officially supporting the repentant Crispin when that wretch was called on the carpet. But Crispin was neither demoted nor suspended. In the subsequent grilling it came to light that he had purchased the goat legitimately from the station *peon*. All the same; if he ever rustled livestock again, it never came to my notice.

For months afterwards L – – was liable to be greeted by clandestine goat-like bleats from his colleagues when about the yard on union business of fomenting trouble. Should he use the selective telephone to confer with other Federation dignitaries he would be unable to hear anything for the bleating from every operator on the line who might be listening in. So chastened was he by this ridicule that my whole attitude towards his plump fireman, Crispin, took a most favourable turn, much to that miscreant's wonderment! …

Between Llocllapampa and Tambo the valley of the Mantaro becomes more and more attractive. Trees appear singly, then in groups. The valley opens out in a funnel-shaped mouth, and ahead is the wide sweep of the Huancayo Valley, its confining hills still fell-like. Right ahead of 401, as the train gallops along the river's edge beyond the final tunnel, lie the eternal snows of Huaytapallana in the Comas range, towering above the far slopes of the *Cordillera* that drop to the eastern forests. The engine's whistle utters its long cry for Tamho station, followed by the four toots calling for 'the board' – in this case the stall – and the switch at the south leg of the wye leading into the half-mile Jauja spur. Jauja is a dead-end station.

Out upon the main again and a meet completed with one of the Huancayo railcars, the *Rapido* sets off down the valley, where there is more tangent track than anywhere else on the system, and the maximum grade of $1^1/_2$ per cent is limited to a few short stretches that in any case are in a northbound train's favour. The river is out of sight on the other side of the valley. Between it and the tracks are extensive fields of corn. The right-of-way is bordered by maguey or century plants. The villages that lend their names to stations are all somewhat remote from the tracks, some even invisible behind encompassing groves of eucalyptus. Huamali is in quite open country; but trees close in about the tracks at Matahuasi, near the end of an eight-mile tangent, the longest on the line. Set in wooded surroundings two miles farther on is Concepcion, where 401 has a meet with Train 152, a railcar running from Huancayo to Oroya. Then on again, clear of the woods, rounding the bluff above the river at Orcotuna halt, and down another long tangent into San Jeronimo.

Between San Jeronimo and Huancayo the Mountain Section reaches its lowest point of 10,643 feet. Afterwards it rises gently to a short but slightly steeper drop into Huancayo, which is 10,696 feet high.

91. *Jauja was once a town of considerable importance and in the 1920's was still a fruitful source of freight traffic. Engine No. 101 leaves Jauja station with a lengthy mixed freight for Oroya in 1927.* (Author)

92. *The Oroya District Officers' private car* Chalaca *on the tail of train No. 2 in Llocllapampa. Wives loved this 'home from home' which had all the dwelling amenities of a small bungalow, plus the services of a cook/steward.* (Author)

93. *Huamali station, and a meet between a Sentinel railcar and a passenger train, at the tail end of which is the Oroya District Officers' inspection car* Chalaca. *(Author)*

94. *Sentinel-Cammell steam railcar No. 1 is seen here at Oroya, but spent most of her life working the Huancayo-Jauja local passenger service, and paid for herself over and over again.* *(Author)*

95. *Hunacayo station in 1937, with Sentinel steam railcar No. 6 and trailer on a Juaja working. These units were designed for one man operation and were automatically fired, with three-drum water-tube boilers pressed to 500 psi.*
(Author)

The last leg of 9½ miles is fast going. The woods that had retired somewhat, close up about the tracks again. No. 401 rushes down under the trees with whistle screaming, while passengers collect their belongings and prepare to detrain at journey's end. Huancayo station platform is crowded with people to witness the train's arrival, to see who is travelling and to add to the bedlam when the coaches disgorge their occupants. Hordes of small boys gather to compete with hopeful adults for the carriage of passengers' baggage. In Peru there is no system of station porters such as on British railways. Station *peones* are employed for freight duties, but not for the convenience of passengers.

Bell tolling, No. 401 rolls slowly up to Huancayo platform, in accordance with the speed restriction within yard limits. The hour is 4.10 p.m. The run has been accomplished in 9 hours and 10 minutes from Lima. No. 1 will arrive at 6.01, after a trip of 10 hours 31 minutes. Tomorrow morning at 6.20 a.m. No. 402 will leave for Lima, No. 2 following at 7.05. Buffet car passengers are advised to have breakfast on the train. It's good!

Huancayo is the prettiest station I have seen anywhere. The yard is triangular, with a wye for turning engines and rolling stock. At the top of the wye is a Spanish-tiled engine house. Tall gum trees cluster thickly about the yard, even encroaching as far as the tracks. At the north end there is a grove of magnificent trees, under which is a rose garden and a bungalow to house visiting railway officials. The middle of the wye is a flower garden crowded with roses, cornflowers, lilies, pansies and numerous other blossoms all carefully tended by the station gardener. The air is full of their perfume, of the aroma of the gum trees, and perhaps also with a tang of eucalyptus wood smoke from the employees' houses on the south side. The station is on the town's edge. There is scarcely any noise – no permanent switching engine, no yard movements, no clamour or the to-do usually associated with railroad termini. Here is beauty and tranquillity. The engines and railcars seem to walk on tiptoe as they go about their business. Only at leaving time do whistles and bells let go, and when they do, all Huancayo hears – and hurries!

96. *Huancayo shed, in its idyllic location surrounded by gum trees. The third rail on the right hand track belongs to the 3ft gauge Huancayo-Huancavelica Railway.* *(Author)*

No. 401 covers the road so fast that one cannot help comparing its hurry with the more leisurely tempo of a generation ago, when the standard-gauge Peruvian carriers were very much looked down upon by the lordly Argentine broad-gauge systems. An unkind twist of fate caused the metamorphosis of the latter, and some of their displaced sons moved north-westwards to the once despised Andean pikes, now well-groomed, dynamic and highly efficient – and still privately owned.

The Central and Southern Railways of Peru, under their common parent, the Peruvian Corporation, have never been static, in the two-strips-of-rust-and-a-mixed-train-daily way. Never have development and improvement stood still. They have ever kept pace with the times, and this has somehow been accomplished without landing themselves inextricably in the red. I have stressed, and repeat, the important point that Andean roads are operated successfully on a slender budget. That this is possible is because the men who run them are educated to it in the hard way; and the railways are not bedevilled by politicians and political nominees, as State systems so often are.

The Central has come a long way since I joined it back in the days of carbon-arc headlights and wooden pilots. These obsolete accessories were still being used, even at that time. The new is not always better than the old; though it may offer attractive advantages. Carbon-arc headlights gave a magnificent, white illumination of the track ahead – while the arc endured. The trouble with them was that the carbon rod feed had a way of sticking, which caused the arc to break, and was apt to plunge the track ahead in darkness just when light was most required. In the event of a collision with rocks, wooden pilots splintered and broke away from the pilot beam with little danger of derailing the truck wheels as tubular steel ones may; but they cost too much money and took too long to build.

In those days the single mountain train ran three return trips a week, arriving in Oroya – if all was well – at 5.30 in the evening, and reaching Huancayo at 10 p.m. The non-superheated 2-8-0's used in this service were still as Rogers had outshopped them in 1906. They crept up the mountain nobly enough, but with no reserve at all of steam. Pressure plunged at once if a tube or two began to weep. On the descents beyond the hard-won summit no liberties could be taken with the Eames simple vacuum brake, which was applied to its utmost limit merely to keep the train from running away. Stops required plenty of steam brake on engine and tender, plus clubbing of coach handbrakes by the four ever-ready brakemen, whose services were summoned by a single sharp toot from the whistle.

Enginemen, stout individualists, were autocratic in the extreme. A hoghead unable to assert his own authority was quickly put in his place by the fireman. Most hoggers, be it said, were not weighed in the balance and found wanting. One of the Chosica freight men was a holy terror – a sphynx-faced Negro of the jettest black, and not, as it happened, a physical giant. This man was never known to smile. I knew him for years, esteeming him as a first-rate engineman, and in all that time I not once saw the slightest expression of amusement on his face. He was also extremely taciturn. The one pleasure he seemed to find in life was to wait for the brakemen of his train after signing off from duty and beat them up singly or together. Police interference eventually robbed him of this diversion.

In the same roundhouse, at a later date, there arose an extraordinarily aggressive fireman, whose aged and well-liked father relinquished a throttle and was promoted to locomotive inspector in the same section (the driver who pulled out of Chosica without his train in Chapter 3, in fact). This fireman had a way of dealing with his engineer at the very start of their partnership. He would take a piece of chalk from his pocket, draw a line down the middle of the backhead, across deck and apron to the tank, and say with menace in his voice: 'What's on that side of the line is yours. What's on this side is mine. Understand? Keep your nose out of my side and there will be no trouble!'

He got away with it for a time only because he was paired with elderly men, but the day came when he found himself in a cab with the sphynx-faced Negro, who for years had refrained from his bellicose pastimes of yore and was in consequence more taciturn than ever, if that were possible. No doubt over-confident from success, the indiscreet fireman pulled the chalk-line gag. Sphynx-face said nothing. He merely stood that fireman up against the tank and hit him slowly and methodically, right-left-right-left, until the man was almost senseless. He then threw the fireman bodily out of the cab and went calmly along to the office to ask for another! Having become more than tired of that fireman's intransigence and the repeated complaints from engineers with whom he was paired, we cautioned Sphynx-face about fighting on duty – but not without a wink. The fireman's lesson was well learned; and while it couldn't make a silk purse out of a sow's ear, it did at any rate relieve us of an irritating source of trouble.

Freight enginemen in those days worked sixteen to eighteen hours a day, six days a week, if not seven. Of course, they pulled in a fat pay packet, but it meant insufficient rest, which sooner or later might (and no doubt did) result in sleeping on duty. At the same time, there was not the snap and bustle to train operation that is achieved today. Highway competition was non-existent. Would-be shippers were expected to approach the Traffic Department hat in hand – excepting only the C de P, in whose presence we ourselves uncovered.

Central freight traffic in 1936 was moving at the rate of some 850,000 tons a year, with passengers transported at – peculiarly enough – practically the same figure. The Southern at that period moved 220,000 tons of freight and 284,000 passengers. Today's annual figures for the Central are over a million tons of freight and nearly a million passengers; while the Southern handles about half that tonnage and a quarter of a million fewer passengers. Cerro de Pasco Railway freight tonnage figures beat the Central's, but their case is rather different, nearly all of it being the Company's own minerals from mines to processing plants.

Traffic handling efficiency grows steadily. Double-heading was anathema to the Engineers' Department of the Central at one time. The mention of such a procedure brought forth immediate howls about concentrated loads, curve displacement and so on. Garratts were received in 1930 with growls of disapproval. Since 1952 double-heading has been an accepted policy, with all-round benefits to the Traffic Department. When diesels can profitably replace steam throughout the altitude range, steam will go. As soon as the money can be found, CTC will open out certain operational bottlenecks on the mountain at present causing continual headaches to the dispatchers.

There is no doubt that the *Andes* type locomotive played a big part in the streamlining of the Central, the Southern and the C de P. With them, with lightweight passenger stock, with aluminium freight cars and roller bearings, with dual-service cars to eliminate empty movement, an upward trend in operational efficiency has been secured.

Lest you think me unduly biased, I shall close this chapter with some words by Charles Irving, writing of the Central in the *(Manchester) Guardian* of January 22, 1962. During his visit to Peru, the Company gave him an 'inside' view of the system and its working.

'It might be supposed, and I believe it quite often is supposed, that the world's highest railways are those freak things that carry sightseers up mountains with the aid of a toothed rack, or a gradient of about one in four. But in fact the world's three very high railways – the Peruvian Central, the Antofagasta and Bolivia, and the Peruvian Southern – were in no sense built for sightseers. They were built to move things, and things more than people, over the bare, rough, jagged and weirdly coloured spine of the Andes. And of this notable trio the highest, the grandest, the most spectacular, and at its summit level the busiest, is the Peruvian Central. It is the most wonderful railway in the world.'

97. Once a 'must' for any self-respecting South American railway was a Funeral Car. This splendid example, taken over by the Central Railway of Peru from the old Lima Railway in 1935, dates from the 1860's.
(Author)

Chapter 12

RUNNING THE MOUNTAIN SECTION

OFF and on – mostly on – I had eight years in the Mountain Section of the Central of Peru where operating conditions were really tough, where materials were shaved down to a minimum, and where reserves of power and personnel were non-existent.

Headquarters of the section were located at Oroya, and there I occupied a bungalow between the roundhouse and the machine shop, right on the job. A nucleus of freight locomotive power was provided by the little 2 8 0's that in an earlier chapter I described as 'misfits', besides which there were several 110-class *Mountains* and 100-class *Mikados*. There were also a couple of 80-class 2 6 2 tank engines taken from the Lima-Callao local service to be used as a relief for the Sentinel railcar in Huancayo and for special light passenger runs. Passenger trains 1 and 2 between Oroya and Huancayo were handled either by rebuilt Rogers 2 8 0's of the 50-class, or 90-class 4 6 0's.

Towards the end of my tenure of office in the section I meticulously kept work logs, and it is from these that the following extracts are quoted. The remarks in parentheses are added now, by way of explanation, and were not in the original entries.

Time must be turned back to the years 1934 and 1935; for the logbooks I still possess cover this period. If it isn't the Central of today, it does at all events provide a taste of steam mountain railroading as experienced by a representative of the Locomotive Department, who with the District Engineer and the District Traffic Superintendent endeavoured more or less successfully to keep traffic on the move in all weathers. We watched and we improvised. Resourcefulness was a necessity if the old power and rolling stock inflicted upon us were to be kept in service.

In the roundhouse of my day we were without an electric welder. Some small oxygen welding jobs were within our capacity, but frame breakages and tube welding meant sending the defective engine to Chosica or Guadalupe. The main shops in Guadalupe were always behind with the schedule of general repairs, which resulted in units being worked that had run out their mileage. The usual cry from the Chief of Traction was: 'Keep her going till the shops can take her!' This we did – but when I look back on it now, I realize how often fortune was on our side.

… Sent to Chief of Traction Driver Guerra's report on dropping of a car in Casapalca because of Eng. 112's excessive slipping. Side rod bushes of this engine are in a foul state; about half an inch play in them. Floating bushes of big-ends also bad. Piston rings due to be examined. We put a new bolt in front end of lower R.H. slide-bar of Eng. 47, and to do this had to take out the piston. An ordinary bolt was perforce fitted.

The boiler of Eng. 112 is remarkably clean inside considering the length of time since the last washing. Scale does not exceed $1/16$in on plates and slightly more on stays. The new piston rod extractor used for the first time on Eng. 112 has got damaged. Seems that in Guadalupe they are not using properly hardened material for these jobs.

Eng. 59 arrived with the tubes pouring water and one stay in throat plate leaking. Am calling in a boilermaker tomorrow, Sunday, to work on these.

Guadalupe has instructed me to consider enginemen's vacations as time worked, so I anticipate argument with the Federation [the Enginemen and Trainmen's union].

Night reports pretty heavy and a long report to do on Eng. 59 [this refers to driver's work reports to be attended by the roundhouse].

Have advised J.T.T. [Chief Dispatcher and Trains Office] that Eng. 112 must be stopped on Monday and Tuesday to repair side rod bushes. Reported valve of water crane to D.E. [District Engineer], as the slow rate of flow is delaying engines when taking water …

… Engine 59 failed between Tamboraque and Matucana with Train No. 1 on account of tube trouble. Am finishing up the rebushing of rods on Eng. 112 and she can go back into service tomorrow. Driver

M – – damaged the track yesterday speeding with Train 207; and today with 208 again exceeded the speed limit, besides failing to obey whistle signal rules.

Phoned Chief of Traction about the piston extractor, and he says that the metal has apparently not been hardened. This indicates gross neglect on the part of the shops.

Piston of Eng. 112, L.H. side, found to have been knocking on the cover, and latter is cracked in consequence. Ordered new one from Sub-Store. Piston rod extension reduced to clear the cover.

Eng. 74 arrived from the coast, which will allow us to stop Eng. 70 as from tomorrow for overhaul of boiler and rods ...

... Wrote to Chief of Traction about putting permanent crews on each engine here.... Made out a table showing how short Oroya shed personnel is in comparison with Chosica and Guadalupe. Guadalupe's total of men per engine is 3.28; Chosica's is 4.28 actually and 3 if the Garratts are considered as each representing two units; and Oroya as low as 2.07, including the Sentinel. The other sheds are also superior in the number of fitters per engine; in fact, Oroya is inferior in every single item, and is under a further disadvantage in not possessing an electric welder. I intend to show this table to the CME when I next go down to Guadalupe, in the hope of convincing him of the urgent need for more men and material here.

Measured flanges of Eng. 105 and find those of leading coupled wheels down to $^5/_8$in and $^{11}/_{16}$in – very bad. Leading truck flanges are also bad ...

... To Ticlio on Extra 74 South. She steamed steadily at 165-170 pounds, but can't reach 180 with the injector working. *Tools:* short of pinchbars. Motion: fair – several pins need changing. *Rods and brasses:* good. Boxes: good. Report: reduce distance between L.H. front sandpipe nozzle and rail. Level up springs. Change spring of R.H. leading coupled wheel. Close crossheads on both sides, as the limit of $^1/_8$in between shoes and slide bars has been reached. Engine smoking rather too much, but is looking good and runs exceptionally smoothly for her class.

Saw truckmen in Galera and Ticlio. Both said a few days ago that they hadn't enough brakeshoes to carry on with, but they now state that they can manage until the arrival of the Chief Car Inspector with supplies.

Eng. 74 pulled to Galera 139 tons in four loads and one empty and made a very creditable trip. On arrival in Ticlio I found Driver L – – and Conductor Lavado quarrelling about a five-minute delay which Lavado wished to blame the engine for but which L – – swore was Lavado's fault. I personally think the time was lost by the two wrangling; though Eng. 105, with 155 tons, made slow time because of several large tubes blowing, no doubt on account of the cracked tube sheet. L – – says he was delayed yesterday by Lavado's having insisted on the sand pipes being dismantled completely when sand wouldn't run. Nothing was found wrong with them. Fireman Durand and Brakeman Bosich confirm this. The sandcar was used today on the Casapalca-Ticlio stretch on account of the vast quantity of oil still on the track from Eng. 110's leaks yesterday. D.S.S. informed me that the sandcar was sanding on one side only, and that oil was dropping on the track from the boxes.

Complained to the D.E. of a bad bit of track at Viscas, and he instructed the Roadmaster to see to it at once ...

. . . Made a house inspection this afternoon with D.S.S. [District Traffic Supt., *Sierra*], D.E., secretaries, Station Agent and Yardmaster. In Driver S – – 's house we found a can containing five kilos of No. 2 (engine) oil, which he says he was keeping for an emergency! In Truckman M – – 's house were two large bits of firewood stolen from the machine shop. In Firemen M – – 's and R – – 's houses we found steam hoses. Fireman A – – had three brakeshoe cotters; Lighter-up N – – , 5 kilos of fuel oil; Fireman C – –, 6 oil cans, 2 torches, 1 padlock, 2 shovels, 1 brakeshoe cotter and a steam hose. Fireman AR – – also possessed a steam hose. Lighter-up C – – had a new grease can and a lighting-up pipe. Mechanic H – – had two padlocks. Fireman C – – is thus an easy winner in this damned annoying racket of filching equipment off engines! The houses, incidentally, were disgracefully dirty, and their occupants have been told to clean them.

The Chief of Traction came up on Train No. 1, and together we investigated the collision in Ticlio, in which Billson's fireman must share the blame for not looking out to see if the line was clear.

... Had Fireman I – – on the carpet for coming to his engine (No. 114) 8 mins. after leaving time this morning. His excuse is that he thought he was off the board, having at his own request been taken off duty on 207. He never took the trouble to see if he was named for another engine. I suspended him for a day, and he promptly asked for six days' leave to go down and kick to the Federation. I told him to get the hell out of the office! ...

... To Casapalca on Extra 102 S., changing to Extra 114 S. at Van Brocklin.... The engine steamed heavily on leaving Oroya but picked up after Yauli with the firedoor slightly open. Springs need straightening. Arrived in Galera at 9.55 a.m. with 107 tons in 7 cars. Inspected truckmen's stores in Galera, Ticlio and Casapalca and found everything okay.

Shortly after 10 a.m. a few rocks fell on the track above Van Brocklin, breaking a rail and blocking the line. Driver Guerra, with Eng. 114, saw them ahead, though at only a short distance, and was smart enough to stop his train in time.

I returned on Train No. 1, Eng. 57, leaving Casapalca at 2.25 p.m. and arriving Oroya at 5.10 p.m. In Cut-Off the joint of the fuel oil pipe beneath the tender tank fractured, allowing a great deal of oil to escape. I did what I could to direct this oil clear of the rails, but a fair amount fell in the middle of the track and upon the L.H. rail. Immediately on arrival I put the engine over the oil dump and emptied the tender. Advised D.S.S. of the oil on the track and arranged to send out the sandcar tomorrow.

Eng. 105 has the superheater header cracked through the rear row of element seats; a bad crack, long and rather open, and I anticipate trouble. The R.H. conn. rod little-end of Eng. 60 has heated up seriously, burning the brass and causing the wedge to seize. The L.H. link pin of this engine suffered in the same way some time ago, and it is obvious that Driver S – – has not been oiling sufficiently. On the last house inspection I found a quantity of oil in his house, which he swore he was keeping for an emergency, but which he probably took to sell ...

An interpolation is necessary here to press the point home that on these tremendous grades oil on the rails could easily cause a breakdown in the service. It happened all too frequently. It might originate in drips from tank cars or tenders – overfilled fuel tanks were a menace in that respect, the oil running down the sides of the tank, over the truck frame to the track, or dropping directly on the tender wheels – and it might be from badly adjusted or worn flange lubricators on the engine.

Central engines were fitted with flange lubricators feeding through a cock and a hose nozzle to the flange near the top of the leading coupled wheels, their presence being required to avoid excessive flange wear on the terrific curves. The design was poor, and when the hose nozzles were worn or corroded, the fuel oil used as lubricant dripped as readily on the tread as on the flange.

I produced and fitted on most of my engines a pivoted swan neck pendulum lubricator bearing squarely against the flange by its own weight, on the front centre line of the wheel, so that any excess oil was thrown off the flange centrifugally before it could creep over the tread. These, with a sight feed for adjustment, were completely successful, and the Mountain Section hogheads swore by them. But better than any flange lubricator on the engine were the automatic curve lubricators installed in the track a a later date. These functioned with grease from a pump actuated by the flanges, and all the wheels got the benefit, rather than only those of the engine.

In addition to flange lubricators, all engines were fitted with rail washers. These were nozzles set over the rails in front of the leading coupled wheels, piped from a point on the boiler backhead well down in the 'wet' region. When the valves were opened, hot water at high pressure issued in a chisel-shaped jet and flashed into vapour on contact with the air, effectively slicing oil off the rail tops. Similar nozzles were fitted on some engines to wash the leading driving tyre treads in the same way. In both cases it was most important that the nozzles be properly positioned to sweep the oil clear of the rail or tyre altogether and not blow it back under the following wheels.

To continue the log:

... I have noticed for some time that Driver M – – 's nephew goes round the Oroya yard every and all day carrying a small grip. I have made enquiries out of curiosity and am told that he sells contraband cigarettes of foreign make [tobacco was a State monopoly at that time]. If this is so he must get them sent up on some engine and I have heard that Driver V – – of Train No. 1 is in on the game. This is quite likely. There are many places on the engine where such things might be hidden – under the sand in the sandbox, for example. I must keep an eye on him …

The Sentinel did her full service yesterday without further axle trouble, I hear; but Eng. 83 was kept in steam in case she might be needed as relief.

Both Drivers Isusqui and Flores were threatened by the officers in command of the troops they transported this week, being told that if they didn't speed up their trains they would be shot. It is probably quite useless to make any complaint about it, but this sort of abuse is hard to bear!

Received a letter from Kramer [Kurt Kramer was the driver of the Morococha railbus] suggesting that explosives are being robbed from the mines in the Morococha district. He has noticed a number of mining people travelling on Omnibus No. 10 with suspiciously heavy suitcases. Am passing his letter over to D.S.S. for investigation …

… Saw Kramer and Omnibus No. 10 in Morococha. Motor is running well, and petrol consumption has improved. The front pair of bogie wheels has a bent axle; so I will arrange for the vehicle to come in on Sunday morning to have it straightened. Unfortunately, we can't swap over the bogie wheels on account of the brake drums on the trailing pair. The new rear brakeshoes ordered last month haven't come and are urgently needed, as the brake is no longer reliable.

I asked Kramer to tell me the name of one of the people he suspected of carrying dynamite, but he wouldn't say. Made a check-up on Driver V – – for illicit packages, but found nothing. Eng. 46 reeked of fish, but I searched tender, tank, etc., without finding it …

… On arrival of Eng. 46 with Train No. 1 today I watched V – – from the corner of the pump house, and after the engine was in the shed three people collected parcels from the cab. The first was a small girl, who went off with a huge package. The second was Yard Brakeman Quinones, who took a medium-sized parcel; and the third was M – –'s nephew, who collected a small one, and – spotting me – tried to hide it under his coat. This lad also had his small grip with him …

… Saw V – – about the parcels collected from his engine yesterday, and he admits to those taken by the child and Quinones, but says they contained only bread. In the brakeman's case, I was able to ascertain that this was so. But V – – strongly denied that M – –'s nephew had received anything other than bread too. I caught a glimpse of the contents of the latter's grip this morning and saw what looked like pamphlets or tracts …

I interpolate once more: this cloak-and-dagger stuff was no mere fiddling. Driver V – – , one of our best passenger engineers, was subsequently caught on two occasions carrying stolen dynamite on his engine; was suspended a month the first time, and the second time, besides a suspension, lost the top passenger run for over a year! In the case cited above, what I was scared of was political dynamite rather than the kind used in mining (and fishing). The last thing we wanted was to have the Railway mixed up in civil disturbances.

Enginemen were never denied the privilege of carrying private stuff for their families or friends, and as long as they were open and frank about it our tolerance was wide. But not fish – fish in the strainer 'basket' of the tender contaminated the feed water with brine and caused priming.

… On account of exceptionally heavy slipping, Eng. 110 ran out of oil and failed this morning on the trip from Huancayo to Oroya. Eng. 105, with the cattle train, brought both trains up from Huari [over 1½ per cent maximum grade], a total of 1,050 tons. As far as I know, this is a record-and damned bad for the engine! I cannot see that anyone is to blame for the failure, or for the resulting delays in getting the southbound trains out of Oroya. On arrival, Eng. 110 had to be serviced and lit up, and left approximately two hours late. [Southbound freights were held awaiting the freight and cattle from Huancayo, which had to be rushed through without holdovers in transit] …

… Inspected Sentinel No. 1 in Huancayo this morning and went with her to Jauja on Train 142. Returned on No. 143, leaving 5.54 p.m. and arriving Huancayo at 7 p.m. She steamed heavily as far as Huamali, where she picked up and was doing well when the pump check valve stuck and the handle of the stop valve blew off, letting the boiler water escape below the gauge level. Lodwig and I got it shut in

98. *The Oroya yard engine and yard crew in 1927. The bull-voiced yardmaster is fourth from the left. His brakemen, on the running board of the diminutive North British 2-8-0, and beside the motion plate, carry the hooked iron brake clubs that were their badge of office.*   *(Author)*

99. *The Alco Mikados of 1923 were good engines, able to take tremendous punishment. Boilers however were rather long for conditions on the Central.*   *(Author)*

time, and with both injectors on and the fire out managed to raise the water level enough to light up again. This caused a delay of 20 mins. The black oil used on this trip had water in it – probably the reason for the poor steaming ...

... The GM [General Manager] wishes a test to be made to Morococha tomorrow with Eng. 83, so I have arranged with D.S.S. to do it. Eng. 114 hit a fallen rock between Casapalca and Ticlio and broke the L.H. front cylinder cover, bent the front steps, the crosshead link, anchor link, union link, eccentric rod and eccentric on that side. Engine cannot work till these are straightened and cyl. cover changed.

Called up J.T.T. to ask when C de P car No. 80, stuck in Saltacuna with a broken archbar, would be brought in. The dispatcher promised to bring her over today; but to make sure I passed a memo. in to D.S.S. on the subject, stating that the same promise was made twice last week. Saw Howard of the C de P about returning our archbar which the Casapalca truckman fitted temporarily, and he assured me it would be handed back as soon as the car arrived ...

... Made the test run with Eng. 83 to Morococha. Filled up the tank and boiler at Chaplanca and left Cut-Off at 11.57 a.m. At the start of the grade it became obvious that time could not be made with both coaches 20 and 15, so coach 15 was left in the safety-switch spur. From there on better time was made; though 83 could not quite hold her steam with the injector on. I did the firing myself and kept a full glass of water while the steam didn't drop below 160 pounds. At Kilometre 10 there were about ten inches of water in the tank [she was a little side-tank engine], and we carried on without taking more. At Kilom. 1 the L.H. injector blew dry, and at the entrance of Morococha station the R.H. one blew dry also. Time from Cut-Off with one coach [15 tons] was 1hr. 3 mins. Both truck boxes on L.H. side ran hot. They are on packing at the moment, but will have to go back to grease. The test shows that two coaches cannot be hauled without taking water at Kilom. 10. I am checking the engine to find reason for poor steaming; although everything appeared to be in order ...

... A slide came down in Kilom. 235 trapping Eng. 58 with coaches on the other side. I rushed out Eng. 92 for a work extra at 5 a.m., lighting her up from cold – she was washed out yesterday – and having 50 pounds of steam to move her within 40 mins. flat. Engs. 58 and 59 got through to Oroya. As soon as she was serviced, Eng. 59 was rushed back again as a slide threatened in Kilom. 249, and I sent Boilermaker Assinas with her to finish the necessary work in Huancayo tonight.

Eng. 71 collided with C de P car 1100 on No. 1 shop track at Morococha plant. The bumper beam of the tender was badly bent, the frame was bent, the rear truck was damaged, and the floor plate underneath the tank was knocked away at the corner. We can't handle the repairs in Oroya. Called up Chief of Traction and told him about it, and he promised to do what he could to get another tender up to us. I also told him about Eng. 110 and my suspicion that there is a fracture starting in the driving axle, asking if I might keep 103 here for a few more days. He replied that I would have to; because the shops could take in no more engines at present.

Eng. 112 opened up a crack in the firebox at Tunnel 34 and the blow from it put the fire out, killing the engine. She was towed to Chosica. This leaves us only two freight engines for southbound service tomorrow, and I wired J.T.T. advising him, with copy to CME.

A slide came down in Kilom. 3 of the Cut-Off-Morococha branch, and Omnibus No. 10 had to return to Morococha by way of Galera. Kramer had insufficient gasoline, but I told him to borrow some from the C de P at Mahr Tunnel ...

... Train No. 2 hit a big rock beside the track between Pachacayo and Oroya. The L.H. south steps of coach 43 were smashed, and the pilot, bumper beam and cylinder cover guard-ring on L.H. side of Eng. 59 were bent, while the front cylinder cock on same side was snapped off. Lacking time to do a proper repair job, I am having the pilot temporarily secured. The clearance remains as it should be. Train No. 2 was delayed in Oroya while we repaired the coach steps, fitting plain boards. I sent the two broken steps down to Lima with the coach ...

Notice was given that on account of a slide in Kilom. 85, which will take a day and a half to clear up, all southbound extras at 8 a.m. tomorrow are cancelled. Eng. 110 was ordered out with four flatcars to work at the slide. Chosica's Eng. 104 is making the transhipment of passengers, and Driver Barraza wired asking for supplies, as all he had are finished. Eng. 58 ordered out also, to change with Eng. 104 on the road and return to Oroya; so I sent the supplies with her ...

... Went to Galera on Extra 60 South. Returned on Extra 105 North. We left Oroya with 209 tons in 10 cars and ran slowly in consequence; while Eng. 105, following closely behind us, had only 150 in 4 cars, and therefore had to run dead slow and stop in order to keep her distance. This was a needless waste of time, and it put unnecessary strains on the tube sheet of 105. It would have been perfectly easy to give 105 the heavier train, and I am reporting the matter to D.S.S. so that he can take it up with the Yardmaster.

On the way back, we had a meet with Train No. 2, Eng. 52, in Rumichaca South, and though fairly well up to time she was smoking very badly. I had no chance to talk to Driver V – – about it, but the Shed Foreman told me that the engine's tubes were not leaking when she arrived in Oroya from Huancayo.

D.E. complained that the engine of Train No. 1 dropped oil on the track between Kiloms. 146.200 and 147.300 on the 18th inst. That day Eng. 57 was on the train, so it is Guadalupe's pigeon ...

... Went to Morococha on No. 122, Eng. 85. She steamed poorly from Oroya to Cut-Off, made too much smoke, and couldn't hold her water level. After leaving Cut-Off we fiddled with the damper adjustment till the right one was discovered; smoke disappeared, steam rose to 180 pounds, and both injectors could be used. The front damper and the firedoor flap must be kept closed. The engine was run with reverse lever one notch from centre and throttle full open. On the return run, Driver C – – , unfamiliar with the automatic brake, had some trouble in holding the train, and handbrakes had to be used. But I gave him full instructions, and he knows more about it now.

Driver L – – in Morococha complained that traffic was giving him excessive tonnage, and that today he had to pull 120 tons. The correct tonnage rating for the five per cent grades of the branch has been accepted as 112 for the 60-class, and I shall speak D.S.S. about it ...

... Had a telegram last night from Driver C – – asking for another engine to be sent down to Huari to help him, as he hadn't sufficient fuel oil to get to Oroya. This was due to traffic delays and a train of 720 tons, plus the fact that Eng. 110 has a small fuel tank. C – – says that the slipping on Saturday last was not due to oil on the track.

Went to Casapalca with Trackcar No. 9 [a 4-cyl. Chevrolet open touring model automobile of 1930 vintage, fitted with steel tyres for rail use]. While in Casapalca, D.E. and I examined the spot where car 1179 derailed. The wheel mounted gently on the straight just after leaving a guardrail, ran for about four feet with the flange on the top of the rail, and then fell outside the track. My idea now is that this car, having the weight of other cars pushing back against it while the engine behind pushed it forwards, tended to slew, and a sudden jolt caused the flange to mount. The explanation is scarcely satisfactory; but the only alternative that occurs to me is that the wheel was forced out of position by a displaced brass, and that is even more unsatisfactory. Truckman Jauregui says that no brass was out of position when he examined the car; but it could conceivably have jumped back in place.

Examined the oil on the track between Casapalca and Ticlio. There is black oil on the insides of the rails, obviously from excessive flange lubrication, and beyond that one can see gobs of No. 2 engine oil on the rail tops flicked off boxes and rods, a result of over-oiling. Enginemen drown their running gear with oil and then complain to me continually that the regulation allowance of lubricants is insufficient! ...

... The D.E. advised me that oil spilt on the track last week between Huancayo and Pachacayo was from Eng. 62. When I inspected this engine on Monday there was no sign of any oil having leaked between engine and tender; and, moreover, Driver Isusqui emphatically denies it. The D.E. also said he had a report from his gang foreman that on the 28th inst., in Kilom. 182, 25 ties were damaged by a fallen brake rod on Eng. 112. Nothing whatsoever was wrong with the brake rigging of this engine on that date, and the damage must have been done by a car. He also complained that on the 27th, Eng. 110 burned five rails in Kilom. 256, in the same spot where Eng. 58 previously burned the rails through excessive slipping ...

The two principal unions on the railway – the Confederation (shops and roundhouse men) and the Federation (engine and train men) – were at that time just beginning to feel their oats. The Federation was represented in Oroya by Driver L – – , bad boy of my section, the same who shot-blasted A. T. Howard's car on the Huaymanta grade crossing, and who later was involved in the adventure of the Llocllapampa goat. There follow now a few extracts that tell of but one of the many engagements between us during a campaign that lasted from 1927 to 1935, when I finally left Oroya.

... Eng. 76 was delayed 2 hrs. 20 mins. this morning for lack of a driver. I – – was on the board to take her out, but refused to have the work train [less money was involved]. L – – also refused. M – – refused too, but eventually went. When I had him on the carpet L – – took a defiant attitude, but I suspended him for four days. Gave I – – two days, in consideration of his better record. The Chief of Traction okayed this. I tried to get hold of O – – to replace M – – in the yard, but he couldn't be found. The GM came up today. He asked what had been decided about the fusing of the lead plug on Eng. 112 and I told him that low water was the cause [these plugs might blow if left in too long; so I was not stating the obvious]. He then asked why Driver F – – was still working and told me to call up the CME and ask what action was being taken. I did so, and CME replied that F – – and his fireman were to be laid off for two days as from tomorrow ...

... L – – got his suspension forms and immediately started to make trouble. As usual, he was insolent and overbearing, and threatened to 'make things awkward' for me. He said that four drivers would go down to the Coast tomorrow to lodge a complaint against me and that I was to give them a pass. I laughed at him, pointing out that if four drivers left the job it would mean that trains would have to be cancelled and traffic would be held up. It would be the same as a strike, I said, and he might find himself in jail. His reply was that my action was such that he could and would declare a complete stoppage if necessary, without the regulation notice. I invited him to go ahead and do it; because I was not on any account going to issue a pass for the four drivers. He then demanded one for himself, which I refused. After talking at some length with the Assistant *Comisario* [who happened to be visiting Oroya] he signed the discipline forms and took his copy.

I explained the whole case to the GM. He said that a strong hand should be taken with L – – and that if matters were as I stated he had no claim at all. He told me to let the suspension stand, but to allow L – – to go down and lodge his complaint to the CME, at the same time sending down my own report covering the case...

... Yesterday afternoon the Federation came to make their claim about L – – 's suspension [this was a visiting delegation from headquarters]. They asked if it was an order that he must go down to Guadalupe to see the CME; because they didn't wish him to go, since the matter could quite easily be fixed up in Oroya. I told them what the Manager had said. L – – is now trying to make out that he was ill, but he won't get away with it as far as I am concerned. I questioned the callboy again, and he is quite definite in his allegation that L – – did not refuse to go out because he was sick, but because he said he was not going to work on that train. I gave the Federation my reasons for laying L – – off, and they were satisfied. Hitherto, they had heard only his side of the story. I saw L – – this morning, and he pulled the 'sickness' excuse strongly. He is back at work now, and is 'on call' today.

The Federation also spoke on behalf of Fireman C – – , who complains that when working on the way freight between Oroya and Huancayo, his driver, S – – , makes him take a bucket and go off up to the villages to collect horse manure while the train is stopped at a way station loading and unloading cars. C – – 's objection is that it offends his dignity to do this in full view of the villagers, and that small boys follow him making insulting remarks.

I pointed out that I personally would much rather be spared the vast accumulations of manure that are washed out of boilers in the shed, but that it is the drivers themselves who insist on putting it in, and that the manner in which it is collected is their own business.[1] I added, however, that the driver does right to stay on the engine and send his fireman, seeing that there is always moving of the train to be done to position cars at the freight room ramp. I gather that it is Huamall that yields the richest hauls of manure. What C – – wants is for a brakeman to be sent out to collect it ...

100. *This North British 2-6-2T of 1907 once worked local trains between Lima and Callao. It must have been quite a shock to be transferred to Oroya, 12,225ft higher, to work a one-coach train as a replacement for Sentinel car No. 1, during repairs to the latter.* (Author)

101. *Engine sandboxes were not large enough to hold all the sand required, and at one time, sandcars such as this one were pushed on the nose of the first early-morning freight out of Oroya for Galera, to sand the frosted rails for the benefit of following trains.*

(Author)

Fortunately, L – – was the only persistent troublemaker in my department. Routine was far less hampered then by labour disputes and restrictive practices than was the case ten years later. Mechanical officers were concerned with the machinery of transportation; in a subsequent era they were obliged to concern themselves more with the machinery of conciliation!

When not spiked in Oroya by the Shed Foreman's absence, which meant working nights as well as days, much of my time was spent out on the line.

... Went to Morococha and made a careful inspection of Omnibus No. 10, to discover the reason for the frequent hub breakages. Both back wheels have about $1/8$-in. lateral wobble, and the R.H. one is also $1/8$-in. eccentric. This is undoubtedly the cause, and we can remedy the trouble by turning off the tyre until true. The omnibus is making good time and running well; though No. 6 big-end is beginning to knock. Found that freight was being carried inside instead of on the roof, and this is damaging the seats. Told Conductor Puente he must stop doing this.

The water in Morococha is clean and is not treated, the filterman stating that D.E. told him to omit treatment. The mixer is in working order. The turntable is very easy and in good condition. The shed roof is in lamentable state and must be repaired before the wet season begins. Sand supply is good.

Found boxcar 1072 with very sharp flanges. A check-up of cars in the yard showed that axleboxes are not being packed properly. I made Truckman Landeo pack a box correctly in front of me and warned him that he must be more careful in future, as half the hot boxes in this section are caused by waste grab. His stores are okay. Some cars had stones wedged against brake yokes to centre shoes on the wheel treads. Must report this to Traffic. as the practice is dangerous.

... Went to Galera on Eng. 75 to check state of water at various tanks. Chaplanca water is not being treated, is fairly clean, and mixer is okay. Yauli has one deposit tank only, no mixer, and water is fair. Went on to Casapalca on Eng. 103. At Ticlio, water is being treated and is clean. Mixer there is working. At Casapalca there is no treatment and water is dirty.

Eng. 75 has the linseed filter condemned, apparently by Guadalupe [this apparatus was a scale inhibitor]. She is steaming fairly well and running gear is good. Found Eng. 105 with flange lubricators and rail washers all out of position, and cab window panes missing. I noted from Eng. 75 that the 105 was running wet, and on examination in Casapalca found that three large flues, a number of roof stays and the crack in the tube-sheet flange recently welded were all blowing badly. Nevertheless, the engine was doing her full duty. Driver Isusqui, on Eng. 102, reports that tonnage from Oroya to Galera was 156, or a slight overload.

Had Eng. 74 in yard service today to loosen up. Chief of Traction wrote asking why this engine had been sent to Morococha yesterday, so soon after being shopped. Speaking to him today over the selective [telephone] I explained that Guadalupe neglected to tell me what repairs had been done on her, and for that reason I had no idea it would be dangerous to send her up there. Told him that the derailment of one pair of wheels was caused principally by the poor state of the track, which should be repaired without delay by the C de P.

Eng. 49 burst a superheater tube shortly after leaving Huancayo with Train No. 2. Eng. 74 was sent down to help bring the train in No. 2 arrived 1 hr. 14 mins. late with Eng. 74, and Eng. 49 arrived light at 11.30 a.m. I find that superheater tube stocks in the Sub-Store are low, and there is only one 50-class 'B' element here. Asked Chief of Traction to send up some more and he promised to let us have three each of 'A' and 'C' elements, and two more 'B's'. Started work on 49 at 1 p.m...

Fitters removed steam pipes and superheater elements during the night, and we found the trouble to have been the small element on the L.H. side, one end of which had blown out of the header [these engines used Robinson type superheaters, with elements expanded in] ...

Eng. 59 left on No. 2 today looking exceedingly smart both above and below the running boards. It is a good thing for the public to see passenger engines thus, and many stopped to look at her ...

... This morning, Eng. 110, on first southbound extra, spread oil on the track between Yauli and Rumichaca. The three following freights were all considerably delayed through slipping, and Eng. 70 opened up the cracks in her tube sheet, which blew so badly that she was forced to give up her train in

Galera and return to Oroya. At J.T.T.'s urgent request I sent out Eng. 61, in yard service, to relieve her, but warned him that the boiler of this. engine is bad, and she can handle only a reduced tonnage ....

... Guadalupe called up to ask why Eng. 110 dropped oil on the track yesterday. I explained that it was due to a loose union on the oil line close to the heater under the firepan, and that this was definitely not leaking the day before yesterday. I also said that several drivers had reported a tank car leaking. The Chief of Traction told me to have a look at the tank car with light oil for Huancayo shed when it came through, as he had noticed that it was wet with oil in several places.

The D.E. reported that Eng. 58 had dropped oil on the track between Kiloms. 227 and 228.500. I saw the piping, which was clean enough; but it looks as though oil has leaked from the firepan, probably from dribbling accumulations when lighting up.

Eng. 112 broke her throttle rod today in Yauli [and not for the first time!]. Driver Lopez told me the break was at the lever itself, so I instructed him how to move the engine. J.T.T. asked for another engine, but this I couldn't give him. However, I told him that Eng. 58 could go out to bring in No. 112. He arranged for her to do this.. .

The trouble with the throttle of Eng. 112 turned out to be the breakage of the stud anchoring the fulcrum of the lever to the boiler. As we were unable to get the bit of broken stud out at once, the engine had to stop in Oroya instead of going back into service, while we drilled it out with a ratchet drill.

Eng. 110 broke her frame immediately behind the R.H. cylinder. On her arrival in Oroya I examined the fracture and wired the Chief of Traction asking him to order her down to Chosica for welding. Also wired J.T.T. advising that a train would have to be cancelled on Monday owing to shortage of power. The reason for the frame breakage was the failure of three of the studs of the supporting bracket at this point. All three stud fractures are fresh.

Received a letter from the CME advising me that K – – would take over from me on June 17, and that I was to transfer to Guadalupe. This officially confirms what the Chief of Traction told me last week ...

Such was the prosaic, everyday background to the glamour of crashing exhausts on the four-per-cent, tonnage snaking upwards through cuts and over fills, crazy mountain ledges, zigzags and man-killer tunnels, and a summit higher than Mont Blanc. Work logs can't be expected to tell of the scene in Oroya yard in the small hours of a wet morning, with the engines for the early freights to the south lined up on the house track with sizzling pops and dynamos wailing their sing-song chorus – of the brakemen's bobbing lanterns here and there like will-o'-thewisps in the heavy darkness – of the ponderous, roaring hiss of a locomotive, still only half awake, clump-clumping out on the table with open cylinder cocks – of the streaking rain seen against the dim glow from cabs where firemen are busy filling oil cans and trimming torch wicks – or of the tang of half-burnt fuel oil and the unforgettable aroma of living steam engines filling the thin atmosphere. Nor can they be expected to tell of the heart-searching cry of a chime whistle echoing and re-echoing back and forth between the high rocky walls of the gorge holding Oroya in its hollow – of the first thunderous blast of the first train out as the engine takes up the slack, feels the pull of what seems like an overload, and struggles with faltering grip to move up the main and out of town – of the impatient double toots from a hoghead convinced that brakes are dragging back there on some empty hopper car – of the sudden roaring volley shaking every neighbouring window as drivers let go on the wet rails and spin wildly.

They make no mention of the warm, fragrant afternoons on the deck of a freight engine lazing down the Huancayo Valley; or the thrilling rush down the long tangent through the eucalyptus woods into Huancayo of an evening, with the mellow whistle announcing the train's arrival at railhead. Yet the idyllic moments were part and parcel of the working pattern. There was no monotony – there could be none. Every day demanded a fresh approach. So it was then and so it is now. Power may change, schedules may be speeded up and CTC may oust the old train orders and tablets, but the game continues to be played in the same old way; because that way is taught by the mountains themselves.

In my day we looked back aghast at the crawling schedules and horrifying accidents of the *Mogul* era. Today, with the *Andes* type engines supreme in Oroya, on both Central and C de P railways, our successors doubtless look back on the days of the old 60-class, the 100s and 110s with much of the same horror, wondering how the dickens we ever got tonnage over the road with them, or dared bring it down those grades with handbrakes alone – wondering also, perhaps, how with the troubles we experienced, there were ever enough engines available to provide an adequate service.

But all those everyday experiences of leaking flues, hammering brasses, hot boxes, dripping fuel oil, broken frames and disconnected throttles added up over the years to one of the most thoroughly successful locomotive types ever built. The *Andes* type, coming as the climax of steam operation, was the product of our aggregate experience – and it beat the Andes!

[1] *Horse manure fed into the boiler through the injectors was considered a sovereign remedy for leaking tubes. But for this useful commodity some of the crocks in my section would never have got over the road!*

102. The robust running gear of an Alco Mikado is typical of Andean steam, where locomotives operated for much of their time at full throttle and long valve travel.

(Author)

Chapter 13

SLIM GAUGE RANK AND FILE

Arica-La Paz Railway

IT has already been mentioned that the shortest rail route from La Paz to an ocean port is the 285-mile Arica-La Paz Railway. It is more or less a straight line; whereas both its competitors – the FCAB and the Peruvian Corporation systems – angle off diagonally from La Paz to Antofagasta and Matarani respectively. The Arica route being 236 miles shorter than the Matarani one, which in turn is 200 miles shorter than the Antofagasta line, *should* take the cream of the Bolivian export and import traffic. That it doesn't can partly be blamed on the higher port tariffs in Arica. But were that obstacle adjusted satisfactorily, the Arica-La Paz (FCALP) would still have to 'tool up' considerably before it could compete in the way of volume of traffic with its two big, foreign-operated rivals.

The construction work was commenced in 1906 in a small way, but not until 1909 did it really get going in earnest, and that was when Sir John Jackson, the British contractor, took it over. At the Bolivian end, construction material was brought in over Peruvian rails and Lake Titicaca. The total cost of the line is estimated as having amounted to £4,063,561, including basic rolling stock and 75 1/2 miles of water pipeline down the Vale of Lluta.

The whole line was originally administered by Chile, but in 1928 a protocol was signed between the two republics for the turning over of the Bolivian section to Bolivian management, an agreement consummated in May of that year. International traffic revenue was split on a 40/60 basis, the larger portion going to the Chilean administration.

The Chilean section comprises 155 route miles, of which almost 26 are rack. The Bolivian section is entirely adhesion, 130 miles in length. Its construction came about through the Treaty of Peace, Amity and Commerce signed by the respective Governments in 1904. The year 1913 saw the line opened to traffic – traffic, be it noted, that failed to materialize in quantities that might have justified the expenditure required to make the railroad a business proposition. It started out as a prestige undertaking, and that is what it has remained.

A normal monthly freight movement of 7,000 tons is hardly impressive, and this has declined with the growth of Southern of Peru traffic passing through the new port of Matarani. Port for port, Antofagasta has the drop on Arica by virtue of its notably lower tariffs, but Arica has hopes that with completion of the new mechanization of its port there will be a marked increase in its share of the international traffic. Given equal port facilities, the FCALP could become a serious competitor to the two giants now virtually taking the lot.

The Chilean section possesses the actual summit of the line, 13,963 feet at General Lagos. From the station of Central, 43 1/2 miles from Arica and 4,852 feet above sea level, to Puquios, milepost 70, at 12,220 feet, is a rack section on the Abt system, but with two racks in preference to the three used on the Chilean Transandine. If you recall, the two-rack system was pointed out in Chapter 5 as being the stronger. The grade here is 6 per cent, while kept to a maximum of 3 per cent on the rest of the line, as on the Transandine.

The Esslingen rack-adhesion steam locomotive came here in a form rather different to those of the Chilean Transandine. The FCALP job possessed a ten-coupled rigid engine at the cab end, and a two drive-pinion rack engine mounted on a four-wheeled truck under the smokebox, the locomotive in working order weighing 92 tons. Another type of engine for the same service was outshopped by Baldwin. This, like the Esslingen, was a tank, but the wheel arrangement was a conventional 2 8 2, with the rack drive in the centre of the locomotive, beneath the boiler, between the second and third driving axles. Adhesion cylinders were 19 x 20in; rack cylinders, 18 x 18in; drivers 37 in. diameter; boiler pressure 200 pounds. The weight in working order was 75 metric tons.

103. *Arica (FCALP) station, with railcar No. 337 forming the thrice-weekly express service to La Paz.*

(Richard Pelham)

MASCHINENFABRIK ESSLINGEN

Locomotiva de Fricção e de Engrenagens, Sistema Combinado para o Caminho de Ferro de Arica-La Paz. Pêso em Serviço, 92 Toneladas.

1926 Esslingen advertisement featuring their extraordinary 4-10-0 rack-adhesion tank.

104. *Pampa Ossa, the mid point of the one-time rack section.*   (Richard Pelham)

105. *FCALP Borsig 2-8-0 No. 107 shunts boxcars at El Alto, on the heights above La Paz, in February 1955. The snow-covered peak of Mount Illimani (21,000ft) can be glimpsed in the background.*   (David Ibbotson)

A smaller Baldwin 2-8-2 rack-adhesion locomotive – similar to the other type but with shorter tanks, and boiler canted to 'level up' on the six-per-cent – carried the rack drive between the first and second adhesion driving axles. Both types had outside bar frames. Baldwin also provided a Mallet articulated compound for adhesion only.

Today, the rack section is worked by three steamers, with two two more in reserve. Six 660 h.p. General Electric diesel-electrics operate on the adhesion sections, with a couple of more recent 1,200 h.p. additions to the stud. These are C C hoods, the smaller ones tipping the scales at 64 tons, with a 10.7-ton axle loading, and geared for a maximum speed of 50 m.p.h.

The 'growlers' have given a good account of themselves mechanically as well as economically. Diesel traction dates from 1953; and at the same time that mainliners went into operation, yard switching was undertaken with 41-ton G.E., 150-h.p., B-B units. Diesel-mechanical railcars supply a special-fare fast passenger service to and from La Paz, with buffet luncheon and 'elevenses' included. Besides these, there are international passenger trains taking considerably longer for the same journey, but at less than half the railcar fare. The annual figure for passengers transported is in the order of 40,000.

My impression of the passenger rolling stock on the FCALP when I saw it just before World War II was that it compared with that of the FCAB in appointments as well as size – not by any means inferior to anything that we in Peru could show. As on all Andean roads, only bogie stock is to be found. Air brakes and MCB couplers are used on the 400 freight cars, as well as on coaches. Trains are operated on the old-type block system.

The Bolivian section possesses some new 2-8-2 tender engines that even on standard gauge would be quite large. German locomotive builders have done well on this system-in fact, both Chile and Bolivia have purchased considerable numbers from Germany. Though perhaps not so dynamic as that of the U.S.A., German sales organization in South America is better than the British, particularly on the score of extended credits and delivery.

Running twice a week in summer, in both directions, and once a week in winter, the de luxe diesel-mechanical railcars leave Arica at 8 and arrive in La Paz at 18.10 – just over ten hours for the journey. From La Paz, timing is the same; but departure from the Bolivian capital is at 9. Passenger trains leave Arica on Mondays at 21 hrs. and arrive in La Paz at 22.40 hrs. on Tuesdays – 25 hrs. 40 mins. of travel. From La Paz, they leave at 10 hrs. on Fridays, arriving Arica at 7.10 on Saturdays. The railcar fare is approximately £7 10s. 0d. First class freight moves at a cost of some £7 3s. 0d. per ton.

Just outside Arica the line passes Chinchorro, where the engine terminal and shops are located. It then runs through the well-cultivated Vale of Lluta on an easy grade, past the stations of Rosario and Poconchile to arrive at Central, foot of the mountains proper, where the 6 per cent rack section begins. From here trains are hoisted to Puquios in a matter of 26½ miles, with three intervening stations – Quebrada Honda, Pampa Ossa and Angostura.

Once again on easy adhesion grades, the line takes off over the *puna*, enlivened by views of distant snow-covered summits, to General Lagos, 45 miles away and 115 miles from the coast. The station is at the foot of the volcano Tacora, where there is a flourishing sulphur business, a snow-covered cone very like Arequipa's Misti in appearance. The line then drops gently for 13 miles to the frontier station of Visviri. Between here and Charana, a mile and a half farther on, it passes from Chilean territory into Bolivian.

The slightly falling grade persists for 64 miles, to the point where the railway crosses the River Desaguadero, whose waters flow from Lake Titicaca. General Pando, just beyond the river, is slightly higher than the previous station, Calacoto. At this point a four-mile branch built in 1914 peels off to the copper mining centre of Corocoro.

Undulating but slightly, the line proceeds for another 48 miles, through General Ballivian, Comanche and Coniri to Viacha, that junction where Antofagasta and Guaqui tracks join on the heights above La Paz. At the Alto, 14½ miles from Viacha, FCALP trackage finishes, and the drop down the mountain into La Paz is made over FCAB metals. Arica management would like to have La Paz consignees collect their freight at the Alto and wheel it into the capital by road, but there is apparently no outstanding eagerness to conform with this arrangement.

106. *Shay locomotive in yard service at La Paz, starting point of the abortive La Paz-Beni railroad.* (J. G. Todd)

Being at the moment on Bolivian State Railways property, mention might be made of a scenically interesting little pike called the La Paz-Beni Railroad, which being unfinished is a long way from reaching the vicinity of the Beni, that immense Amazonian-system river traversing Bolivia's forest region. This too is part of the State-owned network, and since it reaches the considerable altitude of over 15,000 feet in its 42 miles of completed track, its existence could not in all fairness be ignored, even if its traffics are not of much consideration.

The Yungas, or warm highland valleys of eastern La Paz Province, are extraordinarily productive, and it is this region that the railway taps, albeit highways have already opened it up. Railhead is at Chuspipata, from where connection is made with the chief town of North Yungas, Coroico, by means of road vehicles in combined traffic arrangements, linking at the same time Alcoche, 118 miles from La Paz.

Still in service here and there in the Andes where grades are steep, curvature severe and speed of no consequence, one finds a Lima Shay. The La Paz-Beni has one, and it may yet see more years of faithful service before being bumped off the iron by a diesel.

If this little railway is ever completed – and it is not the only partially built slim-gauger in Bolivia – it should prove a glorious line scenically, even if estimates of eventual traffic prove over optimistic.

The Cuzco-Santa Ana Railway

Another similar undertaking to the last is the Cuzco-Santa Ana Railway, well-known to foreign tourists visiting the Incan mountain city of Machupicchu north of Cuzco. Projected in 1905 to open up the rich Vale of Santa Ana, 120 miles distant, this little line began its existence in 1921 and has not yet reached

107. The daily passenger train, hauled by a Henschel loco, crosses a modern railcar used for the tourist traffic to Macchu Pichu, on the Cuzco-Santa Ana line.   *(Gannon)*

its intended destination. Railhead is at present only slightly beyond the bridge over the Vilcanota (which becomes the Urubamba, flowing into the great Ucayali and so to the Amazon) where the old and perilous trail begins its tortuous climb up the sheer side of the mountain to the fascinating ruins of Machupicchu, more than 3,000 feet above the rails. This is 70 miles from Cuzco – little over half way to Santa Ana-but the line so far is scenically stupendous. It is owned and operated by the Peruvian Government.

The railway was originally planned for electrification – rather as a glorified interurban – type line than as a full-scale railroad – but the formidable estimated cost of the venture caused a change of mind. When I last travelled over it there were two Baldwin 2 8 2's of 1927, plus one or two smaller engines of uncertain age. But first class passenger traffic relies more on the Buda railcars, resembling small omnibuses with rail wheels on two rigid axles. They seat only about ten people, and they bounce and jounce their way at headlong speed over a track fit to lift the hair off a railroad man's head!

The professional eye is conditioned to note with some apprehension that many of the ties are contorted as though they had endeavoured to wriggle out from under the rails and escape. It might appear that this has frequently been achieved; for in many places their absence has been made good with slabs of rock. Curves are lengths of straight rail bolted together. If present at all, ballast is meagre. The result is that the roadbed is not one to inspire confidence or engender riding comfort; but the Buda cars cling to it nobly, and the scenery through which the railway runs is of a kind that is likely to distract a passenger's attention from everything else.

From 11,000 feet at Cuzco the line struggles up a thousand feet higher, through two double zig-zags. Near the top, the view of the Cuzco valley is wonderful. Beneath is the city, dominated by the ancient fortress of Sacsahuaman; and behind are the dark crags of the mountain walls interspersed with extensive snowfields. Topping the intervemng mountain range and beginning its easy descent beyond the summit, the track then falls from the treeless region of the *puna*, in a setting of more snowfields and jagged peaks, down to lush water-meadows where cattle wander in large herds. Beyond these it enters the mountain valleys, so closed in and precipitous that rails lie in thick blue twilight, while the mountain sides high above are bathed in brilliant sunshine.

Trains pass within sight of the majestic Incan megalithic ruins of Ollantaytambo at the foot of the steep mountain wall, all the while following the course of the smooth, swift Vilcanota River. A nine-mile branch comes in on the right from the town of Urubamba. When the abundant broom is in flower, filling the air with its heady perfume, the valley is a glory of brilliant yellow. Farther on, beyond Torontoy, broom gives way to pawpaws and tree ferns as the tropical heat of the eastern forests reaches into the Andean foothills. It is the only Peruvian rail route I know where a passenger can look upwards through sub-tropical foliage and see in a single glance the several marked belts of mountain vegetation to the very limit of its range, where it peters out in the perpetual snow of the extreme altitudes. The grandeur of the scenery on this line baffles description. It must be seen to be believed. It may well be unique!

The Cuzco-Santa Ana main iron ceases at some 6,700 feet above the sea. If it never reaches Santa Ana, it does at all events bring the tourist to the vicinity of one of America's most wonderful archaeological treaures. Formerly, the visitor to Machupicchu had no choice but muleback for the punishing climb from CSA track to the ruins; now there is a motor road to the top of that awful trail.

Huancayo-Huancavelica Railway

Between Cuzco and Huancayo, termini of the Southern and Central Railways respectively, is a highland region of great mineral and agricultural potential, of teeming Indian community life, and a pronounced scenic beauty. A 578-mile highway (of sorts) threads through the heart of it, linking the southern city with the central town, and uniting the important centres of Abancay and Ayacucho *en route*. There was at one time a scheme to construct a railroad to link the two standard-gauge systems.[1] A metre-gauge railway was authorized by the Peruvian Government in 1907. The survey for the line was entrusted to Charles Weber, who prepared a trace of it between Huancayo and Ayacucho, entailing a route mileage of 165. By the following year nine miles had been graded ready for track laying.

Construction was still in progress in 1924, when I joined the Central; in fact, by 1926 only twenty-two miles were laid. Huancavelica was now the objective, a mercury mining centre once the source of all the quicksilver required for the production of silver in the great Cerro de Pasco workings and the many others throughout the Peruvian *Cordilleras*. When rails actually reached Huancavelica, two Baldwin *Mikados* arrived from Philadelphia to take over from the tiny engines used during construction and to inaugurate the services. These Mikes constituted only a small order in the books of a builder at the time engaged in turning out giant power for the Rio Grande and the Santa Fe', to say nothing of deliveries to all parts of the world; yet they sent an engineer from the works to see them assembled and stay with them until full satisfaction in service had been established. Routine attention of this sort was more than any British builder offered, and it was a powerful booster of sales.

The Huancavelica line's first principal driver was Don Juan Benavides, brother to Don Enrique Benavides who was running the Central's Oroya-Huancayo passenger engine. The two brothers often met on their respective engines in the Central's Huancayo yard, part of which was third-railed for Huancavelica freight transhipment. Don Juan's little Mike was about half the size of the Central *Mikado* presided over by Don Enrique, but; its whistle was every bit as loud and its bell just as pontifical!

Shortly before leaving Peru some eighteen years later I happened to be visiting the Cuzco-Santa Ana Railway and noted two familiar engines in the Cuzco roundhouse. The Administrator informed me that they were the two Baldwins from the F.C.H.H., where a newer German-built locomotive had made them redundant, and an *International* railcar was handling part of the scanty first class passenger movement. On both lines train brakes were vacuum, clearances and axle loadings identical.

The F.C.H.H. runs down the valley from Huancayo to its head, following the R. Mantaro through the eucalyptus woods, and over the *pampa* or plain, where cereals, potatoes and flax are produced. Entering a gorge cleaving the mountain barrier, it climbs for twelve miles to emerge at a summit, from which it runs south-easterly down another gorge on the other side, over easy grades, to Mariscal Caceres (or La Mejorada, as it is sometimes called), passing Manuel Telleria and Izcuchaca on the way, the latter an old Spanish Colonial village astride the Mantaro in the narrow confines of a valley that leaves little space for river, railroad and highway. Here, 47 miles from Huancayo, these three part company, the line heading

108. One of the original three Baldwin 2-8-0's supplied for the FC Huancayo-Huancavelica is pictured at Huancayo in 1956.

(David Ibbotson)

109. Baldwin 2-8-0 No. 103 of 1920 stands at Telleria with a mixed consist. Local Indians take advantage of the free hot water supply.

(D. Trevor Rowe)

110. Hunslet 2-8-0 No. 107, supplied in 1936, awaits a meet at Mariscal Caceres, on the Huancayo-Hancavelica line.

(Richard Pelham)

up into the mountains southwards through another *quebrada*, while the road goes on to Ayacucho and Cuzco. Thus it rises from 8,000 feet at Mariscal Caceres to over 12,000 at Huancavelica, in a distance of 47 miles, passing Acoria on the way.

Manuel Telleria – under the mountains walling in the valley – was at one time remarkable for possessing a station agent of 94. This, while unusual, was not the whole tale. When *cholos* of the mountains have passed the critical age of 50 or so years, they become desiccated in the dry atmosphere and cease to age. The vast majority die early – to our way of thinking – but the minority who survive may go on to the century mark, and past it, with vigour little impaired. The ancient stationmaster in question was such a one. In spite of his venerable age, he took unto himself as wife a damsel of 18, and soon had by her a fine son. It was his, too. That old man was a terror, and any would-be ravishers kept their distance out of respect for his performance with a gun! He was a good telegraph operator, and ruled his station with an iron discipline (the 'staff' consisting entirely of his own huge family by previous wives).

Though after leaving Huancayo trees are relatively few, the valleys are green and the scenery traversed by the line distinctly beautiful. One can say that the hills resemble the Cumbrian fells, that the section from Mariscal Caceres to Huancavelica is reminiscent of Dartmoor in many places, but it is impossible to convey an idea of the prevailing atmosphere. Andean rails penetrate sparsely populated regions that give the European a feeling of 'remoteness'. It is in this that their extraordinary fascination lies. Mining districts are quite unlike what in England is implied by that term, but are, much in line with their counterparts in the Western U.S.A. and Canada. Towns and villages are completely free of dismal grey and grime, and the more ancient they are, the more picturesque they become. Huancavelica itself appears more ancient than it is, doubtless because rainfall there is abnormally heavy. A railroad seems an anachronism amid those colourful weedcovered buildings of the golden age of Spanish mining in the New World.

Railhead is at Lachoc, some ten miles southwest of Huancavelica. This whole region is pregnant with mining possibilities, as yet scarcely more than scratched. Geoffrey W. Morkill, General Manager of the Central from 1935 to 1951, once said to me:

'The Huancayo-Huancavelica goes where our tracks should be. There would be a great future for the Central if the Peruvian Corporation could hand over to the Government the useless Northern Railways[2] in exchange for the F.C.H.H. We could then convert it to standard gauge and build it on to Castrovirreina where it would open up an incredibly rich mining region. From there it could be extended to Ica to join up with the (standard gauge) Pisco-Ica line. Given proper port facilities, Pisco could become the ocean outlet for the minerals transported over the line, and our position as a railway would be enormously strengthened. The F.C.H.H. is not being exploited as it might be. It could be a regular gold mine if it were properly worked-but not as a narrow-gauge line making transhipment of freight necessary in Huancayo. In our hands, and with the gauge the same as the Central's, it might well become the most important section of the whole system. Everything should be done to get hold of it.' . . . A few days later he repeated to me: 'We must get hold of the Huancavelica line *somehow!*'

Up to this moment the F.C.H.H. remains a narrow-gauge Government railway reaching in to a region where treasure lies buried, but unable to provide the key that would unlock the door to that wealth. G. W. Morkill's dream has so far not materialized.

The Guayaquil and Quito Railway

Up to now, the railroads reviewed in this chapter have been metre-gauge lines. We come finally to another 42-inch road – an unusual gauge for the Andes, found in Chile only on the F.C.T.T., and not at all in Peru – a railway noted for its tremendous grades and curvature. This one is the Guayaquil and Quito, linking the Ecuadorian capital 9,375 feet up in the mountains to the port on the Guayas River that today is the largest port on the West Coast in terms of population. The system is 288 miles in length, and its summit is 11,841 feet – not, perhaps, a giant among Andean railroads, but plentifully endowed with physical difficulties nevertheless. Prior to its advent, two weeks were required to cover the trail. The railroad cut this time to two days for ordinary pasenger trains and twelve hours for the *rapidos*.

Construction work began in 1871. But here there was no Wheelwright, no Meiggs or Clark, to conquer the financial obstacles and carry the line through to a triumphant conclusion within a few years. It was 1908 before the railway was finally ready for through traffic.

This was a Government venture financed with funds set aside for the purpose from national revenue, and one Garcia Moreno set hand to the task of commencing the work at Durán, across the river from Guayaquil. This unsung genius was running into one of the toughest constructional nuts to crack that Andes could show; for the Guayaquil and Quito had unusually difficult conditions to face in its steep climb to the *páramo*, as the Ecuadorian puna is called. The first 54 miles were comparatively easy, over marshy low ground producing rice and sugar, into firmer terrain where the tropical forest thickened and freights of coffee, fruit and tobacco could be expected. The next 27 miles raised the track to 5,925 feet at Sibambe (now called Empalme Cuenca) where the going became hard – exceptionally hard. A fantastic obstruction of rock called the Devil's Nose blocked progress. The projected manner of negotiating it proved impracticable. Money ran out. Work came to a standstill with the rails on the wrong side of the demonic barrier.

So far, two years had gone by. Two more were spent in finding a way past the Devil's Nose. The Government raised more money by selling State bonds in the U.S.A. and England. Another contractor took over the construction, building on and up. Physical difficulties and recurrent shortages of funds delayed the work again and again, until in 1908 Eloy Alfaro finally completed it by reaching Quito.

The Durán-Devil's Nose section had been operated by the Ecuadorians; but thereafter a mixed U.S.-British administration took over the running of the line. From Sibambe to Palmira, where the rails breasted the western rampart of the mountains and came out upon the *páramo*, a climb of 4,701 feet was made in 22 miles, entailing maximum grades of 5.5 per cent (1 in 18) uncompensated for curvature. The total curvature of the line amounts to 16,000 degrees, or the equivalent of 45 closed circles, and many of these curves are of three chains radius. Moreover, there is no rack here. This is an adhesion road pure and simple.

Once on the top, the line undulates across the *páramo* for 185 miles, between 8,435 feet at Ambato and 11,841 feet at the highest point, Urbina. Lakes, fertile valleys, upland ridges and towering snow-capped volcanoes, most of them still active, form a spectacular setting for this remarkable railway. Chimborazo, with its top 21,220 feet high, dominates the scene. Earthquakes play havoc here from time to time.

Ordinary passenger trains stopped for the night at Riobamba, 150 miles from Guayaquil. Possessing neither sleeping cars nor diners, the G & Q arranges halts for meals at convenient waystations, in the old American style. In fact, under foreign administration its whole character was so solidly North American – air brakes, standard code, the train order system, and all – that the U.S. boomer fraternity wrote its name high on their international list. These wandering rails from north of the Mexican border may have lacked a marked sense of responsibility but they made up for it by possessing vast funds of operating experience. The G & Q's completion took place in the heyday of the boomers. The word got round that trainmen were pretty certain to land a job there, and it became a link in the chain along which these restless souls moved in their unceasing peregrinations in search of the sun and adventure.

At this point I hand over to my old friend and colleague John L. Macintyre, lately retired from the Central of Peru, who went to the G & Q in 1910 from the Caledonian Railway. His picture of the line in boomer days is worth presenting in his own words:

'We used to call the G & Q the "Good and Quick". It's almost fifty years since I left it, and my memory these days isn't what it was. They were my happiest railroading times. It was straight, decent working – no intrigue or back-biting. Inspector – Chief Inspector – Travelling Auditor-Cashier and Paymaster – Secretary and Treasurer of the Ecuador Express Co. (a railroad sideline with the baggage cars, and delivery carts in Quito drawn by big Kentucky mules) – Acting Controller of the Railway, and so on – those were the steps I made there.

'The average grade was about 3¹/₂ per cent; but from Luisa (the junction for Riobamba) up to the Urbina pass it was 4¹/₂ per cent. There was one place north of Alausi called *Pueblo Viejo*, for a sunken village in the vicinity, where the grade hit 5¹/₂ per cent. I have often seen engines take several runs at it before they could get up. A permanent track gang was stationed there to raise the track after each train passed, as it was always sinking.

'From Durán to Bucay, milepost 54, was flat; but at Bucay the mountain engine took over the passenger for the climb – they were all mixed trains, by the way. The coaches were very ancient – American Car & Foundry Co., I think – and there was one passenger vehicle (it would be wrong to call it a coach) built in the Durán shops, and known as the *"jaula"* or *"cage"*. It may have been an old stock car. It had no springs and no roof. The other coaches had rattan seats, but this thing was fitted only with wooden benches round the inside and down the middle. It was unsafe for the mountain, and worked only between Durán and Bucay. When riding in it, the vibration kept you dancing around the whole time. How the passengers stood it I don't know; but the coast people seemed to like it for the unobstructed view it permitted – and the fresh air!

'There were some small North British Locomotive Co. engines working between Durán and Bucay, as far as I remember, and also between Ambato and Quito with the milk train that left Ambato at 3 a.m. and returned in the afternoon. But most of the engines were Baldwins, and these worked on the mountain from Bucay up. I don't recall their specifications, but they were big snorters. When I arrived in 1910 there were some old Shays on the riptrack outside Durán shops, but none of this type still remained in service.

'The curves on the line were very sharp in some places. If I am not mistaken, the Devil's Nose had four zig-zags. What a wonderful sight! I never saw anything like it. You came up the grade out of Sibambe and there was that huge "nose" towering above the train. It was by means of those zig-zags that the engineers who built the line got out of the Chanchan Valley and past the *Nariz del Diablo* – a fine and truly great piece of work.

'Plying between Guayaquil and Durán with passengers was a ferry boat called the *Colon*, the usual type of large river boat with churning wheels. Then there was *Saranac*, a tugboat to handle the lighters with

111. Guayaquil and Quito: 1944 built Baldwin 2-8-0 No. 44 has its front end examined for damage at Sibambe, after hitting a fall of rocks while working the mixto to Alausi.   *(Richard Pelham)*

freight over the river. Archer Harman, President of the "Good and Quick", used to come down from New York on visits in a lovely yacht named *Cavalier* which was said to have belonged at one time to royalty.

'The main shops of the railroad were in Durán, and both Ambato and Quito possessed small workshops. At Latacunga was a kind of forge with one or two helpers. The Company had its own doctor and hospital, and this was located at Huigra, 72 miles from Dura'n, where most of the administration was centred – General Manager, Traffic Superintendent, Trainmaster, etc., as well as the Chief Dispatcher's office. They all had Company houses there, and over the GM's office were quarters for employees, and a messroom. Passengers from Guayaquil on No. 1 ate in the hotel at Huigra during the 30-minute lunch stop. On No. 3 from Riobamba to Quito the lunch stop was at Latacunga. No. 1 stopped overnight at Riobamba and No. 3 took passengers on to Quito next day. No. 4, from Quito, also stopped overnight at Riobamba, and passengers continued their journey to Guayaquil next day on No. 2.

'With a single exception, all the drivers and conductors were British or North American. The exception was an Ecuadorian named Ramos, who worked on the mountain now and then, but didn't like it. One of the American hoggers was a coloured man known as Nigger MacRae, who worked on the flat Duran-Bucay run. I asked him once why he preferred to keep off the mountain, and he replied: "Dat ain't no place for a niggah. No suh, boss!" His Deep Southern negro drawl was attractive to listen to. One day we caught a big snake that was alleged somewhat doubtfully to be harmless and tied it to a piece of wood on the tender of MacRae's engine (we were burning wood at the time as a temporary measure during one of the frequent revolutions). When Nigger Mac took over his engine in Durán, the snake was lashing around like a mad thing and hissing angrily. It did its best to attack Nigger Mac, but he settled its hash with a crowbar. Very aggrieved at us, he remarked: "Ah likes a joke as well as any man does; but Ah don' see no joke in puttin' a tremenjous goddam snake like that on a man's tenduh. No suh – dat ain't funny! "

'Strange to say, while I forget some of the technical details of operation, my memory retains vivid recollections of those whom I worked with, and their nicknames. They read like a novel of the old West – the West of the boomer as well as of the gunman. There was Driver Macintosh, known as "Smilie"; and another driver dubbed "Lucky Baldwin". Then there were "Kid" Dalton; "Cat" Jamieson; "Bull" Wilson; "Hurricane Harry"; "Roaring Dick"; "Babe" Markley (also spoken of as "Mad" Markley, because of his custom of clearing passengers off the open coach end-platforms with a brake club). Very few of them could speak any Spanish. Their linguistic attainments were of the "Me Gringo – me no savvy" kind! One of these old-timers remarked to me. "You know, Scotty" – I was always either "Scotty" or "Mac'; to them – "you know, Scotty, I don't savvy this lingo at all. Why in hell they want to say 'naranja' instead of 'orange' beats me! You sure are an educated hombre, speakin' three lingos like you do – Scotch, English an' Spanish!"

'They may have been roughnecks, but all the same they were wonderful chaps and gentlemen at heart – do anything for a pal, even if they weren't above helping themselves to Company property. These old boomers were always drifting about between the various republics, wherever the good money happened to be. There were no restrictions on their movements in those days – no passports or other red tape. When a boomer blew in on the G & Q he would hit the extra board, and one of the other enginemen or conductors would go to the hotel keeper and say: "So-and-So's eats are on me till he gets a regular run". If the extra board was not giving the newcomer enough work, there would be a general whip-round to raise enough dough for him to move on to another republic.

'From time to time even the regular men on the G & Q would feel the itch in their feet and "pull the pin" for a getaway to other places. In six-months or so, perhaps, back they came, a sheepish grin on their faces. There was Mike Browder, Conductor of the milk train – he had a pitch-in one day with the Trainmaster over the switching at Machachi. The Trainmaster was a fuss-pot and wanted Mike to do the switching according to the book, but Mike just went on giving signals to the driver in his own way. The Trainmaster asked him: "Ain't you goin' to do like I said?" and Mike replied: "No, I guess I'll do it my way today, Mr. Jones". When he arrived in Ambato he said to the Trainmaster: "This is my last run, Mr. Jones, an' here's my resignation! " The Trainmaster realized he had been hasty and begged Mike to reconsider it; for Mike was reckoned a good conductor. But all Mike said was: "That's all right, Mr. Jones. It don't make no difference anyway. I've got itchy feet, and a guy gets stale when he stays too long in one place. I'm pullin' the pin an' gettin' out of here!' . . .

'It was all so wonderful to me, going out there as a fresh-faced youngster from the old "Cally". I couldn't believe my eyes when I first saw men pull guns on each other. Everyone carried a single-action forty-four Frontier Colt – no one considered the double-action reliable – and it was a case of pulling back the doghead and letting go, or else "fanning" it. I possessed a Webley .32; and an old-timer said to me: "Say, sonny, if you was to shoot that off at me and I got to know about it, I'd be real mad at you!" Some of the boys favoured shoulder holsters and some the waistband of their pants, but one and all were experts with the gun. There was a freight conductor named Felton who used to practise what he called the "draw" from any part of his person – holster, shoulder or waistband – and he was lightning itself. I have seen him throw a can in the air, draw, and hit it twice before it landed.

'Felton was one for covering the line with his trains faster than anyone else could wheel 'em on the freight runs. "We was rollin' along – just a-wheelin' 'em some!" as he used to say. He pulled the pin and took off down to the Oriente "a-huntin'gold" and was reported killed by a fall from a high rock-though some alleged that headhunters got him. The first time I ever saw him was in Ambato, walking down the street with a gun in each hand, keeping a tin can on the move ahead of him with unaimed shots from the single-action six-shooters. Every time he "threw" his guns, as they called it, the can leaped. I enquired who he might be, and someone told me his name, adding that he had been a sheriff in the Western U.S.A. "Watch him when he takes a seat in a canteen or in the hash-house", I was told. So it was that I noted how Felton always sat facing doors or windows, back to the wall, that he might command all entrances. It was the instinct and "trade mark", as it were, of the genuine gunman. He was the only man I ever

112. *Baldwin No. 44 runs into the street section at Alausi, at the top of the Devil's Nose, with a mixed train.*

(Richard Pelham)

knew to carry a derringer on a band round his forearm. His explanation was that, should he be disarmed, he could snap the band down and "bore" the other man! But there was no boast or brag about him. He was a quiet, slow-spoken chap. I liked him very much, and admired his skill with a gun and his gentle ways. I felt it keenly when we heard of his death. We were real friends.

'Then there were the songs we used to sing at our smoking concerts. One of them went to the tune of "Clementine":

> 'Oh Collectors, oh Inspectors, hear the travelling public roar,
> And when we are gone forever, they'll forget us nevermore!
> Oh the happy days we passed there,
> On numbers one, two, three and four,
> Chuckin' drunks and checkin' chickens
> On the trains in Ecuador.

'We were a carefree lot on the old "Good and Quick" back in those days, and the world was at our feet!' ...

113. Baldwin 2-6-0 of 1900 No.14 leaves Bucay for Duran, on the costal section of the G & Q.
(D. Trevor Rowe)

Under foreign operation, tariffs were still fixed by the Government. The G & Q made no money for those who ran it, but on the other hand deficits were covered by State subsidies. The foreign administration finally begged the Government to take the railway and run it themselves, which they eventually did about 1952.

In 1929 three Beyer-Garratts were added to the locomotive roster. With a tractive force of just under 43,000 pounds, these 2-6 2 + 2-6-2 articulateds were designed to tackle the 5.5 per cent uncompensated maximum grade of the mountain section equal to straight 6.6 per cent (1 in 15) – with trains of 170 short tons. Their cylinders were 15½ x 20in, with 38-in. drivers, and a boiler pressure of 200 pounds. Worthington feed-water heaters were fitted – and, of course, bar frames, the only practicable frame for the Andes.

Today, the condition of the line is chaotic. What freight moves on its rails is mostly Government property. Train schedules are virtually non-existent. So bad are the track and rolling stock that breakdowns and derailments are endemic. Travellers possessing the necessary money fly between Quito and Guayaquil; while those who can't afford to fly travel by bus over a highway that is far shorter and quicker than the rail route. The 'Good and Quick' of the boomer fraternity has become 'Gimcrack and Queer' in the Motor Age.

[1] At the moment there is a plan for the construction of an electrified railway to connect these two. A Japanese firm has started work at the Cuzco Sta. Ana end.

[2] He was referring to the Trujillo, Pacasmayo and Paita-Piura lines, owned and operated by the P.C.

Chapter 14

THE HAZARDS OF MOUNTAIN RAILROADING

ANDEAN railways are subject to the same kinds of accidents as flat systems, plus many that are peculiar to heavy grades and difficult mountain country. However, in the case of derailments and collisions it's likely that results will be less serious on the mountain line because speeds are considerably lower. That is to say, of course, unless the accident takes place in a particularly dangerous spot. So many factors influence the seriousness of the case that one can't be dogmatic about it; but I would personally rather be a passenger in a train that derailed on a mountain at 20 m.p.h. than in an express that comes off the track at 70! The apparent obviousness of that preference will be modified if you consider the chances of a derailed mountain train's going over the edge. I would prefer to accept such a risk, rather less, I think, than the one of being turned over with half-a-dozen burning coaches on top.

Fortunately, the travelling public knows nothing about the majority of the accidents that take place. In any case, most of these are not serious; but some, if witnessed, might excite the imagination and bring rail travel to the state of being considered a risky business, which it is not. Ships' officers are the only other public transport servants who have to undergo as long a training period as enginemen before being entrusted with human lives and property. If road vehicle drivers were as carefully screened, spent so many years gaining experience before being permitted to take control, and were obliged to undergo such stringent physical examinations to ensure that they retained an optimum standard of fitness, there would be no congestion on today's highways.

Unseen by the public, his existence even ignored, is the Train Dispatcher, whose responsibility is far greater than an engineer's, and whose mind requires for the efficient performance of his duties the comprehensive perception of a general's, the instantaneous and correct reaction of a racing driver's, and the foresight and planning power of a chess champion's. For these talents he is awarded a salary that no air pilot would deem worth while picking up. But then, remember, a dispatcher is quite out of the public's sight!

The dispatcher's constant fear is the issuing of 'lap orders'. That is to say, giving a train orders to run between two points and forgetting that an opposing train with clear orders is already occupying the single track. Dispatchers are almost superhuman, but not entirely infallible. It *can* happen. If there is an intervening station there may be time to stop one of the trains and sidetrack it before anything happens. Or, perhaps the enginemen of one train see the other's smoke and appraise the situation in time. At all events, collisions due to lap orders are exceedingly rare. When one does occur on a mountain road there is less chance of escaping disastrous results than on a flat road; as visibility is generally very limited by tunnels and blind curves. A train crew running a meet is perhaps less rare. This means passing the point where a meet is to be made with an opposing train. To bring it about, engineer, conductor, fireman and first brakeman must all have forgotten or misread the train order; for all have copies duly signed for.[1] The human element does occasionally fail, particularly when established custom is being varied. And the Train Order system depends for its safe operation on the human element.

Slides and washouts do occasionally disrupt traffic even on flat roads. On mountain roads they are perennial, fully expected, dealt with by routine. Commonplace though they are on any Andean system, on the Central of Peru their incidence is perhaps greater than on any other railway-in fact, in a report of 1950 to the Peruvian Government by the Morrison-Knudsen Company, Inc., the remark is made that: '. . . the Central of Peru is one of the most difficult and expensive in the world to operate'. The precautions, dictated by many years of hard experience, taken by that road to ensure the safety of passengers and freight have reduced the result of slides and washouts to no more than a slight delay and the possible inconvenience of transhipping from one train to another over the obstruction.

Runaways are the nightmare of the mountain railroader. Rigid observance of precautions, wise choice of equipment and the provision of safety switches can reduce their incidence, but there's no eliminating

114. *Matucana, on the Central Railway of Peru, showing work in progress to clear the tracks which had been inundated with mud brought down by heavy floods.* (C. Crofton Atkins)

115. *Earthquake damage in 1940, with the track at Tambo Viso, Central Railway of Peru, completely buried by the boulders on the left. The 'quake also moved several bridges and cracked their abutments.* (Author)

them entirely. Factors exist beyond human control which, given the usual combination of circumstances, bring about the necessary conditions for a mishap of this sort. More usually, perhaps, the human element fails. Rules are not obeyed – routine is skimped through familiarity – a prolonged no-trouble period encourages the taking of chances. A runaway may end in the most spectacular pile-up of any; and before that end there is occasionally time for those who stay with the train to meditate on the omissions that brought it about! When the cause is the wrong choice of equipment, the people responsible are seldom aboard to reap the benefits of the lesson; though I remember a case where that was so – and vigorous action was taken immediately afterwards to prevent a repetition.

In this particular instance, passenger trains were controlled by the Eames *simple* vacuum brake. *Simple*, mind you – not the automatic! This meant that a leak in one of the old leather brake cylinder diaphragms, in the brake pipe or hoses, put it right out of action. That such equipment could exist on a mountain railroad is incredible, but it is a fact nevertheless. A passenger train was coming down the mountain with the Locomotive Superintendent's private car on the tail, and that exalted functionary inside, when the hoghead lost control of the train through the cracking of a brake cylinder diaphragm leather. His efforts to hold it with the engine brakes caused the drivers to lock, and the train was off like a bullet. A very ugly accident could have resulted, but by good fortune it happened not far above a safety switch with a sand drag. The train shot off the main, was checked effectively by the sand drag, and rammed the mountain only hard enough to throw the enginemen out of the cab windows, shake the passengers to the floor, and stand the Locomotive Superintendent upside-down in his whisky-and-soda. The alacrity with which the simple vacuum brake was stripped from all the railway's stock to be replaced by the automatic brake indicated how well the lesson had been learned by the man who in mechanical matters had the say!

By their very nature, vacuum brakes are inefficient at high altitudes. But even the far more efficient air brakes can be the cause of a runaway if carelessly handled. Retainers help when turned up, holding as they do a determined air pressure in the brake cylinders; though if through poor judgment an engineer 'loses his air' by using it up quicker than the compressor can recharge the main reservoirs, his control is gone. Adverse weather conditions can force even an experienced man to lose his air. The automatic air brake with straight-air control was developed to guard against this contingency.

Crew carelessness in skimping or neglecting brake tests can cause appalling accidents. Seven lives were lost and a 40-car freight totally wrecked through this on Christmas morning, 1954, on a railway I had been closely associated with. The train ran away down a two per cent grade at headlong speed out of control for some twenty miles, and then jumped the track. Of the eight men on the train only one survived. It is almost certain that after switching in the initial station the regulation brake test had not been made, and the angle-cock of the brake pipe behind the tender or on the leading car was closed – either that, or hoses were not connected. The brakes on the train had therefore not been charged and were isolated from the engine. The test before starting would have drawn attention to this. Engine brakeshoes were worn right through, but car brakes had never been applied!

Another hazard is carelessness in the matter of low water level in the boilers of steam locomotives; though these accidents are seldom seen by outsiders. Sometimes it isn't carelessness. For instance, high altitude plays hob with lifting injectors as well as with vacuum brakes. At one time I had my share of troubles with a certain type of injector very popular on British railways, that undoubtedly did its job well at sea level but was the devil to get started at anything over 10,000 feet in height. Engines fitted with a pair of these, and no other, were dangerously vulnerable to low water accidents. On several occasions crownsheets were saved by keeping throttles wide open. The water level rises when the throttle is opened. Lead plugs might be effective enough when they fuse on a coal engine but are not likely to prevent an overheated crownsheet on an oil burner.

Syphons in the firebox are perhaps the most valuable protection against crownsheet collapse from low-water overheating. They act rather like a coffee percolator, and keep up a circulation of water from the bottom of the tube sheet to the top of the crownsheet. Even if the water level drops below the top of the firebox, enough water will 'percolate' from below to keep it wet. They are a standard fitting in *Andes* type engines, and their value cannot be overestimated.

Carelessness comes into it when the hogger deliberately cuts the guns on a grade in order to carry a slightly lower fire without loss of steam, thus clearing away dark smoke in a tunnel, and then neglects to keep a very close watch on the water level in the boiler. What causes boiler explosions is not the overheating of the crownsheet, but the subsequent foolhardiness in starting injectors again to raise the water level, thus bringing relatively cold water in contact with it. It is then that stays and firebox part company and the contents of the boiler come out through the firedoor.

The tilt of the engine on grades requires to be watched too. Going up a four per cent grade you may have the highest point of the crownsheet covered with water, yet bared when the grade levels off. It is often the practice to fit indicator plates beside the gauge glasses showing the highest point of the firebox in relation to the level in the glass on maximum up and down grades. Enginemen like the water as low as they can safely carry it, because too full a boiler invites priming. They also like test cocks on the backhead as well as water gauges of the reflex type. Test cocks are considered reliable indicators of true water level; gauges sometimes lie – and in any case do not show the true level inside the boiler. And reflex gauge glasses do not burst like the tubular ones and fill your ear full of slivers!

My first accident was with a gravity car – that item of equipment so patently useless on a flat railroad. Fresh to a mountain railway, I had been out on an inspection trip up the line with a District Traffic Superintendent, and we were just coming lickety-split into our 'home' yard down a steepish grade. The D.T.S. was working the handbrake when a fly hit him in the eye. On these handcars we were out in the open and at speed a fly or bee could hit one's face like a small pebble! He dropped the brake, yelled to me to take over and clapped a hand to his injured eye.

We were approaching a trailing switch at a clip of about 40 m.p.h. I was new to handcars, and imagined quite wrongly that the switch was 'automatic' – that the blade was spring loaded and would let us through, little knowing that if it had been, a handcar was too light to move it over. It wasn't an automatic switch. The D.T.S. saw nothing, and told me afterwards he thought I knew! Yes – we hit that switch all out and became airborne. By luck we landed right side up; but the D.T.S. and I continued our trajectory while the handcar wrapped itself round a stub switch. When we had picked the ballast out of our hair and assessed damage it was to find no more than a few bruises. From then on I was always mighty careful with trailing switches.

These handcars are used on the Central of Peru to pilot passenger trains down the mountain during the wet season, when slides are prevalent. Slide warning devices are impracticable for several reasons, and track walkers patrol the dangerous sections continually to protect in case of rocks or slides on the track. The pilot handcar is an additional precaution. It precedes the passenger train by perhaps half a mile, this lead allowing the pilot time to put out protection for the train should he find an obstruction on the line. So sharp are some of the blind curves that handcars have been known to hit obstructions before they could be stopped. In any case, dogs are a number one hazard to them. Dogs appear to be unable to resist chasing handcars, often hurling themselves right in front of the wheels in their slavering excitement. And dogs materialize in places where there is not even a sign of human habitation. If the handcar catches up with the dog – and it is generally travelling must faster – there is every chance of being derailed by the animal. Llamas can also be dangerous. There is nothing to protect you in these vehicles – nothing to prevent llamas coming in on top of you if you rush into the midst of a herd of them wandering on the track.

Freight cars running by gravity as 'trains'[2] are a development of the handcar idea. I well recall some 35-ton capacity flat cars, taring at 12 tons, that were fitted with wooden pilots and acetylene headlights to handle milk traffic on a certain Andean railway. They possessed clasp brakes powerful enough to lock the wheels when applied with a club through the brake-wheel spokes, and the speeds they reached on four per cent grades were so terrific that accidents frequently occurred. Most of their runs down the mountain were in the wee hours of the morning; but the headlights, however bright, were of little use on curves, and except on the tangents there was every chance of hitting fallen rocks. Locked and sliding wheels are as bad as no brakes at all. Time and time again these cars were involved in fatal collisions with rocks. It was a great relief for all when their use was eventually discontinued; though not before their reputation as killers had won for them the cognomen, 'Death Cars'.

116. *The driver of Central's No. 40, busy chatting, failed to notice that an ore loading chute was lowered in one of the Morococha mine sidings, and backed his engine under it.* *(Author)*

117. *The Chosica shed foreman, Bert Isaacs, poses with his children in one of the Central Railway's gravity cars in 1927. The handbrake represents the only means by which the car can be controlled.* *(Author)*

Mountain lines often have numerous tunnels and at the same time possess brakemen who take too many chances on car tops. Where cabooses are not operated because of weight and other considerations, there is no way of keeping roofs clear. The danger arises when trainmen have for some reason to pass along the top of the train from front to rear – generally it's the other way about, with the man facing the direction of travel – and if they forget the presence of a tunnel they may be hit at the mouth of it and knocked off. Telltales, to warn of approaching tunnels and bridges, are not normally used in the Andes.

Many are the lost limbs I have witnessed through trainmen falling between moving cars, usually after taking chances for years and getting away with them. The wheels can just as easily lop a head off or cut a body in two as remove a leg or an arm – and often do. The time-honoured procedure with an amputated limb is to apply a tourniquet as soon as possible, and then fill the victim up with all the liquor that he can take. Provided the bleeding has been stopped, if he can be made dead drunk he quietens down and usually reaches hospital in good enough condition to pull through. If no liquor is obtainable he may bewail his fate so much that it finishes him off.

There is nothing much you can do about lost heads other than collect the bits and turn 'em in to the police. Andean Indians have a way of sleeping off periodical drunks on the railroad track, with a rail as pillow. When a curve is chosen for a resting place, their sleep may be violently prolonged. It appears to be impossible for Indians to understand that the railroad track is not a public right-of-way. To them it is a convenient road. They seek it when driving their animals. At night they can follow it by feel, without requiring a light. Blind people prefer it for the same reason. Of all the Indians killed in the Andes by trains, I think quite half of them are blind and deaf people!

Animals killed while wandering about or being driven on the track achieve fantastically high values when their owners lodge claims in court for damages. Railway responsibility is not officially recognized if the accident takes place away from a public crossing; so the claimant and his friends perjure their immortal souls to prove that, (a) it did in fact occur on a crossing; and (b) the regulation crossing whistle (two long toots and two shorts) was not sounded. The scales of justice tending to weigh against a foreigner, the killing of livestock can be very expensive. Enginemen do their best to avoid it; though more because of the risk of derailment than from any regard for the company's resources.

The 'cowcatcher', as the pilot is called by the layman, is a most effective safeguard when it comes to animals; though in the case of heavy obstructions, such as rocks, it can be knocked right under the leading wheels and trip them. I have the highest opinion of these accessories. My life was once saved by one; so I say that with feeling.[3] Also, very early in my career on an Andean railway I witnessed their effectiveness in an encounter with a bull.

The bull was a big one and a mean one to boot, as a track walker up an adjacent telegraph pole was no doubt ready to assert with emphasis. We came round a curve upon this scene at a good speed, as our big *Mikado* was pounding down an easy grade with a passenger train. The bull was trying to push the telegraph pole over to get at the man, and had it wobbling when the yell of our whistle drew the brute's attention to our approach.

Deciding that we had no right to intrude he left the pole, pawed the ballast up a bit and then charged the oncoming train right along the middle of the track. I half expected to feel something when he hit the engine bows on; but of course we never felt a thing – nor did we see where that bull went. But next day, passing the same spot on another train, I noticed that vultures were interested in something amongst the maize quite fifty yards from the track. The pilot had thrown that bull out to one side without a mark on the front of the engine to show that any such encounter had taken place.

On flat roads there may be time for engine crews to 'join the birdies' – to jump – before a collision. On mountain roads a very reduced visibility generally allows no time to unload, or even to slam the brakes into emergency and kick the sanders open. On such occasions, fortunately very rare, the advantage of big cab windows may be seen. When the tender comes in against the backhead, followed by the first car over the tank top, it is as well for engineer and fireman not to be present. There is a good chance that they will already have flown, impelled through those windows by the shock. I remember a very bad 'cornfield meet' in 1927, on a blind curve, with both trains – a freight and a passenger – running fast and working steam. A way station operator had forgotten to put out a red order board for the freight and deliver fresh train orders changing a meet with the passenger. Due to telescoping of the wooden stock the death roll in the coaches was serious, and both engines were completely smashed up. But none of the enginemen was badly hurt. All four men had shot out of their respective windows when the engines hit, and all were thrown clear.

The operator responsible for this accident took to the hills and vanished – a not uncommon method of escaping certain retribution. In countries of wide open spaces and sparsely inhabited mountains it is very difficult to trace fugitives, particularly when their physical appearance conforms to a racial type that seldom varies. Generally speaking, it was the small fry of relatively short service who made themselves scarce in this way. However, I do recall one occasion when an engineer did it. It was low water that time. The tank of his engine went dry on a passenger run through neglect in not filling up at a customary water stop, with the result that he had to cut off his train and run for it to the nearest plug. By the time there was enough water in the tank for the squirts to catch, the crownsheet was yellow-hot and the lead plugs had melted. He decided that somehow the boiler must be filled and an awkward situation saved, but was not inclined to take the risk himself. If the crownsheet held he might claim that the plugs were blowing slightly when he took the engine over – as they sometimes would if not periodically renewed – but if it went, he was not going to be within range. He therefore told his fireman to get both injectors going while he himself went along to the station to advise his home roundhouse. The fireman was a raw youngster who knew no better, and he fell for it. It cost him his life too. The crownsheet collapsed the moment cold water touched it, and the firedoor blew off, killing him as he stood watching the gauge glasses.

When the roar of the explosion had died down, when the dust and moisture had settled, and the tinkling of glass from broken windows had ceased in the neighbourhood of the station, the engineer emerged from the telegraph office, found the coast clear in the direction of the station gate, and departed swiftly to lie low for a discreet period of time. In doing this he of course admitted his guilt and could have been charged with manslaughter if caught. He remained out of sight for a couple of years or more, probably in some remote corner of the republic. But to our chagrin, he made a brazen reappearance after a change of government following a political coup and landed a remunerative post as an assistant in the Ministry of Works, Transport Division, in which he remained for an appreciable time as a thorn in our flesh.

Before getting too far away from the subject of Cornfield Meets, let me say that train v. train is anybody's fight, but train v. railcar invariably means obliteration of the railcar. Diesel units built to a useful power/weight ratio for heavy grade work cannot possess frames and bodies robust enough to stand up to a locomotive ten times as heavy, backed by a number of cars or coaches. The devastating fierceness of the fires often resulting from such collisions might he due to thermit formed from the aluminium and steel in the construction, ignited by the tremendous heat of the blazing fuel oil.

There was a hoodoo railcar that concluded its maleficent career in this way, taking its toll of human victims with it, whom we hoped had been killed in the crash and not burnt alive. My first acquaintance with the unit was when it was a-building, and even then it was a maverick. Once put in service in the Andean foot-hills it was involved in repeated grade crossing accidents, all more or less costly to itself and all extracting their toll of life from the other vehicle. It had begun as a double-ended articulated job with two diesel engines, but before its ignoble finish had been converted to a single-ended articulated. The displaced end was freely 'cannibalized' to keep the unit in service. It was loathed and feared, and all who had anything to do with it breathed a sigh of relief when destruction caused its number to be removed from the roster.

Engine 112 of the Central of Peru was disliked for her recalcitrance. Steam locomotives are perhaps the nearest thing to living creatures that man has devised, and no two are alike in anything but external appearance. This may well be because each is individually built. Even sister engines perform differently. Some are tractable, some are stubborn. But however obstinate, sickly or difficult they may be at work, the moment they are headed for home they become eager and docile. An engine will hate one engineer and oppose him like a mule, but another – even the most rough-handed – can do anything with it.

118. *A rare photograph of one of the 'death cars' (right) which made the nightly gravity run from Matucana to Lima, carrying milk churns.* (Author)

119. *The Cero de Pasco's wrecking outfit was hired to assist in clearing up the derailment of Central's No. 105 at Tambo, the act of a disgruntled ganger, in 1928. Here a C de P Mikado pulls No. 105 on to a temporary track, run underneath as the crane lifts the front end of the loco.* (Author)

We who have spent a goodly portion of our lives on and around steam locomotives have some of us probably seen engines move on their own at night. It is a fact that they sometimes do, and if not stopped at once may tip themselves into the pit of the turntable. Of course, there is a rational mechanical reason for this propensity for straying, but to witness it is eerie in the extreme. Engine 112 was a notorious sleep-walker – a wild, treacherous locomotive. She was the first heavy engine I ever handled – a big 4-8-2 standing 14ft 5in from the rail to the top of her stack – and, feeling my inexperience, she took the bit between her teeth and very nearly managed to push through the back of the roundhouse when I was taking her off the table into her stall. She was always in trouble on the road. Enginemen came to dislike her intensely, and she in turn disliked everybody. On one memorable occasion when she was pulling a freight drag on the Huancayo section where grades are easy and tangents long, the pin came out of the bell-crank of the throttle rig, inside the dome. The throttle valve, instead of falling shut, flew wide open and stayed there. Up till then she had dragged her feet as though barely able to move the tonnage, but the moment she felt that control had gone she was off like a streak, while the engineer, the fireman and myself struggled with the reverse lever – she had the old-type 'Johnson bar' – trying to 'boss' it up the sector into mid-gear and thus cut off steam from the pistons. We did it eventually; but only by dint of fighting it notch by notch. Meanwhile, the speed of the train was beginning to rival the wind, while frantic signals to slow down came via the bell cord from the conductor on the last car. We delivered the train at its destination, but were obliged to give up any thought of a return trip to the home roundhouse. Instead, Engine 112 was blown down and towed home dead.

Years afterwards she was converted to 4-8-0 in the hope of ridding her of a marked tendency to slip common to all her class. She went out of Guadalupe shops with a course cut from her massive boiler and with full air brake equipment on her; for at that time the road was going over from vacuum to air. The hoodoo went into action the moment she entered freight service on the mountain. Coming down through a cloudburst, her engineer thought he saw something peculiar about a culvert not far ahead. He big-holed the brakes rather too late, and the 112 nosed out on a section of track suspended in the air, under which a river of mud from the cliff at one side had washed away all the stone-work and fill. She lifted her back coupler out of the knuckle of the car behind and fell through into the mud, rolling over and over down the mountain to come to rest on her side, boiler downwards. Her bemused engineer clambered out of the cab window. It was his good fortune that his side was above the level of the mud streaming into and about the capsized engine, filling the rest of the cab. Young Jones, the fireman – one of the most promising lads in the section – was drowned in that mud, and with him the conductor, who had been on the engine when it fell. We dug the two of them out hours later. Poor Jones was found with his hands over his face, as though he had died trying to keep the mud out of his mouth and nostrils. Lying as she was, the only way to salvage the 112 was to strip her completely where she lay. No crane could handle her deadweight so far from the track. I never saw her in steam again, having left the railway before she came out of the shops after repairs.

In Andean railroading, wrecking operations are more often than not hampered by space limitations. There may be just not enough room for the crane to swing, let alone to be positioned with the outriggers fully extended. Then again, so much of the line lies on curves that, even if outriggers can be extended, the crane isn't level. This may make lifting on the inside of the curve a tricky business.

I was present when a wrecking crane was set up on a rather sharp curve at the head of a steep gully to lift an engine tender without trucks well down below track level on the inside. It was a bad position, but the weight to be lifted was so well within the capacity of the crane that the risk of capsizing it was slight; moreover, outriggers were fully extended towards the lift, and clamps were attached to the rails at each corner of the crane's underframe. The tender was lifted into the air and the operator began to swing it towards the track in order to load it on a positioned flatcar. This accident took place at 15,500 feet above sea level, and the crane had come up from the coast with its operator, a coast man. He was inadequately clad for the bitter night cold at this altitude; half bemused, also, from mountain sickness. Possibly because of this, he became confused and opened the throttle full instead of closing it when the tender came over the flatcar. The crane at once rotated faster, till the tender was standing out from the boom at a considerable angle from the vertical. As it swung thus over the higher ground outside the curve, the massed gandy-dancers (section gang men) and fitters scrambled back into safety, yelling to the crane driver to stop. We watched helpless as the tender swung past over the track again, knowing full well what was going to happen when the effect of the crane's tilt towards the inside came into play. When the tender was over the spot from which it had been lifted there came a rattling and banging as the ground under the outrigger packing balks crumbled and the balks collapsed.

Then the crane started to fall over, dragging the groaning rails and ties with it. A prolonged cry went up from all the watchers as it fell on its side boiler downwards on the steep slope of the fill. But for the fact that the rail clamps still held it to the crazily twisted track it would have slid down out of sight. As it was, from where I stood with the District Traffic Superintendent we could see the wheels uppermost and a corner of the underframe. For a moment after the noise subsided there was a breathless hush. A face appeared in the light of the flares over the edge of the underframe as the crane driver crawled out from under. His ancient straw hat – a black-and-white 'boater' – was still on his head, but the crown had parted company with the rest, standing open like a lid. The eyes underneath were wide in amazement, as was the mouth when that too came into sight. It was like a scene from an ancient slapstick comedy. I was unable to contain myself and doubled up with overpowering laughter. That set the D.T.S. off too. Fortunately, the surrounding darkness hid us from sight of the other watchers, some of whom were by now surging forward with cries and yells to extract the unhurt but dazed crane driver from the wreckage.

The task of picking that crane up, righting it once more and putting it back on the rails was no subject for mirth during the next two or three days. The C de P wrecker was hired from Oroya, its passage of the Galera Tunnel at the summit of the main line resulting in an adventure that shall he told in the appropriate chapter, and on reaching the scene of the disaster – where the capsized crane had been shored, the clamps removed and the track returned to the ballast – it was decided that the working position was too risky to warrant its use.

We righted the crane and re-railed it with the use of a 'dead man'. After jacking it up to rail level and about eighty degrees from the vertical – the boom had already been detached – a pit was dug well up on the other side of the track. In this pit were placed a number of old rails lashed together. The pit was then filled in and the earth well tamped round the rails leaving their ends protruding for about four feet. To this anchorage we shackled two double-pulley blocks and tackles. Slings were attached to the underframe of the crane, taken over the superstructure, and hooked to the tackles. The cable ends were connected to couplers of locomotives above and below the site.

When the engines moved away, the pull came on the slings via the 'dead man' and the tackles. The crane rose slowly and steadily towards an upright position till the centre of gravity was past the vertical, when it then settled gently on a nicely calculated cradle of ties. All that remained to do was to lower it to the track with jacks.

I have mentioned these details to explain the use of a 'dead man,' an ingenious aid little known to those who have done no wrecking. On light work a 'dead man' could sometimes be used with a *'Lidgerwood'*. This was a steam winch mounted on one end of a flatcar, a hauling device at one time popular throughout the Americas.

There was another occasion when I laughed at the wrong time. The GM of the Central came down to the works from Lima in a splendid limousine of American make fitted with the first Firestone pneumatic rail tyres we installed. This trackcar was really a very fine job, and the GM was justifiably proud of her. When he had gone with the Chief Mechanical Engineer into the latter's hideout at the other corner of the general office building, the chauffeur of the trackcar ran his charge into a side track in front of my office window, leaving it close up against a cut of empty boxcars. He then went off up to the Light Units section, probably to scrounge something, leaving the trackcar unattended.

Down the yard from the roundhouse came the goat, a small but chunky 0-4-0, in the charge of the half-English throttle-jerker whom I call Billson. This class of switcher had a well tank, with the fuel tanks at either side of the firebox, and the back of the cab was open. The yard brakeman, on the rear footboard, was thus able to join freely in cab conversations. On this occasion Billson was doing most of the talking, letting the engine run itself. The idea at the moment was to go into the side track and snake out the cut of boxcars, putting them over on the team track. The engine came down the yard cab first, cleared the switch of the track where the cars were, and then advanced boiler first into the siding. Billson and his fireman were meanwhile deep in conversation, faces towards the back, paying not the slightest attention to where they were going.

When about twenty feet from the cars Billson slammed the throttle shut and reached for the brake handle. He knew without looking where the cars were. They had been there all week. There was no need for him to break off the conversation till only a few feet separated the couplers. What he did not know was that the GM's favourite trackcar was between these cars and the engine. I saw it all happen and could do nothing to prevent it – only watch with an awful fascination. The limousine folded up with a noise like a crushed biscuit tin, and Billson – horrified into belated action – flung the Johnson bar back. The stop he made was quick, but the damage was already done.

I was Acting Chief of Traction at the time. Billson was one of my headaches, and I rushed out of the office building with every intention of having a gallon or two of his blood on the spot. But as I came up to the scene of the disaster there was disclosed to my vision the spectacle of the trackcar, its erstwhile proud fifteen feet of wheelbase compressed into about half that length, its back arched like that of a tomcat confronted by a terrier. From underneath, a medley of struts, shafts and rods protruded at crazy angles. The engine's coupler had gone through the rear of the body, and the car coupler had punched the radiator and motor back into the driver's seat. Billson regarded me from the cab with an expression of wistful apprehension.

Recalling the funny noise it had made on being crumpled up, the sight of that trackcar proved too much for me. I tried to bite back the laugh coming up, and couldn't. Greatly relieved at my guffaw, Billson began to laugh too. The fireman looked mystified and then joined in. The brakeman had vanished, no doubt to establish an alibi. There were the three of us, helpless with mirth, when the GM and the CME came out of the general office, moving in our direction. They had neither heard the collision nor were aware of it till they came up, by which time we had succeeded in assuming suitably grave expressions.

It was a relief to me that justice was summarily administered by my superiors. After my unfortunate lapse I could never have caned Billson as he deserved. He drew a month's holiday without pay, and the fireman and brakeman a fortnight each. Let the story end there, omitting the pungent remarks of the GM as he gazed on the foreshortened remains of his trackcar, still on the rails but fit only for the scrap heap!

One wet February morning in 1909, the American Bridge Company was renewing girders of a bridge over the Chaupichaca gorge on the Central. There were several American engineers, but most of the labourers were Jamaicans. The 33, a Rogers *Mogul* of 1900 vintage, was detailed as engine of the work train attached to this job. She had been to Tamboraque, a water station a few miles up the line, and was returning to the bridge down the four-per-cent when she got out of control and ran away at headlong speed towards the bridge. At that time a small smelter was operating in Tamboraque. Smoke from this smelter flattened down on the track, mixing with the rain to form a soapy solution on the rails, causing braked wheels to lock and slide.

The bridge gang had a crane out on the span when the 33 came in sight on the short tangent giving on to the abutments from a tunnel. There was no time for the black labourers and their white bosses to scramble clear. The runaway engine plowed into the crane full tilt, with so severe a shock that with a shriek of rending metal – the whole bridge span collapsed, falling into the river at the bottom of the ravine in a tangle of twisted girders, machinery and human bodies.

Passengers crossing the gorge on today's trains may see from the bridge the wreckage still half submerged in the foaming white river beneath. The 33 lies upside-down, water cascading through the spokes of her naked driving wheels. To salvage her would have been more costly than she was worth; so she was stripped of most of her running gear and left where she lay. But there is some evidence, too, that she was a hoodoo engine, and was better down there in the river than working mischief on the line. It seems she had formerly been numbered 37, but after repeated derailments was considered so unlucky that her number was changed. If that is true, the ruse in no way broke the hoodoo. A new span was put in and Chaupichaca Bridge was again ready for traffic in April 1909, a remarkably smart bit of work; but the old girders are to be seen sticking up out of the river beside the dead engine as a terrible reminder of what could happen in mountain railroading if routine precautions were relaxed.

The Morococha-Cut-Off branch of the Central has grades that very nearly touch five per cent. This section was always notorious for runaways in the bad old days of steam – jams on the engine and 'armstrong' brakes on the cars. At the Cut-Off end, near its junction with the main stem, there was a safety switch with a spur about forty feet long, ending up against a rock wall. This protected the junction, but was hardly reassuring for the crew of a train belting down that grade out of control!

Frost, mist and thin rain were the conditions usually responsible for wheel slip resulting in loss of control on the down run. A Mountain Section engineer one day felt his train getting away from him, and disliked the thought of being plastered up against the end of the safety switch spur at the bottom with four cars of zinc concentrates on top of him; so he opened the sanders, reversed his engine and unloaded. The rest of the train crew had the same idea. Speed at the time was no less than alarming, and as they all chose the safest-looking spot to jump for – the choice was strictly limited in any case – the tangle of limbs and bodies took some sorting out, by which time the now unmanned train had vanished from sight round a curve. After making their tally of cracked ribs, black eyes and missing teeth, the seven disconsolate men set off limping in the direction of Cut-Off, when to their amazement they heard a train coming up the track round the curve where theirs had disappeared not long before. It proved to be their own! They clambered aboard as it passed them, were soon jogging down to Cut-Off as though nothing had happened, except for their own scars, and were resolved by mutual assent to keep mum about it.

120. *The remains of No. 33, involved in the Chaupichaca Bridge disaster of 1909, were still visible in 1938, in the river bed below the reconstructed bridge.* (*Author*)

But truth will out. The slackened driving tyres and flats on all the car wheels demanded investigations which occasioned prevarications so barefaced that official suspicions were aroused. Then one of the brakemen decided to make a clean breast of it. That the train should have backed up the line to fetch its crew after coming to a stop by itself was not easy to swallow, but the evidence was too strong to ignore. When wheels slide brakes must be released and tied down anew. The 'shacks' had released car brakes to do this when the urge to jump hit them. Engine brakes were not applied because when the engineer reversed the engine and widened on the throttle his intention was to win a retarding effect by having the drivers rotate in reverse. The well sanded track plus an easing of the grade did the rest. Had the abandoned train piled up at the bottom, no one would have blamed them for jumping. Their guilty consciences at having jumped needlessly, and a realization that all those flat wheels and loose tyres were not going to be overlooked, caused a clumsy attempt to 'cover up' that wouldn't have deceived a child!

Cars running wild down grade are another hazard of mountain railroading. They may escape from a siding where some careless switchman has forgotten to replace a derailer; they may have cut off from the rear of a climbing train, their air brakes unchanged through neglect. Whatever the reason for their escape, if they meet a following train the result is likely to be a mess-up!

Let me quote a case of this sort from my diary:

'What a day! At 2 p.m. an awful accident took place. The 12.30 railcar from L – – to C – – was hit, in Y – – by 40-ton gondola 960, a runaway from a train switching in C – – . This loaded car, out of control in C – – yard, was allowed out on the main *through the safety switch* by the yard pilot. It is hard to believe that anybody could be so stupid! Car 960 hit Railcar No. 2 (a diesel) a tremendous blow that completely destroyed the cab, engine and the whole front end. It knocked the 31 passengers into a state of semi-consciousness, and all the seats broke away. With the railcar impaled on the gon's coupler both vehicles then ran off towards L – – at a rapidly increasing speed. The last $9\frac{1}{2}$ miles down that grade were covered at a speed of 80 m.p.h. They rushed under the V – – bridge (where the main line enters the first of the city yards), jumped the track at the switch, and 960, turning over, threw its load of gypsum all over the station yard. Luckily, No. 2 kept on going, and clearing 960 came to rest still upright. Two passengers who jumped from railcar windows while it was rocking through the station were cut to pieces. Two others had their brains bashed out inside the car (most of it was on the walls!). G – – , one of Milne's accountants, has his leg shattered and a foot torn off, but is still alive. Of the 31 passengers, five were killed and eighteen seriously injured! All the same, had there been another train following them on the way up to C – – it's doubtful if any would have survived.'

No railroad likes to have its mishaps advertised, hence the discreet dashes. The amazing things about it are that the railcar stayed on the track when hit by the gon; and that the two, locked together, ran nearly 30 miles without coming off on one or other of the sharp curves with such necessarily slight superelevation. The maximum permitted speed on this section was 50 m.p.h.

To conclude a chapter that personal experience could extend almost to book length, I shall return with you to the perilous five per cent grades of the Morococha cut-off on a freezing wet morning in the pre-airbrake era many years ago. I was riding one of the big *Mikes*, No. 101, with a hogger named Flores, and we were on the way down from the Morococha mines to Cut-Off with four 35-ton hoppers loaded with zinc concentrates for Oroya. Just in front of us the track fell away out of sight with a suddenness reminiscent of one of those spine-chilling descents on a fun-fair switchback railway. As we breasted the top and started down the longest and most crooked stretch of maximum grade, the brakeman on the cars behind tightened already taut brake chains with their clubs to check the surge forward, while the fireman took advantage of a steam brake application to screw on the tender handbrake. Four loads were few enough to hold one of these heavy engines on such a grade. The brakies put their backs into it to steal another tooth on the brake shaft ratchets and all of a sudden we shot forward as though kicked in the rear by another train! A link had snapped in the foundation rigging of one of those hoppers, putting its brake out of action.

Flores at once began to use the steam-jam on the engine, but fifty tons of unbraked weight were now pushing us from the rear. Our speed increased rather than diminished, until Flores, becoming alarmed, lugged the sanding rod back and gave the engine all the braking power it possessed. There was a sudden ominous glide as the drivers locked and slid.

Had the sanders been working properly we might have regained control. But those old manual sanders were always unreliable. Sand slightly damp from condensation inside the boxes on the boiler top had a way of forming a bridge over the outlet valve or in the pipe itself which required determined hammering on the outside to break. Sliding wheels were a menace. Flores released the steam brake, yelling to the fireman to get out along the 'towpath' – the running board – with the hammer and shake the works up quick. Then the jolting tender became quiet as its wheels locked, skidding along the icy surface of the rails. We had hit a bad frost patch – just when we most needed clean rail to grip on! One by one the three braked cars behind us lost their feet. Speed increased dangerously. Up in front the fireman clung to the handrail with one hand and hammered the sandpipes with the other. Flores did all he could to graduate the engine brake applications, an almost impossible task with a brake valve having no lap position. It was either all on or all off, and all on meant locked drivers. Meanwhile, I was at the tender handbrake, releasing it to get the wheels rolling again and then screwing it up anew, while the brakemen back on the cars were similarly engaged.

The old engine began to rock dangerously on the curves and I wondered how many moments would pass before we took off at a tangent. If we jumped the rails on the outside there was a giddy drop down the mountain to the bottom of the gorge; if on the inside, the hoppers were likely to pile up on top of us. About a mile away down the track was the safety switch protecting Cut-Off yard. Reach that out of control and the wreck would be a shambles !

Everyone was too busy to think of unloading. By the time some sand was running through the sander pipes the wind of our speed and the flailing rods was enough to blow most of it away from the nozzles without its reaching the rails. We teetered at the utmost limit of stability on the last of the bad curves, got round it somehow, and found ourselves on a stretch of fairly straight track ending at yard limits. At the same time we emerged from the gloom of the high, narrow gorge into a burst of unexpected sunshine, watery but effective enough to lick the frost off the rails.

Driving tyres found a grip at last. The menacing smoothness of our long slide ended in a wild jolting as the enormous counterweights taking up half the driving wheel centres lifted those wheels up and banged them down again at each crazy revolution, with the force of eight steam hammers. Flores had the Johnson bar in reverse and was cracking the throttle, leaving the steam-jam off so that I might the more easily coax the tender wheels back to reason. The question now was, would we be able to check ourselves in time to avoid piling up on the safety switch spur ?

Tender and car wheels bit on the dry rails. There was a noticeable lessening of our headlong rush – but at the same time, Flores was yelling that the warning board for the safety switch was now in sight, only a few hundred yards ahead. It was now that we really had our hearts in our mouths. Speed was dropping, and if wheels could keep their grip we might escape with only a minor wreck. And still no one had thought of unloading. The reduction in speed from a rush to a run and from a run to a walk seemed to take an interminable time – but it was progressive. We had passed the board and must be just about at the switch! At no more than an easy crawl, Engine 101 kicked on the turnout and ground to a stop ten yards from the wall of rock at the end of the spur. Scarred tyres, blue hot, filled the air with their acrid tang.

That wasn't the last runaway I rode, but in none of the subsequent ones was disaster averted by so narrow a margin.

[1] There are local modifications of this operating rule. I speak here in terms of Standard Code.

[2] The Standard Code definition of a train is: 'One or more locomotives or self-propelled vehicles, coupled together, with or without cars, displaying markers'. The deciding factor is conveyed by the last two words. if the markers are missing, a hundred-car freight drag ceases to be a train, and a responsible observer would undoubtedly consider it only part of one.

[3] The episode is related in Ruins in the Sky, by the same author (Hutchinson, 1958).

Chapter 15

RAT-HOLES

IN flat railroading the tunnel is a mere incident. On Andean roads it is an event, if not an ordeal. I speak, of course, from the point of view of the trainman; though passengers are not entirely insulated from the circumstances that make it so.

What a world of difference there is between the neat portal of a well-lined bore on the orderly route of some ballast-scorching highliner of Europe or North America and the jagged, broken-toothed maw of an Andean rat-hole chiselled and blasted through the solid rock! The first, spreading comfortably over two or more tracks, is scarcely inconvenienced by the soft blast from valves hooked up to about fifteen per cent, and the undiminished rush of a hot-shot generating more noise from its running gear than from the engine's exhaust. On the other hand, the Andean tunnel awaits the train's approach with menacing deliberation. Its walls and roof embrace the rake closely as though ready to crush engine and cars into tangled wreckage. It thrusts the heavy smoke back into every aperture of the struggling vehicles, bombards the eardrums of the crews with the fearsome cacophony of the blast; showers particles of loosened stone or icicles on tender, roof and deck; makes itself in every way as terrifying as possible until the train finally escapes its grasp and staggers out into daylight once more, shaking free of the enveloping pall of smoke as a terrier shakes the water from its back. It lays artful traps of moisture or solid ice on the rails within its frozen belly, yelling with mad laughter when driving wheels lose their precarious grip on the four-per-cent, and heavy drags begin to slide backwards, forcing the half stifled enginemen to relinquish the protection of sacks or wet waste in order to calm the engine's panic. It is the merciless amusement of Andean tunnels to drive trains out the way they entered, unable to win through. Engines and the men at their throttles fight to beat the obstacles – somehow. Thus it is that every tunnel negotiated by a mountain train is a triumph.

Except for its length, one flat-road tunnel is very like another. Not so the mountain tunnel. Each of these has its peculiar characteristics. Prevailing winds play queer tricks with the ventilation; one, though long, may hold fumes high beneath the roof, while another, far shorter, clogs up with smoke moving in the same direction and at the same speed as the engines. Curves – moisture – temperature – all play a part in making each tunnel different. Enginemen and others intimately acquainted with the road come to know the behaviour of exhaust fumes and the vagaries of sound within each bore so well that blindfolded they could say with complete certainty where they were.

There are bad tunnels, and tunnels less bad; but for steam power no heavily graded mountain tunnel was ever good. The fearsome rat-holes negotiated with such travail, such discomfort, by trains heading up grade lose all significance for those descending – in fact, they become almost friendly, allowing trainmen, as they do, to check by vision in the darkness if any heavily-braked car wheels are sliding. Even the diesel cannot escape the threats from mountain tunnels, however.

Passengers on mountain trains hasten to close coach windows as soon as they hear the crashing reverberations of the engine's exhaust in the tunnel's mouth. Should a wisp of oil smoke find its way in through chinks or ventilators, handkerchiefs are at once whipped out to mask mouths and nostrils against the poisonous fumes. These same fumes, such rumours of them as ever reach the sensitive membranes of a passenger's nose, are largely blamed for the onset of mountain sickness when steadily increasing altitude begins to make itself felt. Actually, they serve as a tonic. Loaded though the exhaust gases from oil fuel may be with carbon monoxide and the products of the imperfect combusion of Bunker-C, they never killed anything but germs! It is my contention that a diet of good, oleaginous tunnel smoke from the stack of an engine with weeping flues will ward off the pangs of mountain sickness and all the ills that the human nose and throat are subject to. Contemporary expert assertions that lung cancer can be caused by exhaust gases from diesel motor vehicles fail to convince me. For years I regularly countersigned the reports of enginemen's physical examinations by the railroad's doctor, and there was never a single case of lung cancer – yet these men, mark you, inevitably inhaled the fumes from their oil-burning engines in tunnels for about 260 days in the year! Deafness was the chief trouble with the mountain men, never chest or throat diseases.

Deafness is understandable. One must experience it to believe the noise that a large steam locomotive's exhaust can make when working a full rated tonnage in a restricted bore on four per cent grade, with the reverse lever down in the corner and the throttle back over the tank. Piston-valve engines are bad enough in this respect; but the old balanced slide valves gave an exhaust as sharp as the crack of a whip,[1] which under a low tunnel roof was like a succession of gunshots within inches of the tympanum. The ground bass, as it were, for this well-nigh unbearable racket is the heavy drumming of the fire, severe enough to loosen the very lining of a tunnel – where such perfection exists. Even in the open the racket on the deck of an oil-fired engine being really pushed is remarkable; but the moment the stack noses in under the jagged portal of a tunnel a metallic ring is added to the explosive roar of the blast. The sound is flung off the walls into the cab, exciting every loose steel plate into sympathetic vibration, together with the thunder of the fire producing an aggregate of crash, boom and clatter enough to shatter the eardrums. Many enginemen stuff wads of cotton-wool in their ears the moment they put their seatboxes in the cab at the start of a day's work, and leave them there till they sign the report book on return to their home shed.

Before reaching one of the more lengthy and unpleasant Andean tunnels, the procedure is for the fireman to 'sand her through', putting a funnel-load of sand through the tubes to remove any soot deposits. This he does with enough anticipation to allow the resulting cloud of inky smoke to clear from the stack, and for himself to be back in his seat, well enveloped in a sack, before the first tunnel fumes waft into the cab. The hoghead in the meantime has turned himself into a shapeless mound of sacking, deaf and blind to all that goes on about him, like a would-be saint detaching himself from the naughty world. Free of human interference, the engine dives into the bore and has things its own way till well out in the open at the other end. But if the scheming spirit of the tunnel manages to win a trick by laying a slippery patch and bringing about a mad flurry of wheel-spin, the besacked mummies must perforce emerge from their protection to fan throttle and oil latch and work the sanders – perhaps even the rail washers – until the frantic engine finds its feet again, by which time the circumambient atmosphere, often deficient in oxygen from altitude, has assumed a plastic consistency.

Should a sizeable lump of tunnel roof detach and fall on the track, the engine hits it; for if daylight reigns outside there is no headlight on to show it up, and no eyes to see it even if there were light. I have personally never been derailed thus inside a tunnel; though engines I have been riding on suffered buckled pilots now and then. But when I was new to Andean rail customs this blind running worried me more than a little – and I never did lose the habit of keeping an eye on the water glass when the two enginemen had gone to earth.

Forty years ago, when engines were 'owned' by their crews, some of the mountain hoggers carried pets with them. Not for men of the power working in the rat-hole sections were the lace curtains, flower-filled sconces and gold-framed icons beloved of the proud engineers on easier, open runs where there was no tunnel smoke to muck up their cab décor. Instead, they had their canaries, their dogs, or their ring-tailed coatis. The dogs and coatis could look after themselves by wriggling under the deck floorboards or in behind a seatbox when, always on the lookout, they saw a tunnel coming. But canary cages had to be meticulously covered every time, and this was always done by the hoghead while his fireboy was sanding her through. Whatever species the bird or animal attached to the engine, it invariably loathed tunnels and looked thoroughly miserable until the ordeal was over. I remember once a very large, hairy spider that dropped into the cab from over the mouth of a long tunnel into which we were slogging. I watched it in the stabbing light of the fire. When smoke and heat came in it cringed and drew its legs up about itself. At the other end it was dead.

The temptation is strong on a smoky engine with leaking flues and scant of steam to shut off 'the gun' (as the injector is called in the vernacular) before a bad tunnel and pinch down on the oil to get a clean stack. This might make for easier living conditions in the bore, but it has its risks. If a dry crownsheet comes of it something will probably happen. Syphons will usually save the crownsheet, but even a lead plug fused will draw for the indiscreet hogger anything from a fortnight's unpaid holiday upwards. I well recall an occasion when little Billson – the same who pancaked the GM's favourite trackcar – took a big *Mike* through a succession of tunnels thus, and then forgot that the squirt was off. And the 102 had no syphons. He was well beyond the last of the tunnels when recollection dawned and in panic he and his bakebrain slammed on both guns, shooting two streams of ice-water over that red-hot firebox. Of course, the crownsheet came out through the firedoor; the cab – a wooden one – splintered outwards, the tender stood on end, the engine leaped into the air and came down obliquely across the track, the fireman was blasted away and reappeared five cars back up to his waist in zinc concentrates, and Billson – with undeserved luck – was projected through the window by the explosion before the boiler water reached him. That was the last time Billson ran an engine on the main line. From then on it was yard goats and railcars for him!

By the way, there's another tale about Billson in connection with tunnels. He possessed a deeply-rooted fear of the supernatural, and firmly believed that the Central of Peru's Chaupichaca Tunnel was haunted by the ghosts of the Americans and Jamaicans who perished in the disaster of 1909. The body of the engineer of the 33 was never found, so it was said. It was a spectacular accident accompanied by heavy loss of life, and naturally stories were woven round it in sandhouse and switch shanty. One of these was that the vanished engineer 'walked' in the tunnel, climbing aboard approaching engines in search of old acquaintances to whom he might tell where his mangled remains lay. Billson believed this tale implicitly – in fact, it was he who told it to me. He was a fireman at the time, and his cab mate was a wag who loved a practical joke.

Chaupichaca Tunnel was one of the bad 'uns. Not only was it long, but within it the air currents had a trick of wrapping the engines in a snowballing blanket of their own smoke and holding it there. One day, Billson as usual went head down in a generous allowance of damp waste at the entrance of the bore and crouched on his seat to ride out the ordeal, his imagination no doubt toying with the awful thought of other-world visitants waiting somewhere in the reverberating darkness to seize the passing handrails and swing aboard. Just where the blackness, the noise, the blistering heat and the almost solid smoke were at their worst, an icy hand was laid gently on the exposed nape of his neck.

With a piercing shriek Billson shot through the front door of the cab to the running board, and hurled himself along to the pilot beam, where he crouched trembling beside the brakeman's box (containing lamps, detonators, fusees, and so on, and always carried there for lack of a caboose), defending himself as best he could from the searing blast thrown right down upon him from the belching stack immediately overhead. And there he stayed, until the engine was out of the tunnel, across the bridge and through the next tunnel on the other side of the gorge, and the others which followed closely on that. They had to lift him off in Tamboraque, so nearly dead was he from suffocation. Meanwhile, the waggish hogger restored the circulation in the hand he had held under the tender water-cock, and made sure all was well on the fireman's side. Billson's subsequent assertion to me was that he had turned at that icy touch to confront the gesticulating spirit of the mangled, long-defunct engineer, and the sight unnerved him.

You will know by now that some Andean tunnels have nothing over them but a roof. Their purpose is to carry wet slides, streams or washouts safely over the track – a 'snowshed', as it were, for flash floods and falls of mud. It may be remarked that the washouts invariably choose the places not so prepared for them! But whether you have a yard of concrete or a mile of rock over your head, a tunnel is still a tunnel.

On the Southern of Peru they like to tell you that Meiggs, hearing that the Arequipa-Juliaca section avoided the use of any bore, swore that no mountain road worthy of the name could be without a tunnel and ordered one to be built, whether necessary or not. There certainly appears no real reason why the Southern's one and only tunnel should exist. But if the Southern is deficient in these uncomfortable accessories, the Central makes up for it by possessing no less than sixty-three within seventy-four route miles.

Meiggs's merry men building the Central worried little about ventilation, probably considering that trainmen were a hardy breed anyway, and most of the tunnels were not long enough to starve them entirely of air. They did make occasional concessions, all the same, by leaving open the side holes in some of the longest where tunnelling had been commenced in the middle as well as at the ends. But this slight relief was impossible in the world's highest railroad tunnel, the Galera, where the Central passed over the Continental Divide on an underground mainline summit of 15,694 feet.

When the U.S. 'Great White Fleet' visited Peru 'way back in the days before world wars were thought of, Admiral Evans and his flag officers were taken up to Oroya in a special train to see something of the Andes. Assured that the freezing water dripping from the roof at the apex of the Galera Tunnel drained away, some to the east and some to the west of the Divide, he insisted that the labouring train be stopped in that exact spot while, groggy with mountain sickness, he descended alone to the track beside the luxurious private car placed at his disposal for the journey. The earnest pleas of the GM who was responsible for his welfare and safe return to the U.S. Navy were waved aside as he vanished rather unsteadily into the surrounding darkness. In a minute or two he reappeared, looking rather pleased with himself as he adjusted his fly buttons, and to the anxious GM he remarked:

'That's dandy! I've always wanted to pump ship into the Atlantic and the Pacific at the same time. Now I can say I've done it. Let's go!' ...

In the more thickly populated regions between the *Cordilleras* of the Andes – the productive valleys at ten- to eleven-thousand feet – tunnels are frequently regarded as the legitimate right of way for man and beast as well as for trains. It is impossible to convince the mountain Indian that this is not the case. For untold centuries he has used the paths and roads provided by authority, whether that of the State, the Spanish vice-regal government, the Inca and his *curacas*, or the local power that existed before the Incas. His communal idea of property goes back beyond history, and he possesses no inkling of even the most elementary safety precautions. The railroad track is to him a highway for the use of all; tunnels and bridges are merely ways of extending that highway for his personal convenience. It is by no means rare in these districts, then, to meet with herds of llamas being driven through a tunnel in the face of an unwitting train. Fortunately for Andean railways, the llama, most common of domestic animals, never causes a derailment. Horses and cattle very seldom do. But pigs are different. Pigs are dangerous; they get under the pilot, and a wheel will lift on their rubbery flesh. Engineers will do all they can to avoid running over a pig.

When I was still fairly new to Andean railroading it used to be my joy when riding freight trains down from Oroya to Huancayo to get right up in front on the pilot beam of the engine and sit in solitary glory on the brakemen's box, with the warm smokebox door behind me and a splendid panorama of colourful scenery ahead. The grade dropped gently enough to make only a touch of steam now and then enough to keep the moderate speed steady. The soft click and hiss of the pistons on either side bespoke peace and contentment. Flies of some particularly hard-shelled species occasionally hit me like pellets in the face, but the crystal-clear air, bringing perhaps the faint tang of aromatic eucalyptus smoke where a village was in the offing, was sweet enough to make any insect bombardment worth while. The flanks of the surrounding hills were generously carpeted with wheat, golden ripe, rippling to every zephyr. The track followed the Mantaro River, ice-cold at this altitude but as like the ideal of a Scottish trout stream as any northern heart could desire. The skies in these regions were always a miracle of cloud formations; and from time to time one could catch a distant glimpse of gleaming snow ranges against a setting of deepest blue.

It was in this appreciative mood that I sat one day in the usual vantage point as we approached a tunnel. This tunnel was on a curve. I liked it because the grade was not more than one per cent and even with a tonnage drag in the opposite direction to our present one it posed no difficulties – moreover, it sounded inside very like the Central Line at Lancaster Gate. I used to shut my eyes and imagine I was in the Tube. We headed in. I shut my eyes and imagined, listening to the rumble of wheels, the soft clatter of running gear and the occasional clink of a brake beam. Then some hunch made me open them.

We were almost round the curve, and against the daylight at the far end I saw something that caused me to lift myself off that box and jump for the running board pronto. There was a herd of llamas almost under us, and a *cholo* in a poncho was between the rail and the wall waving us down madly! I was scarcely off the pilot beam before there were llamas, all legs and necks, rolling and kicking where an instant ago I was seated dreaming blissfully. We killed about five of them and damaged a number more. If the owner's entire family had been liquidated by us he couldn't have made more fuss! The front of the engine was a shambles. My overalls were liberally spotted with fids of bloody hide and wool; but for the grace of God I would have had them right on top of me! From that day on I was cautious about riding the pilot in a tunnel.

On the whole, however, accidents in tunnels are remarkably rare. There are so many awful things that could happen, but they seldom do. Supposing one met a runaway car inside a tunnel – supposing the dispatcher issued lap orders (the Sword of Damocles hanging over every dispatcher's desk) and there was a cornfield meet followed by a cave-in! How could one survive such a calamity – or, if not directly involved oneself, how the devil would you clear the mess afterwards? Such conjectures were apt to permeate the imagination in the racket and darkness of a bore; and the day finally came when my number turned up, as shall be related in a minute. I have also seen the results of a cornfield meet – a head-on collision – at the very mouth of a tunnel, when a train heading out on a blind curve was hit by another just about to head in. The cars of the one heading out were still inside, and two big empty gondolas on the end of the train jumped so with the shock that the coupler knuckles lifted out and parted. Cut free from the rest of the train, these cars started off back down the grade of nearly five per cent and emerged from the lower end of the bore like bullets from a gun. The tail-end brakeman tried to hold them, but he had no club. Their speed was soon beyond stability limit and they shot off at a tangent from a curve, turning over and over in mid-air. Of course, the brakeman was pulped! Meanwhile, at the front end, the engineer and fireman of the same train had no time to join the birdies or even brace themselves. The fireman was flung out of the window when the crash came, but the engineer was impaled through the stomach on the brake valve handle and pretty well broken up generally. He died screaming a few minutes later. The crew of the other engine had not been swathed in sacks, and they saw the danger in just enough time to jump.

This same tunnel was a particularly bad one for heat. It was the second longest on the Central of Peru, built in 1925 after the floods of that year, as I have already told. Our Beyer-Garratts worked up the mountain from Tornamesa cab first to avoid cooking the enginemen in tunnels, but this particular bore caught them with the boiler leading.

The union to which enginemen belonged had agitated for, and won, asbestos hoods and gloves for the crews of Garratts, and these were made up in the Upholsterers' Shop in the works and duly distributed. They were most effective. Protected by the hood and gloves you could sit in the cab and laugh at the searing heat in the Purhuay Tunnel, which was indeed severe enough to hurt where any bare skin was exposed. Moreover, you could see where you were going; for the hoods had a window in front, like a welder's mask. And yet – our enginemen would *never* use them. They would raise the roof with their complaints if new ones were not issued at regular intervals; but in service they obstinately stuck to their sacks and wet waste, while the hoods reposed unwanted in their seatboxes! Enginemen are a perverse lot, and the breed is the same the world over.

The worst tunnel I ever knew was the Galera bore, where Admiral Evans achieved his feat of linking Atlantic and Pacific. In actual length it was a mere 3,860 feet, but on occasions it was to us more like that number of yards. From Ticlio, this brute of a tunnel climbed on a grade of some 4.5 per cent for about three-thousand feet of its length and then dropped on an easier grade to the other mouth, where Galera station was situated. Traffic through the tunnel was controlled by tablet. Smoke tended to travel upwards towards Galera, due to prevailing winds outside – but I shall have more to say about that in a moment. The great snags about this dreaded rat-hole were twofold. A subterranean stream somewhere under Mount Meiggs and over the tunnel's unlined roof kept a deluge of water dropping on the track right at the vertical curve at the apex, this water trickling along the rail-tops and freezing into a steel-like coating of ice; and a train pulling away from Ticlio station on the main to enter the bore had no chance to get a run at it. My Oroya 60-class 2-8-0s could scarcely ever get through to Galera without coming to grief on the ice, even when given a good start by backing their trains away up the Morococha branch towards La Cima and coming down with throttles wide, hell-bent for election through Ticlio yard and into the tunnel. The roaring blast would grow slower and slower, would begin to labour, and then – all of a sudden – their feet would fly out from under them and they would come to a halt dancing madly. As the whole train began to slip back the engineer would coax that throttle with all the art he knew, opening up rail washers and sanding, trying to win a grip for the drivers. Apprehensive of losing control on that grade, brakemen would take up the slack of car brake chains in anticipation. Perhaps the engine would manage to dig its heels in and stop the backward slide, lurch forward a few metres while driving

121. *East portal of the Central of Peru's Galera Tunnel, under the Continental Divide, at Galera station. This is the highest tunnel in the world, its peak being 15,690ft above sea level.* (Author)

tyres growled ominously, and then suddenly burst into another flurry of slipping. Meanwhile, the smoke stayed with the engine, and the act of breathing – always a kittle matter at nearly 16,000 feet – became a major problem.

Twenty-five minutes was the limit of endurance in this ordeal. Freights often took two or three shots at the tunnel before winning through, returning each time to Ticlio and backing up the Morococha branch for a fresh run at it. Now and then an engineman might be overcome in that smoky rat-hole, but it was a rare occurrence. I was present once on a Cerro de Pasco *Mogul* returning from loan to a construction company in Callao when the fireman and coalpasser collapsed between Casapalca and Ticlio from over-exertion and mountain sickness. Firing a coal-burning 'muzzle-loader' (non-stoker engine) on these grades was pure hell! I was forced to wield the scoop in their place over the top, including the passage of the Galera Tunnel. We were double-heading a Central 60-class, and it was the crew of that engine that got the bulk of our smoke in the bore, as well as the incandescent cinders; but for all that, what with the exertion of scooping slack into the firebox and the lack of air, I wouldn't care to repeat the experience. It took us nearly twenty minutes to get through, and the hogger, Harry Wall, had just about shot his bolt when we finally emerged into clean air and pulled up in Galera.

That tunnel had its perils for descending trains also. In the old days of the 'armstrong' brakes (so called because the braking power was applied by strong arms on the brake wheels), before the installation of air on all our freight cars, brakemen had to be on their toes to prevent trains getting away as they topped the summit and dipped on the terrific falling grade. Over-enthusiasm with brake clubs might slide car wheels on the icy surface of the rails, and that was worse than no brakes at all.

South of Ticlio station there was the safety switch turning off the main into a sand-drag, and this brought many a runaway to a stop without much damage being done. If the crew of a train out of control in the tunnel stuck to it they were fairly safe, but if they jumped they generally got hurt. The urge to jump was enhanced by doubts about the main iron's being unoccupied between the tunnel's mouth and the safety switch; for if another northbound train were standing in the station waiting for the tablet a pile-up was unavoidable.

My worst moments in any tunnel were spent in the Galera inferno, and the cause was our friend Billson, on the occasion of his dropping the crown-sheet of Eng. 102. The wreck was about a mile below Ticlo station. I mentioned the accident in the last chapter. Down the bank was the tender, with our own wrecking crane upside-down on top of it.

Normally, wrecking operations came under the Engineers' Dept.; but it happened that the District Engineer was away at the time. I was therefore called upon to pick up the mess and clear the line for traffic. The GM phoned me from Lima to get hold of the C de P wrecking outfit, including that splendid Brownhoist 60-ton 'Big Hook'. This was all arranged satisfactorily in Oroya, and in due course the outfit was delivered in our yard with C de P No. 6 on the head end, one of the big Alco 2-8-0 coal-burners, with the mighty Bill Williamson at the throttle.

The Brownhoist looked very lofty to me, even with its boom reposing on the boom car, and the stack removed to lower the overall height. To make sure she'd clear in the Galera Tunnel, the Roadmaster and I checked her with a tape and found her just six inches under the official height of the tunnel's roof above rail level. She'd do it, but only just!

Bill Williamson was inclined to be scornful of our Central institutions on the drag up to Galera. In retaliation I twitted him on the Six's lack of guts. Meanwhile, the two firemen worked madly to keep the *Consolidator* hot. The real estate they scooped into that firebox did everything but stay put. As usual, half of it came right out of the stack without hitting the grate at all, and a goodly proportion of the remainder fused into enormous lumps of slag that had to be sliced and hooked back through the firedoor to be jettisoned from the gangway.

'You got a swell track though,' Williamson remarked rather reluctantly. It was indeed a handsome track with its gleaming ballast innocent till that moment of falling ash, neatly walled throughout most of its extension. The District Engineer and his zealous roadmaster had recently done wonders in the way of ballasting with that metal and rip-rap taken from Mahr Tunnel which was said to contain a high proportion of silver. Work trains were spreading this argentiferous ballast every day throughout the whole of the Mountain Section. From Oroya to Casapalca it was already laid. Even the track through the Galera Tunnel was resplendent with it.

Darkness was falling by the time we reached Galera, and what little fuel was left in the tender consisted of earthy dust; but there was just enough to take the Six-spot back to Oroya if she dropped the hook in Ticlio and departed homewards at once. Steam was low. To bring it up as we stood waiting for the tablet the coalpasser scooped some of the muck up from the corners of the bunker and the fireman hosed it over and spread it in the firebox. The blower pumped clouds of billowing black smoke from the stack, but the needle began to edge up towards the red line.

Behind the tender was the cab of the crane, boom facing aft along the separate boom car. There followed two flats with slings, chains, jacks, ties and blocks; a tool car; and finally the combined kitchen and bunk car. The crane crew had already started firing up, and the foreshortened stack flush with the crane's roof was erupting its own quota of black *pampa*-coal smoke and live cinders. When Williamson cracked the Six's throttle and we lumbered forward it was with the anticipation of having a smoky passage of the bore, but not one unduly trying. The grade southbound to the summit was fairly easy, and the air currents blowing through from Ticlio towards Galera tended to move smoke back clear of the engine. In any case, in this direction train speed was much greater than when dragging up from the other end.

We galloped into the tunnel at a fair clip with glaring headlight, secure in the knowledge that the fully air-braked train would be completely under control when we breasted the top and started down. We were just over the summit and Williamson had pushed the throttle home and was reaching for the air latch when there came a tortured, grinding noise from somewhere behind us. At the same instant the engine checked so violently that we who stood on the cab deck pitched forwards against the boiler backhead in a shower of fire-irons and slack from the tender. There came a succession of heavy thumps and startled shouts, and we stopped as suddenly as though we had run into the tail of another train.

'We're on the dirt!' roared Bill Williamson, lapping the brake valve. His instinctive reaction had been to big-hole the air and wipe the clock at the first hint of trouble. But the yells and excitement in the dark behind us made us think the crane had jumped the track-not the engine. I had a torch and together we climbed down for a look. The Six was all right. The crane, too, was on the rails as far as we could see – but for all that, there was something wrong with her. The hook's cab frame and outriggers were just about filling the bore from wall to wall. No space remained for big men to squeeze past. There was something strange about the way the cab was canted. Then we saw the reason. The crane was jammed solid against the jagged roof of the tunnel.

By the time we were back in the engine's cab there was a slowly rising tide of woolly-looking coal smoke building up from the track beside the engine. I remarked on it to Bill Williamson, surprised that it should accumulate down there instead of up under the roof. The air currents were playing weird tricks with it. Then it struck me that with what was belching out of our own stack and from in and around the imprisoned crane's cab, that carpet of smoke was going to thicken more and more till it eventually filled the whole area of the tunnel. It couldn't escape past the crane, and the air currents prevented its exit the other way. If we stayed where we were it would soon rise high enough to suffocate us! Breathing was difficult enough at this altitude in any event; and as the smoke reduced the area of available air, the more the fire on the Six's wide grate would rob us of what oxygen remained. Already it was noticeable.

'Maybe I can back her out of it,' Williamson remarked. The Conductor was with us on the engine and he agreed. The three sharp toots of the whistle sounded deafening in that confined space. Then the Six lunged back against the crane, faltered, and lunged again. Nothing happened. Williamson widened on the throttle, and with a roar the drivers lost their grip on the ice. Opening the air sanders, Bill tried once more – unsuccessfully. The Brownhoist was stuck as fast as a seized piston in a cylinder!

By that time the smoke layer had risen almost to the gangway.

'We'll have to cut off the flats behind the boom car,' I said: 'then try to pull the hook forward. With the grade in our favour she may make it.'

'Supposing the crane is holding the tunnel roof up,' the Conductor said. 'If we shift her it might bring the roof down on top of us!'

I had thought of that, but it didn't appear likely. A reconnaissance on the Six's tank top disclosed that already a fair amount of stone had been brought down. Broken rock was scattered all over the tank; but the crane's roof did not appear to be wedged behind any sizeable protrusions. If we could move her at all it would most probably pull the cab right off her, without precipitating any serious fall of rock from above. But at the same time, the source of that water that poured from the roof must be close above, and if we did tear more rock out, it might open up an inrush that would cause a complete cave-in.

We discussed the matter in the cab, while the level of that deadly smoke rose relentlessly.

'Let's try to pull her free. If we can't, we shall have to cut the engine off and run for it down to Ticlio. The first thing is to uncouple those cars behind the boom.'

That was easier said than done. I went down into the smoke with the Conductor, our faces masked in wet waste, and we felt our way back to the crane. The torch was useless now. The smoke was quite opaque. While the Conductor, a little man, somehow wriggled between the hook's frame and the wall, I climbed up behind the tender and yelled through a hole in the plating to the crane crew in the cab what we intended to do, warning them to get out in case the whole cab parted company with the superstructure. They told me the smoke wasn't so bad on their side. After an anxious interval they relayed two items of news: the train behind the boom car was cut off; and the Conductor had passed out.

I returned to the Six's cab over the tank, to find the smoke almost breast high on the deck. Steam was dropping too. Like ourselves, the fire was being starved of oxygen; moreover, nothing more had been put into the firebox since we pulled out of Galera, and the injector had been started to raise the water in the boiler enough to cover the crownsheet when the engine tilted downwards on the falling grade. It was now or never. If we couldn't move the crane it would have to stay there till the roof frame could be cut free with oxyacetylene torches.

'Well, let's go!' said Bill Williamson, using the same words that his compatriot, Admiral Evans, had used twenty-five years before in almost the same spot. The double toot of the whistle smote our eardrums; the front air-sanders hissed softly; and I gripped the cab handrails hoping that something would happen.

It did. The drivers let go, the blast thundered, and Williamson latched the throttle home prior to having another try. This time driving tyres bit on the sand. We jerked forward a little, and there came an unearthly groaning and grinding from the crane. We had moved, but not more than inches. Williamson swung the heavy Johnson bar into reverse with his left hand – against the pressure in the valve chests this was an unconscious exhibition of extraordinary muscular power – kicked the engine back against the crane to gather all the slack he could get in the couplers, and then slammed her into forward gear again, widening on the throttle as he did so. The Six flung herself against the collar, and the wheels gripped. There came a tearing, grating sound and loud bumps from behind – and we kept going!

We had pulled free. No serious rock fall followed. There was another heavy bump as the remains of the hook's cab roof struck a projecting tooth of rock, but it never checked us. The smoke in the cab dwindled away in wisps, and sweet air poured in upon us. The air brakes bit and held us smoothly till we emerged into the cold, sparkling night at Ticlio, only too conscious of the fact that we had escaped just in time from a distinctly perilous situation.

The crane was superficially damaged but not disabled. Most of the cab roof had been ripped off, but the boom tie-rods had not been touched, nor had the boiler shifted. Once in the open air the Conductor came round, little the worse for his experience. The Six returned to Galera, shifting the remainder of the wrecking train back into the yard; and a gang started in at once to remove the rock falls from the track in the tunnel.

When in due course investigations were made into the reasons why the C de P wrecker had jammed when there should have been enough clearance for her to pass through the bore safely, the District Engineer found the answer. It was the new ballast. Goaded by that zealous little roadmaster, the section gangs had tamped so lustily that the whole track was raised. None of our own rolling stock had fouled the roof in the tunnel because all of it was well within the loading gauge.

---

[1] *Steam distribution with slide valves actuated by Stephenson gear is superior to that with piston valves and the Walschaerts gear, but the problems of maintaining them are considerable. Slide valves, particularly with superheated steam, are difficult to lubricate properly, and require tremendous power to drive even when of the balanced type once standard in N. American practice.*

"HUNSLET"
STEAM and DIESEL
LOCOMOTIVES

The modern power, backed by world wide experience

This metre gauge 2-8-0 superheater mixed traffic locomotive has just been supplied to the Guaqui-La Paz Railway in Bolivia. Tractive effort 20,000lb at 75% B.P.

The Trinidad Government Railways have had many years of economical and reliable service from this standard gauge 275 H.P. diesel locomotive on shunting and local freight service

"Hunslet" steam and diesel locomotives are giving efficient, reliable and economical service–in countries between the Equator and the Arctic, on high mountain railways and in deep mines. Outstanding in design and construction, they are the result of specialised experience in meeting and overcoming the particular problems that local conditions present. "Hunslet" have built all types of steam and diesel locomotives for most classes of railway and for the widest range of gauges, and at present are dealing with orders from every continent–ample proof of "Hunslet" superiority.

THE HUNSLET ENGINE COMPANY LIMITED
HUNSLET ENGINE WORKS • LEEDS 10 • ENGLAND

Chapter 16

ANDEAN RAILS IN THE NEW AGE

I would personally be inclined to pick the middle 1920s as the Golden Age of South American railways. As far as Andean systems are concerned, I feel sure it was the culmination of undisputed monopoly in the field of transport. Teething troubles had been ironed out. Fat traffics were assured, with adequate rolling stock to handle them, and steam power that was not far off reaching the top of the efficiency curve for its own kind of prime mover. Unpredictable 'acts of God' in the way of Dame Nature's seasonal pranks were all that could disturb the stability of the railroad official's routine.

Of course, there were few who saw their existence in this glorious light at the time. The consensus of opinion was that the grand old days before the upheavals of 1914-1918 were indisputably the best of all days. Setting aside the bias in favour of the days of one's youth, the columns of annual net receipts bear out the contention that it was those years immediately prior to the great slump of 1929 that shone with the most golden lustre. It was then that the summit was reached and the down grade began, slowly at first but steepening more and more until it plunged into the era of competition. The King of the Castle, shaken from his eminence by an economic cataclysm beyond his control, recovered his balance only to find that others besides himself were scrambling towards the position that for so long had been his own.

Road competition came to the Andes long after its presence had been felt elsewhere principally because the building of highways in the mountains was such a costly and difficult matter. How motor vehicles might perform at extremely high altitudes was not a problem that kept anyone awake at nights until the highways had become fact. There were troubles in plenty at first. Prevailing winds blowing up the valleys of the western side moved at about the same speed as the vehicles, with the result that overheating was pronounced. As altitude increased the boiling point fell, which aggravated the trouble. The railroads, chuckling at the sight of those stalled trucks and cars enveloped in clouds of steam and their fuel pumps inoperative for vapour locks, experienced the same troubles when they in their turn began to use the internal combustion engine on the mountain. Power loss was a secondary problem, North American practice being generous enough in the matter of horsepower to overcome most of the deficiency. Trouble-shooting techniques were quickly evolved by the ingenious drivers on the highways. True, there were ghastly accidents, but there was no lack of drivers with commercial vehicles bought on hire purchase to replace each one eliminated by fate.

With cheap fuel, with facilities for purchase, and no conception of overhead costs, the wildcat truck driver of the Andes rushed in his hordes to compete with the railroads, undercutting existing tariffs with an abandon that the organized trucking companies dared not emulate. Rules and regulations laid down by Government for the safety of passengers and freight were flouted with brazen contempt. If one driver was caught, there were hundreds more equally irresponsible doing the same thing. The individual wildcat operator couldn't last long in the business. He killed himself, or defaulted on the payments for his truck – never, perhaps, made any payment other than the initial one. But where one dropped out, two more were ready to take his place.

The authorities inclined to look on all this as progress. It was the pattern of today. Railroads were old-fashioned. The pace was set by Detroit, and South America must follow suit if it were to hold up its head unashamed. It was that first onslaught of wildcat competition that provided an impetus impossible to arrest. As the years passed things shook down into a more orderly form, but the old days were gone. An era had vanished; the Golden Age was over.

It says much for the men administering the railroads that they rose, albeit stiffly, from their ruts, braced themselves and set about meeting the challenge. An outcome of the slump, 'retrenchment' was already a familiar word with these rail systems operating on the proverbial shoestring. Doubtfully remunerative passenger services could not be wiped off the card because of legal obligations, but losses could in many cases be cut, and hopes were focused on the railcar as the means of doing so. The competitor's own weapon could be used to win back some of the lost high-class freight traffic, and also to attract new traffic not so far exploited by the rails. The figure of the shipper was magnified and adored. Propaganda stressing the railroads' servitude to the former victim of monopoly aimed at bolstering goodwill. Few stones were left unturned. The weakness of the wildcat trucker – irresponsibility – gave the railroads the wherewithal to spotlight their own reliability and powers of restitution in the event of damage or loss, to counterpoise the opponent's advantages of cheapness and speed. Combined traffic – road and rail – together with door-to-door delivery, quickly found the railroad companies with truck fleets of their own to advertise their growing sense of public service. No one would dare to say now that competition was a bad thing! Efficiency became the watchword. The go-get-it traffic man appeared in the picture, and all of a sudden everyone was wide awake.

Many passenger services with conventional trains were supported almost entirely by revenue deriving from freight operation. The slither towards the red may not have been reversed – at the start, at any rate – but it was arrested by the advent of the railcar. However, the railcar created stiff problems for the mechanical man, who, like his traffic colleague, rose to the occasion nobly. Vituperation in plenty was directed at the self-propelled unit, but once established it was there to stay. As a matter of fact, there was no choice but to accept it. When the 1930s came in, the railcar had become part of the roster, and General Managers were already perusing with heartfelt relief the figures of spectacularly reduced operating costs where formerly losses had been staggering.

Grandaddy of the self-propelled units was the steam inspection saloon, in remote times a perquisite of top brass. The younger generation may never have seen one in the flesh, as it were, but will be familiar enough with the style from old rail pictures. Briefly, a tiny locomotive, usually four-coupled, shared a frame with a small coupé or coach. Décor tended to be lavish on both sections of the whole, and maintenance was as befitted a vehicle used by the highest rail dignitaries for their periodic inspections of the system they directed. It took four men to run these little crates, but operating costs were of small consideration in those lush days. Besides the engineer, fireman and conductor, a brakeman was generally taken along to perform such chores as throwing switches and protecting the rear end as flagman.

The Central of Peru had a fine example of this species of vehicle in an inspection saloon named *Favorita,* the leading end of which was a Rogers Forney dating from earliest construction days, when the renowned Henry Meiggs and his brother John G. scuttled about the main iron in its well-appointed interior. Fifty-three years later, when I joined the Central, it was still in service, though retirement to the riptrack was imminent. By that time it had been bumped out of managerial inspection service by motor track cars, and was on hire to honeymoon couples or diplomats for speedy private transport to one or other of the seasonal resorts. A peephole had been discreetly bored through the bulkhead separating the cab from the coupé, so that the fascinated enginemen could take it in turns to watch the antics of the honeymooners during the trip. This was shown to me when I squeezed into the cab with the two enginemen for *Favorita's* final run with a happy couple bound for Ancon. I was already aware of the little engine's reputed feat of covering the nine miles from Callao to Monserrate in seven minutes flat, a remarkable performance (if true) with wheels of no more than three feet in diameter. *Favorita* had once possessed two younger sisters, outshopped by Rogers in 1890 and 1891, named *Chalaca* and *Limeña* (names perpetuated in today's business cars), but these I was too late to see.

The internal combustion engine made its debut on the Central in the form of a stately Drewry inspection motor car. This too was still in commission when I joined, but it was by that time the cherished conveyance of a roadmaster. Vehicles of the same kind were chugging up and down the Andes in Chile and Peru alike. Then came a road automobile sturdy enough to withstand the punishing vibration of steel wheels on steel rails, and, suitably modified, it became the most effective inspection vehicle to date. This was the big six-cylinder Hudson, a car built like a battleship, already proven in numerous pick-up services over murderous trails and dirt roads, through mountains and over deserts.

From these sturdy Hudsons there evolved the custom of adapting suitable road vehicles to rail requirements. The pomp and ceremony of the old steam inspection saloon was lacking, but the cost sheets justified the loss of dignity. The Model-A Ford and its contemporary Chevrolet rival both proved well up to the exigencies of rail service. Then Firestone brought out a pneumatic rail tyre that doubled the life of back axles and provided a soundless, smooth ride. Today, the station wagon equipped with pneumatic rail tyres is the preferred inspection unit.

The commercial road truck chassis fitted with a passenger body and rail wheels began the railcar idea in the Andes. Many of these railbuses still operate. Such husky units as Mack and Buda produced were capable of standing up to the work; but to say that they gave no trouble would be to lie. The weak point was the back axle, and the greatest hazard they faced was overloading. In handling lightly patronized passenger services they allowed of the withdrawal of heavy locomotives and coaches. They cut down stand-by expenses to a minimum, and released crews for other and more remunerative work. And they caused management to want something even better.

The steam railcar had the advantage of being designed for its purpose. It was sturdy, reliable, and familiar to roundhouse forces trained in the lore of steam traction. The drawbacks were, that two men were required in the cabs, and that engine power was not sufficient for heavy grades. Its first cost was of course considerably more than that of the home-made body on a commercial truck chassis; but then, its passenger capacity was also considerably greater. Where the nature of the line permitted, and the volume of traffic required it, the steam railcar was a winner. Those early chain-driven or cardan shaft steam jobs of the 1920s performed a magnificent service. In the next decade ambitious attempts were made to adapt them for one-man operation by providing automatic oil firing and boiler feed arrangements. Instead of a fireman, drivers frequently had the enforced company of a fitter or electrician struggling head downwards in infernal temperatures with relays, valve adjustments and coordinated functions. The reliable old simple engines were re-placed with small axle-mounted compound engines rotating at such high speeds that when anything gave – as it all too often did – the whole works exploded into tiny fragments! The promising start to serious steam railcar development dissolved in chaos. Eyes turned hopefully to the diesel engine, now coming to the fore in other parts of the sub-continent and elsewhere.

Diesel railcar experience had been gained on flat or easily graded roads. A unit suitable for operation from sea level to a vertical height of three miles was another, and quite different, matter. Power-weight ratio became all-important, while cost could not be ignored. Electric transmission was too costly, too bulky, too complicated – also, its efficiency looked poor on paper when compared with straight mechanical transmission. Early experiments in lightweight construction to improve that vital power-weight ratio showed that safety was being sacrificed. The strength was lacking to withstand the hard knocks to which any Andean rail unit is subject. Collisions were disastrous. The whole affair just folded up on the luckless passengers inside, and was also liable to ignite and consume itself like a magnesium flash.

Another fault of the lightweight was the lack of sturdiness in the small diesel engines designed primarily for road vehicles. Experiments with various automobile engines showed that rail service requires a prime mover with more stamina than road vehicle engines possess.

The fall-off in power output of some 45 per cent at 15,000 feet appeared to call for supercharging. The gasoline engines fitted with blowers sacrificed a considerable measure of power in driving these appendages, and the altitude loss was not compensated enough to justify it. Where railcars were put to work at fairly constant altitudes, however high, the problems could be met to a great extent by allowing for the loss when calculating the necessary power required. The greatest problem came to the fore when cars were to be operated through a wide altitude range. If power were calculated for maximum altitude, there was excess power at the lower ranges, with a consequently uneconomic operation. 'Derating' was practised, but this could never be anything but a doubtfully satisfactory compromise, involving as it does the provision of an engine with more power than actually required and then cutting down the output in order to reduce its differential at top and bottom of the altitude range.

A sturdy frame and trucks designed for rail service allowed of fitting larger, comparatively slow – $1/8$ running diesels, and these brought with them another headache – the exhaust turbocharger. The rotational speed of these turbo-chargers is so high that early ones had an unfortunate way of shedding rotor vanes from sheer centrifugal stress. The failure of any moving part usually destroyed the charger. Moreover, the apparatus failed to put back that 45 per cent loss from the diminished atmospheric

Argentina's "Northern Transandine Line" Reports:

G-E Diesel-Electrics Maintain High Efficiency at 14,700 feet

In Argentina, the "Northern Transandine Line" hauls freight as well as passengers from sea level to thin-aired 14,700 ft. passes. Operating conditions are among the most rugged in the world. To meet them, five 96-U. S. ton, meter-gage, G-E diesel-electric locomotives were recently placed in service.

Time will tell *exactly* how much the General Electric units have saved through increased efficiency and reduced operating costs. But they have successfully pulled over four hundred U. S. tons per unit on 2.5% grades, at altitudes up to 14,700 feet.

- Continuous rating 25,500-lbs. at 14.5 mph.
- 1,200-hp. to generator for traction.
- Starting tractive effort: 57,600-lbs. at 30% adhesion.
- Top speed: 50 mph.
- Designed for multiple-unit operation.

All G-E diesel-electrics are built to withstand the toughest railroad service, making them profitable for use under operating conditions in your country. General Electric has more than fifty years of locomotive building know-how. This experience is used to design and build locomotives which employ service-proved, standard components to fit *your* operation. International General Electric Company, Transportation Sales, 570 Lexington Ave., N. Y. 22, N. Y., U.S.A.

IA-54-27E

GENERAL ⒼⒺ ELECTRIC
— U. S. A. —

pressure at peak altitudes. One after another, these delicate and perilous accessories vanished from the diesel engines they had adorned, and the bereft engines continued to slog their way about the mountains with more reliability than before, albeit feebler.

Railcars are operating in regular services on the Chilean Transandine, the Arica-La Paz and elsewhere, through altitude ranges from sea level to the summit; but these summits are considerably lower than that of the Central of Peru. On the Central, the critical range was from 12,000 feet to the top. Below 10,000 feet there was little trouble if overheating could be avoided – with the engines, that is; for transmissions presented troubles of their own. After years of hopeful but unsuccessful experimenting, the Central left the mountain in the efficient care of conventional steam trains and relegated its railcars to services over reasonably level track. By that time, the old steam railcars had been converted to diesel – except for one unit – with generally beneficial results. The success of these was largely due to their solid construction. No one was sorry to see the steam components go, least of anyone the author, who had been the victim of the explosion of a high-pressure three-drum watertube boiler in a large double-engined unit which customarily operated with a trailer. There were two of these big fellows: one passenger and one baggage or express freight. The latter was converted for passengers when fitted with a diesel engine later.

The old railbuses with their familiar road truck engines and transmissions were maintained easily enough by the personnel of the day, and driven by chauffeurs who had been put through 'the book' thoroughly enough to pass the necessary examination in train operation. The modern diesel railcar, with its fluid drive, electromagnetic or selective gearbox, its reversing gear arrangements and so on, called for specialized personnel, separate shops and a new breed of drivers. They initiated the diesel era in the Andes, preparing the ground for the inevitable day when steam would vanish completely. The roundhouse fitter working to fractions of an inch, and a Stillson wrench handy for use on any nut of awkward size, had no place in the diesel shop where micrometers and thousandths-of-an-inch were the order of the day. Similarly, the old hog-mauler who had spent his working life with steam was generally found unsuitable for running railcars, particularly if he belonged to that race which having acquired certain habits cannot by any means be broken of them. A new and younger lot took the railcar throttles. Some graduated from the railbuses, some from trackcars; some were young, ambitious firemen anxious to advance in their calling more rapidly than was possible in locomotive service.

Suitable steam enginemen who might not have taken kindly to railcar operation have, nevertheless, proved quite the right stuff for running diesel-electric locomotives, which goes to show that the handling of train consists is another matter altogether. In any case, there was no choice. When it comes to running trains on Andean grades experience is essential, and all the experience was possessed by the steam men. The complexity of the diesel-electric discourages any inclination to 'tinker', and troubles are left for specialist fingers to rectify, which is as it should be.

The battle between diesel and steam is being won on the score of low operating costs. Altitude, against the diesel, favours steam. The higher you go, the lower the boiling point of water. Rarefied atmosphere affects steaming to a slight extent, but not enough to offset the advantage of the lower boiling point. To raise steam enough from cold for switching within the hour on a big road engine is commonplace at 12,000 feet and over. The steam locomotive was therefore in its element at high altitudes, while its diesel rival could barely drag itself along. But the victory was only temporary. The inevitable day might be staved off, but it had to come. Moreover, ways and means were evolved for compromising with the natural shortcomings of the diesel, reducing them to reasonable proportions.

The mechanical officer on an Andean railroad, in all probability basically a steam man, is a jack of all trades. There are not the resources to provide supervisory specialists to cover all the ramifications of present-day locomotive practice, and the man on the job is expected to be an electrical engineer, a motor engineer, a diesel engineer and a steam engineer all combined in one, to say nothing of possessing an intimate knowledge of shop practices and processes plus a wealth of ingenuity in the way of making do with what is to hand when the nearest source of spare parts is thousands of miles away. Resourcefulness is an integral part of his nature. Andean conditions make it obligatory.

INAUGURATION OF THE FIRST OF THE NEW LOCOMOTIVES IN LA PAZ

On the 29th December 1950, a very impressive and enthusiastic inaugural ceremony was held at the Central Station in La Paz, capital of Bolivia, In connection with the arrival of the six new locomotives described in the preceding pages. These locomotives were erected in record time at the Mejillones Works of the Chilean section of this Railway and the first locomotives arrived without incident.

This ceremony was attended by His Excellency the President of Bolivia, Don Mamerto Urriolagoitia, many Cabinet Ministers, heads of the Armed Forces, Government officials, the British Ambassador, the Mayor of La Paz and numerous Senators and Deputies, whilst a great gathering of enthusiastic Bolivian citizens thronged the station and its surroundings.

The locomotives were blessed by the Archbishop of La Paz, whilst His Excellency the President of the Republic, after donning a suit of overalls, personally drove the first of these new locomotives in the extensive station yards.

The above pictures refer to the event.

INAUGURACION DE LA PRIMERA DE LAS NUEVAS LOCOMOTORAS EN LA PLAZ

El dia 29 de Diciembre de 1950 se celebró una ceremonia inaugural muy impresionante y entusiasta en la Estación Central de La Plaz, Capital de Bolivia, relacionada con la llegada de las seis nuevas locomotoras descritas en las páginas anteriores. Estas locomotoras fueron montadas en tiempo record en los Talleres de Mejillones de la Sección Chilena de este Ferrocarril y la primera locomotra llegó a La Plaz después de haber recorrido los 1173 kilómetros sin el menor incidente.

Esta ceremonia fué presenciada por Su Excelencia el Presidente de Bolivia, Don Mamerto Urriolagoitia, muchos Minstros de Gabinete, Jefes de las Fuerzas Armadas, Altos Funcionarios Gubernamentales, el Embajador Británico, el Superintendente de La Paz y numerosos Senadores y Diputados, mientras que una gran multitud de entusiastas ciudadanos bolivianos presenciaron el acto en la estación y en sus alrededores.

Las locomotras fueron bendecidas por Su Ilustrisima el Arzobispo de La Paz, mientras que Su Excelencia el Presidente de la República, después de vestirse con un mono de tabajo, condujo personalmente la primera de estas nuevas locomotras en las extensas vias de la estación.

Las fotografias arriba reproducidas fueron tomadas durante ese acontecimiento.

Following successful employment of the Beyer-Garratt type on the Potosi-Sucre line, the FCAB ordered six more as late as 1950. An official Beyer-Peacock booklet was published to publicise this prestige order. (Collection – Keith Taylorson)

The future is obscure of such Andean railroads as have not been placed on the skids by reversion to State operation, expropriation or nationalization, primarily because of the pronounced depreciation of currencies. Discounting Chile, which has had a State-operated rail network from the start, none of the South American systems formerly in foreign hands has been the better for national administration. Some lines, State-owned, were administered by foreign concerns on behalf of the Government; some were sold up through force of circumstances beyond the control of the administrations; some were taken over more or less by decree in the interests of national prestige. Splendidly-run systems of world-wide repute, in optimum conditions of maintenance, became almost overnight the playthings of politicians and providers of jobs for the boys. Naturally, their deterioration was rapid.

The chief Peruvian railroads are the property of the company that operates them. There is no question of their reverting to the State when agreements expire, as has been the case with certain railways elsewhere, and would have been the case in Peru also had not their ownership been secured in exchange for the guano rights. But there hangs overhead the sword of Damocles in the shape of Operating Ratio – the ratio of operating expenses to revenue.

Where potential traffic is descried, any railroad manager worth his salt is out to get it. That is the stern business of privately-owned systems and the professed object of State-owned ones. If his line is already working close to full capacity he must find ways and means of utilizing his main iron more fully, must be able to meet new demands for car space and motive power requirements. His track and his rolling stock must be in top condition; and this means adequately equipped maintenance facilities. All this calls for a keen eye on modern developments, a regular pruning of deadwood in the shape of obsolete stock, constructions and permanent way, and no vestige of the idea that, 'what was good enough for grandpa is good enough for me'. To maintain a railroad in efficient operating condition and in a state of expansion costs money anywhere, and where physical conditions are as extreme as in the Andes it costs proportionately more than on flat systems. The West Coast of South America is still in industrial infancy. Practically everything required to run the railroads must be imported from industrial countries whose currency exchange rates are unfavourable to the consumer countries. Railroad revenue is taken in the national currency. The material from abroad is paid for in the currency of the country of supply. Rampant inflation throughout South America has aggravated the unfavourable exchange rates, while internally hoisting the cost of living and causing unceasing clamours for pay increases quite out of step with the permitted rises of tariffs. To worsen the already serious situation, the cost of railroad material at the source of supply has risen astronomically since the last war and is still rising; besides which, there is an enforced swing to motive power with a first cost about double that of steam.

To increase traffic over existing single-track lines operated on the train order or *via libre* systems may require lengthy sections of CTC (Centralized Traffic Control), wonderfully effective but fabulously expensive to install and maintain. Nature permits nothing to remain static; and that goes for railroads as well as for everything else. What is not in a state of development must deteriorate. Therefore, a railroad operating as a money-making business cannot afford to button up its pockets.

How easy it is, then, for the most efficient of today's Andean railroads to find its operating ratio on the wrong side of 100 per cent. It is obviously a condition that cannot be endured indefinitely. When the tonic of loans is exhausted without a marked change for the better, there remains the final step of unloading the property on the State at a bargain price and getting out from under. Shareholders may heave a doubtful sigh of relief when this step is taken; but what of the generations of railroaders whose sweat and talent have made the system what it is?

Their life work – their ambitions, skills and devotion to duty – goes down the sink from one day to the next. Landslides bury the tracks they tended so carefully; their bridges rust away; their cherished rolling stock becomes swaybacked and rickety; their proud locomotives vanish one by one to keep a nucleus of crocks tottering about in drastically reduced services. The railroad they lived for becomes a national joke, such as the once renowned 'Good and Quick' up there on the Equator. And it isn't only the displaced foreigners who suffer. The clockwork regularity of the pay packets under private management is gone, and a multitude of bereaved nationals bemoan the fact.

There is a tendency for South Americans to regard railroads as obsolete and to bestow their favours upon the latest fashion in transport, regardless of its suitability for the job in hand. Hence there may be no grief from the public when a railroad ceases in its function as a common carrier, however inconvenient the gap it leaves. Eyes turn to more and better roads, larger trucks, the last word in aircraft. Rocketing tariffs for the restricted movement of freight may be shrugged off as the price one has to pay for being up to date. In flat country where there is little bulk freight the wound may heal sufficiently to be overlooked, but in the Andes – where the important freights are in bulk and highway capacity is strictly limited by physical difficulties – a railroad's passing may be no less than a national disaster.

Chile has already absorbed a number of foreign-operated railroads into the national network, and is capable of running them adequately. Bolivia attempted it but failed. It scarcely seems likely that Peru will deliberately kill the goose that lays the golden egg and make a similar attempt; but what could happen is that prolonged operation in the red might result in the owner company's selling out to the Government.

Mining was the prime reason for most of the railways in the Andes. They came into existence to move minerals from the heights to the coast over tracks that for sheer daring have no equal anywhere. Mining has been the lifeblood of these lines down the years, enabling them to weather the recurring cycles of depression and wartime exigency. Mining still has them looking for ways and means of increasing traffic movement over tracks operating to capacity. Mining is the source of bulk freight that no other form of transport can handle so efficiently and cheaply as a railroad.

Prophecies are dangerous; for in this era of sweeping changes so much can happen that is impossible to foresee. All the same, I shall accept the risk and conclude with the prediction that railroads will continue to operate in the Andes as long as the mining and processing of minerals continues there-and that, by the look of it, is going to be a long time!

BIBLIOGRAPHY

Two Years in Peru. Thomas J. Hutchinson, 2 vols. London, 1873.

Peru in the Guano Age. A. J. Duffield. London, 1877.

Life of Richard Trevithick. Francis Trevithick. London, 1872.

The War Between Peru and Chile, 1879-1882. Clements R. Markham. Sampson Low, Marston & Co.

Henry Meiggs, Yankee Pizarro. Watt Stewart. Duke University Press, 1946.

Ferrocarriles de Chile, Historia y Organización. Editorial 'Rumbo', Santiago, 1943.

Railways of South America, Part III, Chile. U.S. Dept. of Commerce, Washington, 1930.

Inst. Civil Engineers (London). Proc., Vols. 195 and 202.

Railway Gazette. 1st and 2nd S. American Railway numbers, 1926.

The West Coast Leader of Lima, Peru, and its successor, Peruvian Times.

Facts and Views Concerning the Change of Gauge,
        published by the Antofagasta (Chili) and Bolivia Railway Co., Ltd., June 1929.

Ferrocarriles y Caminos, No. 69, Lima, 1951.

Atlantic and Pacific Breezes,
        Spring and Summer 1960. House organ of the Pacific Steam Navigation Co., Ltd.

The Beyer-Peacock Quarterly Review, April 1931.

Reseña Historica de los Ferrocarriles del Peru. Ministerio de Fomento, Lima, 1908.

El Ferrocarril de Arequipa. Lima, 1871.